The Oxford History of New Zealand Music

To the memory of my parents

Frances Jean Wemyss and Arthur Mansfield Thomson

who sang contralto and bass respectively, in the Blenheim Combined Choirs' performance of Handel's Messiah on 14 December 1922, three years before their marriage.

The Oxford History
of New Zealand Music

John Mansfield Thomson

Auckland
Oxford University Press
Oxford   New York   Toronto   Melbourne

Oxford University Press
Oxford University Press, Walton Street, Oxford OX2 6DP

OXFORD   NEW YORK   TORONTO
DELHI   BOMBAY   CALCUTTA   MADRAS   KARACHI
PETALING   JAYA   SINGAPORE   HONG KONG   TOKYO
NAIROBI   DAR ES SALAAM   CAPE TOWN
MELBOURNE   AUCKLAND
and associated companies in
BERLIN   and   IBADAN

Oxford is a trade mark of Oxford University Press

First published 1991
© John Mansfield Thomson 1991

Published with the assistance of the Historical Branch
of the Department of Internal Affairs

ISBN 0 19 558176 8

Jacket designed by Chris O'Brien
Photoset in Bembo by Wright and Carman
and printed in Hong Kong
Published by Oxford University Press
1A Matai Road, Greenlane, Auckland 5, New Zealand

Contents

Introduction

Like America, Canada, and Australia, New Zealand's European musical culture had British origins. By the 1890s a vigorous choral, orchestral, brass band, and domestic musical life had taken root, enlivened by visiting opera companies, singers, and instrumentalists. From this ambience there emerged the first professional composer, Alfred Hill (1870-1960), whose experiences in the Gewandhaus Orchestra and at the Leipzig Conservatorium were not always appreciated in a colonial environment. Hill began explorations of Māori music, his cantata *Hinemoa* (1896) and subsequent ballads drawing world-wide attention to the musical gifts of New Zealand's indigenous people, although touring Māori concert parties and singers had, on a smaller scale, already revealed their music's power.

The Māori showed similar curiosity about European music and soon tackled sailors' shanties as well as hymns, folk-songs and operatic arias, a process which has continued to the present day. Māori vocal skills won the accolades of musically sophisticated Europeans such as Sarah Harriet Selwyn, wife of the first Anglican Bishop, and Lady Martin, wife of the first Attorney-General. That incomparable tradition of Māori singers, which began in the nineteenth century with Princess Te Rangi Pai and Princess Iwa, has continued in the careers of artists such as Inia Te Wiata and Kiri Te Kanawa.

The musical relationship between the two cultures is an important theme in any historical account and it is set forth here quite extensively. It plays a part in answering the question so often asked, 'Is there a New Zealand music?', to which there are many answers. For there exists a strong performing tradition which began in the later nineteenth century when the first New Zealand musicians set forth. Subsequently, their numbers have gathered strength, until today there are many New Zealand-born artists who have won international recognition. This aspect of musical life, particularly important to a young country, extends to choral groups such as the National Youth Choir, to brass bands, and to contemporary music ensembles, each of which has achieved outstanding success abroad. If it still requires dedication, hard work, and ingenuity to pursue the career of a professional musician within New Zealand, this is related to the small population of the country, just over three million people, and the relatively modest, not to say meagre amount the state is prepared to pledge to the arts, not to any reluctance on the part of audiences to sustain them.

Those who ask 'Is there a New Zealand music?' mean, of course, 'Are there any New Zealand composers?', a question often put to the author. The second part of this book tries to provide a convincing answer. For following Hill—whose active life centred on Australia from 1915 onwards—there emerged in the late 1930s the composer Douglas Lilburn (b. 1915), at a time when a group of poets and writers were also articulating their responses to New Zealand society and life. Lilburn's career as composer, teacher, and advocate of New Zealand music is central and crucial to the tradition. His works, encompassing so many fields, are at the heart of the New Zealand repertoire. The following generations have benefited from his tilling of the soil. They have endeavoured in their own ways to develop further a musical language with a distinctive New Zealand style, aims Lilburn himself delineated in his two seminal talks 'A search for tradition' (1946) and 'A search for a language' (1969). The New Zealand composer today can be found in the electro-acoustic studios of Europe, the concert halls of Edinburgh, London, or Sydney as readily as in his or her own land. In this international world of contemporary music, which often obliterates personal styles, he nevertheless retains something of his origins. When the *New Zealand Times* wrote of the young Alfred Hill in 1892 as being 'indeed among the first of what we believe will be a long line of musicians destined to rise in this colony', it may have been merely another example of the euphoria common at the time, a vein which had reached its apotheosis in J. A. Froude's *Oceana* of 1886. But in fact history has given substance to this prophesy. Perhaps it is time to risk another.

This book was commissioned by the Composers Foundation and the Queen Elizabeth II Arts Council. In practical terms it soon became apparent that the material was far more extensive than had been imagined. It might seem that 150 years of music-making in a remote part of the world would fit easily into some 300 pages, the limit set by the publisher. The fact that this was not feasible is testimony to the vitality of the inheritance and to the renewed impetus music found in a new environment. Therefore, a number of topics have had to be passed over, and considerable condensation has been made of others in the interest of making this as much an overview as possible.

Subjects that I have already written about elsewhere have, therefore, been dealt with more briefly. *Into a New Key* covers the origins and history of the Music Federation of New Zealand from 1950-1982 (Music Federation of New Zealand, 1985), the career of Alfred Hill is fully described in *A Distant Music* (Oxford University Press, 1981), and most recently the *Biographical Dictionary of New Zealand composers* (Victoria University Press, 1990) supplements the material in the latter part of this book and adds lists of works, writings and bibliographies.

I have seen my prime task as that of recovering as much of the buried history of music in New Zealand as possible to provide a perspective and restore the continuity of the tradition. The book has been brought up to 1990 to meet the requirements of the publisher. These later sections which have had to concentrate on highlights and the most significant personalities could have been three times as long, and many names worthy of mention have had to be omitted. The chapter on the New Zealand performer, expanded at the request of the publisher, nevertheless had to concentrate on artists of international stature. An exception has been made in the chapter on choral music. As amateur music-making in New Zealand is predominantly choral the publisher felt that this should, therefore, be treated in more detail.

A work which could have extended to two or three volumes, if Māori music had been included, has here been compressed into one, thus making it, in a sense, a 'Concise Oxford History of New Zealand Music'. I hope, nevertheless, that it will do justice to its subject, will prompt explorations of areas that could only be touched on here and that it will stimulate pride in our musical achievements.

John Mansfield Thomson
Wellington, November 1990

Acknowledgements

Many people who have been extremely generous during the preparation of this book I now thank collectively and most warmly for their help. I am deeply conscious of my good fortune. I mention by name only those who have assumed a particularly arduous role, either in institutions or by reading sections of the manuscript. New Zealand librarians show a great spirit of initiative and the staffs of the Alexander Turnbull Library, the Wellington Central Library, National Archives in Wellington, the Auckland Public Library, the Auckland Institute, the Canterbury Museum, the Public Library in Dunedin, the Otago Early Settlers Museum in the same city, and the University libraries in Auckland, Wellington, Christchurch and Dunedin have all earned my gratitude. To the Turnbull Librarian of the time, Mr J. E. Traue, and Miss Jill Palmer, Music Librarian, I owe a special debt, as to Miss Margery Walton who set the enterprise on the right path so long ago and to Margaret Loftus and other staff of the Ephemera Collection. The project has in many ways become indissolubly related to the Turnbull.

The Turnbull Endowment Trust, the Lilburn Trust, the Research Grants Committee of Victoria University of Wellington and the University of Otago have each contributed to the venture. I have an immense debt to the Stout Research Centre of the Victoria University of Wellington who appointed me as their first David Stout Research Fellow which allowed me to further several projects, notably this one, and lay foundations for others such as the recent *Biographical Dictionary of New Zealand Composers*.

I have depended greatly on the expertise of colleagues, friends and scholars who at various stages have read chapters of this book. These are Mary Boyd, formerly senior lecturer in Pacific history at Victoria University of Wellington, Dr John Steele, Professor of Music at the University of Otago, and Professor William R. Roff, of Columbia University of New York, each of whom responded to an earlier version. Subsequently Adrienne Simpson devoted her considerable musicological skills to pruning this into a shape which fitted the required limits. Richard Bolley carefully read this same earlier draft for the publisher, and subsequently I thank my publisher Anne French of Oxford University Press and my editor Ian Watt for their skills with the manuscript. Janet Paul has given it an elegant design.

The following kindly read and commented on individual chapters: Adrienne Simpson, Peter Downes and Jeremy Commons on opera; William Renwick, Guy Jansen, Judith Clark, Alan Thomas, Elizabeth Kerr, Warren Drake, David Sell, Hugh Price, John Drummond, David Farquhar and Peter Walls on education; Rona Bailey and Ashley Heenan on folksong, Dr Mervyn McLean,

Alan Thomas, Charles Royal and Helen Fisher on the meeting of the two cultures, Mervyn McLean and Alan Thomas on the frontier, Lyell Cresswell, Philip Liner, John Harrison and Dean Goffin on the bands, the late Walter Harris on silent film music and Helen Young on broadcasting. Nevertheless in a work of this kind the author is ultimately responsible and takes sole responsibility for his omissions and errors: he further begs readers to send any corrections to him care of the publisher.

Radio New Zealand Concert Programme staff have been constantly supportive and their resources constitute a major research archive of New Zealand music as do those of Radio New Zealand Sound Archives at Timaru which I first explored in the days of Angus Miller and A. M. Thomson. Other organizations which have similarly helped have been the Music Federation of New Zealand and the Orchestral Division of Radio New Zealand. John Casey and Brett Robertson of the Photography Department of Victoria University have provided invaluable services.

I thank my predecessors who wrote their pioneer theses, Margaret Campbell, Julia Moriarty, Angela Annabell and other such writers mentioned in the bibliography. It is a loss that much of their earlier work has never been published and certainly significant that much of it has been done by women. To those working in similar fields today such as Philip Norman, Ross Harvey, Martin Lodge and Valerie Harris, who with Philip Norman produced the Lilburn Festschrift, I give warmest thanks. We are fortunate indeed that New Zealand music is becoming so well documented. This book was commissioned by the Queen Elizabeth II Arts Council and the Australasian Performing Right Association and I acknowledge the constant support in a variety of ways, of Ashley Heenan and Douglas Lilburn, which has been crucial to its realization.

To my colleagues on *Early Music* in London during the periods when I was away from my editorial desk pursuing research in New Zealand, I owe a special debt: the smooth continuity of the journal was miraculously maintained. This was a feat perhaps less obvious to those who have never been involved in such an intricate specialist journal. Margot Leigh Milner spiritedly led the team, with Millicent Elliott, Jenny Cole, Robin Maconie, Richard Bolley, Mirka Zemanova and Richard Abram, all of whom staunchly held the fort with the co-operation of Mr Milbery of Headleys, a devoted printer of the old school and as good a friend of the journal. Our Advertising Manager Arthur Boyars and designers Roger Davies, Peter Campbell and Paul McAlinden, each played a notable part.

This may be one of those times when an author does not need to thank his secretary but instead give recognition to his particular brand of word processor. In initiating this regime Judith Binney of the History Department of the University of Auckland was a valued mentor and subsequently Forrest Chambers and Lisa Larkindale have kept the keys endlessly busy in a stimulating and highly valued dialogue. Suzanne Aspden also gave much help with research, I am appreciative of the contributions to the choral chapter made by John Rosser,

Peter Averi, Martin Setchell, Peter Adams and L. C. M. Saunders.

A book such as this is no individual enterprise but a bringing together of a network of collaborations: I thank each one of you who has made it possible.

JOHN MANSFIELD THOMSON
Wellington, August 1990

The Māori World of Music

Ko te korimako ki te ngahere
Ko te tangata ki te whenua

The song of the bellbird
fills the forest with gladness
Man sings and fills the land
with joy.

In waiata (traditional songs) both the incidents of the past and their high-born composers live again. Songs are not just formulae of notes and words, however beautiful, but a reforming of the community of the present, and in performance, a recollection of the community of the past. These songs put us in touch with ourselves, our identity, and our roots, for as we sing them the scenes of history and visions of ancestors pass dimly before our eyes and for a brief moment time coalesces and we and they are one. Songs are an indispensable part of community life and culture. They have the power to reach down into us to wrench our inner selves from their moorings and cause the world to glisten and we are reborn, reshaped, and revitalized.

The Māori world of music lies in two camps; traditional and modern. Within the traditional camp choices are limited but the modern camp opens up unlimited choices for absorption, adaptation, and reshaping within a bicultural dimension.

In early Māori society, all growth and creativity were under the influence of the gods. One created songs for a social or religious reason. It would be a bad omen if one sang without an obvious functional purpose. There were many opportunities to sing. The waiata chants were group expressions even though composed by an individual provoked in some way. The words would invariably allude to symbols of pride affecting the people. Their singing of the waiata would support those things with which they and the composer would identify. This would be performed in unison, with a melodic range of a 4th or a 5th. In these traditional songs the central melody returns to the droning note each time the melodic pattern is stated. A listener would note this pattern at the outset and settle back to give attention to the words and their message. Movement is mainly by steps upwards or downwards from the droning note with occasional leaps of a 3rd or 4th. Sliding microtonal embellishments and grace notes give interest and shape to the melodic pattern (rangi). There are songs which do not fit this general description but they are the exception to the rule and perhaps influenced by later cultural contacts.

Today there is a tendency not to produce the little 'niceties' that give the

A pūtōrino, a Māori flute from the North Island, detail. *National Museum, Wellington*

songs their special character but to concentrate on the words and the rhythmic pulse that drives the song along. This probably arises from group learning in cultural clubs and a measure of unfamiliarity with waiata style and language.

Traditional songs may be lullabies, laments, love songs, or justifications. They may confine themselves to simple expressions of their subject or range over complex accounts of history, geography, or genealogy. In an oral tradition these songs are an important record of the tribe and have been used effectively to counter contending land claims. Such songs were considered to be an important accompaniment to the whāikorero (formal speech). An appropriate song would give a stylistic finish to it.

Māori people loved the flute and held those who played them in high regard. Wondrous romantic tales were woven around them. It is claimed that players could literally make them talk and that words breathed into them could be carried by the simple notes of the song. Universally, love may be blind, but in the Māori world it apparently had a heightened auditory effect. The most common flute was the kōauau. Crafted in wood or bone, it was a stumpy tubular instrument with three holes bored into the top of it. Its piping but penetrating voice was sounded when air was blown across the opening at the top of the tube. In recent years there has been an upsurge of interest in the making and playing of the kōauau. There are three other kinds of flutes, the pūtōrino, the pōrutu and the nguru, each with a distinctive timbre; these have not enjoyed a popular revival, but may in time do so.

Modern music had its beginnings at the colonial stage of the country's development. There were two sources of influence; sailors and missionaries. Both were to contribute to the expanding diatonic horizon of Māori musical life. But from the beginning when the two cultures met, the greatest musical influence came from the missionaries. They built churches and set up schools in the villages and pursued the teaching of the gospel and the singing of hymns. They became proficient in the Māori language and used it as the medium for teaching. In no time they had the Māori on the road to literacy in their own language. They were solicitors of the welfare of their converts in view of the impending colonization that would inevitably follow. Thus they exerted political pressure to safeguard Māori interests and their own in terms of land acquisition. The Māori's trust of the missionaries virtually guided his footsteps to the signing table of the Treaty of Waitangi.

The land wars fomented by the colonial government's neglect of the Treaty caused severe dislodgment of Māori life style. Without a shared power base as provided for in the Treaty, and the reality of legislative victimization, and loss of traditional resources, the Māori were at a great disadvantage. It was impossible for them to adapt effectively and naturally to the imported culture and its entrenching institutions on Māori terms, and they were reduced to a state of dependency and forced to accept a policy of assimilation.

During the early period the churches remained the strongest European

institution to influence and modify Māori cultural patterns. This was done on
Māori terms. Indeed the Māori people formed their own churches to serve their
cultural aspirations more closely. The language for the service and hymns was
Māori. Some churches adopted the chanting of scriptures waiata-style rather
than diatonic hymns.

In the transition to hymn tunes the Māori had difficulty in negotiating widely
spaced intervals and coping with extended melodic range while keeping in tune.
The carry-over of sliding techniques proved disastrous to the melody. They
were blissfully unconcerned with timing but dragged their way to an agonizing
end. How the missionaries must have suffered. But with the patience of Job,
and judging that the redeeming end would justify the painful means, they
persevered. The Māori today still tend to drag their hymns which they immensely
enjoy singing. In the long run, hymn singing had the effect of opening up
possibilities of a new and exciting range of tonal experience.

This was certainly the case of the adherents of one church in particular. By
1881 when the Church of Jesus Christ of Latter Day Saints (Hunga Tapu)
opened its Māori mission, the Māori converts were prepared to embrace both
the doctrines and the choral tradition of the church. In 1886 the first annual
conference (Hui Tau) was held. In later years music was to become an important
feature of the Hui Tau, and in time influenced the choral development of the
annual conferences of other churches. The church school, the Maori Agriculture
College (M.A.C.) at Korongata, Hastings, opened its doors to students in 1913.
On its staff was a teacher of vocal and instrumental music. The following year,
a well known Māori music teacher who had trained in the States joined the
all-American faculty. The music department featured a band, a choir and a glee
club. In 1915 the band went on an extensive tour of several towns in Manawatu,
Taranaki, King Country, Bay of Plenty, Auckland and Northland. This was
probably the first time that many Māori in the audience had seen Māori
instrumentalists in a band, and realized that this was an attainable goal. On
3 February 1931 the buildings crumbled in the Napier earthquake. Luckily the
school had not convened for the new term. It was never rebuilt. However
its influence had been felt in the musical life of a large number of Māori
communities. Many instrumentalists of brass, wind and piano emerged to form
bands and to conduct choirs. Meanwhile the annual church conference (Hui
Tau) was going from strength to strength and featuring a cultural and choral
competition. The choral section format would include a ladies' trio and ladies'
chorus, and a men's quartet and chorus. The choir competition would be the
crowning event and the massed choir the *pièce de résistance*. These competitions
generated enthusiastic response and the announcements of the selected pieces,
which might include selections from musicals and oratorios, would be eagerly
awaited and worked on for the rest of the year.

The Hui Tau is no longer held, but the choral tradition has passed to the
annual conferences of other churches modelled after the Hui Tau format. These

A pūtōrino. *National
Museum, Wellington*

A kōauau or Māori flute.
*Brian Brake. National
Museum Wellington*

were the Anglican Hui Topu (1946), the Catholic Hui Aranga (1947) and such like.

Other groups in their time have shared the choral glory: The Ohinemutu Rotorua Maori Choir founded in the late 1920s provides an interesting example of vocal transition from the melismatic waiata singing to western choral techniques, while the memory of Seymour's Methodist choir still lingers after the sound of their disciplined singing has faded. The Te Arohanui group's 150 voice choir displayed the best of the Hui Tau choral tradition when they attended the opening of the Polynesian Centre in Hawaii in 1963 and the American mainland. In 1974 the backing group to the winning Commonwealth Games song went on to form the New Zealand Maori Chorale for recording purposes with overseas markets in mind. The choral section of the Aotearoa Festival of Arts shows some innovative groups using original compositions, movements (choralography) and artistic positional changes (choreography), imparting a strong feeling of theatre. 1989 saw the formation of the National Māori Choir. In 1990 it featured a massed choir singing a repertoire of Māori 'favourites'. Perhaps this group may yet take up the kākahu (cloak) of massed voices which was once the feature of the Māori choral scene.

Today there is a renewed interest in Māoritanga. It originated early this century in the work of a group of young men which became known as the Young Maori Party. The three giants of the group were Te Rangi Hiroa (Peter Buck) anthropologist; Maui Pomare, medical practitioner; and Apirana Ngata, lawyer. All saw parliament as holding the key to Māori grievances. All became parliamentarians. Apirana Ngata retained strong links with the Māori world during his forty years in parliament. He was able to regenerate pride in Māori culture through the revival of Māori arts, crafts, songs and oral traditions.

With the cultural resurgence, interest in the collecting and learning of waiata tawhito (ancient songs) ignited. This flame was fanned by the formation of cultural clubs, beginning with Ngati Poneke of Wellington in 1935 which had been functioning under the Anglican Maori Mission welfare services for a number of years. Since then there has been a proliferation of culture clubs throughout the country. These clubs are found everywhere in communities and schools, all serving the same purpose in fostering the performing arts and taking part in ceremonial occasions.

A sense of theatre has always been part of Māori community life responding to the ritual imperatives of oral traditions. The marae was a theatre in which all players, following strict protocol, would play their part, and the performances would be eagerly watched and critically appraised. The presentation would be in oratory, song and dance. The occasion could be a pōwhiri (welcome), a tangihanga (funeral) or a hui (conference) called for a specific purpose. The marae was the centre-point of public display. It is not a wonder then that when Maggie Papakura of Rotorua toured with her concert party to Great Britain in 1911, a carved meeting house went with her. The stage would become a marae in very essence. It is only in the last thirty years that this cultural concept has been replaced by an awareness of the stage as being theatre and not necessarily subject to marae protocol. This was undoubtedly influenced by the expanding experience of live theatre by the Māori in drama, musicals and opera in the 1960s.

The Arawa people were the first to see the commercial possibilities of the tourist trade; they were located in the thermal sights and spas of Rotorua, a popular tourist area. The concert party was the response to this situation. Other areas followed this example but went on tour to find their audience. Invariably the aim would be to raise funds for some worthwhile project, which could be marae related. But seldom would a concert party endure beyond the achievement of its goal. It would disband and regroup whenever the need arose. Not until the culture clubs became established with the aim of promoting the performing arts as a heritage, was the reason for its continued existence sufficiently strong to retain interest and ongoing commitment. Also the advent of the regional and national competitions (the Aotearoa Festival of Arts) became a powerful incentive for clubs to produce original works and strive to raise their standard of performance to a high artistic level.

The instrument favoured by the early concert party and club was the piano. This gave a reassuring framework of broad chordal accompaniment and carried the singing forward in strength. With this backing there was no need for harmony. The focus was on the projection of melody, the words and movements and the haka effects to give tension and excitement, until the final release in the exultant expiration, 'Auē Hei!'

The piano was ideal when the audience came to the marae, but its transportation was a problem when the group performed at another venue. Guitars replaced the pianos in the late 1940s when the concert parties travelled to their audiences; to hotel venues and tourist ships. Their continued popularity across the broad spectrum of contemporary music has assured them of a permanent place in the Māori performing arts. Even earlier, in the 1920s and 30s, most of the dance bands in the eastern provinces were Māori or had Māori participants. In every Māori community the marae dining hall would double as a dance hall on Saturday nights. A pianist would be the sole orchestra or be assisted by a saxophonist and drummer. There would be many celebratory occasions which would bring the whole community to the hall and would provide opportunities for local musicians with a variety of instruments to make music. Today many halls have an ageing piano pushed into a corner as a relic of a bygone florescence, which no longer hears the shuffling feet of dancers, as the succeeding generations have moved on to other social diversions.

The pop scene brought new amplified instruments, new exciting sounds, new combinations of instruments. The glittering pathway from the village hall to the fantasies of a world stage was starlit by television and glamour promotions. This resulted in a flow of Māori musicians and singers onto the Australian and Asian entertainment circuit. Others went on promotional programmes to countries targeted for local products while some culture clubs linked into the summer folk festivals of Europe.

Beat music had brought to the fore many Māori top bands. One of the most popular bands to dominate the entertainment awards was 'Herbs', with its particular style of Pacific reggae. 'Ardijah' won the first Rheineck rock award in 1988. In the same year a group of unemployed youths, 'Mokai', formed under a work-skill programme, won the band section of the television programme, Star Quest. Bands like the popular 'Aotearoa', the all-women 'Black Katz', 'Dread Beat', the access training troup, 'Kahurangi', 'Mana', 'Meg and the Fones', and 'Styx and Shanty', endorsed their reputation with successful record releases. From these groups have come a wealth of original music in either English or Māori or a mixture of both. These groups are among those who perform throughout the country where people gather to drink, muse and mutter, or on talent shows, showcases and festivals.

Puatatangi, the music advisory committee of the Council for Maori and South Pacific Arts and the Queen Elizabeth II Arts Council, have joined together in a promotional project to assist emergent Maori bands to break into the recording scene. Their 'Rourou e Rua' (two baskets) project launched in 1989 attracted a number of new bands. These were featured at the Indigenous Music Festival during the Waitangi celebrations of 1990.

One important genre, that of the brass band, should receive a mention in a survey such as this. The brass band has had a strong and continuing association with the Ratana church. Brass bands also appear with the Kingitanga movement, and there is the historical attachment of a brass drum accompaniment to the poi dance of Te Atiawa of Taranaki. One significant recent development has been the formation of the 'Te Peene o Aotearoa', the Aotearoa Maori Band in 1989. Although promoted mainly by brass band enthusiasts of the Ratana church it has drawn its membership from a wide sector of Maoridom. At the Waitangi celebrations of 1990 this national band impressed with its high standard of musicianship and drill.

In conclusion, it can be confidently said that today Māori music is in good heart. At best it is still community music with a strong traditional heritage and an active adaptation of new music in a variety of situations. The question arises 'Why is this Māori music?' The answer may lie in the historian's observation: 'The two races came to live largely in separate worlds.' For the past 150 years this has been so, and no more so than in the field of music. Cultural survival makes it imperative that Māori people preserve those things which contribute to Māori identity.

TE PUOHO KATENE

Part One

Growth of a Performing Tradition

Alfred Hill, about to
launch into the music of
his *Exhibition Ode* at the
opening ceremony of the
New Zealand International
Exhibition, Christchurch,
1906-7. *Alexander Turnbull
Library*

I

The frontier: explorers, sealers, whalers and missionaries

1 Explorers

The first European music to be heard in New Zealand was that of the baroque trumpet, then at the zenith of its powers. Abel Janszoon Tasman's expedition of discovery had set sail from Batavia on 14 August 1642 in the flagship *Heemskerck*, and the *Zeehaen*, a long and narrow ship known as a flute. Both were small and in no more than moderate condition. By late November, they had reached Tasmania, or Antony van Diemens Land, where they planted a post and a flag. Proceeding in a south-easterly direction, they saw at noon on 13 December 1642 'a large land uplifted high', the west coast of the South Island of New Zealand, between Hokitika and Okarito, where lofty mountains crowd down on a dramatic coast. Two days later they had rounded Cape Foulwind to the north and by midnight on 17 December had anchored outside a sandspit, beyond which there stretched a large open bay which they entered next morning, anchoring at sunset in fifteen fathoms. As lights appeared on shore, two canoes approached, thus forcing the ships' boats, launched in readiness for a landing, to be hauled back on board. The natives called out in a 'rough loud voice' in no known language, and in answer to the cries of the Dutch would come no nearer than a stone's throw, but they blew instead 'many times on an instrument which gave sound like the moors' Trumpets.[1] We had one of our sailors (who could play somewhat on the Trumpet) blow back to them in answer, those of the *Zeehaen* had their under-mate . . . do likewise: after this was done several times on both sides, and the dark evening was falling more and more, those in the vessels finally stopped and paddled away . . .'.[2]

The next day seven canoes moved out from the shore, when despite friendly advances from both ships, one rammed the *Zeehaen*'s cockboat, which had been acting as intermediary. The quartermaster, struck violently several times in the neck with a long blunt pike, fell overboard, the others being attacked with clubs (patu). Four men died; three, including the quartermaster, saved their lives by swimming to the ship. Tasman named the place *Moordenaers* or

Tasman's ships *Heemskerck* and *Zeehaen*, from Tasman's *Journal*. *National Museum, Wellington*

A pūtātara, or shell trumpet. *National Museum, Wellington*

Captain James Cook,
FRS., by William Hodges
(1744-97), artist on the
second voyage, 1773.
Author's collection

Murderers' Bay, later changed to Golden Bay. He then sailed north, celebrating Christmas in gloomy weather in Cook Strait, before resuming his exploration of the North Island coast. He named the new country after his province in Holland, Zeeland, an area of islands and water, so 'New' Zeeland it became. For over 120 years it remained a mere straggling short line on the map, until on 6 October 1769, Nicholas Young, a boy at the masthead of James Cook's *Endeavour*, sighted land, and two days later the first Europeans stepped ashore on the east coast of the North Island near today's city of Gisborne.[3]

Cook's three voyages (1769, 1773, and 1777), provided many opportunities for Europeans to study Māori life and music: 'In their song they keep time with such exactness, that I have often heard above one hundred paddles struck against the sides of their boats at once, so as to produce but a single sound at the divisions of their music', wrote Cook, who admired their superb rhythmic sense.[4] The young James Burney, son of the great music historian Charles Burney, sailed as a Second Lieutenant on the *Adventure* during Cook's second voyage, and wrote in more detail:

> As yet I have not mentioned their Music. I shall say but little on this subject for very little will suffice. Their Instruments are Flutes and Trumpets—the flutes are more curious for their carving than for any music that can be got out of them. I shall bring home a Specimen. The Trumpet is a Tube about 7 feet long—they make these & the flutes by getting a piece of wood fit for their purpose. They then shape it on the outside & afterwards split it in 2. These parts being hollowd are woulded [sic] together & are sure to fit exactly. I saw but one of their Trumpets the whole time we staid here and that Captn. Furneaux got—the notes on this vary according as you blow more or less. I question whether a man who understands the French horn might not be able to play a Tune on it—as to the New Zealanders they constantly sounded the same Note.[5]

Captain Cook himself thought Māori songs 'harmonious enough but very dolefull to a European Ear',[6] a view held by several subsequent explorers.[7] Only two months after Cook's arrival, a French ship *St Jean Baptiste* under the command of J. F. M. de Surville, visited the New Zealand coast, unaware of their predecessor. On Saturday 30 December 1769, 'Three young women came and danced for over an hour very lewd and immodest dances; even more so than the Spanish dance called Mosquito Bag', wrote First Lieutenant Guillaume Labe.[8] A vivid description of a haka is given by M. de Sainson, officer on the notable French explorer d'Urville's 1827 *Astrolabe* expedition:[9]

> Little by little their bodies are thrown back, their knees strike together, the muscles of their necks swell, and the head is shaken by movements which look like convulsions; their eyes turn up, so that, with horrible effect, their pupils are absolutely hidden under the eyelids, while at the same time they twist their hands with outspread fingers very rapidly before their faces. Now is the time when this strange melody takes on a character that no words can describe,

but which fills the whole body with involuntary tremors. Only by hearing it can anyone form an idea of this incredible crescendo, in which each one of the actors appeared to us to be possessed by an evil spirit; and yet what sublime and terrible effects are produced by this savage music![10]

As the eighteenth century drew on, more European musical instruments began to be heard. Elie le Guillou, surgeon on the *Zélée*, which accompanied the *Astrolabe*, described how in 1827 they found a Māori tribe in Otago whose wealthy chief had purchased *'une orgue de Barbarie, dont il amusait son oisiveté'* ('a barrel organ with which he entertained his idleness').[11]

Barrel organs, musical boxes and Jew's harps (the latter commonly used in barter, a gross of them forming part of the New Zealand Company's payment for lands in Wellington), were followed later by violins, flutes and pianos.[12]

2 Sealers and whalers

'There she blows!', aloft on a whaler, from *Nimrod of the Sea* (1874) by W. M. Davis. *Alexander Turnbull Library*

The arrival of sealers and whalers in the late eighteenth and early nineteenth centuries has left a literary and visual mark in the form of writings, paintings, drawings, and some vestigial remains of buildings and equipment, but musically the legacy is slight. The anonymous ballad 'David Lowston' is about a sealer who is left marooned on a forlorn outpost.

> My name is David Lowston, I did seal, I did seal,
> My name is David Lowston, I did seal.
> Though my men and I were lost,
> Though our very lives 'twould cost,
> We did seal, we did seal, we did seal.[13]

Lowston and his team were set down in Open Bay (near Jackson's Bay, South Westland), on 16 February 1810. Their ship foundered in a gale, but meanwhile they had cured 10,000 skins of fur and fallen ill. Eventually the schooner *Governor Bligh* rescued them, the moral being: 'Never seal, never seal, never seal'.

A small sealing trade existed for a decade or so from 1804, concentrated on the extreme south of the country. Whaling proved far more important. With the growth of the industry in the south Pacific, ships based in Sydney had begun to explore New Zealand waters by the end of the eighteenth century, and whaling stations appeared in tiny inlets around the coast, notably in the extreme south and at Port Underwood and Te Awaiti in Cook Strait, through which the whales passed in their hundreds.

It was a brutalizing experience. A song believed to have been composed in the 1830s at Heberley's station at Port Underwood is a bitter expression of the sense of exploitation felt by the whalers towards the agent. Many were paid 'in kind', in commodities; without ready cash they found it almost impossible to get a passage out on a supply ship:

> I am paid in soap and sugar and rum
> For cutting in whale and boiling down tongue
> The Agent's fee makes my blood so to boil
> I'll push him in a hot pot of oil.[14]

Most ships seemed to have at least one or two players of musical instruments aboard:

> . . . then the Captain came on Deck and called for the Cook and his Fiddle, then the Steward fetched up a Bucket of Rum and sang out Grog O, then the Captain said now for a Dance, the Steward took the Captains Flute and played, so they danced away, although the decks were greasy with the Blubber . . .[15]

In his novel *The Whalers*, Alexandre Dumas describes how a barrel organ strongly appealed to the Māori when heard on a whaling ship.[16] At some stations musical life proved to be extraordinarily civilized. Dr Edward Shortland (1812-1893), private secretary to Governor Hobson and later interpreter and native adviser during the South Island land claim investigations of 1843-44, wrote of his arrival at the Sydney entrepreneur Johnny Jones' southern settlement at Waikouaiti Bay, the 'Ultima Thule' of the colony: 'my ears were astonished at the sounds of a piano, and my eyes at the black "cutaway" and riding whip of a young gentleman, lately of Emman. Coll. Cantab., but now acting tutor to Mr J's son and heir'.[17]

3 Missionaries

In 1814, there stepped ashore at Rangihoua in the Bay of Islands the first three missionaries to begin work in New Zealand: Thomas Kendall, schoolmaster and Justice of the Peace, William Hall, carpenter, and John King, shoemaker. Following the lobbying of the noted New South Wales chaplain, the Reverend Samuel Marsden, at Parramatta in Sydney, a post of the Anglican Church Missionary Society (popularly known as the CMS) was set up—what has been described as 'a nucleus of artisan missionaries'.[18] John Liddiard Nicholas, a former London ironfounder who accompanied Marsden, describes the first church service which began with the Old Hundredth Psalm. Afterwards, some four to five hundred Māori, 'surrounding Mr Marsden and myself, commenced their war dance, yelling and shouting in their usual style, which they did, I suppose, from the idea that this furious demonstration of their joy would be the most grateful return they could make us for the solemn spectacle they had witnessed'.[19] In 1823 the Reverend Henry Williams arrived to set up his mission at Paihia, and was joined by his brother William in 1826.

In converting the Māori to a 'higher' religion, the most powerful agent, apart from language, was music.[20] The Reverend E. G. Marsh sent his nephews

Natives assembled to celebrate the Lord's Supper. at Orona Taupo New Zealand.

Maori assembled to celebrate the Lord's Supper. Lithograph in *The Eccelsiologist*, v4n11, March 1845. *Alexander Turnbull Library*

the gift of a pipe organ, powered by foot bellows, a fine example of the English church barrel organ. It could play three hymns; the player stood at the back and turned a handle.[21] The Reverend Henry Williams recorded its arrival 'without the slightest injury . . . It is sufficiently powerful to fill a much larger chapel than ours.'[22] Mrs Henry Williams considered it a little sensual for church use: 'I was glad [that] the overpowering sensations which its full and melodious sounds produced and all the recollections it roused were a little moderated before the Sabbath.'[23] The limited repertoire could be expanded by sending to England for more interchangeable barrels. Such instruments filled the gap before the arrival of proper organs. The Williams brothers had a strong influence, as did subsequent CMS men such as William Colenso, printer and Māori scholar, George Clarke, A. N. Browne, Octavius Hadfield, and Richard Taylor.

By 1831 there were eighty-three Europeans (including fifty-four children) in the Church Missionary Society stations. Meanwhile the Wesleyans had established themselves on the Hokianga and the Roman Catholic Bishop Pompallier had arrived in 1838, eventually to set up his mission at Kororareka in 1841. When the one-and-a-half ton Gaveaux printing press was hauled up the beach along with other supplies for the mission, an eyewitness described how 'Maoris, Missionaries and Sailors all pulled together on the rope to the measured strains of the sailors' cry'.[24] William Yate of the CMS had 117 closely printed pages of a selection of scripture, the liturgy, catechisms, and hymns translated into Māori and printed in Sydney: 'Nothing could exceed the gratification with which these books were received on my return, by those who could read them. They were willing to receive them as wages, or to purchase them with anything they possessed of a saleable nature.'[25] The efficacy of music in the ritual of conversation was as well known to Pacific missionaries as it was to the home sects in England, to the Wesleyans especially, with their chapel enthusiasms which often proceeded from fervour to a state bordering on hysteria and delirium. The Māori gradually began to familiarize themselves with western music, principally through psalms and hymn tunes, although the range of the National Anthem also lay within their grasp.[26]

From 1840 onwards settlers, among whom were historians, amateur anthropologists, and members of Her Majesty's forces, now began describing Māori life (including music) to their friends, relatives, and the outside world. These include Edward Jerningham Wakefield's description of the ceremonies following the deal in which the Company acquired Wellington. Natives from Wanganui, distinguished 'by their ferocious appearance', took part: 'They had blackened all round their eyes with charcoal, and painted themselves copiously with streaks of red ochre and oil; they performed their part with excessive vigour and gusto, and looked, when in the ecstasy of the dance, like demons incarnate.'[27] The celebrations ended with a haka performed by about 150 men and women. In a more classical tone is the description of an evening spent at Lake Taupo in May 1842 by Ensign Best, a young English officer of the 80th Regiment, who showed an intelligent interest in Māori language and culture, collecting a number of songs:

> . . . we were now a large party, the Moon was nearly full and all night we amused ourselves singing round our large fires. The Mauries entered into the spirit of the thing and chanted their Akas or songs with unusual glee. The Taupo women far surpassed those of our party in the grace and voluptuousness of their movements but our war song was decidedly superior in fire and wild ferocity. An English chorus greatly delighted them and had Te Tipa and another chief had their way we might have sung to the day of judgement. At length the moon went down and we retired to our Tents.[28]

Notes

1. Probably the pūkūea (wooden trumpet), or pūtātara (shell trumpet)
2. Sharp, *Voyages*, 121ff.; also Beaglehole, *Discovery* 10ff.
3. See chapter VIII, 2 for details of the collaboration between the poet Allen Curnow and the composer Douglas Lilburn to mark the tercentenary of Tasman's visit, with *Landfall in Unknown Seas*
4. Quoted in Annabell, 'Music in Auckland', 144-5, from Hawkesworth, *An Account of the Voyages*, vol. 3, 468
5. Burney, 56. See also McLean, *Maori Music*
6. Quoted by Beaglehole, *Cook Journals*, vol. 1, 285. See McLean's account of Māori instruments in *New Grove*, vol. 13, 194ff.
7. See René Primavère Lesson in 1824: 'The New Zealander's singing is solemn and monotonous, and is composed of slow, broken, guttural notes; it is always accompanied by movements of the eyes and measured, very meaningful gestures.' Duperrey, *Visit*, 94
8. *Early Eyewitness Accounts of Maori Life 1, Extracts from Journals Relating to the Visit to New Zealand of the French Ship St Jean Baptiste in December 1769*. ATL Endowment Trust, Wellington (1982) 83
9. See especially McLean, *Maori Music*
10. Wright, *New Zealand 1826-1827*, 208
11. le Guillou, E., *Voyage Autour du Monde*, Paris (1844) 244
12. Wakefield, *Adventure*, 34
13. Wedde, I. and McQueen, H. (eds) *Penguin Book of New Zealand Verse* (1985); also in Colquhoun, *New Zealand Folksongs*
14. Anonymous shore-whaling song 'Come All You Tonguers', quoted in Morton, 241, from Harkness thesis
15. Quoted by Thessman J., from his great-great-grandfather Worser Heberley's journal describing celebrations on the *Caroline* after the capture of eleven whales in the Pacific in 1826, in 'The heyday of chasing the whale', *Dominion*, 13 January 1988, 11
16. Maynard, F. and Dumas, A., *The Whalers*, tr. Reed, F. W. London, 1937
17. Shortland, E., *The Southern Districts of New Zealand*. London (1851) 108
18. Sharp, A., in *ENZ*, vol. 2, 505
19. Nicholas, *Narrative*, vol. 1, 206
20. See, for instance, Thomas, A., 'Acculturated Music in Oceania' *JPS*, June 1981, 183-91
21. Made by A. A. Bulkingham, organ builder of Frederick Place, 39 Hampstead Road,

London. The instrument, now in Wanganui Museum, is listed in Langwill, *Church and Chamber Barrel Organs*, Edinburgh (1967, 1970) 107

[22] Annabell, from Williams, H., *Williams Papers 1822-1864*. APL, 203, 210

[23] Williams, H., *Williams Papers 1822-1864*, 215

[24] Quoted in Annabell, 'Music in Auckland' from extract in *NZ Herald*, 23 March 1968, 9

[25] Yate, *Account*, 231-2

[26] See Annabell, 'Music in Auckland', ch. 5 for an excellent account of this process

[27] Wakefield, *Adventure*, 98

[28] Best, Ensign, 308. See p. 369 for an account of collecting four songs

II

Music in the first settlements

1 Music on the voyage

The London headquarters of the missionary societies usually advised their young men going overseas to take with them some means of diversion, such as a musical instrument. Early handbooks and guides to New Zealand did likewise: the bugle and cornet-à-piston 'would be heard to advantage among the echoes of the beautiful scenery', wrote Edward Jerningham Wakefield in 1848.[1]

In 1849 J. Willox offered a first-rate pianoforte as an inducement to sail on *The Prince of Wales* with its 'magnificent' poop, saloon 'of substantial elegance . . . varnished all round in richly decorated and pleasingly tinted panels and pilasters, in shades of Parisian and pure white, heightened in effect with ornamental carvings hatched in gold . . .'[2]

Wakefield felt music was 'an accomplishment of infinite value to the possessor and his or her friends, as a recreation in the intervals of a Colonist's labour, and as relief to the solitude of a distant location. It should be learned *before* starting on the voyage. Nothing is so disagreeable as a fellow-passenger who is *learning* to sing or to play some instrument.'

To E. B. Fitton, writing in 1856, music was a special solace in a bark or wooden hut, 'for in moments of gloom and despondency, of vain regrets for the past, or useless longings for the future, the mind is often diverted and aroused from its morbid state by [its] cheerful and soothing influence'.[3] A piano was essential: '. . . if a lady were hesitating whether to pay the freight for her piano or a chest of drawers, I would decidedly recommend her to prefer the piano. It will afford more gratification and cheerfulness from associations aroused by its music than can be supplied by more practically useful furniture, for which, after all, it is easy to get a substitute from any skilful colonial carpenter.'[4]

In his popular *The New Zealand 'Emigrant's Bradshaw'* (1861), Charles F. Hursthouse was even more eloquent: 'We do not go to New Zealand to live in a tree, or to eat from a tub; and some little plenishing for a house and home is just as necessary there as here. The sight, too, of some old article of furniture, piano, book, or picture, often lends a homely charm to the new dwelling in the new land which is actually *profitable*.'[5] A relative had recently received fifty acres of fine land for an old piano.[6] The cottage cabinet piano seemed especially suitable: it could either be freighted or taken on board to be played in the evening for polkas, songs and waltzes: 'I would advise any fair emigrant to take a piano with her as part of her battery of charms . . .'[7]

Charlotte Godley (1821-1907), wife of John Robert Godley, prominent in the founding of Canterbury, believed

> that if anyone wanted to bring out a pianoforte, a square one is the best, because the machinery is much more simple than in one like ours (a low cabinet P.F.), where, if anything got broken, a mere tuner cannot repair it as he can in the square ones, and I think, too, that for anyone coming out for good, it would answer to bring out a more expensive kind than ours (£28 in its packing case from Wornham [Wornum]), they seem to bear the voyage far better; Mrs Eyre's, Mrs Gold's and Mrs Fox's, hardly suffered at all, while I can afford to say now that ours was very bad. Our friend Mr Giblin was drumming away at it from six to ten p.m.[8]

The New Zealand Company mounted a number of spectacular public functions to farewell colonists and emigrants, where some of the earliest of musical compositions with New Zealand associations appeared. At a grand ball in the Theatre Royal at Plymouth in 1841, attended by 600 people, with 450 spectators, a new set of dances by a Mr Rowe called *The Taranaki Waltzes* and *Gallopade* were 'considered beautiful and danced twice during the night'.[9] The ball raised money to supply poorer emigrants with clothing.

The voyage usually began with sea shanties: 'I was awoke this morning by the most strange noises about 4 o'clock', wrote young Alfred Fell (b. 1817) on his voyage to Nelson in the *Lord Auckland* in 1841-1842. 'Could not tell what in the world to make of it; dressed myself as soon as possible and went on deck. It was the weighing of the anchor, and the noise was a huge capstan used on that occasion, in which is placed a dozen large bars, and men work it round singing all the time a strange wild ditty, of which I could make nothing more out than that it was about "Nancy O" and "Cheerily Men, cheerily O"; not very musical, and yet not very unpleasant withal.'[10] On the *Sir Edward Paget* in 1852, the male passengers helped the crew bring in ninety fathoms of chain cable: 'Then again the catting [anchor-raising] song . . . the boatswain performing the priest's part in the curious litany with various fancy ejaculations as "heave up the devil", "We'll make him civil", "Another pull", "All with a will", "That pull will do" whilst the response of "Heigh, oh, cheerily men" followed each . . . The passengers all very merry this afternoon. One of the intermediates plays the flute and cuddy [saloon] and steerage were jigging away at a great rate.'[11]

Voyages tended to fall into a pattern, made up of an emotional farewell, succeeded by an initial alarm at the discomforts of shipboard life, exacerbated on many occasions by storms around the English coast, a phase usually followed by a delight in its novelty. There was invariably relief at crossing the Bay of Biscay, and pleasure at the more clement weather as the ship approached the tropics. Dancing, singing, hymns on Sundays, and informal music-making enlivened the journey. 'Henry commenced learning the clarinet', wrote the spirited young Mary Anne Eleanor Petre of her husband on her voyage to Wellington in the *Thomas Spark* in 1842-1843, in apparent contradiction to Wakefield's advice. A few days later 'Henry seemed to have made great progress . . .'[12] This phase was almost invariably succeeded by another, when the stifling heat of the tropics, the becalming of the ship, and the absence of stimulation afflicted almost everybody.

Throughout the journey sickness was a constant companion, often rendering passengers (no less captains and crew) prickly and overwrought. A great deal depended on the captain: 'We are occasionally treated to an Irish jig or hornpipe from one of the sailors, the irrepressible steward or the captain', wrote Norman Hunter of his voyage to Dunedin in 1882. 'He plays for the most part on a flageolet though he has also performed on a concertina and fiddle.'[13] A new mood set in with signs of approaching land as drifting seaweed, or a new species of bird lifted the spirits. 'Going out for a glass of water saw the Commodore making ready to go on to the poop, which I took for an indubitable sign of land, so alarmed the others', wrote C. W. Richmond in his journal. '"Long looked for come at last!" There it lay faint in the moonlight of a delicious night . . . I have felt it impossible to believe that here at last is New Zealand.'[14]

Notes

[1] A Late Magistrate of the Colony [Edward Jerningham Wakefield], *Hand-Book*, 437ff.

[2] Willox, J. *Willox's New Zealand Handbook*, 1849

[3] Fitton, 273

[4] Ibid., 283

[5] Hursthouse, 259

[6] Ibid., 260

[7] Ibid., 295

[8] Godley, *Letters*, 101. By 1840 square pianos had lost favour in Britain, being hard to keep in tune. Robert Wornum produced the first 'cottage' piano in 1811. Just over a metre tall, it proved to be musically unsatisfactory.

[9] Quoted in Ward, L. E. *Early Wellington*. Wellington (1929) 448, from *The New Zealand Journal*, 25 December 1841

[10] Fell, 4

[11] Richmond, C. W. Journal, 8 December 1852. Richmond-Atkinson, vol. 1, 118

[12] 'The New Zealand Diary of the Hon. Mrs Henry Petre 1842-4', Petre Ms, Saturday 3 September 1842, ATL

[13] Hunter, N. Logbooks: New Zealand and Back. ATL 091, letter 21 June 1882

[14] Richmond-Atkinson, vol. 1, 123

2 Music and the New Zealand Company: Wellington 1840-1870

When the *Aurora*, first ship of the New Zealand Company, nosed past the jagged rocks at the entrance to Wellington harbour, past the bare promontories, the steep wooded hills and brown tussock-clad cliffs, it seemed to many of those on board like Scotland, only harsher. On 22 January 1840, 'the first emigrants were deposited in a bewildered huddle at the edge of the sand . . . In confused heaps lay casks and bales, beds and pianos, clocks, cruet stands, warming-pans, family portraits and packages, some of them "washing about on the sand, having been thrown on shore considerably below high water-mark"' wrote John Miller.[1] From the nearby bush came the sounds of birds, arresting in their power and clarity, to mingle with the sonorous chants, hakas, and war cries of the Māori, who paddled by furiously in their great canoes, mounting a mock-heroic display.

Soon afterwards, on a sunny day without cloud or wind, the settlers held their first church service under a clump of karaka trees not far from Petone beach. Under the offices of the Reverend John McFarlane, the only clergyman on the first ship, about thirty worshippers sang the hymn 'All People that on Earth Do Dwell', gave thanks for their safe arrival, heard a short sermon, and ended the service with the 23rd Psalm 'The Lord is my shepherd, I shall not want'. Off the outcrop of Somes Island lay several vessels, the British Ensign hanging limply at their peak.

After the removal of the principal settlement to Thorndon Flat across the harbour, to escape the storms and flooding which had marred Petone, there grew up by degrees a small settlement, of shops, inns, houses, and churches, clinging to the thin line of the shore, nudging the bushclad hills that dominated the site. With it there grew also the lineaments of a musical life that had as its cultivated core the singing and playing of the wealthier settlers, especially their wives. On 2 January 1841 a governess advertised in the first newspaper, the *Spectator*, which had begun publication on 27 March 1840, that she could teach 'music, harp, pianoforte and singing'.[2] On 27 March a Mr and Mrs Fitzgerald offered private lessons in music. Musical life also gravitated towards the vociferous taverns which had sprung into being. By 10 October 1840 twelve were listed in the *Spectator*, seven on the Thorndon flats and five at Petone. The mysterious figures of accomplished itinerant musicians soon drifted in and out, footloose creatures wandering the world, playing exotic instruments. And there was always the uproar brought by the outsiders of the town, by the bands of sailors and strays from the whaling stations, in uproarious carousal.

The settings for many musical evenings had an infinite charm: 'As the sun

The Hon Mrs Mary Petre (1825-65). *Alexander Turnbull Library*

went down behind Tinakori, casting shadows across the English green of Thorndon Flat where small boys flew kites, the gentlemen played cricket, and the military band played on Wednesday afternoons, the little colonial township, with its single-floored wooden houses and gables on the street, came alight' writes Miller. On 25 February 1843 young Mrs Petre and her husband dined with their friends Dr Fitzgerald and his wife: 'Such a squash. Mrs Fitzgerald sang and played on the guitar very nicely. Baron Alsdof sang some good German songs'.[3]. Charlotte Godley describes these two ladies some seven years later: 'Mrs Fitzgerald sings very well . . . She has a most beaming, good-natured face, besides being very good-looking only figure, hands etc, unsuccessful.'[4] Mrs Petre is 'very young-looking and with wild spirits, and enjoys a ball or a ride, or a scamper of any kind and is sometimes very pretty'.[5]

Musical life continued between the Fitzgeralds and the Petres, with the ladies playing the guitar and singing. On Saturday 20 May they had a French commander to dinner with Irish guests. When the Frenchman left 'we broke out with two Irish comic songs from the Taguta with stage dancing from Mr St Hill and Henry. We kept going till twelve when Dr Fitzgerald played "God Save the Queen" on a bad clarinet we all standing round him singing out of tune. Never was there such discord before.'[6]

Social life tended to be divided into an inner and outer circle, corresponding

'Thorndon flat and Petiea (sic) taken from Wellington terrace'. Ink and watercolour from the John Pearse Album (1851-156). *Alexander Turnbull Library*

to the 'Select' and the 'Popular' balls of 1841.[7] A miniature *salon* revolved around musical settlers such as the Crawfords, who had ample means, or Mrs Gold, wife of the Lieutenant Colonel of the 65th Regiment. Good singers, pianists, violinists, and flautists took part. To visit Colonel Gold's to borrow music could mean being ushered in by a footman in blue plush to hear music played on a Broadwood semi-grand.

Band concerts on Thorndon Flat in the centre of the town, which had begun in 1846 with those of the 65th Regiment, took place twice weekly on Wednesdays and Fridays. Charlotte Godley's description has become justly renowned: 'It is a very tolerable band, and they play a great number of very pretty things, and altogether reminded me almost *too much* of home. There we met everyone, walking or sitting about in summer dresses, bonnets with feathers and flowers etc., and two or three parties of natives, rolled in their blankets and *squatted* just behind the great drum.' Chairs and camp stools were placed on the green sward around the musicians' snowy white uniforms, picked out with red, and their gleaming instruments.[8]

The town's musical occasions were diverse. St Paul's Church and St Peter's provided simple settings for unpretentious services similar to those of an English village. Government House balls were held with music by the band of the 65th Regiment under Colonel Gold, or by bandsmen from visiting naval ships. Barrett's Hotel, the most famed hostelry in the town, had opened on 24 October 1840 with a toast list and musical honours that would have seemed generous in England, including 'Home, Sweet Home', 'The Fine Old English Gentleman' and 'The Merry Month of May'. From September 1843 Wellington possessed a theatre, the Royal Victoria, 'lighted with gas', the gas lighting manufactured especially for the occasion by a Mr T. Saint. The theatre was opened by J. H. Marriott (1799-1886), whose multifarious talents included those of optician, instrument maker, journalist, and, in hard times, chiselling tombstones and fitting ladies' teeth. His short drama season at the Royal Victoria, which lasted until November 1843, presented favourite comedies and melodramas interspersed with songs, recitations, and occasional dances, usually ending with a farce. On the closure of his theatre he kept his hand in as an entertainer and singer of comic songs, beginning a new venture in 1846 at the Britannia Saloon, and in 1858 he compiled a collection of songs, *The Constitutional Budget*.[9]

In May 1843, an unidentified French naval officer on board the corvette *Le Rhin* wrote warmly of Wellington's musical life to an unidentified correspondent in France:

> The town presented us with a magnificent address and a banquet at the hotel. There followed dinners, balls, parties in the countryside, receptions on board; there was no end to it. The music which we organized amongst the crew plays an admirable role in all the *fêtes*; although it may not be irreproachable, it seems a wonder given the situation: everybody wishes to have it, everybody

wishes to hear it, and it has even been played this evening on the promenade at the unanimous request of the ladies.[10]

Contemporary newspapers advertised imported music, manuscript paper, and a widening range of instruments. By 1854, Smith and Wilcox could offer a 'superior' harmonium in rosewood with three stops and patent percussion etc.; violins, cellos, cornopeans (cornets), bass cornopeans, Koenig post horns, clarionets, flutes etc., and a supply of tutors. They also had an oak harmonium with five stops suitable for a church and a mahogany semi-cottage piano with an elegant oil painting in the front panel.[11]

In due course, musical associations such as the Philharmonic Society (1848) arose, their lives dependent on the talents of particular individuals. Its successor, founded in 1856, performed works by Rossini, Bellini, Kucken, with glees, polkas, marches, horn solos, and Cramer's Fantasia from *Lucia di Lammermoor*, a programme not dissimilar from those of the 65th Band. Anthems by Weldon and Boyce featured in a recital of sacred music at the Atheneum on 7 February 1856, with compositions by Marcello, Handel, and Mendelssohn. The Wellington Amateur Musical Society gave concerts for 'worthy causes' in the 1850s — extracts from oratorios and operas, sacred works, movements from symphonies and sonatas, ballads, glees, madrigals, and folksongs.

The magical words 'overseas artist' soon appeared in newspapers. Ali-Ben-Sou-Alle, after a stormy crossing of Cook Strait, gave a concert the same evening on his 'Turkophone', a mechanical wonder. He claimed to have performed in Paris and London, as well as before Queen Victoria at the Great Exhibition of 1851, the instrument being awarded a special medal. Over three hundred people heard his unfortunate lady accompanist struggling to keep up with him. He remained nearly two weeks in Wellington, arranging a 'Concert for the Million' in which he sang two French songs; his 'Earthquake Polka' and 'Wellington Mazurka' were first performed by the 65th Regiment Band.[12]

Other visitors included the pianist Mrs D'Alton (said to be a pupil of Garcia and Crivelli in London), who gave a 'Grand Evening Concert', with 'gentlemen amateurs', at the Atheneum on 12 February 1856, her rendering of 'Annie Laurie' earning vociferous applause. Mr and Mrs W. H. Foley, with their 'permanent' troupe of four, backed by local amateurs, presented drama with songs and duets, and eventually arranged a regular 'circuit'.[13]

Visiting artists often found themselves at the mercy of coastal shipping, which brought about some extraordinary fusions: Mrs Foley merged with a circus on one occasion, Klaer's Canine and Equine Hippodrome of eight monkeys, four collie dogs, two poodles, and one King Charles spaniel. Jean Klaer and his fellow artist Louis Rossignol leaped over twenty members of the 65th Regiment with their bayonets drawn — thus raising £38.10s for the new Oddfellows' Hall fund, which after its opening on 24 May 1860 became a focal point in the town's musical life.[14]

The first visit by 'The English Opera Company' in 1863, directed by the celebrated Marie Carandini, promised rather more than it gave. Mme Carandini, a tall handsome woman of distinctive appearance, specialized in arranging shortened versions of popular operas, such as *La Sonnambula* and *Lucia di Lammermoor*, linking them with a spoken libretto and presenting the principal arias without orchestra or chorus. She had performed these to great acclaim in tours of Australia, San Francisco, and India. J. C. Richmond, writing from Nelson to his wife Mary in New Plymouth on 1 March 1863, describes her company of four singers as 'not great artists, but safe and moderately skilful and with good voices and quiet respectable manners . . . you should hear them shout bits of *Trovatore* and *Ernani* in the most approved Verdi style'.[15] She toured New Zealand at about four-yearly intervals, retaining the loyalty and affection of her audiences; at each of her concerts she gave out 'likenesses', to be preserved as souvenirs. On this first Wellington occasion she offered rough Australian songs in the style of the goldfields balladeer Charles Thatcher, bagpipe imitations, flageolet pieces and a miscellaneous selection, perhaps imagining herself in some outback frontier town. She did not make the same mistake again.

Wellington was no more fortunate with its second operatic occasion when in 1864 William Lyster's Opera Company tried to fit itself into the Oddfellows' Hall, with its restricted lighting and stage facilities. Meyerbeer's spectacular *Les Huguenots*, which Lyster had advertised, proved an impossibility, so he substituted selections from *Lucrezia Borgia* and *The Barber of Seville*, interspersed with popular songs such as 'The Village Blacksmith' and 'Sally in Our Alley', without scenery or costumes. Lyster more than made up for it later.

Wellington's balls throw light on early attitudes to class. In 1841 Edward Jerningham Wakefield experienced difficulties in arranging an anniversary celebration to the mutual satisfaction of the 'working classes' and 'the democracy and aristocracy of the place'. In the end, he held two balls on separate days, the 'Popular' and the 'Select'.[16] Ensign Best describes a novel means of transport: '[I] most opportunely discovered a conveyance for the Ladies in the shape of an Amunition waggon with Tilt which we *horsed* with *four bullocks* . . . I was installed as on board the London M.C. & dancing commenced (Band, Piano violin flute) we kept it up untill five & then the weather being moderate walked home. At one time we had seven couple waltzing and the show of Ladies was generally creditable.'[17] Charlotte Godley wrote in 1850: '. . . in short everyone dances here; even my husband was very near doing it, to keep himself warm'.[18]

'The delights of music' as Charlotte Godley put it, characterized early Wellington. At one end of the town was the glitter of a Government House ball—'at other times the little port vibrated with a joyous din, to the tune of tavern fiddle and hornpipe, as the various Ishmaels, Ahabs and Queequegs from Cloudy Bay and Te Awaiti sailed away to the Happy Isles on roaring seas of grog'.[19] The first tentative beginnings of a musical life had emerged: by the 1890s Wellington could describe itself as truly musical. Yet our sympathies are still held by those who made music in the first few decades; their occasions still hold an indefinable glow.

Notes

1 Miller, 45
2 Ibid., 167
3 Petre Ms, ATL, entry for Saturday 25 February 1843
4 Godley, 77
5 Ibid., 68
6 Petre Ms, ATL, entry for Saturday 20 May 1843
7 See Wakefield, *Adventure*, 171
8 Godley, 35. See also Blake, A. H. *Sixty Years in New Zealand*, 43-4, quoted in Moriarty thesis, 30
9 Marriott had arrived on the *Thomas Sparks* in 1842. His artistic skill is revealed in his drawing of the dinner to celebrate the passing of the 1856 Constitution Act, afterwards engraved for the *Illustrated London News*, 12 January 1850
10 *Le Magasin pittoresque*, vol. 11, no. 47 (November 1843) 375. I am indebted to Dr R. D. J. Collins of the French Department of the University of Otago for this reference
11 Cited by Moriarty from the *Spectator*, 28 January 1854
12 14 April 1855, Moriarty thesis, 41ff.
13 Foley's Victoria Circus had made a successful début in Nelson in 1855; their New Zealand tours continued until December 1866. Downes, *Shadows*, 27ff.
14 See Moriarty, 45ff.
15 Richmond-Atkinson, vol. 1, 25
16 Wakefield, *Adventure*, 171
17 Best, Ensign, 276
18 Godley, 57-8
19 Miller, 131

3 Music in the capital:
Auckland 1840-1865

'After mature consideration', Governor Hobson had chosen Auckland for his capital in preference to the Bay of Islands, much to the dismay of the New Zealand Company settlers of Cook Strait. The young town's musical and social life revolved around Government House and the personality of the Governor's wife. The building, which had cost an alarming amount of money, was said to have been modelled on that used by Napoleon Bonaparte in his exile on St Helena, with embellishments by the New Zealand architect William Mason. Unlike Mrs Felton Matthew, wife of the acting Surveyor General, whose piano resided in its case under a tarpaulin, Mrs Hobson could house hers in the drawing room. When the colonial artist Edward Ashworth visited, he admired the gilt chandelier, the paintings, the handsome piano, and the highly ornamented books—not to mention the charm of Mrs Hobson and her children, whom he had found 'young, beautiful, most amiable and unaffected'.[1]

Auckland's social life consisted of dinners, musical evenings, and the occasional ball, enlivened by the band of the 58th Regiment. Talented amateurs of the town included a flautist, Major Thomas Bunbury (1791-1861), commander of a detachment of the 80th Regiment, who had secured many of the southern signatures to the Treaty of Waitangi.[2] William Bambridge, an artist and writing master at Bishop Selwyn's St John's College, played the flute with Thomas Outhwaite (1805-1879), the Bishop's solicitor and secretary, later first Registrar of the Supreme Court of New Zealand.[3] Outhwaite, also a violinist, later distinguished himself as an inspired choral director.

Charles John Abraham (1814-1903), Archdeacon of Waitemata, first Bishop of Wellington 1859-68, with his cello. Drawing by Caroline Harriet Abraham. *Private collection*

Mrs Gore Browne, wife of Hobson's successor, Sir Thomas Gore Browne, made the new Government House the centre for balls, dinners, plays, and readings. Haydn and Beethoven were performed at her concerts and her weekly 'At Homes' became celebrated throughout the colony.[4] On 3 October 1860 Jane Maria Atkinson wrote to her friend Margaret Taylor: 'You meet everyone worth knowing, and have excellent music in one room whilst there is dancing in another. Mrs Gore Browne has weekly meetings in her drawing room for the practice of glees, madrigals and masses. There are many people here with real musical taste; the performances are excellent. Some beautiful quartettes for four men's voices were sung last Monday, and one of Haydn's symphonies well played.'[5] When Mrs Gore Browne left in 1861 Jane Maria declared: 'There will be a complete breaking-up of Auckland society . . . all ranks have met sociably [at Government House] and with enjoyment and benefit. She is quite without snobbishness . . .'[6]

Musically talented settlers included the solicitor Francis Dart Fenton

(1821-1898), tall and aristocratic-looking with an abundant sense of humour. An accomplished violinist and cellist, he participated fully in Auckland's musical evenings until he was appointed resident magistrate in Māori districts of the central North Island, where the Reverend Robert Maunsell persuaded him to teach music to his Māori pupils.[7] William Swainson (1809-1884), a strong humanitarian, especially bent on upholding Māori rights, and an effective legislator, who had arrived in 1841 as Attorney General, summed up the social scene:

Auckland from the west side of Commercial Bay, 12 February 1844. Gilbert Bros. after John Adams. Engraving. *Auckland Public Library*

> Once a week, during the summer, a regimental band plays for a couple of hours on the well-kept lawn in the government grounds; and with the lovers of music, and those who are fond of 'seeing and being seen', 'the band' is a favourite lounge. Three or four Balls in the course of a year, a Concert or two, an occasional pic-nic or water party, a visit to the Gold field, or to the island of Kawau, a trip to the Waikato, or the lakes of Rotorua, are among the few amusements which aid in beguiling the lives of the Auckland fashionable circle; while dissipation in the milder form of temperance and tea-meetings, school-feasts, stitcheries and lectures, suffices for the recreation of the graver portion of the Auckland community.[8]

This 'faithful picture of Auckland' may seem uninviting 'to the frequenters of Almack's, the Opera, Ascot, and the Highlands . . . but, on the other hand, it may be doubted whether those accustomed to the easy freedom of society in New Zealand, would gain much addition to their enjoyment by exchanging it for the chilling atmosphere, and the stiff, cold, formal usages of English fashionable life'.[9]

Gradually musical societies arose, such as the Philharmonic of 1842, choral

Thomas Outhwaite (1805-79), founder of the Auckland Mechanics' Institute Vocal Class and the Auckland Sacred Harmonic Society. *Auckland Institute and Museum*

rather than instrumental, the latter being mostly confined to the interludes of pot-pourris and medleys in the Royal Victoria Theatre which opened as the Fitzroy in 1844. Outhwaite began conducting a vocal class at the Mechanics' Institute. He also lectured on music, and on 17 February 1848 started public rehearsals of a lighter kind with English glees.[10] From this grew the Auckland Sacred Harmonic Society, which gave its first concert, styled as a 'Public Rehearsal', in November 1849, at which the 'Hallelujah' Chorus from *Messiah* was boldly attempted.[11] In September 1850 the Society included 'Ethiopian Melodies' sung with 'contortions and grimaces' by 'gentlemen with their faces and hands blackened', a popular type of show.[12] Modelling his programmes on those of the Sacred Harmonic Society at Exeter Hall, London, Outhwaite drew on Handel's oratorios and Haydn's *Creation*, followed by English sacred works, miscellaneous duets, trios, and quartets in his concert of 14 May 1851. This ambitious 'Public Rehearsal' could boast Sir George Grey as patron. From 1843 to 1851 Outhwaite worked vigorously to establish vocal music in Auckland. 'With nothing at the beginning but raw material to work upon, insufficiently supplied at first even with that, he has organized a well-appointed school of vocal music, which now bids fair to endure as long as the colony itself.'[13]

Outhwaite's persistence in training voices and in giving concerts made possible the founding of the Auckland Choral Society by Joseph Brown (1818-1883) in 1855, the year of his arrival in Auckland to take up a position at St John's College, Tamaki. Formerly organist of Holy Trinity Church, Windsor, and conductor of the Musical Society at Eton, he formed the choir of St Matthew's Church and trained the classes for St Andrew's Presbyterian Church, when psalm singing was introduced. His courses for the public offered fifty lessons for one guinea, reduced to 15/- when more than one member of the family attended. He based these on Dr John Hullah's system of sight singing.[14] By the end of 1855 the Auckland Choral Society existed, which soon grew from sixty to 200 voices with an orchestra of sixty. Brown introduced works by Haydn, Mozart, and Beethoven, but maintained glee and madrigal singing, incorporating both in mixed programmes which often included a flute solo as well. The choir comprised 'respectable' members of the community such as the clergy, merchants, and the ladies of their families.[15] Outhwaite's Sacred Harmonic Society and Brown's Auckland Choral Society established Auckland's choral tradition.

The scarlet-coated band of the 58th Regiment lent lustre to these performances and from 1845 to 1858 formed an integral part of Auckland's musical life. It was a far cry from the lack of ceremonial surrounding the official arrival of Hobson as Governor in 1841, when he and his wife and a small group of officials had 'landed on the reef in Commercial Bay and walked up still fern-clad Shortland Street with a grand band of one fife and one drum playing'.[16] The band not only played in church (which aroused controversy), but essayed operatic airs on the weekly Sunday march to and fro, which led Mrs Selwyn to write: 'The tramp of the men is very spirit-stirring but the Opera airs sounded rather out of keeping with the time and place. I think George would have waxed wrath.'[17] 'Nehemiah' in the *New-Zealander* noted 'Jullien's Polka' on the way to church, 'the Old Hundredth' inside, with 'Lucy Long' on the march home.[18] The band performed at a Total Abstinence Tea Party, at an Anniversary Dinner of the Oddfellows' Lodge, at the consecration of St Patrick's Catholic church, and at funerals, where on one occasion they played 'Auld Lang Syne'.[19] Their programmes included popular operatic overtures and selections, dances, ballads, and songs.[20] When the Regiment was withdrawn in late 1858, some members stayed behind to become prominent in local bands.[21]

Visiting artists began to appear, such as the pianist Mrs John Bell, who gave two concerts in 1851. At the second of these, an unsold harmonium was demonstrated before being raffled. Ali-Ben-Sou-Alle (familiar from Wellington) played on his 'new and wonderful Turkophone', the 'Turkophonini', and the 'Petite and Grande Clarionettes'. Mr Swain, an English baritone educated at the Chapel Royal, Windsor, pleased his audience in 1853 by singing in a fine falsetto in the true glees manner. Several music teachers advertised their services and sometimes visiting artists would give lessons. Mr W. H. Barry (1819-1907) stands out among these early teachers: from 1850 until 1852 he organized the St Patrick's Band, founded a 'Mercantile Academy and Grammar School', and a Music School.[22]

Music at St John's College

In 1842 Bishop George Augustus Selwyn had first established his training school for natives, St John's College, at Waimate, housed in attractive but apparently inconvenient wooden buildings leased from the Church Missionary Society.[23] When his wife, Sarah Harriet, arrived later the same year, the Māoris welcomed her as 'Mata Pihopa', 'Mother Bishop'. Her 'poor dear Piano, which was badly banged about in the Tomatin, came, perforce in a waggon only over such a road!' she wrote. 'It had a nest of ferns to soften its fate but the keys are much loosened and the treble is in a bad state—the bass is as fine as ever.' When she played it to a benevolent old Māori in a blanket, 'he thought that I had got a man inside clamouring to get out'.[24] She also brought a fine collection of music, including manuscript copies of Handel operas and oratorios by her mother, Lady Richardson, and her own green leather notebook with its minuets, German tunes, folksongs, and dances, now part of the collection in St John's library.[25]

After unsatisfactory negotiations with the Church Missionary Society, which owned the Waimate building, Selwyn moved St John's to Tamaki, outside Auckland, less than two years later. Unsuccessful experiments with stone led him to engage the architect Frederick Thatcher (1814-1890), who worked brilliantly in wood. His simple buildings, notably the chapel (1857), established

A Māori policeman in
Auckland, 1850. Pen and
ink drawing on coloured
paper by Cuthbert Charles
Clarke (1818-63). *Hocken
Library, Dunedin*

an architectural style, which nurtured an equally distinctive musical life.

St John's became a place of religious and useful education for all classes of
the community, especially for candidates for holy orders. It served also as a
hostelry for young settlers on their first arrival in the country and a refuge
for the sick, the aged, and the poor. Selwyn called it 'the key and pivot' of
all his New Zealand plans. Every scholar was required to practise one active
and one sedentary trade: music in the form of singing for services, hymns, psalms,
and chanting had an important place. Selwyn ran it as a Collegiate School
'conducted upon the plan *(Mutatis Mutandis)* of Eton'.[26] Selwyn had been trained
at Cambridge, was a dedicated Tractarian, thus a High Church believer
supporting a primitive sacramental Catholicism, but he was essentially a practical
man, not a theologian. 'In his view, God was better served in the mission field
than in doctrinal debate', writes Ruth M. Ross.[27]

'There was no sermon or address: none was needed', wrote Canon Frank
Gould, who served at St John's from 1848 to 1852, of a Sunday service. 'One
felt as if the whole college was wound up to concert pitch. Every Sunday was
the same, yet always new. We never had an organ or anything of the kind
in the chapel: no need for it when the chants "Veni Creator", "Sanctus", etc.,
could be rendered by the whole college for a choir.'[28]

Lady Mary Martin, wife of the Chief Justice, describes the singing at a wedding
attended by pupils of the College:

> The Maori boys and girls between the speeches sang English glees and catches
> with great spirit. It was a pleasant surprise to find that the New Zealanders,
> when properly taught, had much musical talent and very good voices. We
> had noticed, from the first, the perfect time that they kept, not only when
> responding in church, but when singing songs as they paddled. But their native
> music, when they chanted their old songs, was harsh and monotonous, and
> their attempts to follow our hymn-tunes most deplorable. No sooner, however,
> were the young people in the school taught to read music by the figure system
> [tonic-sol fa or Hullah], and trained by regular practices weekly, than we found
> out the gift of song that was in them. The girls used to sing some of
> Mendelssohn's Chorales with great spirit and accuracy. It is quite common
> nowadays for young New Zealanders to play the harmonium and act as organists
> in their native churches.[29]

The arrival in 1846 of Arthur Guyon Purchas (1821-1906), gifted in many
directions, as clergyman, surgeon, and musician, gave music-making at St John's
fresh stimulus: '. . . ere long we had singing in the chapel which was popular
and greatly enlivened the services . . . the Maoris boys learned many catches
and glees; used to sing "Bacon and Potatoes" (Fra Martino) as a dinner bell
in default of a real bell or gong'.[30] Purchas wrote his *First Lessons for Singing
Classes* (1849) while styled 'Precentor of St John's College, Bishop's Auckland',
played a leading part in compiling the *New Zealand Church Hymnal*, and arranged

its *Tune Book* (1866). He also gave music lessons to the blind and invented a speedy method of preparing metal plates for printing Braille.[31]

When St Stephen's School for Girls was opened in 1850, the Reverend Vicesimus Lush, MA, who lived with his family at Ewelme Cottage, gave a vivid picture of the ceremonies involved. These illustrate the wide range of skills achieved at St John's. Bishop Selwyn, in fluent Māori, introduced the native part of the College, according to their different occupations, to the girls of St Stephen's, who were lined up in two rows before him:

> First the printers and bookbinders came forward — six fine intelligent Maori lads. These brought an offering to the girls of books they had printed in the college press and bound with their own hands. After them the weavers and spinners were called upon, and they presented a large quantity of excellent cloth they had spun. Then the shoemakers from the college gave according to their craft, and the farmers from the estate gave a large quantity of fresh butter, the proceeds of their industry. Lastly, the carpenters, two very fine Maori lads, were summoned by the Bishop, who said that their gift to their country-women was the noble building in which they were all assembled, for the large proportion of the edifice had been made by their hands . . . All this proceeding excited considerable interest; when ended they gave us many specimens of their singing, English and Maori songs alternating, and certainly you might have gone to many an advertized concert in London and not heard such sweet music and such skilful management of the voice.[32]

In February 1865 the capital was moved to Wellington, and with the departure of the Governor and his retinue much of the life and sparkle went out of the town. No longer did the members of the General Assembly flock north. Gradually the main body of imperial troops, stationed in Auckland during the early part of the Land Wars, moved south. 'The old Auckland had passed away.'[33]

Notes

[1] Annabell, 'Music in Auckland' and Platts, *The Lively Capital* have proved invaluable sources in this chapter

[2] Annabell, 29. See Bunbury's *Reminiscences* for entertaining glimpses of Auckland's musical life

[3] Platts, 116

[4] Ibid., 192. The Gore Brownes arrived in 1855

[5] Richmond-Atkinson, vol. 1, 641

[6] Ibid., letter of 7 July 1861

[7] Platts, 208

[8] Swainson, 68

[9] Ibid., 83

[10] He did not always adhere to the strict form of the glee, presenting some as choruses, which brought comment from the local press. He did, however, seem to have a counter-tenor available. See Annabell, 42 and Phillips thesis, 247ff.

[11] The *New-Zealander* critic, his head filled with the sounds of London performances by Costa and Hullah, found it artistically too ambitious, although later he changed his mind. Annabell, 53

[12] See Thomson, *ADM*, 15 for a description of the Hill family's 'Christy Minstrelsy' of 1879, a variant of the Ethiopians; also review quoted in Annabell, 59, from *Southern Cross*, 20 September 1850, 3

[13] Annabell, 62, quoted from the *Anglo-Maori Warder*, 24 August 1848, 2

[14] John Hullah (1812-1884) devised an important system of sight singing used by many English amateur choral societies after 1840. It had a fixed doh, whereas that of tonic sol-fa was movable.

[15] Most of the Society's concerts took the form of 'public rehearsals', although at occasional special performances the public could purchase tickets, as with *Messiah* (see Annabell, 71)

[16] Quoted in Annabell, 74, from Sir John Logan Campbell's *Reminiscences*, entry for 9 March 1841. The 58th is believed to have consisted of a minimum of twenty-five players, stringed instruments being added for social occasions such as balls

[17] Annabell, 97, from Selwyn, *Reminiscences*, 24 January 1846

[18] Annabell, 97

[19] Ibid., 74

[20] See Annabell, 89 for list of operas from which the band most frequently drew its selections

[21] The band of the Royal NZ Artillery formed in 1864 claims descent from that of the 58th Regiment (see Annabell, 74)

[22] See Annabell's excellent chapter on music teachers, 124ff.

[23] See Standish, M. W. in *Bishop Selwyn at Waimate*, ch. 3, 28-33

[24] Selwyn, *Reminiscences*, 18

[25] This includes Byrd's 5-part Mass, works by Handel, Greene, Boyce, Arne, and Scarlatti, madrigals, early Victorian catches, and glees. Allan Thomas compiled a preliminary list for use in his radio programme 'Music in Colonial New Zealand'

[26] Quoted in Evans, 99

[27] See her fine essay 'Bishop's Auckland' in *Historic Buildings of New Zealand*. Auckland (1983) 80-9

[28] Quoted in Evans, 110

[29] Martin, 70

[30] Ibid., 31

[31] See Thomson, J. M. 'A colonial bouquet: music to please Sarah Harriet Selwyn', *EMNZ*, vol. 3, no. 4, 2-8; also Limbrick, *Bishop Selwyn in New Zealand*, especially his 'A most indefatigable man'

[32] From the diary and journals of Rev. V. Lush, prepared by Miss A. L. Ruddock, printed in *Weekly News* 1939 (typescript from St Stephen's)

[33] Platts, 243. Selwyn's High Church advocacy of the organ and the choir, especially strong in Auckland, remained influential, for it indirectly led to a fierce confrontation between the organist and the tuner of St Paul's in the late 1860s and later quarrels between the organist and vicar. This was a microcosm of greater conflicts between the High and Low Church. (See Thomas, A. 'Facing the music, a social history of church music and the organ in a 19th-century New Zealand church', NZ Musicological Society Conference, Wellington 1984.)

St Mary's, Parnell, built in 1860 and cathedral church from 1887-1973, also became a notable centre of musical activities. What is known as Bishop's Auckland endures to this day.

4 Precentor's pipes and Scottish piety: Dunedin 1848-1865

Dunedin shared more than its name of 'Edinburgh on the hill' with its Scottish prototype, for it lay at the head of a then idyllic harbour, whose hills, notwithstanding the bush, closely resembled those of the northern hemisphere. Settled in 1848 by the Otago Association, a product of the Free Church which had broken from the established Church of Scotland, it was founded by William Cargill, veteran of the Peninsula campaign and India, then in his sixties, and the Reverend Thomas Burns, cousin of the poet Robert Burns.

Before leaving Scotland, many of the 247 emigrants attended a service in Glasgow on board one of the first two ships, the *Philip Laing*. After prayers for 'comfort, prosperity and happiness' in the new land, the ship echoed with the sound of the second paraphrase of an austere old Scottish hymn 'O God of Bethel'.[1] On the voyage itself, 'the enjoyments consisted principally in singing national songs, and in practising church psalmody', wrote the Otago historian Thomas Morland Hocken, a musical fare far more puritanical than that of the other emigrants.[2] The precentor's pipe, which sounded the note for the psalm-singing on board, was to continue to lead the church services in the new settlement.

Music played a minor role in the Presbyterian Church—except for psalmody. The *Psalms of David in Metre* and the *Translations and Paraphrases in Verse* made up the staple musical diet of church congregations, who rejected 'human hymns' and the organ, choosing for many years to stand for prayer and sit for singing. It was left to the Anglicans, of whom there were a moderate number by 1850, to use instruments. A young girl who attended an Anglican service was astonished to hear two flautists accompany the singing of the small congregation: 'when the hymn was given oot,' she declared, 'up stood the lang, lanky, young men, pat the sticks to their mooths and tootled out siccan a whustling as ye never heard'.[3]

The Reverend Burns, a theology graduate from Edinburgh and a strict disciplinarian, visited every family and household and noted the details in his diary. He organized the building of the first modest wooden church, which offered two services each Sunday, and he saw that the psalmody was properly sung. James Adams served as precentor and bell-ringer of the First Church for an annual salary of ten pounds. His tasks included holding classes, leading the Sunday singing, and publishing announcements and marriage bans. As precentor, he was expected to stand in front of the congregation and give them the pitch with his pipe or a tuning fork. 'Many a precentor, starting too high, floundered to the end of a verse in a trying and distressing solo', writes Margaret Campbell.[4]

A Scottish precentor's pipe, maker unknown. *Castle Collection, Wellington. Photography by Alexander Turnbull Library*

Dunedin from Little
Paisley, 1847, by E. J.
Abbot (1799-1865). *Hocken
Library, Dunedin*

James Adams, however, had a fine voice, sang accurately and forcefully, and
won praise for the excellence of the music in his church.[5]

At the First Anniversary Ball in 1849, between forty and fifty ladies and
gentlemen danced to the music of a quadrille band until 'morning's grey light
was beaming'. Musical life had a simple rustic variety:

> Wedding parties went on late into the night in cramped kitchens and cleared
> barns, with violins, concertinas or bagpipes supplying the music for the polkas,
> mazurkas or reels. 'Harvest Homes' were gatherings approved by the settlement
> founders. The entertainment would consist of dancing, singing and recitation,
> interspersed with announcements of the yields in bushels of wheat, oats and
> grasses, and in tons of potatoes and turnips. An address by Dr Burns on 'the
> benefits of steadiness, industry and sobriety' would conclude the evening. Such
> an address might well have been more appropriate at the Public Dinners which
> some gentlemen were privileged to attend. At these 'the band kept playing
> lively airs until the approach of the wee sma' hours against the twas'. Local
> parodies were delightedly received, while toast after toast was followed by
> 'prolonged and vociferous cheering and applause' and by such frivolous and
> patriotic songs as 'The Ratcatcher's Daughter', 'The Votaries of Bacchus' or
> 'The Bonnie Hills of Scotland'.[6]

Early Dunedin concert programmes usually contained popular ballads and
folk-songs which reflected the homely tastes of the settlers, rather than the light
classical programmes found in Wellington or Auckland. As Hocken writes:
'The opportunities for what may be called public sociality or entertainment
were yet scanty enough, and pleasure of the sort was taken circumspectly, if

Bugle used by Jock
Graham, postman on the
goldfields in the 1860s,
made by Henry Distin
(1819-1903), London.
*Otago Early Settlers'
Museum, Dunedin*

not sadly . . . But the record was quite broken, and a new departure made
in 1858, when Miss Redmayne, aided by amateurs, gave three or four grand
instrumental and vocal concerts in the school-house, the admission to which
varied from half-a-crown to four shillings.'[7] Miss C. Redmayne also helped
form the first musical society, the Harmonic, which from 1856 gave concerts
of glees and ballads, and visited other towns.[8]

Dunedin's unsophisticated, church-orientated musical life reflected the tastes
of the original settlers, who had been drawn principally from the lowland Scots.
They were carpenters, bricklayers, shoemakers, Paisley weavers (whose trade
had gone with the coming of machines), and farm labourers. An élite of a kind
did exist, consisting of farmers' sons, small shopkeepers, and self-employed
tradesmen. Later immigrants followed this pattern, all imbued, according to
Cargill, 'with the principles and habits of Scotch piety'.[9] They bought copies
of *The Parlour Song Book, Dance Music of Scotland, Burns' Songs* and a variety
of tutors for accordion, violin, flute, and concertina. They were less interested
in purchasing Haydn, Mozart, or Beethoven. The *Otago News* offered for sale
pianos, harmoniums, fifes, musical boxes, and 'newly-invented' organ-accordions,
the self-help nature of Dunedin's musical life being reflected in the offers of
handymen to tune instruments and keep them in order.

The elders of the community were not unaware that their peace and stability
might be threatened. Modest discoveries of gold were made quite regularly
in Otago and a prize had been offered for the first substantial strike. When
Gabriel Read, a prospector from Tasmania, discovered a rich seam at Gabriel's
Gully in 1861, miners in their thousands flocked from Australia and California.
They turned 'Edinburgh on the hill' into something its prototype had never seen.

Diggers arrived on every ship, making their way hotfoot to the interior.
Within a few months musical life changed too, as the first of the touring
companies arrived. 'We come, we come with songs to greet you', sang the
San Francisco Minstrels, who advertised themselves as a 'Mammoth Sable Operatic

Troupe' of seven performers, giving five concerts at the Provincial Hotel in 1861 before heading off into the teeming hinterland.[10] In 1862 two theatres, the Princess and the Royal, opened within a month of each other, complete with private boxes costing two guineas, dress circle five shillings, stalls, pit, and orchestral well. Rowdy audiences poured in to listen to excerpts from operas, plays, and theatrical compilations which might include *Romeo and Juliet* followed by *The Celebrated Bob Ridley Breakdown* or *Hamlet*, succeeded by 'that laughable farce', *The Secret*. Presbyterian psalm-singing and Scottish ballads were overwhelmed by exotic cosmopolitan entertainments. Messrs Poussard and Douay advertised themselves as from the Paris Conservatoire and performed violin music. A German Club that met bi-weekly for unaccompanied singing at Muller's European Hotel attracted fifty members. Italian organ-grinders and German bands appeared in the streets to oust the supremacy of the Scottish fiddle and bagpipe. Monsieur Achille Fleury, leader of the nine players of the Princess Theatre Orchestra, energetically conducted two brass bands, and led a quadrille orchestra that not only played at bazaars and balls (funerals by request), and at more serious 'recess' concerts during theatre intervals, but also at Catholic church music festivals, now much livelier thanks to the stream of touring musicians.[11]

Gold turned Otago into New Zealand's richest province and Dunedin into its wealthiest city. Capital flowed south to finance importers, whisky-makers, brewers, clothing companies, banks, metal and engineering trades, and the manufacture of all manner of equipment. In November 1861 the colony's first daily newspaper, the *Otago Daily Times*, appeared, and in 1865 prosperity took visible shape in New Zealand's first Exhibition of trade, industry, and the arts, with orchestral and chamber concerts, and celebrity occasions featuring artists from the visiting Lyster Opera Company, which had so impressed Dunedin during its first visit a few months earlier.[12]

The trades section of the Exhibition included musical instruments, some by English manufacturers, but also the first pianos to be made in New Zealand, the achievement of Charles Begg, a highly successful piano manufacturer who had arrived in 1861 from Aberdeen, where his monthly output averaged thirty-five instruments. He began his new career as a piano tuner, but following experiments with New Zealand woods, he resumed manufacturing and entered four pianos in the Exhibition. 'It would be invidious to institute a comparison between this instrument and its English rivals' (such as Chappell's versatile 'School-room Pianoforte' and harmoniums), concluded the Report of the jurors, 'but as an example of local industry, it is deserving of the highest commendation. Mr Begg has not aimed at anything extravagant, but simply to produce a sound well-constructed instrument, and he has succeeded in a degree certainly not previously attained by any colonial manufacturer.' It won a bronze medal.[13] Begg himself had constructed all the parts, with the exception of the metalwork. The case was of Otago rimu, the string and sounding-board of Swiss pine.

VAUXHALL GARDENS.
THE steamship NUGGETT will leave the New Jetty as follows:—
From 9 a.m. till 12 p.m. every half hour.
Fare, there and back, 1s.
The proprietor has determined to give the public of Dunedin such a reception, combined with Christmas sports and prizes that will astonish both Old and New Identity.
Ladies come early to enjoy the fresh air and a dance where you will not be disappointed in a good cup of tea with cream in it.
H. FARLEY, Proprietor.

The *Nugget* carried passengers to Vauxhall Gardens, opened in 1862, modelled on the famous London gardens. *Otago Daily Times*

Charles Begg's piano with
scarlet-coloured velvet
backing on the front panel.
Otago Early Settlers'
Museum, Dunedin

He had used Broadwood's action—'the workmanship throughout is very
creditable indeed'. Begg decided, however, to turn from the making of pianos
to developing a retail trade, principally through the chain of well-stocked music
shops which perpetuated his name until 1986, and he also played an important
part in establishing bands and orchestras. His handsome, late-nineteeth century,
two-storeyed brick building in Dunedin rivalled anything in provincial Britain
and perhaps in London.[14]

Begg's contemporary, George R. West, an English immigrant who also arrived
in 1861, founded a music emporium of exceptional quality.[15] West, a conductor,
singer, teacher, and player of many instruments, published numerous popular
pieces as well as the *New Zealand Magazine*, which contained popular songs
such as 'My Grandfather's Clock'. He conducted the choir of St Paul's and
organized the concerts at the 1865 Exhibition given by the Philharmonic Society
and local bands. He imported pianos from the world's leading makers, English
and European, harmoniums from London, Stuttgart, Paris, and Boston, and
church and parlour organs with up to twenty-four stops and one or two manuals.
Each month he added to his prodigious list of publications, which he advertised
as 'The largest stock of sheet music and books in the colony'. The most austere
musical ambience in New Zealand had become the most flamboyant.

Notes

[1] Campbell, M., 'Music through the century' in Tombs, H. H. (ed.) *A Century of Art in Otago*. Wellington (1948) 102-10

[2] Hocken, 95

[3] Ibid., 133

[4] Campbell, 54

[5] Ibid., 13

[6] Campbell, 'Music through the century', 103

[7] Hocken, 176-7. See also John Drummond, '"Choirs and Clogs, Mr Ballad and Mr Bones", Musical and other entertainments in Dunedin, 1860-1862.' Hocken Lecture, 1989

[8] See Beattie, *Calendar* for details of Canterbury concerts, viz., 'Three Vocal Entertainments' in Lyttelton in March 1860

[9] Olssen, 34

[10] Campbell, 'Music through the century', 104. The party consisted of a violinist, a contralto, a tenor, a banjo player, a clog, boot, and pump dancer, a tambourine player, and Mr Harry Leslie, 'Inimitable Delineator of Ethiopian Character'

[11] Ibid., 105

[12] See chapter III, 4

[13] *New Zealand Exhibition, 1865. Reports and awards of the jurors*. Dunedin (1866) 204-7

[14] *Cyclopaedia of New Zealand*, vol. 4 (1905) 223ff.

[15] Macandrew, *Memoirs, Musical and Otherwise*. Auckland (n.d.) 1

5 Canterbury: The English inheritance 1851-1900

Prelude: 'The night watch song of the Charlotte Jane'

The *Charlotte Jane* was a splendid, three-masted ship of 730 tons, described at her Bristol launching in 1848 as 'one of the finest . . . which we have ever seen'. In 1850 the Canterbury Association hired her to carry 151 passengers to Lyttelton, the first of four 'Canterbury Pilgrim' ships to sail. She held 27 passengers in the chief cabin, 19 in the intermediate, and 105 in the steerage.

'The Night Watch Song of the *Charlotte Jane*' is a conventional type of ballad which crystallizes the way in which mid-Victorian musical culture transplanted itself to New Zealand. The words were by a brilliant young Irishman, James Edward Fitzgerald, and the music by a former English wine merchant, James Townsend, who was said to have resembled the Vicar of Wakefield. The words presumably were written on or shortly after the long voyage to Lyttelton, the music being a later, somewhat plagiarized addition.

James Townsend (1815-94). *Canterbury Museum*

The cover of the published edition of the ballad shows the *Charlotte Jane* in full sail, spanking away from the English coast, probably near Plymouth.[1] The words of 'The Night Watch Song of the *Charlotte Jane*' became extremely popular, for they touched on feelings common to many at the time. They encapsulated the sense of loss emigrants felt at leaving England as firmly as the expressions on the faces of those in Ford Madox Brown's classic Victorian genre painting, *The Last of England*. They also evoked the spirit of the colonists' English and Irish ancestors, whose bodies lay in distant country churchyards and metropolitan mausoleums. The Polynesian voyagers who discovered New Zealand had left their homelands in the same way, loaded with provisions and animals (like the cow brought out by Fitzgerald). They too had expressed similar sentiments, as it was almost impossible for them ever to return:

'Tis the first watch of the night, brothers
And the strong wind rides the deep;
And the cold stars shining bright, brothers,
Their mystic courses keep.
Whilst our Ship her path is cleaving
The flashing waters through,
Here's a health to the land we're leaving
And the land we're going to . . .[2]

The succeeding verses reinforce this elegaic strain, until at length the mood is dismissed:

> But away with sorrow now, brothers,
> Fill the wine-cup to the brim!
> Here's to all who'll swear the vow, brothers,
> Of this our midnight hymn . . .
>
> The wine is at an end, brothers;
> But ere we close our eyes,
> Let a silent prayer ascend, brothers,
> For our gallant enterprise.[3]

Edward Robert Ward (1825-51). *Canterbury Museum*

The cabin passengers in the *Charlotte Jane* included Edward Robert Ward, 25, an Anglo-Irish landowner, a graduate in law from Trinity College, Dublin, who kept a journal which reveals a warm personality and an observant eye, and recorded many of the musical activities which softened the boredom, misery, and discomfort of those on board. He describes the pianos being played in the cabins, the dances and promenades to 'Sir Roger de Coverley', 'Lucy Long', and 'the Boatman's Dance'. He sympathizes with the brave attempts at a chorus from Mendelssohn's *St Paul*, and applauds the formation of a glee club. From the steerage, packed mainly with Irish immigrants sponsored by the Ward family, including three printers and a stonemason, came other convivial sounds. The agriculturalist James Stout, when invited to the upper deck, 'managed in spite of the evident difficulties, to set a dozen pair of feet jigging it to a country dance and polka', played on his three-stringed fiddle.[4]

Under Captain Lawrence the ship made a fast run of ninety-nine days to Lyttelton, her arrival on 16 December 1851 being watched with keen excitement by Charlotte Godley, who had been anxiously waiting with her husband John Robert, leader of the new settlement. The son of an Irish landowner, he was educated at Christ Church, Oxford, whence Christchurch derived its name.[5]

The following Sunday, by which time the other three ships had anchored in the harbour, the first church service took place in a two-storeyed warehouse on Norwich Quay full of sugar, tar barrels, tarpaulins, and coils of rope. 'Strange it was to see the bright summer costumes and the pink and blue ribbons of the Pilgrim mothers and daughters, contrasted with those rough planks and cases, and that dingy cob-webbed, lowering roof. Not less marked was the excellent singing and chanting . . .'[6]

On 11 January 1851 the first issue of Fitzgerald's *Lyttelton Times* announced regular meetings to practise church music.[7] The Canterbury tradition of choral singing had begun.

The Canterbury settlement: 1851-1900

Lyttelton, a vigorous seaport, remained the centre of the settlement until the 1860s, when the advent of the telegraph in 1862 took the *Lyttelton Times* and the Chamber of Commerce across to the plains. Christchurch gradually consolidated itself as the financial, political, and artistic capital of the province, strengthened by the completion of the rail tunnel linking it with the port in 1867.

The musical accomplishments of the first settlers included glee- and psalm-singing, a ready knowledge of the oratorios of Handel and Mendelssohn, and the latest operatic arias, especially those of Rossini, Donizetti, and Meyerbeer. Under the impetus of a succession of able English immigrant organists and choirmasters, Christchurch soon excelled all other settlements in the vitality of its church and choral music. Orchestral societies took root with more difficulty, yet domestic music-making flourished, so that although the town lacked a Government House, balls and similar festivities occupied an important place alongside horse racing, ploughing matches, boat races, and cricket.[8]

Charles Merton (1821?-1885). *Canterbury Museum*

Early musical societies tended to be short-lived. Such proved to be the fate of the Lyttelton Choral Society, directed by J. F. McCardell, well known as a singer, auctioneer, bookseller, stationer, and band organizer, who held the Society together from 1852 to 1858. On its formation only three or four members had any knowledge of music. He depended upon gifts of scores, and even after three years, still had no piano of his own. He rehearsed and gave 'public rehearsals' in a small room unkind to voices. People took babies in arms to concerts, which caused frequent complaints, and the audience often interrupted the performance.[9] As people moved to Christchurch the Society collapsed.

McCardell reappears as one of the founders of the celebrated Canterbury Vocal Union on 20 August 1860, which after many permutations finally became the nucleus of the Royal Christchurch Musical Society. A leading figure of his time, he conducted, played the violin, formed a glee and madrigal society, engaged in photography, and gave readings from popular authors and magic lantern entertainments. He was often responsible for the decorations at balls. After a number of benefit concerts over the years, he left for Australia in 1888.

Charles Merton (1821?-1885) played a similarly significant role, inaugurating the Christchurch Choral Class in 1857, which met weekly to practise. It gave its First Public Choral Meeting the same year with a band and chorus of forty performers in a mixed programme of glees, overtures, hymns, and choruses, concluding with 'Rule Britannia' to an audience estimated to number 300.[10] Merton gave singing lessons on the Hullah system,[11] taught many instruments, and became a master at Christ's College from 1858 to 1859. The following year he left for Rangiora, where he again invigorated musical life.

As elsewhere, many lively musical evenings took place. Lady Barker describes how the hands of her Christchurch friends are 'as skilful on the piano or with

Temple of Truth, Latimer Square, Christchurch, c. 1895, a popular concert venue. *J. G. Lamb. Canterbury Museum*

a pencil, as they were in handling a saucepan', probably even truer in the 1850s.[12] At the other end of the scale were the songs, often bawdy, rough, and coarse, sung in the hotels and at smoke concerts from which ladies were excluded. At an evening Lady Barker spent amongst working-class men, in deference to her presence there was 'no smoking, no songs, no conviviality of any sort'.[13] Reviewers of the first concerts often felt them to be superior to what might have been heard in an English provincial town, thus boosting the morale of performers. Mr and Mrs Foley, well known throughout the colony, gave a concert in a theatre in 1857 when 200 witnessed their musical *burletta*. Miss Redmayne from Dunedin became a favourite ballad singer. In 1864 the All-England cricketers beat Canterbury, Cobb & Co extended their coach service to the region, and the Lyster Opera Company, despite high admission prices, filled the theatre. But more significantly for the town's musical life, it was also the year the Bishop of Christchurch, using the customary silver trowel, laid the foundation stone of the Cathedral, commissioned from the doyen of English Victorian gothic, Giles Gilbert Scott. Afterwards, 'Christ, our Corner Stone, is Laid' was sung by the choir and everybody joined in the 'Old Hundredth'; 'the company then went to luncheon in Coker's new room in Cathedral Square'.[14]

Development of church choirs

The foundations for Christchurch's achievements in church music were laid in the mid-nineteenth century. The pro-church of St Michael, the first to be established, provided free musical training for its choir. Church choirs soon raised the standard of the choral societies.[15]

From the late 1850s onwards the choirs grew and established themselves as an alternative to weak congregational singing. In the following decade they grew in strength and musical merit and the congregation became subsidiary, as happened in English churches and cathedrals during the same period. In Christchurch this was due largely to the inspired leadership of fresh arrivals such as Robert Parker (1847-1937), a highly trained young organist and choirmaster, who had emigrated for reasons of health. As the cathedral began to dominate the town's choral activities, so the choirs began to decline after 1879. The rise and fall of the Christchurch church choirs, the internecine conflicts that beset them, the way they responded to the changing political, economic, and social factors within the settlement, make a microcosm of New Zealand musical history.

At B. W. Mountfort's fine stone church of St John's, Latimer Square, a determined effort was made to give brighter services with a full choir in the Broad Church tradition of Jebb and Wesley. The church, which seated 600, retained its fashionable status throughout the century, its choir wearing long surplices, buttoned or tied at the neck and almost covering the boots. Poetry readings were held: 'An Evening with Tennyson' or 'An Evening with Longfellow'. The two-manual organ by G. M. Holditch of London had twelve draw-stops. Robert Parker began his long and distinguished career in New Zealand musical life at St John's, where he was organist and choirmaster from 1869 to 1872, bringing a love of discipline and ceremonial as well as 'an unrealized desire to enter the priesthood'.[16] He had what Bornet describes as 'a great mission' to spread and improve the choral service.

Parker abhorred badly performed solos, but praised the part-song. In 1871 he set out his views in a series of articles in the *New Zealand Church News*, and was rewarded by overflowing church attendances. Without Parker there would probably have been no outstanding achievements in church music. Dissension, rife elsewhere, appears never to have spread to St John's.[17]

Parker's work came to maturity when he moved to St Michael's in 1872. Whereas St John's had involved the congregation by simplifying the choral side of the services, St Michael's placed its emphasis more on choral excellence. Parker formed a choir guild in 1878 to train singers and to give musical experience to those in the congregation who wished it, introducing Handel and Bach and regularly performing cantatas.[18] Criticisms of the elaborate services appeared in the newspapers, and in 1878 at the annual meeting an unsuccessful attempt was made to limit the expenses of the choir to £100. These standards did not long survive Parker's departure in October 1878. He eventually became organist and choirmaster at St Paul's Pro-cathedral in Wellington. Subsequent organists included Henry Wells, an excellent English musician with an erratic temper, and Davis Hunt, under whom the relationship between a fine choir and congregational participation reached a point of balance.[19]

The first precentor of Christchurch Cathedral, the Reverend W. H. Elton, opened a choir school, the first outside Britain, on 16 March 1881. To do so, he used his own resources.[20] Acrimonious disputes followed, and when the Cathedral Chapter appointed Henry Wells as first organist, taking him from a position he had just accepted at St Michael's there followed an unhappy period of rows between the cathedral and the other churches. Before long 'the cathedral enforced a dull uniformity on predominantly non-congregational parish worship'.[21] Nevertheless, fine musical results were achieved by other denominations, such as the Wesleyans, who held an ambitious music festival in 1872, repeated in subsequent years, in their Durham Street Methodist Church.[22]

During the latter part of the nineteenth century, specialist choirs arose such as the Christchurch Liedertafel, founded in May 1885, and the Liederkränzchen. Their intentions were similar to their European counterparts, to perform part-songs for male voices in a light-hearted festive atmosphere. From 1887 until the 1900s, the Motett Society, founded by Henry Wells, reached notable heights. By the turn of the century the Musical Union and the Motett Society had nearly 400 voices out of a total city population of just over 50,000.

The oldest and best-known choral society began on 20 August 1860 as the Canterbury Vocal Union through the initiative of nine dedicated musicians.[23] Early concerts followed the familiar pattern of glees, part-songs, operatic choruses, and chamber music, until the first performance of *Messiah* took place on 23 May 1864. On 26 May 1865, the *Lyttelton Times* published a lengthy leading article on the Society and praised its wide and permanent influence on musical tastes. Soloists were still not up to London standards but the choruses excelled.[24]

By the 1870s oratorios regularly appeared in programmes, and in December 1874 Haydn's Imperial Mass was performed. Conductors changed quite frequently until the advent of F. M. Wallace (1888-1904), who was succeeded by Dr Bradshaw (1905-1912). Similarly the Society's name changed a number of times. It remains one of the outstanding choirs of the country.[25] The Christchurch choirs, like their British counterparts, had made of singing 'a way of life'.

Orchestral music in Christchurch in the nineteenth century

Instrumental music acquired a leader with the arrival in 1871 of Alexander Lean (1823-1893), who had practised as an architect in England, becoming Under Secretary for Public Works in the Provincial Executive of Sir John Hall. Influenced by the achievements of August Manns at the Crystal Palace, Jullien at the Proms, and Charles Hallé in Manchester, he set out to work along the same lines in Christchurch, idealistically underestimating the magnitude of the task. He formed the Christchurch Orchestral Society (1871) and became music critic to the *Press*. Lean performed Haydn's Symphony No. 17 to a small audience on 1 May 1872 with an orchestra of less than fifteen, led by Carl Bünz.[26] His supporter, Charles Bonnington, had a music shop and music rooms in Cathedral Square and composed popular pieces such as the 'Mount Cook Waltzes'.[27] Lean, determined that the symphony should be the centrepiece of his programmes, from 1872-1878 featured those of Haydn and Mozart, which found a hesitant and critical response as being too 'heavy': his vision, formed in London, faced insurmountable obstacles in a colonial environment.[28] Lean felt keen disappointment when after seven years' work he was forced to disband. He was strongly inclined to blame the failure on the low level of public taste, nurtured on the piano.[29] He felt there might perhaps be a potential audience of around 100 in Christchurch: improvement might come through the establishment of a university chair of music. At his death, his devotion to the highest musical ideals was lauded in the *Press*.[30]

Alexander Lean (1923-93). *Canterbury Museum*

The Christchurch Amateur Orchestral Society (1881-1890) trod a more popular path, but one beset with its own difficulties, especially in finding enough instrumentalists. When F. M. Wallace (1852-1908), a cousin of the English composer Sir Alexander McKenzie, settled in Christchurch as a violin teacher in 1887, he dominated the city's musical life. He had led the Philharmonic and Crystal Palace Orchestras in London for ten years, and had earlier studied with the renowned violinist Ferdinand David at Leipzig. He became conductor of the Christchurch Musical Society in 1881, which amalgamated with the Orchestral Society in 1894 as the Musical Union. This gave him the resources he needed, and he embarked on a full season of two choral, two orchestral, and one mixed concert each year. This was an altogether productive period: the chorus swelled in numbers and many new works—by Greig, Dvořák, Tchaikovsky, Cowen, and Alfred Hill—were introduced, as well as the major compositions of Haydn, Mozart, Beethoven, Schubert, and Mendelssohn.[31]

In the nineteenth century the beginnings of a unique Christchurch phenomenon can be seen, a capacity to form rival societies in similar fields, which waged internecine war against each other:

The story of choral societies in Christchurch during these twentyfive years (1860-85) is marked by a somewhat monotonous regularity. As soon as one society was formed, on what seemed a satisfactory basis, and had prospered for a short time, a split in allegiance, either to conductors, or to different principles of programme organization, would lead to the establishment by the discontented of a rival society. But up to 1885, it was invariably found that the population of Christchurch was not large enough to support two societies, and one of them was forced to disband, or a union was arranged between the two.[32]

Such conflicts have continued until the present day, and it is virtually impossible to find their basis in class, educational, or historical affiliations: 'All my early life in Christchurch was marked by division', wrote Frederick Page. '. . . there were two piano clubs, there were two choral societies, both at each other's throats, there was a symphony orchestra that struggled on and collapsed . . . Someone should have knocked our silly heads together.'[33]

Notes

[1] The drawing is adapted from a watercolour by J. E. Fitzgerald, an accomplished artist. For details of the *Charlotte Jane* see Ward, *Journal*, 214

[2] Words given as printed in the original song. Fitzgerald himself probably modified them slightly to the form in which they appear in Alexander, W. F., and Currie, A. E., *New Zealand Verse*, London (1906) 4, and other anthologies

[3] The music was printed lithographically by Messrs Ward and Reeves of Christchurch, pioneers of the process, and won a bronze medal at the 1865 Dunedin Exhibition. The publication bears no date. See *New Zealand Exhibition 1865: Reports and awards of the jurors*, Dunedin (1866) 237-8, 516

[4] Ward, *Journal*, 27. Although the young men kept watches throughout the voyage, Ward does not mention any night watch song nor any singing while carrying out these duties. Edward Ward and his brother Henry were drowned in Lyttelton harbour on 23 June 1851

[5] 'He was certainly not a Great Victorian, but among the lesser figures of his day he stands high', wrote A. H. McLintock of him in ENZ, Vol. 1, 818

[6] Innes, 6-7

[7] This had been brought out by The Canterbury Association

[8] See 'Music in Canterbury' in Gardner, W. J. (ed.) 440-64; also Pritchard, *Selected Source Readings*

[9] See Watson, thesis 'Music in Christchurch', chapter IV, 'Choral Societies in Christchurch'

[10] Beattie, 1469, 1506

[11] See chapter II, 3, note 14

[12] Barker, *Station Life*, 46

[13] Quoted in Watson thesis, 29

[14] Innes, 147

[15] The factors which brought a new era into being are graphically told by C. P. Bornet in 'Anglican church music in Canterbury 1850-1900'. See also Peters' excellent *Christchurch — St Michael's, a study in Anglicanism in NZ*

[16] Bornet, 92

[17] Ibid., 108, for a discussion of Parker's influence

[18] During 1877 he performed selections from Bach's *St Matthew Passion* on Good Friday afternoon, and he brought in a clarinet and a cornet to accompany him at the organ in Handel's 'Pastoral Symphony', both innovations to the city

[19] Peters, 68

[20] See Bornet, 186ff., for a good description of how this was achieved

[21] Bornet, 199

[22] An audience estimated to number at least 1,600 heard a chorus of 160 voices, conducted by Arthur Landergan, and an orchestra of 29, led by C. F. Bünz, in Handel's *Dettingen Te Deum* and excerpts from *Messiah*

[23] See Holcroft, M. H., 'The uninterrupted song' (editorial on the 100th anniversary of this occasion). *NZL*, 15 July 1960

[24] Quoted in the 500th concert brochure of the Royal Christchurch Musical Society in 'Half a Thousand Concerts' by P. D. B. Christchurch (1975) 20

[25] See Barrie Greenwood's valuable list of dates, works, meetings, journeys, and notable events of the Royal Christchurch Musical Society. Unpublished (1975)

[26] *Lyttelton Times*, 2 May 1872

[27] Lean had purchased scores from a defunct Sydney society. As nearly all of these lacked a conducting score, he prepared them himself from the parts

[28] Watson, 129, from the papers of Colonel Lean, July 1882

[29] Watson, 136. See Pritchard, *Sources* 47, for comment on the unsophisticated musical background of early settlers

[30] *Press*, 21 November 1893

[31] Wallace left for Wanganui in 1905

[32] Watson thesis

[33] *NZL*, 28 April 1979, 14. See also Page, 39

6 The Regions and the West Coast goldfields

Music outside the principal centres depended on talented musicians whose arrivals and departures caused great fluctuations in events. At its best, musical life in the smaller towns had its own drive and vitality. In Rangiora for instance, Charles Merton's concert troupes gave regular performances of vocal and instrumental items in quite remote North Canterbury township schoolrooms during the winter months of the 1860s. His mid-Canterbury counterpart H. A. Gates, organist and choirmaster at St Stephen's Anglican Church in Ashburton from 1881, took his group to schoolrooms and wool sheds, to give settlers accustomed to a rigorous and sparse life, what was described as 'the pleasant oasis in the desert of their existence'[1].

Of the three further New Zealand Company settlements which followed Wellington, both New Plymouth (1841) and Nelson (1842) outshone Wanganui (1840), where musical activities remained relatively modest. A choral society (1864) gave its first concert two years later with sixty-five singers and the second band of the 57th Regiment. An Orchestral Club (1890), a Liedertafel (1898) and an intriguing Sash and Door Brass Band illustrate the range of activities.[2]

New Plymouth soon acquired a reputation as 'a musical place' through its domestic music-making and its public concerts which began in 1844, many of the personal associations behind these having been formed on the voyage. The New Plymouth Philharmonic Society became active in 1856, pursuing a busy life. Its music inventories contain oratorios, overtures, Haydn and Mozart symphonies, dance music, glees and part songs.[3] After the land disputes of the 1860s followed by the military campaigns, most women and children left the town, which came under siege, nearby settlements being sacked. On 9 December 1860 J. C. Richmond described the lonely scene to Margaret Taylor:

> I am leading a desolate bereaved life. None of our ladies are left us . . . The white and gold arabesque paper has been torn from the walls, the windows smashed, and fires lighted on the floors in the middle of the rooms . . . Our pianos and pictures we brought away, and our books, but not all the furniture . . . Music and paintings are gone to sleep for me . . .[4]

Some of Nelson's small cultivated group of lawyers, doctors, retired military and naval officers, younger sons of the gentry and county families, had had a classical education, knew French, German and Italian, could sketch in pencil and watercolour, and were fine musicians. The Nelson Institute and Philosophical Society opened its first library and reading room in 1842. A short-lived Philharmonic Society, conducted by Charles Bonnington, arose in 1852 as did

Music group in Roxburgh.
Hocken Library, Dunedin

the Nelson Amateur Musical Society. The Harmonic Society founded in 1860 built itself a modest hall in 1867. It survived for 95 years and established a tradition of engaging directors direct from Germany. Elizabeth Pringle Caldwell, who arrived from Edinburgh in 1851, found that there was no teacher of music in the town: 'I was beset to give lessons tho' pianos were very few.'[5] At dinner parties, noted for their spirited conversation and music, she accompanied herself in Scottish and Italian songs and sang at the first public concert, which was held to defray the expenses of acquiring instruments from Europe for a band which Charles Bonnington was forming. Nelson's most brilliant musical period began in 1893 when Michael Balling unexpectedly arrived as conductor of the Harmonic Society, to succeed Herr von Zimmerman. (See Chapter III, 7)

Around the bay at Motueka, the Greenwood family of thirteen sang nightly: 'The family glees and catches are excellent, and so also are the fluting of father and son to the mother's accompaniment', wrote Mrs Selwyn on a visit.[6] One evening in 1850 the family gave 'the first Quadrille Party ever known in these shores amongst us *respectables*'.[7]

Invercargill, an offshoot of Dunedin, became renowned for its choral society under the direction of Charles Gray, known as 'the father of music in Southland', whose concerts used to bring Mr Baeyertz, editor of the *Triad*, hustling down, especially where questions of ornamentation and authenticity in *Messiah* were concerned.[8]

By the turn of the century musical life throughout New Zealand had reached a peak of activity, although unevenly spread, as the pages of the *Triad* and the *Cyclopaedia of New Zealand* (1897-1908) show. Hastings might describe itself as 'the Leipzig of New Zealand', but its early orchestral, vocal, operatic and dramatic societies proved as fluid as elsewhere: 'the same few patrons and performers were involved time and again', writes Mary Boyd.[9] Gisborne, because of its isolation, was compelled to develop a vigorous musical life of its own. Its Theatre Royal, opened in 1873, lit by three quadrate kerosene burners suspended from the ceiling, played host to many theatricals and musicians, including the Pollard Opera Company and those of J. C. Williamson.

The pattern of New Zealand provincial musical life echoed that of Britain, with mixed vocal and instrumental concerts, choirs, amateur orchestral societies and brass bands. This varied only in settlements by other ethnic groups such as the Scandinavians at Norsewood and Dannevirke, the Yugoslavs of the northern gum fields and subsequently the vineyards of Auckland, and the Bohemians at Puhoi, who had arrived from the German-speaking district of Staab, about sixty-five miles south-west of Prague, in 1863. This courageous founding group of just over eighty were granted sixteen hectare lots by the Auckland provincial government. Isolated by geographical and linguistic barriers, Puhoi remained a pocket of Bohemian dance and music unique in New Zealand, with Dudelsack (bagpipe), fiddle and accordion, and from 1896 onwards for several years, an exceptional choir directed by Father Smiers, Puhoi's parish priest, with the help of his brother.[10]

On the West Coast the decade 1860-1870 has been described as its 'high noon', for the whole region swarmed with diggers from England, California, Australia and other parts of New Zealand, with Hokitika as its thriving goldfields capital. By the mid-1860s its bigger hotels could be luxurious, with dance rooms in which their publicans promoted monster balls. Greymouth followed suit. On 13 June 1868 the *West Coast Times* announced that Jules Guerin of the Victoria Hotel and Dancing Saloon in Greymouth 'had been at home, seen the Great Paris Exposition, and learned a few wrinkles, not only in the adornment of his Saloons, but in the style in which they should be conducted, which will be a pleasant surprise to his visitors'.

Joseph Harding, recently arrived from Dunedin, built in 1865 the first concert hall in Hokitika, the California, a long, low structure of corrugated iron, lacking flooring, seats or furniture apart from a bar partitioned off in each corner. Here Charles Thatcher and his wife Vitelli that same year performed a new repertoire of goldfield songs which brought down on him the warmth and contempt of the Hokitika correspondent of the *Lyttelton Times*. Thatcher left after a farewell banquet during which a local merchant he had pilloried substituted a toy watch for the gift originally intended. In March 1866 James Bartlett opened his Prince of Wales Opera House, a huge wooden building which could hold 1400 and seat 1200, papered inside, decorated with raised ornaments and lit by vast gas chandeliers. Australian vaudeville companies, gymnasts, minstrels and ventriloquists peopled it most frequently, adding on occasions singers and other musical 'numbers'. On Saturday 4 May, 1867 the *West Coast Times* advertised Harriet Gordon 'Queen of Song and Burlesque', in a 'thrilling drama in three acts', *The Rake's Progress* and in a new burlesque *Ill Treated Il Trovatore*.

More than a few visiting artists risked their lives in crossing rivers, gorges or in edging coaches around precarious heights. The large and commodious theatres which arose in the early 1900s, several by the noted architect Henry Eli White (1877-1952), and most at the behest of Williamson or Fuller, extended from the cities into the provinces and thereby attracted singers and pianists, as well as light and grand opera companies.[11] Most of these fulfilled a dual role and functioned also as cinemas. Sir Benjamin Fuller (1875-1952), the best known member of the English theatrical family, eventually established a permanent Fuller vaudeville circuit in each of the four main centres.[12]

By 1918 a touring pattern for artists and companies was well established thanks to the chain of theatres in both islands and the organizations which ensured they were filled. Choirs, semi-professional and amateur orchestras existed in the main centres and in most towns. Above all, brass bands proliferated. During the war these activities continued, but frequently with heart-breaking difficulties, and after the War musical life entered a testing period as musicians struggled to rebuild the fabric. Both then and now, the quality of musical leadership remains the most important single factor in any consideration of music in the regions.[13]

Notes

[1] Quoted in Gardner, W. J., ed., *A History of Canterbury*, vol. 2, 449

[2] See Chapple, L. J. B. and Veitch, H. C., *Wanganui*. Hawera, 1939

[3] Moriarty thesis, 9. The Minute Books of the Philharmonic Society are held in the Taranaki Museum, MS 065

[4] *Richmond-Atkinson*. v11, 666-7

[5] Miller, 174-6. Elizabeth Pringle Caldwell, 'Reminiscences', ATL, 16

[6] Quoted in Miller, 175

[7] Ibid. 176

[8] Charles Gray arrived in Invercargill from London in 1885 and became conductor of the Invercargill Musical Union which performed a wide repertoire and gave extremely successful orchestral concerts

[9] Boyd, 157-8

[10] See Father Daniel Vincent Silk's *A History of Puhoi*. Dunedin, 1923

[11] These include His Majesty's, Courtenay Place, Wellington (1911), built by White, now the St James; His Majesty's, Blenheim (1911), now demolished; Wanganui (1912), and the Municipal Theatre in Hastings (1915), which withstood the earthquake and is still standing. See Rob Ansell, 'Empires lost', *New Zealand Architect* n4, 1987, 49-51

[12] Downes, *Shadows*, 146ff; *Top of the Bill*. 34ff.

[13] See for instance John Schwabe's talk 'Music in provincial centres' to the AGM of IAML (International Association of Music Libraries), Palmerston North, 1983 and numerous papers by a variety of speakers at subsequent conferences

III

Themes and variations

1 The colonial ball

Couple dancing, detail
from George Cruikshank's
La Promenade. Engraving.
London 1835.

The elements of the ball are beyond rational analysis: the clothes, the perfumes, the hairstyle, the lace, the flounces, the visits to the milliners, and the perusal of the latest fashions from overseas; the programme card, (the *carnet du bal*), originally of silver or tortoiseshell, velvet or satin, and finally paper, and the gold pencil which became a mere wooden artefact with a tassel finish; the preparation of the supper, the ordering of wine, port, champagne, and the best madeira, the putting up of the decorations; and above all—who to invite and who NOT to invite. The ball was the most invigorating single phenomenon of nineteenth-century colonial life. It made and unmade matches, it mixed together in some kaleidoscopic whirl all elements of society, it gave isolated communities a sense of cohesion and purpose, it kept unbroken the musical bonds with Britain and Europe.

The key to its popularity lies in the dances and the music. Once learned, the basic steps scarcely changed and could be employed from one end of New Zealand to the other. Simpler dances, such as the polka, the schottische, and the Roger de Coverley, could be learned on the spot. The tunes, whether played by a regimental band or by a lone instrumentalist, had a hypnotic appeal: at the first strains of a quadrille, dancers became possessed as the music of Strauss, d'Albert, Lanner, Jullien, or lesser mortals unfolded.

By the early 1800s, formal dances such as the Minuet had virtually disappeared from the ballrooms of England, as had country dances, except for the Sir Roger de Coverley, a favourite throughout the century. The waltz, the first of the new dances to sweep Europe, seemed a simple, robust, even vulgar dance of the people. That couples actually clasped each other around the waist, while essaying vigorous movements, made it seem extremely erotic.

The quadrille, which almost always opened a ball, appealed 'to the old, the young, the robust and the slender',[1] it gave sets of four, six or eight couples time to speak to each other, it offered a plentiful exchange of partners. Originally a group of five French country dances of different rhythms and tempi based on folk-tunes, it soon became sophisticated and could attain considerable

'"The horrors of war",
NZ, October 64', the title
of one of the few surviving
dance cards, an ironic
commentary by an
unknown artist on a
convivial occasion in the
midst of the land wars.
*Private collection, photograph
held by Alexander Turnbull
Library*

complexity, as surviving dance patterns show. In 1819 Joseph Hart devised a simplified version called the Lancers.

There followed various 'novelty' dances, such as the lively polka for couples, in 2/4 time. Of peasant origin, its short heel and toe steps were easy to learn, and following its début in Prague in the 1830s it soon spread all over Europe. On 14 March 1844 the Paris correspondent of *The Times* wrote that it combined 'the intimacy of the waltz with the vivacity of the Irish jig'. An 'Emigrant Polka' appeared in England, and in New Zealand the conductor Angelo Forrest wrote his 'Porangi Polka' in 1880.

The quick, show-stopping galop usually ended the first half of a ball and became its finale. Its simple steps made it the least complicated of ballroom dances.[2] Couples held each other as in the waltz, but both faced the line of the dance and proceeded with rapid springing steps down the room: 'When avid ballroom dancers heard the eight-bar introduction they probably reacted like thoroughbreds at the starting gate', writes the American dance historian Cynthia Adams Hoover. 'As the musical momentum increased (especially towards the end in the eight-bar passage of ascending and descending quavers) the couples would sprint during the final notes and then rush toward the chairs along the wall, panting with excitement and pleasure.'[3] Sometimes dancers ended with the Roger de Coverley, or with its Australian variant, a circle dance called Stockyards, adapted from the last figure of the quadrilles.

The reel, a survivor of the old country dances, occasionally appeared in fashionable ballrooms, more often in its Scottish form in New Zealand. Some of these, such as the Reel of Tulloch and the eightsome, are still danced today, as is the version known as the Highland Fling. In America the reel became the basis of square dancing, often known as 'Breakdown' or 'Hoedown'. An occasional polonaise might appear.

Charlotte Godley had already attended balls in Wellington while she and her husband awaited the arrival of the Canterbury settlers. At Lyttelton, she welcomed the newcomers with tea, coffee, and dancing—the first ball to be held in the settlement. Thereafter she attended balls regularly, even at outlying farms. She describes a lady who danced so much she got hysterics, and a Mrs Russell, who danced forty times and wore out the only tidy pair of thin boots she had.

Lady Barker, shocked by her first Christchurch ball in January 1866 where the music was 'very bad and the decorations desolate',[4] had recovered her enthusiasm by December, decorating her own farmhouse, and commenting on an 'unfortunate five ladies who had been nearly killed with incessant dancing'.[5] On one occasion out visiting, she encountered an unusual set of quadrilles:

> . . . in a short time I heard something like music and stamping . . . I stole softly down to see what was going on: when I opened the door of the general sitting room a most unusual sight presented itself—eight bearded men, none of them very young, were dancing a set of quadrilles with the utmost gravity and decorum to the tunes played by a large musical box, which was going at the most prodigious pace, consequently all the dancers were flying through the figures in silence and breathless haste. They could not stop or speak when I came in, and seemed quite surprised at my laughing at them; but you have no idea how ridiculous they looked, especially as their gravity and earnestness were profound.[6]

But the most unusual of such experiences occurred on her verandah in the cool of the evening as a full moon arose. The young men of the house decided to hold 'a servants' ball':

> . . . I was forced to gallopade up and down that verandah till I felt half dead with fatigue. The boards had a tremendous spring, and the verandah . . . was very wide and roomy, so it made an excellent ball-room. As for the trifling difficulty about music, that was supplied by Captain George and Mr U——— whistling in turn, time being kept by clapping the top and bottom of my silver butter dish together, cymbal-wise.[7]

The Richmond-Atkinson Letters discuss the perennial shortage of women, who is on 'flirting terms' with whom, how to get rid of an unsuitable partner, and the merits of the musicians, offering some sharply etched character vignettes: 'The Miss Murrays, the insufferable daughters of the Commanding Officer were as supercilious and bouncing as usual.'[8] Miss Park's eyes 'show very well through a dark veil',[9] and a Dr McKinnon in a Highland costume of rich materials 'showed his manly form to great advantage'.[10]

Dancing teachers practised throughout the country. One such was a Mr Lewis, a professor of dancing, who offered his services in Picton in 1863 for 'Fashionable Dancing and Calisthenic exercises', with private lessons in all the newest dances of the day—polka, mazurka, La Varsovienna Waltz, schottische, lancers, etc. Katherine Mansfield describes one of these exotics and reaches the heart of the occasion in the short story 'Her First Ball'.

Notes

1 Record sleeve-note to '19th-century American Ballroom Music 1840-1860' (Nonesuch H-71313) 1975
2 Chassés [dance step in which one foot appears to chase the other] with occasional turning movements in 2/4 time
3 Record sleeve-note (Nonesuch H-71313)
4 Barker, *Station Life*, 36
5 Ibid., 98
6 Ibid., 146
7 Barker, *Station Amusements*, 218-19
8 Atkinson, A. S. 24 June 1856
9 J.C. to Mary Richmond, 3 September 1862
10 Maria Richmond to Emily Richmond, New Plymouth, 25 April 1863

2 Military and brass bands

The origins of today's flourishing brass band movement go back to the city waits of the Middle Ages, to the church bands described by Thomas Hardy, and especially to military bands. The movement in New Zealand, however, owes most to the brass bands that arose in Britain last century. Following the invention of valves which made the instruments easier to play, bands took root vigorously in the Midlands and north of England, with the more humanitarian industrialists setting up recreational and choral groups. The adoption of the cornopean (cornet) in the 1830s introduced an infinitely versatile instrument, somewhat similar in sound to the clarinet, especially in its sweeter registers, but much easier to finger and blow. The cornet solo came to represent the high point of many a bandsman's career, and eventually the instrument moved inside to the concert hall, a development Bernard Shaw castigated repeatedly: 'The vulgarity of the cornet is incurable . . .'[1]

Brass band contests began in Britain in 1845, the first taking place at the home of Sir Clifford Constable as part of a festival which also included medieval games, falconry, archery, and tournaments.[2] John Henry Iles, an ardent British bandsman, began commissioning British works as test pieces for a national festival contest, first realized at the Crystal Palace in 1900. Not until the late 1920s, however, did leading composers such as Holst, Elgar, and Vaughan Williams write for brass band, opening the way for a rejuvenation of the repertoire.[3]

When the military band of the 58th Regiment played itself ashore in Auckland, having disembarked from the *Royal Sovereign* on 2 June 1845, Major Cyprian Bridge recorded the event in his journal: 'The Light Company, Band and Drummers landed at 8.00 am, and marched into barracks: first band that ever landed or played in New Zealand.'[4] The 'Black Cuffs', as they were known, soon found themselves at the heart of the town's music-making.[5] The band of the 65th Regiment arrived in Wellington in 1847 to give promenade concerts, play at balls and other functions, and take part in domestic musical evenings.[6] During the period of the Land Wars, from 1860-1870, eleven of the fourteen British regiments in New Zealand had their own bands, at least six of which had foreign bandmasters, mostly German or Italian, this being considered extremely fashionable. Signor Philip Galea of the 57th Regiment in Taranaki, for instance, encouraged the cultivation of music among young people in the town and composed numerous ballads, including 'The Maids of Auckland'. Herr E. Bergmann of the 18th (Royal Irish) Regiment composed 'The Waikato Waltz', dedicated by special permission to Miss Cherry, niece of General Cameron, commanding officer of the British Imperial Forces.[7] After the founding of Kneller Hall in 1857, home of the Royal Military School of Music, British-trained conductors gradually replaced continentals.

On the expiry of their term of service or the recall of the band, some musicians

First New Zealand
Representative Band to
tour Great Britain, known
as 'The Hinemoa Band',
1903. *Hocken Library,
Dunedin*

elected to settle in New Zealand. Thus the Royal Artillery Band, formed in
Auckland in 1864, included members of the 58th and 65th Regiments. The
land conflicts had also brought into being settlers' bands associated with the
militia, such as the Taranaki Volunteer Rifles (1859), which, after a year's tuition,
marched through the town using their new instruments.[8]

Many of the immigrants who had brought brass instruments with them formed
groups. In May 1844, for instance, a small band of ten amateur musicians took
part in the ceremonies attached to the laying of the foundation stone of the
Mechanics' Institute in Wellington, and the festivities attending the departure
of Governor Fitzroy in October 1845. 'Bonfires were lighted and, as the Governor
stepped into the boat, his effigy was burned, while the Wellington Band played
"The King of the Cannibal Islands".'[9] Similar ensembles, including flute and
drum bands, grew up in various parts of the country, a number associated with
the gold-fields. In Central Otago, the band in Queenstown was generally regarded
as the best in the area. Bands sprang up in Westport, Greymouth, Reefton
(organized by a body of Cornish miners), and notably Charleston. The most
unusual of all West Coast groups, the Kokatahi Band, neither brass nor military
and originally formed by miners, still plays today.[10]

More important for the bands' subsequent development was their association
with the military forces. In the late 1870s gazetted regulations allowed for the
formation of garrison bands associated with the volunteer corps, the Government
providing an annual grant of £20 towards their upkeep. Sixteen garrison bands
had been established by 1900; many of them were very small, twenty being
considered a creditable number. The Invercargill Garrison Band led the field
in 1878, later to be reorganized by Captain W. E. Heywood, a professional
army man of excellent musical ability, known as 'the father of the New Zealand

brass band movement'. He rapidly brought his group to a leading position in the colony, thanks to a full complement of experienced brass players, including an outstanding young cornettist in William Valentine Siddall.[11]

Nineteenth-century bandsmen, splendidly alert behind their beards and elegant moustaches, took keen pride in their uniforms. The famed Kaikorai Brass Band (1881) dressed in 'Hussar-style' uniforms, with extravagant braid adorning the front of their tunics, and neat pill-box hats. The Sydenham Brass Band of Christchurch had bright scarlet tunics with white facings, black trousers with scarlet stripes, and shakos—a more or less cylindrical form of military hat with bright red plumes. The Thames Hauraki Brass Band (1898) boasted two outfits, a navy-blue street uniform with red facings, and an all-white summer one with black facings, nicknamed 'The Ice-Cream Band' at New Plymouth in 1902. Bands could be identified by their colours, which ranged from the green and gold of Masterton, and the khaki and maroon of Woolston, to Nelson's black and gold (also favoured by Palmerston North).

Bands sponsored by private industries and national organizations began to appear in the 1870s. Among the first were the Christchurch Engineers Band, conducted by Ernest Oppenheim, under the patronage of H. Toomer & Sons, Bootmakers, and the Railway Band. Such bands played on every conceivable occasion: accompanying the imperial troops when they marched out of Albert Barracks for the last time in 1870, taking part in the endless civic procession that farewelled Governor Lord Bowles in 1873, and the same year welcoming home the unbeaten Auckland Provincial Cricket Team.[12] They played at regattas, annual Caledonian games, race meetings, and rugby and cricket matches. They could be hired for holiday excursions or special celebrations. Their forte, however, was the summer outdoor concert. In January 1871 the band of HMS *Galatea* played to a crowd of over 2000 by moonlight on the Albert Barracks green, with sky-rockets ascending every few minutes.

The most unusual nineteenth-century ensemble was the Christchurch Bicycle Band, described as 'a rolling ginger group' of the Christchurch Professional Band, which had been formed in the 1890s by Fred Painter, well known as a long-distance runner and a record holder for the 'high bike' (penny farthing). These were the years of bicycle fever. The penny farthing had been superseded by a variety of cycles such as the Safety and the Ordinary. Women began to ride in the 1880s as the bicycle became a symbol of freedom.[13] Painter spent much time training his group to mount and dismount at a command, keep correct intervals between players and learn how to play while cycling—difficult for the slide trombonist and snare drummer. At the Opera House, 'they cycled on stage from the wings, and after performing an elaborate figure-of-eight manoeuvre, repeated the movement playing their instruments', to thunderous applause. On an outdoor occasion an unwary lady cyclist crossed their path. The band took evasive action, the lady fell off her bike, but the music continued uninterrupted.[14]

Brass band contests, which began in New Zealand during the 1880s, produced notable groups, especially in the South Island, where a Balclutha-based magazine, the *New Zealand Musical Monthly* (1888-1890), catered for their tastes. The balance shifted to the North Island in 1895 when the Wellington Garrison Band, to the South's dismay, won the contest, which subsequently took on the air of the battlefield.[15] There soon arose the concept of the test piece, as in Britain. The first New Zealand Band Association was organized by an Oamaru journalist and musician James Mitchell, followed by the United Brass (and Military) Band Association of New Zealand (UBBA), which subsequently split into North and South Island sections. By 1900 the New Zealand brass band movement had reached a high point; its circles of influence widened as district associations formed to encourage bands in smaller towns.

New and accomplished bands appeared as time went on. The Sunday recital or evening promenade remained a highlight of social life.[16] 'Oh listen to the music in the park . . .', wrote J. A. Lee nostalgically. 'I have lain on dry grass in the sunshine listening to many a band concert.'[17] City and borough councils voted funds for open-air concerts; Christchurch, for example, in the 1900s gave £100 to be divided between the Garrison and Stanmore bands.

Most New Zealand regiments in World War One had bands, and towards

Painter's Bicycle Band in Dean's Avenue, Christchurch, 1897. J. N. Taylor, Canterbury Museum

the end contests of a kind were held behind the lines in France. Despite the grievous casualties inflicted by the war, bands gradually re-established themselves afterwards. Some long-established groups disappeared, but within a few years the movement had recovered much of its vitality. In 1920-1921, for instance, two A-grade bands (the 2nd South Canterbury Regiment and the Kaikorai Brass Band) competed in the Australian competitions at Ballarat.

The split between the North and South Islands continued, with separate contests being held. Agreement between the two was reached in 1925, followed by a merger in 1931. The New Zealand Brass Bands' Association 'heralded the beginning of a new era in the history of the brass band movement'.[18] Newcomb believes bands reached their peak in the 1920s, largely as the result of dedicated practising. During the depression the Kaikorai Band and others gave concerts almost every week.[19] Novel types of bands emerged, such as the fine group at the Institute for the Blind in Auckland. In 1936 a ladies' band was formed in Auckland, followed by others in Dunedin and elsewhere. In 1958 the Dunedin Ladies' Band became the first of its kind in the world to win a national contest.

When General Booth, founder of the Salvation Army, discovered that the Fry family's modest ensemble of two cornets, a valve trombone, and euphonium could calm exceedingly hostile crowds, he engaged them for a trial period to accompany his own campaigns. In March 1880 the General directed officers and men to learn to play and to send instruments to Headquarters, asking for 'violins, bass viols, concertinas, cornets or any brass instruments, drums, or anything else that will make a pleasant sound for the Lord'.[20] Booth said of the bands in 1884:

> They are to work for the salvation of souls, and for nothing else. We are not going to stick them up on the platform, nor march them through the streets for them to perform and be admired. They are to go there and blow what they are told, and what the commanding officer thinks will be best for the salvation of souls, and if they won't blow for this object, let them stop playing. The man must blow his cornet and shut his eyes, and believe while he plays that he is blowing salvation into somebody.[21]

In 1883 Captain George Pollard, then twenty-one, a violinist and fine concertina player, and Lieutenant Edward Wright, aged nineteen, an excellent cornettist, founded the Salvation Army in Dunedin. Within nine months five bands headed a march of over 500 new recruits at their first National Congress.[22] As the bands were prohibited from playing in the streets, many bandsmen were arrested and gaoled, to be welcomed back to the local barracks with a thanksgiving service. In 1899 General Booth himself toured New Zealand with the Federal Band, which included H. Gladstone Hill, later musical director of the celebrated wartime RNZAF Band.

New Zealand Salvation Army bands reached high standards, more than comparable to their British counterparts.[23] The many fine conductors and composers who grew up within the movement include Brigadier Henry Goffin and his son Commissioner Dean Goffin, whose *Rhapsody in Brass* (1942), written in the Middle East, became the test piece for the Belle Vue (Manchester) Contest in 1950. In 1956 he became National Bandmaster of Great Britain. Thomas Rive, Ronald Tremain, Neville Hildreth, and Ray Cresswell of Motueka all wrote successful band music. Lyell Cresswell's orchestral work *O!* celebrated the centenary of the Army in a full-throated manner that would have satisfied Booth.

The British tradition of writing for brass band continued in New Zealand through the Rimmer family (especially William and John), Alex F. Lithgow, of 'Invercargill March' fame, and Charles Trussell, who wrote the 'Wairarapa March'. Others include Thomas B. and Thomas Gray, Llewellyn Jones *(Maori Rhapsody)*, H. C. A. Fox, Vernon Griffiths, John Ritchie, W. Francis, and Larry Pruden *(Haast Highway)*. New Zealand's first composer, Alfred Hill, began his career on the cornet. A photograph shows him at the age of eight in the livery of the Wellington Garrison Band.

Among notable New Zealand groups, the RNZAF Band, directed by H. Gladstone Hill (who was appointed on 26 June 1940 at the age of sixty), has left an indelible impression. With borrowed instruments that were twenty years old but in quite good condition, Gladstone Hill began welding his players into a fine ensemble. '. . . I marvel that the band ever played in tune, for we had the most cosmopolitan set of instruments one could imagine. All had to be high pitch which precluded many clarinets and saxophones that were available in the shops', he writes. 'We had to fight all along the line to get decent uniforms and shoes instead of service boots in order to be at least presentable on a public platform.'[24] His players included John McCaw on clarinet, later to make his name in London orchestras, and several who went into the National Orchestra after the war, such as Ken Wilson, Frank Gurr, and Peter Glen. Frank Callaway, who played bassoon, later became Professor of Music at the University of Western Australia. The band aroused intense enthusiasm; it played at rugby matches and liberty bond rallies, and gave symphonic concerts on a special three-tiered platform built at the insistence of their director. On the arrival in Wellington of the first American troops on Sunday 14 June 1942 the band created a sensation: 'When the cheering ceased they called for more music', wrote Gladstone Hill, and so the band gave its famous Drum Corps special, at the halt, playing the Maori Waltzes. No words of mine can recall that historic morning . . . we played for over an hour.'[25]

A tradition of outstanding brass virtuosi might be said to have begun with the nineteenth-century cornettist of the Invercargill Garrison Band, William Valentine Siddall. He was followed by such players as John Robertson[26] and Gordon Webb.[27] Ken Smith junior's meteoric career as a cornettist aroused widespread admiration,[28] as did Errol Mason's.[29]

The Hinemoa Band made the first overseas tour by a New Zealand band

E. R. Schreck, champion cornet soloist of the Kaikorai Band, Dunedin and South Seas Exhibition, 1889-90. *Hocken Library, Dunedin*

in 1903, in black uniforms with silver fern badges. They visited over 100 cities and towns in Britain in six months, with Princess te Rangi Pai (contralto) and Chieftain Rangiuia (tenor) as soloists. Its direct successor, the 1953 New Zealand National Band under K. G. L. Smith, consisted of thirty-eight players in virtually the same style of uniform. It also included Māori artists.[30] The National Band of 1962, again under Ken Smith, won the brass band section of the World Music Contest in Kerkrade, Holland, and further honours at the Edinburgh Festival. It was especially praised for its prowess in marching, which became an outstanding feature of New Zealand contest bands.[31] On the 1974 tour of Canada and America the band won standing ovations for its unique sound and style. The National Band again toured Britain in 1978 and 1985, winning world championships. In 1985, under Ken Smith jun., son of K. E. L. Smith, the band returned to Kerkrade and gained the highest points ever awarded at this contest. The Māori groups accompanying the band, now more polished and professional, proved an invaluable asset.[32]

Conversely, leading British bands (and one American) have electrified New Zealand audiences. The famed Besses o' the Barn Band, conducted by the distinguished bandsman Alex Owen, played at the Christchurch Exhibition in 1906-1907, when its tone was held to resemble an immense organ or a very strong concert orchestra.[33] Sousa's tours in 1910-1911 demonstrated the precision of the American military band. The Royal Artillery Band formed the centrepiece of the 1914 Auckland Exhibition, and at Dunedin in 1926-1927 the Argyll and Sutherland Highlanders, conducted by Major Ricketts (composer of 'Colonel Bogey'), won the admiration of the entire city. The previous year the Newcastle Steelworks Band under H. Baillie had toured. The Grenadier Guards captured the public imagination in 1934-1935, especially through their traditional uniforms, although their marching disappointed.[34] Their second visit in 1984 was highly successful.

New Zealand bands may have started as predominantly working-class groups like their British counterparts, but today they attract members from a wide range of occupations. In 1983 the Skellerup Woolston Band included a chartered accountant, a clothes designer, an export manager for a transport company, and a mechanical engineer.[35] 'Banding is something that gets into your blood and you can't get rid of it', declared Ernie Ormerod of his lifelong passion.[36] The same could clearly be said by the many thousands who share this potent musical addiction. The flourishing New Zealand brass band movement has stimulated many areas of national musical life. It has provided a training ground for orchestral players and composers, and through international recognition New Zealand has become one of the leaders in a world-wide movement.

Brass bandsmen pursuing the writer A. R. D. Fairburn, who had compared their activities to 'bear baiting and pole-squatting'. Caricature by Russell Clarke. *New Zealand Listener*

Notes

1. *Shaw's Music*, vol. I, 573
2. A typical competing band might include three cornopeans (cornets), two keyed bugles, trumpet, two trombones, ophicleide, and three serpents. The music might include selections from a Mozart Mass, a Weber or Rossini opera, and a pot-pourri of country folk-songs
3. Holst's *A Moorside Suite* (1928), Elgar's *Severn Suite* (1930), Vaughan Williams' Overture *Henry the Fifth* (1933-1934) and John Ireland's *A Comedy Overture* (1934)
4. Quoted in Newcomb, *Challenging Brass*, 13
5. See chapter II, 3
6. See chapter II, 2
7. See Newcomb, *Challenging Brass*, 14-15. Bergmann wrote many other pieces
8. Ibid., 16ff.
9. Ibid., 16
10. See chapter II, 5
11. Newcomb, *Challenging Brass*, 77
12. Elphick thesis, 209ff.
13. Around 1900, Malcolm Ross, a Wellington journalist and an enthusiastic cyclist, caught the spirit of the Ladies' Cycling Race in a photograph taken at the Basin Reserve, ATL [17551 1/4]
14. Newcomb, *Challenging Brass*, 38
15. For details see Newcomb, *Challenging Brass*
16. See Prescott, E. 'Places where music was made in Christchurch', *Historic Places in New Zealand*, December 1987, 16-17
17. Lee, *Early Days*, 105
18. Newcomb, *Challenging Brass*, 46
19. See Walter Sinton's account of one such occasion, *ODT*, 19 April 1975, 12
20. Quoted in Taylor, A. R., 335-6
21. Quoted in Boon, B. *Play the Music, Play!*, a history of Salvation Army music (1966). I am indebted to Lyell Cresswell for bringing this to my attention
22. Newcomb, *Music of the People*, 95ff.
23. Notably the Citadel Bands in Wellington, Newton, Dunedin, Christchurch, and the Auckland Congress Hall. The Wellington Citadel Band made several recordings for the BBC in 1953
24. Gladstone Hill, H. Autobiography, Acc.76-251, ATL, 151, 195
25. Ibid., 178
26. Originally a cornettist, he became trumpet player, then principal trumpet of the Toronto Symphony Orchestra. He later joined the Melbourne Symphony Orchestra, eventually becoming principal trumpet under Goossens in the Sydney Symphony Orchestra, where he was well known for his recordings
27. Principal trumpet in the London Symphony Orchestra for ten years
28. He also conducted the St Kilda Municipal Band, which won the national A grade title in 1955, and the National Band in 1985. See Newcomb, *Challenging Brass*, ch. 19, 'The virtuosos', 81-4
29. He probably won more cornet championships than anyone else and became the distinguished conductor of Continental Airlines Brass Band
30. This band won the championships at Belle Vue and at Edinburgh
31. Taylor, *Brass Bands* 233. See also Ansley, B. 'Class brass', the story of the Skellerup Woolston Brass Band, *NZL*, 10 September 1983, 21
32. Communication from Philip Liner, broadcaster, who accompanied the National

Band on its 1974 tour as compère. The author is indebted to him for several helpful suggestions for this chapter

33 *Press* report quoted in Newcomb, *Music of the People*, 69, See also *Triad*, 11 April 1910, 44

34 Newcomb, *Music of the People*, 47

35 Ansley, 'Class brass' 21

36 Interview with author

3 Folk-music

New Zealand's diffused and slight folk-song inheritance is due not to lack of invention but to historical circumstance. By the 1840s, British folk-song had virtually been destroyed by the inroads of the industrial revolution or been driven to seek refuge in the remoter agricultural districts of England, to be rediscovered and recorded by Cecil Sharp, Maud Karpeles, the Kennedys, and others in the earlier years of this century. In 1946 Douglas Lilburn perceived that most of the tradition had already been lost: 'I feel that the English and Scots and Irish folksongs are no longer the real influence on our music that they might have been even twenty years ago', he said in recalling his childhood experiences of hearing such songs sung night after night.[1] Nor did New Zealand have any equivalent of the convict settlements in Australia, which produced such a pungent vein of bitter and sardonic protest. Instead, it is as if the archetypal figures of the bullocky, the outback shearer, the overlander, and the gold-digger metaphorically strode across the Tasman, to mingle with New Zealand shearing gangs, swaggers, labourers, and gold-miners, bringing with them familiar tunes which simply acquired new words. For Australia acted as a reservoir of New Zealand popular and folk music: even the most individual figure of the period, the balladeer Charles Thatcher, cut his teeth on the Victorian gold-fields.[2]

New Zealand folk-song encompasses familiar themes, beginning with the sealers and whalers. Most songs have to do with the land, with farming or shearing, with life on the gold-fields, with the digging of kauri gum in the north, and later in the nineteenth century, with the local equivalent of the sweatshops of industrial Britain. And most have derivative tunes, with suitably adjusted words.

A fresh interest in what remained of this heritage arose in the 1950s. Stimulated by a radio programme presented by Arnold Wall jun., a well-known broadcaster, Rona Bailey, began collecting songs throughout the next decade. With the help of others she gathered a small group of 'traditional New Zealand songs' and a larger one of 'folk-style' music on such subjects as life in the bush and the gold rushes. She concluded that her own efforts and those of her colleagues had taken place 'too late': 'People had become too old, much material had been tossed away and burned and the cumbersome recording equipment of the time would put them off no end.'[3]

The New Zealand Folklore Society (1966) sponsored field trips and research studies, which resulted in publications such as *Shanties by the Way* (1967), edited by Rona Bailey and Herbert Roth with musical arrangments by Neil Colquhoun, and the latter's *New Zealand Folksongs* (1972).[4] The New Zealand tradition as a whole lacked the instrumental music common to the Irish and Scottish,

Accordion player, detail of photograph by Frederick Tyree of flaxmill workers, Paturau, Nelson, c. 1906. *Nelson Provincial Museum*

as it did the protest songs found elsewhere and any body of love songs. It shared the first and last of these characteristics with Australia.

Nevertheless, surviving folk material highlights aspects of colonial life which might otherwise have disappeared. These are found most abundantly in the works of a London orchestral player and music-hall entertainer Charles Thatcher (1831-1878), who recreated the English topical street ballad. Having abandoned his intention of staking a claim on the Bendigo gold-fields in 1852, he turned to his original occupation, the singing of topical songs to his own words, setting them to popular music-hall tunes of the day. He lampooned local personalities, scandals, and events, on occasions ending up in public brawls or the police court dock. Some of his songs became so popular they were passed on from singer to singer until their origin was forgotten and they had become genuine folk-songs, such as 'The Song of Ballarat', which could still be heard in the 1960s from the lips of old Australian bush singers.[5]

In February 1862 there appeared *Thatcher's Dunedin Songster*, the first of his New Zealand songbooks.[6] Thatcher, self-styled 'The Inimitable', had easy targets:

> The streets here in Dunedin are now a sea of mud,
> This place is very much the same as 'twas before the flood,
> Everything's so primitive, improvement is ignored,
> By that Provincial Guilded Sham, the Old Town Board.

He labelled the dour church-going founders 'The Old Identity', in a song which made them look absurd and won him renown.

> Go on in the old fashion,
> And ne'er improve the town:
> And still on all new comers
> Keep up a fearfu' 'down';
> Don't alter your Post Office —
> Let that old jetty be —
> And thus you'll be preserving
> The Old Identity.[7]

This was sung to the tune of 'Duck-leg Dick', a music-hall song by Charles Chilton.

Thatcher revisited Otago on two further occasions during the decade, lambasting the same targets and attacking the Chinese, parasites, monopolists, and pretentious capitalists who belonged to the 'Dunedin Loafing Society'.

Although Thatcher held a unique place on the gold-fields and in the theatres, other entertainers introduced songs of more local origin. 'Bright Fine Gold', part of the oral tradition since the 1860s, versions of which were sung as lullabies and used by children for games, tells of the harsh winter climate of the Tuapeka gold-field which killed off a number of miners:

Charles Thatcher reciting in Thatcher's Concert Room, Mapier Hotel, Ballarat in 1860. A view of the stage and audience. 1860? Pencil. *Mitchell Library, Sydney*

Spend it in the winter
Or die in the cold.
One-a-pecker, Tuapeka,
Bright fine gold.

Some are sons of fortune
And my man came to see,
But the riches in the river
Are not for such as he.

I'm weary of Otago,
I'm weary of the snow,
Let my man strike it rich
And then we'll go.[8]

'The Tents of Chamonix' commemorates the fate of a party of miners caught out in the snowstorm (a monument marks the place), and 'Paddy's Fight with the Chinamen' describes a typical gold-fields incident. Its author, Joe Small, toured with Thatcher several times, specializing in 'Irish' songs and 'characteristic comicalities' portraying a colonial type dubbed 'The Unfortunate Man'.[9]

One of the best-known folk-songs, 'Shanties by the Way', began as an Australian poem, 'The Public by the Way', by E. J. Overbury, published in Victoria in 1865. It is believed to have crossed the Tasman with diggers heading for the West Coast in the late 1860s, and thereafter it travelled widely throughout the country. Various versions exist:

Men and maids are dancing lightly
To the music that they play
Kerosene lamps are shining brightly
In those shanties by the way.

Māori boys searching for gum with spades and gum spears, Northland, c. 1910. *Alexander Turnbull Library*

The gold-fields were alive with music, played on everything from violins and concertinas to cornets and tin cans.[10] The surviving instruments in the Arrowtown museum for instance include a fine set of Irish pipes, a chalumeau, and brass instruments. The postman, Jock Graham, would give a loud blast on his bugle to announce that he was about to deliver mail to Gabriel's Gully. R. V. Fulton describes an evening concert when there were about 5,000 miners in the Gully:

> Some good concertina player would have around him a number of good voices, and situated, on a prominent point of one of the short spurs, . . . would give the signal that he was ready by a vigorous shout 'Jo Jo'. This would be taken up by one and all of the miners until the whole population was notified that the concert was about to commence. All flys and doors of tents would be opened and then such airs would be introduced as 'Away down the Swanee River', 'The old folks at home', 'Oh, Willie we have missed you', 'Constantinople', 'The old log cabin in the lane' . . . Their hearts would be full and their feelings genuinely stirred with the memories of the past, and all that it meant for them.[11]

This vivid description of a gold-fields concert also emphasizes the derivative nature of most of the gold-fields songs.

The loneliness of the life of the gum-diggers in northern New Zealand from the late nineteenth century onwards, and the daunting physical circumstances, created a genre of harsh songs that spoke of 'that slighted blighted north' where the earth was 'bare and barren'.[12] Many Māori worked in these gum-swamps in appalling conditions which completely undermined their health. In the 'End of the Earth', the toils of 'hooking' for gum are described, when the digger had to scrape the gum clear of dirt before he could sell it. By 1885 about 2,000 gum-diggers were at work, mostly in areas north of Auckland, although the best gum came from the Coromandel Peninsula. By 1900 many hundreds of Dalmatians (originally Austrian) flocked to the gum-fields, camping together in groups. The export of kauri gum reached its peak in 1899 (11,116 tons), gradually tailing off thereafter.

Little remains of early immigrant and settler songs, beyond a few published ballads such as 'Altered Days', by John Barr (1809-1889) of Craigielee, a Scots migrant to Dunedin:

When to New Zealand first I cam,
Poor and duddy [ragged], poor and duddy . . .

He struck a vein to be repeated with many variants by labourers, especially those indentured in the back country, suffering physical hardships and loneliness. John Barr 'was a general favourite, and had a face as soft and sweet as his poetry', wrote Thomas Hocken. 'At a gathering, he was pretty sure to come down and sing one or two of his new compositions for the good of the company.'[13] He styled himself 'Poet to the Caledonian Society of Otago'.[14]

Some Australian songs became adapted to the New Zealand environment. 'The Old Bark Hut' became transmuted into 'The Old Mud Hut', and other songs appeared with titles such as 'Rise Out of Your Bed' and 'The New Chum'. Although New Zealand has not produced a rival to the Australian 'Click Go the Shears', a number of evocative rural songs exist. 'Shearing', a song with words attributed to David McKee Wright (1867-1928), but with an anonymous tune, portrays the ebb and flow of shearers between Australia and New Zealand. Tony Simpson quotes a shearing song by Mick Leracy, first secretary of the New Zealand Shearers' Union, written around 1900.[15] The predominant mood of these songs is one of cynicism, coupled with anger directed against the employer (often 'The Company'), but tinged with hopes for better times. Charlie Hammond, an English artist who worked his way around Australia and New Zealand, drew 'The dance of the shearers' in his *Sketch-Book*.[16] Shearers dance together at Otakapo Station in the Rangitiki in 1894, as Bob Craig plays Highland dances on the violin and Charlie Hammond accompanies on his small harp — 'They had never heard such music on the station before.' In 'Macintosh's lament' Cameron walks over in moonlight from the outstation with his pipes and plays the piece in front of the long room.

Conditions in nineteenth-century 'factories' in the main cities and in the West Coast mines showed that the oppressive practices of Britain thrived in the colony, as demonstrated in the 1890 *Report of the Sweating Commission*. 'In the dressmaking and millinery trades in particular, the practice of children or young persons working for 12 months without payment had persisted unchecked', writes Jeanine

Graham.[17] These young employees, usually girls, gave their services free of charge in return for the opportunity to learn a skill which would stand them in good stead later. When the year was up they were usually put off and exchanged for another batch. Seddon reckoned 90% were discharged as soon as they became entitled to wages. 'The Sweater', a song with anonymous words and music, is an antipodean equivalent of Thomas Hood's poem 'Song of the Shirt'. Publication of the words in the *Lyttelton Times* in March 1889 led to public meetings, sermons by the Reverend Rutherford Waddell in Dunedin, and a press campaign in the *Otago Daily Times*, resulting in a royal commission and a seamstresses' union:

> Who robs the widow of her right
> By work that takes her day and night,
> To earn his poor starvation mite?
> The *sweater* . . .
>
> He is society's disgrace
> And must be told so to his face.
> So out with him. Leave him no place,
> The *sweater*.

Hymns were borrowed for political and prohibition songs: 'Strike Out the Topline', the theme song of the Prohibition Movement of the 1890s, was modelled on the revivalist stalwart, 'Throw Out the Lifeline'.

When the old folk-songs were uncovered in the 1950s and 60s, some poets and musicians found themselves adding to the repertoire, so that after a lapse of around fifty years a type of topical ballad was revived. Peter Cape, an ardent folk-song devotee of the 1960s, wrote cattle-drover songs — celebrating the solitary figure with his scurrying dogs, following large herds of sheep or cattle on unsurfaced gravel and dirt roads. He also described the scourges of the deer, opossum, and rabbit, and sang about the man who takes the shopping money and spends it on the races, about State houses, dances, and the civil service. There are nostalgic songs like the 'Ghosts of Arrowtown' and 'At Martin's Bay'. 'The Stable Lad' tells of a coaching company employee who falls in love with a West Coast hotel dance girl but dies before he can declare his love.

Many of the characters from the few genuine folk-songs and ballads reappear in contemporary verse such as Denis Glover's *Sings Harry* sequence, celebrating a romantic, tough, back-country character. Some of these poems have been set to music by Douglas Lilburn (see chapter VIII, 3), as have those of the whalers set by Douglas Mews. The folk tradition continues to influence art music as well as generating new and accessible genres, exemplars of which can be found in the Hocken Library Archive of Popular Music.

Notes

[1] Lilburn, *A Search for Tradition*, 21

[2] See Jones, T., 'Australia: Folk music'. *The New Grove*, vol. 1, 711. Also Arnold, R., 'Some Australasian aspects of New Zealand life, 1890-1913'. *JNZH*, April 1970

[3] Interview with author, January 1986

[4] Rona Bailey gave the known antecedents and the sources of each song, whereas Neil Colquhoun 'modernised the source', which cast doubts on the validity of the material. Hybrids such as 'Now is the Hour', a fusion of Māori and European traditions, survive in the modern popular folk field

[5] Ward, R. 'Songs of the Goldfields', a review of Anderson, H. *The Colonial Minstrel* (1960), *Sydney Morning Herald*, 25 November 1960

[6] See Hoskins, *Annotated Bibliography* for an excellent summary of Thatcher; also earlier *Goldfield Balladeer*, and review of *Annotated Bibliography* by Thomson J. M., *Music in New Zealand*, Spring 1989, 51-2

[7] An instance of this is quoted in Olssen, 63, from Bathgate, A., *Random Recollections*, 17

[8] The first known version of this song occurs in Reeves P., (ed.) *Canterbury Rhymes* (2nd edn. 1883), accompanying a poem 'The Lament of Canterbury', described as a lullaby. It was attributed to Crosbie Ward in 1862 and is quoted in Ruth Park's gold-field novel, *One-a-pecker, Two-a-pecker*

[9] See Hoskins, R., 'Joe Small, colonial songster', *EMNZ*, December 1986, 17-21

[10] Angela Annabell discusses gold-field music in 'New Zealand's cultural and economic development reflected in song'. See also the extensive literature of gold-field reminiscences

[11] Fulton, 89-92

[12] Words of 'Trade of Kauri Gum', attributed to William Satchell, Colquhoun, 22

[13] Hocken, 201

[14] See his *Poems and Songs* (Edinburgh 1861) and *Poems* (Dunedin 1874)

[15] Simpson, T., 'The folk culture of the dispossessed'. *Maorilander* (Journal of the NZ Folklore Society), 14

[16] See Fry for Hammond's lively illustrations

[17] Graham, J., 'Child employment in New Zealand'. *NZJH*, April 1987, 67-8

William Saurin Lyster.
Weekly Times, 12 September 1874

4 Opera: William Saurin Lyster to the present day

The beginnings

It could be said that opera was the lingua franca of the nineteenth century. It enjoyed a popularity that has never been surpassed. Piano transcriptions of famous arias sustained countless domestic evenings, just as libretto books, with their plot summaries and principal themes, encouraged a widespread understanding of works before they were experienced in the theatre. It was also the age of the travelling opera company, some of which, such as those of James Henry Mapleson (1830-1901) and Carl Rosa (1842-1889) in England, achieved the status of an institution.

For the twenty years following settlement, New Zealand lacked the experience of live opera, although operatic arias with a linking commentary had been successfully presented by Marie Carandini and her company on her 1863 tour and thereafter.[1] The first full-scale operatic ensemble arrived from Melbourne the following year, when on Saturday 27 August 1864 Lyster's Royal Italian and English Opera Company opened a twenty-four night season with twenty different operas in gold-rush Dunedin.

William Saurin Lyster (1827-1880) was born in Dublin into a family of Protestant gentry, deprived of their lands by the 1849 Encumbered Estates Act. Forced into exile, Lyster had to make his own way, and after many escapades as sailor, soldier, and actor, he became an entrepreneur, forming an opera company around 1857 in America, with his brother Frederick as musical director. In 1859 he engaged two American singers who had returned home after distinguished careers in Europe, the dramatic soprano Lucy Escott and the tenor Henry Squires. He already had two prima donnas—Rosalie Durand, a light soprano who took soubrette roles, and Georgia Hodson, a mezzo with an exceptionally wide range, well able to sing as a contralto. Georgia Hodson married William Lyster, and Rosalie Durand wed his brother Frederick. The new arrivals, Escott and Squires, were to take the company to unprecedented heights.

Lyster was a tall man with a black beard, a hot temper, but a great deal of tact, who read widely, talked well, and was said to combine 'the Irishman's love of a cause, with the vision of a saint and the temperament of a gambler'.[2] In 1861 he took his company across the Pacific to Melbourne, which, after the discovery of gold in Victoria, had become the largest and most prosperous of all colonial cities. The enthusiastic welcome he received led him to choose Melbourne as his base.

The new Princess Theatre, Dunedin, 1876, replacing the original theatre which had burned down. *Hocken Library, Dunedin*

Lyster believed passionately that opera must be presented with accomplished singers, chorus, and orchestra, and effective costumes and sets. To this end he employed the best theatrical artists in Australia. He summoned brilliant stage effects from his machinists, such as aerial flights, sudden disappearances, ships in full sail, cathedrals disintegrating, and magical transformations. He had the latest opera scores sent out from Europe and secured full details of their original productions.

Lyster had organized his Dunedin season on the basis of a guarantee against loss, underwritten by Shadrach Jones, a former Sydney entrepreneur who owned various hotels which he had converted into theatres. Jones had become insolvent by the time of the company's arrival and could not meet his commitments. Lyster tried to interest the banks but they turned him down: he therefore proceeded at his own risk.[3] In preparation for his arrival, the Princess Theatre had been thoroughly refitted. The interior had been painted in faint mauve, and the front of the dress circle ornamented with raised scrollwork in gilt, the ceiling resplendent with radiated bands in crimson and gold. Seating was increased: 'the stall seats have been divided, in ample proportions, even for ladies . . .'[4] In the *Otago Daily Times* Herbert Haynes and Hay advertised evening dresses in 'rich broché and chené silks, French glacé silks in all the new and fashionable shades', lace dresses, opera cloaks, wreaths (presumably to throw to the singers), and white kid gloves.

Lucy Escott and Henry
Squires in costume for *La
Favorita*. *State Library of
Victoria*

The season opened with condensed versions of Donizetti's *Lucrezia Borgia*
and *The Daughter of the Regiment*, the former one of Lucy Escott's show-pieces.
Heavy rain fell unremittingly on the first night, as every available cab drove
back and forth from the theatre and the less fortunate struggled through the
mud. Around a hundred people were reported to have been turned away from
the stalls. The audience was 'the most enthusiastic we have seen in Otago',
wrote the *Otago Daily Times*. Their anonymous critic, who was well versed
in European opera, and had heard the famous Grisi and Mario a score of times
in *Lucrezia Borgia*, as well as Jenny Lind and Ronconi in *The Daughter of the
Regiment*, declared Lyster's performance 'an unqualified success': '"Thorough"
is evidently the motto of every woman and every man in the company; and
that means an evenness and effectiveness, the secret of which although enjoyed
by all, is not discoverable except by those who watch performers very narrowly.'
Lucy Escott's Lucrezia was 'capital . . . her acting is superior to that of most
operatic performers'.[5] Her voice seems to have been that of an unusually wide-
ranged mezzo rather than that of a true high soprano. Squires did not make
so strong an impression; he was 'light and fluty, instead of robust or sympathetic'.
He seemed to be a soft, rather than dramatic tenor, elegant and stylish, although
his characterizations, especially in Meyerbeer, were to develop dramatically.
Georgia Hodson 'sang "Il segreto" most correctly as to notation and feeling,
[but] the *brindisi* [drinking song] sounded somewhat thinly'. In *The Daughter
of the Regiment* Rosalie Durand presented 'a clear firm mezzo-soprano voice,
a perfect *abandon* (where such is necessary for effect), and a generally prepossessing
appearance, which made her a favourite from the moment of her appearance'.
E. Armes Beaumont, a handsome and melodious tenor, 'has within his reach
the position of the Sims Reeves of the Southern Hemisphere'.[6]

A brilliant *Il Trovatore* on 31 August sealed the high reputation of the company,
with tumultuous calls for the principals. Their repertoire, astonishing in its
range, included *Maritana, Martha, La Traviata, Norma, The Daughter of the
Regiment*, Meyerbeer's *Les Huguenots* and *Le Prophète*. Although they lacked
the full complement of scenery and effects, and had only a small orchestra
conducted by George Loder, they presented a different opera each night. It
was a regime that gave their principal singers, numbering around twelve, little
respite, as there were no alternate casts. Most operas were sung in English,
but Escott and Squires preferred to give Italian works in their original language.

The *tour de force* of the season proved to be Meyerbeer's grand opera *Les
Huguenots*. Lyster had taken particular care in its production, ordering costume
designs from Paris. His scenic artist John Hennings excelled himself, as did
the resident machinist.[7] It was 'placed on the stage and performed throughout
with an ability we scarcely expected to find', wrote the *Otago Daily Times*.
Lucy Escott's Valentine was 'one of her greatest triumphs . . .' In the renowned
Act IV duet between Valentine and Raoul, 'Madame Escott fairly brought down
the house . . . Mr Squires fairly shared the honours . . .'[8] Following a triumphant

Faust, the season ended with the last of several benefits, at which William Lyster thanked the gentry and public of Dunedin for their liberal support.[9]

He intended next to visit Auckland, but when news of his success reached Christchurch a local group of investors offered to share in a season, which opened with the same versions of *Lucia di Lammermoor* and *The Daughter of the Regiment*. In the former, Lucy Escott was 'not only an excellent singer but a first-rate actress', and in the latter, Rosalie Durand 'made an excellent Marie, acting the part with a lively *abandon* evidently natural'.[10] Emboldened by these successes, Lyster proceeded to Wellington, where as we have seen, he was frustrated by the small stage and meagre equipment of the Oddfellows' Hall.[11]

His spirits restored by a successful Auckland season, Lyster returned to Dunedin, playing for a month in conjunction with the 1865 Exhibition, the first to be held in the colony. On the way back, he made amends to Wellington and gave a memorable if basic performance of *Faust*. At the conclusion of Act V, as the singers were about to reach the climax of the trio, the stage suddenly began to glow with blue light from chemicals ignited in the wings. The audience sat in stunned silence before breaking into furious applause.[12] Lyster promised to return when the town had 'a more commodious house', a resolve he fulfilled on his next visit in 1872.

Dunedin welcomed him back warmly. After opening with *Il Trovatore*, he presented the first New Zealand performance of Meyerbeer's *Le Prophète*, with augmented orchestra, 'a large number of supernumeraries . . . and every care with the scenery'. The grandiose effects required must have stretched even his ingenuity. 'The introduction of skaters upon the ice was much applauded, and the fierce determination and stirring chorus of the soldiers of John of Leyden, with which the scene opens, were highly effective.'[13] The Company then introduced Weber's *Der Freischütz* (1821) and Auber's *Masaniello* (1828), both first New Zealand performances, and ended with a Grand Complimentary Benefit of *Norma* and *The Lily of Killarney*, given to Lyster by the citizens of the town. Once more he spoke feelingly of the kindness and encouragement he had received, and wished 'a warm-hearted, cordial, generous and music loving people' all future prosperity.[14]

He returned in 1872 with Lyster and Cagli's Royal Italian Opera, Escott and Squires now having retired in Paris, and again in 1880, the year of his death. His twenty-four night run at Wellington's Theatre Royal included Verdi's *Aida* in Italian and Bizet's *Carmen* in English, the orchestra and chorus being acclaimed as the largest and best ever brought to New Zealand.

Lyster's achievements place him at the heart of Australian and New Zealand opera. He had built up and maintained a nucleus of experienced professionals in Melbourne, including Australians like the tenor E. Armes Beaumont. He had embodied the best of the European tradition in his own productions. He had inspired other impresarios, such as the Italian Martin Simonsen and George Musgrove.[15] 'It was a bold thing to bring over an opera company to Dunedin',

Henry Squires as Raoul in *Les Huguenots. Mitchell Library, Sydney*

remarked the *Otago Daily Times* in 1864. 'The advent of the Lyster Company marks a new era in our social history.'[16]

Lyster's successors

Fanny and Martin Simonsen

On 19 August 1865, Martin Simonsen (1830-1899) introduced his wife Fanny, (1835-1896) a singer from the Opéra Comique in Paris, to an appreciative Melbourne audience. Fanny joined the Lyster Opera Company in June 1866, where she and Armes Beaumont later took over the roles sung by Lucy Escott and Henry Squires. She had a warm personality, and soon won a following both in Australia and New Zealand, for 'although her voice lacked the natural beauty of Lucy's, she possessed a consummate mastery over it', writes Love.[16] Martin Simonsen, often billed as 'solo violinist to the King of Denmark' and an itinerant opera director, also worked for Lyster, holding the position of principal conductor for a year in 1866, before being demoted to the first violins. Among the first to follow Lyster to New Zealand, Simonsen began with operatic excerpts interspersed with songs and piano solos, as on their 1868 Wellington visit when they introduced Weber's *Der Freischütz* (advertised as being performed 'in character'), a work which later entered the Company's repertoire.[17]

Having expanded into a full-scale ensemble, the Simonsen Grand Opera Company made several New Zealand tours, that of 1876 being the most spectacular, even outclassing Lyster in the size of its orchestra and the number of singers. On one of these Jennie Macandrew (1866-1949), daughter of George West, founder of Dunedin's famed musical emporium, played a small organ in *Faust*:

> Standing in the wings with my score on a small desk—by candlelight—and waiting my call, I was much alarmed at one Wood, the scene shifter etc, calling out to me 'Look out missie, there is the devil', and turning with a cry I saw Mephisto in all his array, scarlet suit and sword etc. My fears were allayed when he said 'Don't you know me my dear?' This was Riccardi, one of the finest singers to visit New Zealand.[18] He had a glorious heaven-sent voice and was the most courtly of nature's gentlemen . . . Simonsen himself was conductor and his asides and stage whispers were very funny: 'Benham, come to zee front', 'Oh my dear Fanny, what a bad house', etc.[19]

In 1881 the Simonsens visited Nelson. 'There is an opera company here', wrote Dorothy K. Richmond to Ann Shaen on 4 June:

> I have been to *Der Freischütz*, the fireworks in the incantation scene were a marked success, the fire brigade were in waiting outside the theatre, the hose was prepared, we wished we had brought our umbrellas. In the programme

we were requested to keep our seats as there was really no danger whatever. I think the fireworks took even more [applause] than the huntsmen's chorus. Mr Briggs, the man who undertook pyrotechny was twice called before the curtain with uproarious applause. *Norma* I also saw . . .[20]

The Simonsens were undoubtedly an excellent if uneven professional company, as was evident on their 1889 Dunedin visit, when they gave a successful *Il Trovatore* and a disappointing *Faust*.[21] Their repertoire ranged from Gilbert and Sullivan, through lighter works such as *Les Cloches de Corneville* to serious or grand opera. Yet much of the Lyster magic and professionalism must have brushed off, and with Fanny as principal singer they did not lack a star. An Australian colleague remembered her as 'not only a great artist, but a woman of a singularly generous nature — temperamental perhaps, and prone to rash utterances, but moved by an abiding impulse to give only of her best to the public'. Her husband Martin was 'impatient of interference, and in some respects difficult to get on with, but single-hearted where music was concerned and an accomplished conductor'.[22]

On Fanny's death in 1896, the *Evening Post* paid tribute to the honour and respect she universally enjoyed: 'So the curtain has fallen at last upon poor Madame Simonsen, after an operatic career of so many, many years. Her name was but another way of spelling MUSIC . . . Her opera of life contained many acts, and a sprinkling of sweet music, but the discords, or, in other words, her ups and downs with Fate — were many, and so severe in late years that she abandoned the stage and tutored pupils.'[23]

Just as the Simonsens had kept a love of opera alive, so did several other short-lived groups, including the Cagli and Pompei's Royal Italian Opera Company of the 1870s, which later merged with Lyster. They played a four-week season in Auckland from November 1871, including *Il Trovatore, La Traviata, Lucia di Lammermoor*, and *Don Giovanni*, winning ovations, enthusiastic notices, and bouquets, with net profits exceeding £1000.[24]

J. C. Williamson (1845-1913)

The American-born actor and impresario J. C. Williamson, who became one of the wealthiest and most influential managers in Australian history, had in his youth bought for $100 a 'sketchy' script called *Struck Oil*, which his friend Clay M. Greene had rewritten. In 1873 Williamson and his wife, the comedienne Margaret Virginia Sullivan, who played as Maggie Moore, performed the play with phenomenal success and subsequently took it to Australia. After it had brought in £7000 at the Theatre Royal in Melbourne, Williamson moved to Sydney and beyond. This early commercial flair remained dominant throughout his professional life. It has been attributed to his non-theatrical middle class background which allowed him to identify with public taste, but it is also associated with a childlike view of the magic of the theatre which he is said

J. C. Williamson (1845-1913). *Alexander Turnbull Library*

to have retained throughout his life.[25] Following his second Australian success with *HMS Pinafore* in Melbourne in 1879, he settled there to form his (Royal) Comic Opera Company in 1880, turning the Theatre Royal the following year into the best-equipped in the antipodes. Williamson's first New Zealand tour of Gilbert and Sullivan, whose sole Australian agent he became, opened at the Princess Theatre, Dunedin, on 27 February 1882 with *Patience*, followed by *HMS Pinafore* and *The Pirates of Penzance*, featuring Alice Rees. In Nellie Stewart, later to marry the impresario George Musgrove, he had a spirited and popular leading lady.[26]

Williamson's companies toured New Zealand regularly, covering almost every genre, but concentrating on Gilbert and Sullivan and light opera. In this context his 1910 productions of *Madama Butterfly, La Bohème*, and *Carmen*, with Amy Castles, Bel Sorel, and Rosina Buckman, proved operatic highlights.[27] Recalling productions he had seen at the Metropolitan and Manhattan Opera House in New York, Rudolph Baeyertz of the *Triad* arts journal found the Christchurch performances somewhat uneven, partly due to the indisposition of Amy Castles, who did not appear, and Rosina Buckman, who did. Madame Bel Sorel, however, 'has a sensitive musical organization, and her enunciation is quite remarkable for an artist singing in a foreign tongue'. Rosina Buckman sang with obvious difficulties but 'made a genuine artistic success'.[28]

Williamson later favoured visual spectaculars such as *Ben Hur*, arranged tours for artists of the calibre of Henry Irving and Dame Nellie Melba, and developed an intense interest in racehorses. He had a sure sense of public taste, never lost his love of the theatre, disliked the experimental, and remained happiest with the star system he had created and the long runs it engendered.[29]

The Heralds of *Lohengrin*, from the Musgrove Opera Company's 1907 production, with A. Crump, S. Sullivan, and H. and J. Oakes, members of a prominent Wellington musical family. Visiting opera companies enlisted the help of local musicians for the larger works, even if the costumes did not quite fit. *Alexander Turnbull Library*

George Musgrove (1854-1916)

William Lyster's *artistic* successor proved to be George Musgrove, whose family connections had led him to emigrate to Melbourne and become Company treasurer.[30] Musgrove's own career as entrepreneur began in 1880 with a spectacular production of Offenbach's *La Fille du Tambour Major*, which ran for 101 nights in Melbourne, later bringing Nellie Stewart to stardom and marriage with her producer.[31]

After a split with J. C. Williamson, Musgrove continued on his own, developing a passion for opera. Like Lyster, Musgrove frequently had costumes and sets made in Europe. He held auditions for singers in Hamburg and Berlin, and commissioned scenery and costumes from the noted Berlin firm of Baruch and Company. This could prove so intricate and magnificent that often twenty-five minutes were required to assemble it between each act.[32]

In 1901 Musgrove took eight operas to New Zealand, including Wagner's *Flying Dutchman, Tannhäuser*, and *Lohengrin*.[33] 'Opera has never been produced in New Zealand on a scale so rich and ornate, and with such affluence of musical resources, both vocal and instrumental', wrote the *Free Lance*.[34] And of the entire three weeks: 'Such a season has never been known in Wellington. It has been at the flood-tide from the start . . .'[35] The singers included Barron Berthald, Lawrence Mooney, Clarence Leumane, and Madame Slapoffski as Elizabeth in *Tannhäuser*.

On his 1907 tour Musgrove added *Die Walküre*: 'The audience was absolutely spellbound and as the wonderful drama and music progressed, culminating in the Magic Fire music, the curtain fell to thunders of applause', wrote Nellie Stewart.[36] The alarming expenses and the difficulties that erupted among the German singers on this tour spelt Musgrove's downfall: 'Alas! the character and disposition of the German artists was not on a par with their abilities. Jealousy and internecine strife became the order of the day—and night—and a great artistic scheme which had commenced so brilliantly was doomed, bringing to ruin a great man with splendid artistic ideals.'[37] Herr Mohwinkel had proved an outstanding singer but the orchestra was severely criticized.

Musgrove was an outstanding entrepreneur. His principal conductor, Gustav Slapoffski, likened him to Carl Rosa, Colonel Mapleson, and Sir Augustus Harris (the great Wagner impresario at Covent Garden): 'I had worked for long periods with these operatic giants so was able to make comparisons.'[38]

The Hon. R. A. Loughnan, in his book *New Zealand at Home* (1908), sums up the impressions left behind by these companies whose singers created what was undoubtedly the 'golden age' of New Zealand opera:

> The survivors of those times still talk with warm respect of Lucy Escott, the charming prima donna, and Squires, the brilliant tenor, the Grisi and Mario of the Antipodean lyrical world, as they were called.[39] In the seventies Italian

Tom Pollard in his youth.
J. & P. Cooper collection,
Alexander Turnbull Library

companies brought Italian opera to the country in the best Italian manner, with artists who, though not in any instance of European celebrity, were all capable singers, with beautiful voices and stage experience of the right kind . . .[40] Crowds followed the misfortunes of the *Sonnambula* with sympathy, listened spell-bound to the great sextet in *Lucia*, were fascinated by the death scene in *Lucrezia*, and greeted with uproarious delight the immortal *Barbiere* . . . They left behind traditions of sprightly Rosinas, rollicking Figaros, comical Bartolos, of a really great Mephistopheles, a charming Marguerite, a Valentine of sonorous energy, of true nobility of declamation, and the agreeable balance of great voices.[41]

The word 'opera' in the titles of several companies denoted light or comic opera, or Gilbert and Sullivan, as with Signor Riccardi's English Opera Company (1879), mentioned earlier, and the Lingard Opera Company (1879). Although only one company with strong New Zealand connections arose during this period, that of Tom Pollard, others emerged fitfully, such as those organized by Luscombe Searelle (1853-1907),[42] composer and impresario, whose *Estrella* (1884) and *Bobadil* (1884) launched him into the international world of comic opera, or *Opera Bouffe* as it was then called. His music is today totally forgotten.

Tom Pollard. *J. & P.*
Cooper collection, Alexander
Turnbull Library

The Pollard Opera Company

On 24 December 1896 the *Evening Post* wrote appreciatively of Tom Pollard's Opera Company: 'We have seen these young people develop from precocious children into capable and finished artists, and so much of their time has been spent in New Zealand that they are looked upon as almost a local institution.' This description exactly fitted the facts, for Tom Pollard was born in Tasmania, and the ensemble's beginnings lay within the family of James Joseph Pollard, a northern English piano tuner who had emigrated to Australia in 1860. Twenty years later James presented a juvenile version of *HMS Pinafore*, the group incorporating his fifteen Tasmanian-born children.[43] Such ensembles had already proved popular in London, where an official junior Gilbert and Sullivan company existed alongside others such as Robey's Midget Minstrels and Warwick Gray's Juvenile Opera.

The Pollard Lilliputians were soon to make a unique impression both in Australia and New Zealand. Children who were not part of the family were legally apprenticed to the company, and a formal agreement set out the length of the engagement from one to four years, the salary being paid to the parent, not the child. The Pollard organization, in return, 'guaranteed to teach the apprentice the theatrical profession, educate and clothe him, provide him with pocket money and return him to his parents at the end of the specified period'.[44]

Tom Pollard (1858-1922), born in Tasmania as Tom O'Sullivan, married the daughter of James Joseph Pollard and joined the company, initially for three months as an orchestral violinist. He remained for thirty years, however, changing his name and achieving fame when he took over direction. The original Lilliputians began their first New Zealand tour in Invercargill in 1881, followed by an unprecedented three weeks in Auckland, and an enthusiastic farewell crowd on the Dunedin wharf. After the death of his father-in-law, Tom Pollard directed the second tour of 1884; the repertoire contained eight popular comic operas.[45] Despite enthusiastic receptions, cheering crowds, and bands leading them to the theatre, it now proved an inescapable fact to audiences and critics that the Pollards were growing up. An Australian tour reinforced these conclusions, where the problem became so acute that the company, already beset by family disagreements, disbanded in 1886.[46]

'Auntie May' Pollard, an original child star of the first company who died in Sydney in 1970, aged 102. *J. & P. Cooper collection, Alexander Turnbull Library*

In 1891 J. C. Williamson invited Tom Pollard to form a new group, which began a New Zealand tour in July. But as the prevailing depression took effect, Williamson withdrew his support, leaving the company to continue touring under their own steam in Australia. Fortunately, a nearby gold strike brought full houses for their Adelaide season of *The Gondoliers*, which prompted Williamson to re-engage them to perform *The Mikado* and *La Mascotte* at his Princess Theatre in Melbourne in October 1892. This patronage proved crucial. Reviewers enthusiastically praised the young artists, some of whom, including the New Zealand-born Marion Mitchell, quickly became Pollard celebrities. The choruses were well sung and the dancing admirable.[47] Lily Everett made a spirited heroine in *La Mascotte*.

A new arrangement with a more eager J. C. Williamson now ensued, followed by another New Zealand tour in 1893 featuring the pantomine *Aladdin*, notable for the triumph of the sixteen-year-old Marion Mitchell, especially in her home town of Wellington. The company virtually became self-supporting, designing and making most of the costumes and scenery themselves. 'I learned to paint on the print-frames of old theatres . . . We carried our own limelight plant and made our own gas' wrote W. S. Percy.[48] In 1895, a disastrous fire at the Theatre Royal, Palmerston North, destroyed everything—music, prompt-books, costumes, and scenery. Ingenuity alone saved the day, as they improvised performances. But the company also faced another crisis, the familiar one of children growing up. Tom Pollard and his senior associates now decided to reconstruct completely. All association with juveniles was dropped, and an adult Pollard Opera Company set out on a New Zealand tour in 1896 with a new repertoire and another pantomime, *Djin Djin*, whose spectacular scenic effects helped ensure that resounding success remarked on by the *Evening Post*.

Unidentified member of the Pollard Opera Company. *J. & P. Cooper collection, Alexander Turnbull Library*

After a further series of negotiations with Williamson, the Pollards evolved into a full and complete light opera company, taking into their repertoire works such as *La Poupée, The Belle of New York* and *The Geisha*. The company numbered seventy, with an orchestra of ten.[49] They entered new fields when they launched Alfred Hill's romantic opera *Tapu* in the Wellington Opera House on 16 February 1903, and turned this improbable combination of Māori themes and musical

Marion Mitchell as Nell
Gwynn, her favourite
Pollard role. *Collection of
Peter Downes*

Poster for the Pollard
Opera Company
production of *The Belle of
Cuba. Hocken Library,
Dunedin*

comedy into a highly successful venture within New Zealand and beyond. In
Alfred Hill's eyes the Pollard production of *Tapu* was the best.[50]

After another disastrous fire, this time in Durban, South Africa, they lost
their wardrobe, scenery, scripts, and music (including *Tapu*). Tom Pollard
returned to New Zealand, where he became Director of Entertainments at the
Christchurch Exhibition of 1906-1907. Later he organized a new Pollard Juvenile
Opera Company which toured from 1907 to 1910. But the times were against
him as the taste for vaudeville and moving pictures grew. Despite his latest
attraction, *Miss Hook of Holland*, the Pollard Company finally closed in Timaru
on 13 April 1910. Tom Pollard, with his two brothers, opened two cinemas
in Greymouth and Hokitika, and became a producer for amateur operatic societies
until his death in 1922.

The Pollard Company had provided an invaluable training ground for theatrical
and operatic talent from which many stars emerged. In addition to Marion
Mitchell, renowned for her Nell Gwynne in Planquette's operetta of the same
name,[51] Lily Everett, Lily Stephens, Maud and May Beatty were outstanding,
and among the men W. S. Percy, the male lead in Alfred Hill's *Tapu*, who
had joined the Pollards as a boy. Photographs recreate the stylishness and vivid
personalities of these artists, and that indefinable quality, verging on pathos,
that attends the well-drilled and joyous theatrical ventures of youth.

'As a producer of opera, Tom Pollard had no peer', wrote Stan East in the
Triad:

> He seemed to know intuitively every stave of any opera that one could mention.
> His interpretation of Gilbert and Sullivan was unrivalled, and with it all he
> possessed a rare quality of tact and patience that added in great measure to
> his success . . . He did a great work in cultivating musical taste in the small
> towns of New Zealand, and there will be many a journalist, many an amateur,
> many a noisy, inglorious Melba, and many a parson, too, who will pause to
> think with regret that no more shall we see his tall figure coming up Main
> Street, and turning into the right-of-way behind the Oddfellows' Hall, there
> to work prodigies of productions in the cavernous, gas-lit recesses behind the
> musty stage.[52]

The end of an era and a centennial Faust

The changed musical life following World War I was nowhere more apparent
than in opera. With the deaths of Williamson (1913) and Musgrove (1916),
two commanding figures had left the stage, but 'The Firm' continued to flourish,
as did other theatrical enterprises, notably those of the Fuller family, now led
by Sir Benjamin (1875-1952), who had begun his stage career at the age of
nine in a minstrel troupe and sung in the chorus at Covent Garden. In 1895
he worked his passage to Australia and joined his father's variety show. The

family later settled in New Zealand, where they established permanent vaudeville theatres in each of the four centres. What became known as the Fuller circuit also embraced revues, dramas, pantomimes, and latterly films.

In 1916-1917 Benjamin Fuller rescued the Italian Gonzales Grand Opera Company,[54] which had been stranded in South Africa at the outbreak of the war. Singers included Scamuzzi, a notable baritone, the tenors Capelli and Balboni, and the sopranos Visoni and Gonzales. Madame Gonzales sang Violetta one night and had a baby next day, a feat earlier achieved by Fannie Simonsen.

The day of the touring opera company was almost over, to be replaced by shorter, more select tours of 'Grand Opera', with carefully chosen 'name' artists, usually organized by Williamsons or Fullers. It was also the period of musical comedy, of *Chu-Chin-Chow* (1921), Gladys Moncrieff in *Maid of the Mountains* (1922), and in the same year Williamson tours of *Merrie England, The Chocolate Soldier*, and Gilbert and Sullivan. The Royal Comic Opera Company presented *Lilac Time* (1926) and *Lady Be Good* (1927). In 1936 *The White Horse Inn* introduced a revolving stage. 'Our Glad' became a celebrity: 'My wish is to be remembered by theatregoers as "that favourite of the people" because of that image that has always meant so much to me.'[55]

Familiar names appeared in the cast of the Williamson Grand Opera Company of 1920. Gustav Slapoffski, Musgrove's chief musical ally, was in the pit, and the principals included Amy Castles, Strella Wilson, and Browning Mummery.[56] In 1928 the Fuller-Gonzales Grand Opera Company returned with fourteen operas,[57] featuring different casts from those on their earlier visit. Their principal singers included Rosita Silvestri (dramatic soprano), Maria Menkina (coloratura), Matilda Pfrimmer (mezzo), and Brandisio Vannucci (lyric tenor). The conductor was Ernesto Gonzales.

The world-wide depression had deeply affected the fortunes of artists in Europe, which led a number of distinguished Italian singers to accept an engagement to tour Australia and New Zealand in 1932. The Williamson Imperial Grand Opera Company opened in Auckland on 5 October with outstanding artists, in a generous offering which included such favourites as *Madama Butterfly, Carmen, Tosca*, and *La Traviata*.[58] Lina Paliughi, their leading coloratura soprano, proved outstanding as Lucia and Gilda. Among her colleagues were Molly de Gunst, a young Australian dramatic soprano, Cesarini Valobra, who had sung at La Scala as the original Liu in Puccini's *Turandot*, and Carlo Alfieri, a young lyric tenor who was compared to John McCormack.[59] The Australian singer Joan Hammond, who later had a notable operatic career, was in the chorus. It will already have been noticed how each generation tended to single out one particular operatic season as the finest. In this vein the 1932 Company was held to be the most splendid galaxy of talents ever to visit New Zealand. The overwhelmingly enthusiastic reception was expressed in innumerable reviews.[60]

Sir Benjamin Fuller's Opera Company tour of 1935 proved to be the highlight of his career as an opera impresario, with principals Florence Austral, Muriel

Brunskill, Horace Stevens, Browning Mummery, and Frederic Collier. Lucien Cesaroni was artistic director and Frank Crowther the conductor. A resounding artistic success, the season nevertheless cost Fuller £30,000.[61]

As a centennial opera for 1940, the organizing committee had chosen Gounod's *Faust*, engaging an eminent cast of overseas soloists to tour, supported by local choruses. Despite the outbreak of war, these plans continued. Isobel Baillie, Gladys Ripley, and Heddle Nash set out on an epic wartime journey from Britain with some 600 refugees, crossing the Atlantic on a ship which was shelled by a U-boat, killing two seamen. Their own vessel's superior speed allowed them to escape.[62] Small wonder that Peter Fraser, in welcoming the soloists at Parliament Buildings (where they were joined by the New Zealand bass Oscar Natzke and the Australian, Raymond Beatty), described the visit as 'a memorable one in the history of culture in the Dominion'.[63]

Isobel Baillie (1895-1983), renowned for her serene and radiant voice, made a rare operatic appearance as Marguerite (her customary realm was oratorio). Gladys Ripley (1908-1955), a leading English contralto, sang Siebel, Heddle Nash (1896-1961), a tenor of unique natural gifts, performed Faust, and Raymond Beatty (1903-), replacing Oscar Natzke (1912-51), was Mephistopheles. Natzke, an apprentice blacksmith from the Waikato, who had become one of the world's great basses, was compelled for contractual reasons to withdraw from the role (as Isobel Baillie nearly did). Sir Thomas Beecham, unexpectedly present on a visiting ship in port, was invited to conduct an entire performance, but chose to direct Act II (limited to the principals): 'Stepping down to the orchestral pit, he glanced at the score, closed it up, had a word with Maurice Clare . . . and proceeded to give an electrifying performance.'[64] The soloists made such a strong impression in everything they undertook that they were urged to remain in New Zealand, at least for the duration of the war.[65] But after a month's recital tour with the NBS String Quartet, they elected to repeat their hazardous journey, this time without incident, except that on berthing safely at Liverpool, they saw 'that brave city being badly blitzed', and when Isobel Baillie reached Manchester, 'a land mine fell close by and the doors and windows of my home were blown in; a fine return to England'.[66]

Since 1940 opera in New Zealand has had a stormy, frustrating history. It has encompassed an NZBS *Carmen*, with English soloists Janet Howe and Arthur Servent (1948), and a tour by J. C. Williamson's notable Italian company (1949), which gave 104 performances, made possible by yet another instance of direct intervention by the Prime Minister [Peter Fraser]. Under a distinguished conductor, Franco Ghione, with twenty-five principals and 180 performers, it presented eleven operas.[67] In 1954 Donald Munro formed the New Zealand Opera Group, which became the New Zealand Opera Company, renowned for its performances of chamber opera by Pergolesi, Mozart, Wolf-Ferrari,

Menotti, and others. This developed into a full-scale opera company under different direction, eventually to be cut down by the withdrawal of subsidies. Since then opera has been deemed too expensive to receive more than modest state patronage and has developed on a regional basis.

There have been brilliant periods in New Zealand's operatic history, starting with William Lyster. There have been many outstanding artists who have won admiration and devotion. Tom Pollard encouraged New Zealand singers and championed works such as Hill's *Tapu*. There have been the sumptuous Wagner productions by George Musgrove and the brilliant Williamson Italian Company of 1932. Rosina Buckman and Frances Alda helped initiate a rich vein of New Zealand opera singers which continues to this day. But a fuller performing tradition of opera has not yet reinstated itself, to parallel that of ballet. New Zealand opera cries out for patrons. In no sense does it lack anything else.

Notes

[1] See chapter II, 2

[2] Moriarty thesis, 72

[3] Seats cost 10/6d, 7/6d, 5s, and 3s. Precautions were taken against the best seats falling into the hands of speculators, *ODT*, 26 August 1864, 1

[4] *ODT*, 27 August 1864, 4

[5] Ibid., 5

[6] Sims Reeves (1818-1900) was a famed English tenor

[7] See Harold Love's descriptions of *Les Huguenots* in *Studies in Music*, vol. II, 1977. Lyster's flautist Julius Siede (1825-1903), who conducted from 1865 to 1871, re-orchestrated the work

[8] *ODT*, 13 September 1864, 5

[9] *ODT*, 22 September 1864, 1

[10] *Lyttelton Times*, 8 October 1864, 4

[11] See chapter II, 2

[12] *ODT*, 4 February 1865, 5

[13] *ODT*, 18 February 1865, 5

[14] See Love, 273-4, for a fine tribute to Lyster, and 84 for the Wellington *Faust*

[15] *ODT*, 26 August 1864, 4

[16] Love, 89. Fanny Simonsen, née Hay, was born in France *c*. 1835 and died in Melbourne on 18 September 1896. She sang at the Opéra Comique in Paris as Madame Françoise Dehaes, and became leading soprano of her husband's opera company in which her son and daughters also performed

[17] See Moriarty thesis, 73, and quotes from *Independent*, 1 February 1868. Other members of the company were Miss Rebecca Jones, Mr G. F. Price, and M. Eugene Arlot, pianist

[18] Riccardi later formed Signor Riccardi's English Opera Company which in 1889 toured a pirated *HMS Pinafore* in NZ. He succeeded J. C. Williamson as Sir Joseph Porter in the February 1880 Melbourne production. See Downes, *Shadows*, 81-2

[19] Macandrew, 4. Simonsen's NZ tours included those of 1868, 1876, 1881, 1883; Alfred Hill probably joined the orchestra as cornet player in 1881, having previously had lessons from William Mathias, a member of the Company. See Thomson,

ADM, 16 See also Simpson, A. 'The Simonsen Opera Company's 1876 tour of New Zealand', *TLR* October, 1990

20 Richmond-Atkinson, vol. 2, 484

21 *Triad*, July 1889, 83

22 Love, 279

23 *Evening Post*, 26 September 1896; see also the tribute in the *Melbourne Age*, 30 June 1928, quoted in Love, 279. Fanny's pupils included Ada Crossley and Frances Alda. See also Crossley entry in *ADB*, vol. 8, 1871-1929, 15

24 They also played in gold-rush Thames for two weeks to good houses. See Elphick thesis, 205ff.; Love, 204; and for a disapproving response to an Auckland *Don Giovanni*, see diary of Colonel Feilding, Feilding Borough Council, extract in Dominion, 29 December 1986, 7. See also Thomson, J. M. 'William Saurin Lyster and his influence' in Simpson, A. already cited

25 See Helen M. van der Poorten in *ADB*, vol. 6, 1851-1890, 407

26 See Downes, *Shadows*, 115-20

27 The cast also included Frederick Blamey and Arthur Crane

28 *Triad*, 10 August 1910, 9. Baeyertz also criticized the lack of sophistication of the audience, the poor stage management, and the unbalanced orchestra, indifferently conducted by Signor Hazon. See also Thomson, J. M., 'Rosina Buckman', in Simpson, A. already cited

29 See *ADB*, vol. 6, 1851-1890, 407 and Downes, *Shadows*, 79-88. Williamson's companies visited New Zealand more frequently than those of anybody else — between 1881 and 1910 over fifty tours took place

30 Musgrove's English mother Fanny Hodson, a much idolized opera star, had connections with the acting families of the Kembles and Siddons. Musgrove's sister, the singer Georgia Hodson, had married William Lyster

31 See *ADB*, vol. 5, 324

32 Nellie Stewart's autobiography, *My Life's Story*, gives an absorbing background to Musgrove's achievements

33 The complete repertoire also included *Carmen, Faust, Il Trovatore, Maritana*, and *Mignon*

34 *Free Lance*, 24 August 1901, 14

35 *Free Lance*, 31 August 1901, 14

36 Stewart, N. 190 For a detailed criticism see *Triad* vol. 15 no. 6, September 1909, 37ff.

37 Ibid., 190. For a detailed criticism see *Triad* vol. 15 no. 6, September 1909, 37ff.

38 Ibid., 123. See references to Slapoffski in *ADM*. Musgrove made a 'smalls' NZ tour with a full company headed by Nellie Stewart in 1910-1911, visiting thirty-two towns

39 Mario (1810-1888), a great Italian tenor, formed one of opera's most memorable partnerships with Giulia Grisi (1811-1869), a distinguished Italian soprano with an exceptionally wide range of roles. Idols of their day, they had been heard by the critic of the *ODT* in 1864-1865

40 Companies such as the Cagli-Lyster tour of 1872 and the Simonsens

41 Loughnan, 105-7

42 See Jeremy Commons 'Luscombe Searelle' in Simpson, A. already cited

43 See Downes, *Shadows*, 123-41, also in *Aspects of New Zealand Opera*, ed. Adrienne Simpson (forthcoming)

44 Ibid., 124

45 *HMS Pinafore, Les Cloches de Corneville, The Little Duke, La Fille de Madame Angot, Fatinitza, The Princess of Trebizonde, Sweethearts* and *Patience*

46 Downes, *Shadows*, 127

47 See the Melbourne *Argus*, 17 October 1892, and *Age*, 24 and 27 October 1892

48 Percy, W. S., 'The Story of the Pollard Opera Company' (September 1941) MS 61482, Percy, ATL

49 Downes, *Shadows*, 138

50 Thomson, *ADM*, 72ff.

51 She married Ernest Davis in 1899 and retired from the stage, becoming Lady Mayoress of Auckland in 1935. See 'Darling of the nineties' in Downes, *Top of the Bill*, 28ff.

52 *Triad*, 10 October 1922, 28-9

54 Their repertoire included *Faust, Il Trovatore, La Bohème, Un Ballo in Maschera, Lucia di Lammermoor, Rigoletto, Mignon, Carmen, Cavalleria Rusticana*, and *I Pagliacci*. See ATL Ephemera Collection and Mackenzie, *Singers*, 281

55 Moncrieff, 145

56 Their repertoire included *Tales of Hoffmann, Cavalleria Rusticana, I Pagliacci*, and *Faust*

57 *Norma, Lucia di Lammermoor, Il Trovatore, Rigoletto, Faust, Carmen, La Traviata, Mignon, Un Ballo in Maschera, Barber of Seville, Lohengrin, La Favorita, Fra Diavolo, Ernani*

58 The Company also performed *Tales of Hoffmann, Rigoletto, Lucia di Lammermoor, Il Trovatore, La Bohème, Cavalleria Rusticana* and *Pagliacci*

59 Other artists included Bruna Castagna, a mezzo who gave over seventy performances of Carmen, being described as 'petite and coquettish', the dramatic tenor Pedro Mirassou, Apollo Granforte, Primo Montanari, Ilio del Chiaro, and Michele Fiore, a comic bass who excelled as Don Pasquale

60 See, for instance, *Dominion*, 8 November 1932: 'the sumptuous mounting and costumes left nothing to be desired'. Similar praise was expressed to Jeremy Commons by John Gordon, who also assiduously attended performances

61 Campbell in MacKenzie, 281

62 Baillie, 124ff.

63 *Dominion*, 16 April 1940

64 Jensen, 19. Part of this performance is held by RNZ Archives, Timaru

65 Besides the opera, they sang in a concert version of *Carmen, Elijah*, and other works

66 Baillie, 129

67 *La Bohème, Rigoletto, Aida, Tosca, Madama Butterfly, Il Trovatore, Cavalleria Rusticana, I Pagliacci, Faust, Barber of Seville, Manon*, sung in Italian

Opera since 1946 — a survey

The New Zealand Opera Company (1953-1971) arose through the enthusiasm of the baritone Donald Munro, who had travelled to England in 1939 on his own resources to study opera. After a period at the Royal College of Music, where he won the Tagore gold medal and a Leverhulme Scholarship, he spent two years in Paris with Pierre Bernac, and appeared with Sadler's Wells, the Old Vic and in BBC operas. Following his return to New Zealand he took part in performances of Pergolesi's *La Serva Padrona* with piano accompaniment for the Auckland based Community Arts Service, then directed by Owen Jensen. Their resounding success encouraged him in 1953 to form the New Zealand Opera Company supported by the newly-formed Opera Society. With an orchestra of ten, he presented *La Serva Padrona* and Menotti's *The Telephone*, the effervescence of the former becoming a leitmotif of the new ensemble. More than 5,000 people attended the nineteen performances, many of which were given in small sparsely equipped halls. This grass-roots approach to opera had a kinship with the English Opera Group founded by Benjamin Britten and Eric Crozier in 1947 for whom Britten wrote several chamber operas including *The Rape of Lucretia* and *Albert Herring*.[1]

Munro financed the Company from his own resources, losing heavily in the process and being forced to recoup by working in wool stores and freezing works. In 1955 James Robertson, director of the National Orchestra, became an enthusiastic principal conductor as the repertoire expanded to include Wolf Ferrari's *Susanna's Secret* and Menotti's *The Medium*. The New Zealand Players' Trust lent stage properties and the services of Raymond Boyce, a gifted young English stage designer. In 1956 the Company presented Mozart's *The Impresario* and Menotti's *Amahl and the Night Visitors*, adding *The Consul* the following year. In 1958 *The Marriage of Figaro* included Honor McKellar and Donald Munro, the conductor being John Hopkins. In 1959 sponsorship of £5,000 per annum from The Department of Internal Affairs offered the Company a new lease of life, especially when it was matched by a similar sum from New Zealand Breweries. In 1961 Cabinet set aside £40,000 to sponsor a second orchestra for opera and theatre, to be conducted by James Robertson and led by Ruth Pearl.[2]

Over succeeding years the Company gave many fine performances which included Joyce Blackham's Carmen in 1962 and the première of David Farquhar's *A Unicorn for Christmas* the same year. A largely Māori *Porgy and Bess* with Inia te Wiata in 1965 proved a highlight. 'Inia te Wiata played with great authority; he is a natural actor with a most sympathetic voice', wrote Frederick Page.[3] By now 73% of the Company's revenue came from box-office receipts and private sponsors and 27% from Arts Council grants. 'This is a record of public support unsurpassed by any professional opera company within our knowledge',[4] stated Phyllis Brusey, a company director.

Despite severe orchestral problems, productions such as Britten's *Albert Herring* (1966) continued at a high artistic level. A disastrous warehouse fire in March 1967 destroyed costumes and props of nearly twenty operas but public donations and help from as far afield as London and Australia kept the Company on the road. A cut in the Arts Council funding of $100,000 affected it more seriously: subsequent further cuts placed severe stresses on planning and organization. Nevertheless the Company continued to develop their resources. They sold their Hill Street headquarters profitably to the Ministry of Works and they adapted the Regal Theatre at Karori to suit their purposes. Artistically they continued to grow. Inia te Wiata's Osmin in *Il Seraglio* (1968) showed memorable acting and singing and *Fidelio* which opened the new premises in Karori the same year, went on to a successful tour.

Despite excellent singers and production, Stravinsky's *The Rake's Progress* in 1969 brought a poor box-office response (as had happened with Britten's *Albert Herring*). It became clear that New Zealand audiences still predominantly supported the standard repertoire. The Company restored their fortunes dramatically through Kiri te Kanawa's Carmen, under James Robertson, although subsequent administrative problems soon came to overshadow all else. The Arts Council instructed the Opera Company to amalgamate with the Ballet Company in 1970, a directive that gravely strained its strength and independence, the aims and requirements of the two companies proving incompatible. Unlike Sadler's Wells Opera and Ballet they had not evolved together. The New Zealand Ballet and Opera Trust began its activities in February 1971. Following a successful *Aida* and *The Marriage of Figaro* the Arts Council withdrew its financial support. After a prolonged, public and bitter dispute, the New Zealand Opera Company went into recession. Nearly twenty years of dedicated endeavour and high achievement had been destroyed.

The gap was partly filled by the New Opera Company of Wellington which mounted professional productions in the main centres and toured the provinces, being sustained by small Arts Council grants until its demise in 1979. The National Opera Company of New Zealand (1979-1983) was then formed. Based in Auckland, it toured several fine productions. In 1983 two contemporary works appeared rather closely together, Kurt Weill's *Mahagonny* and Britten's *Turn of the Screw*. Despite their quality, audiences failed to respond. The National Opera Company in its turn was disbanded. Opera thereafter was deemed a regional responsibility, the bulk of the available funding being entrusted to Auckland's Mercury Theatre. Strong pleas for greater equity have so far proved unsuccessful (1990).

As opera in New Zealand continues in its present truncated form, the high standards of many regional productions cannot disguise the paradox of the situation. A constant flow of young talent emerges in the biennial Mobil Song Quest and elsewhere, but has no permanent professional company in which to work. Instead, singers must seek positions throughout the world, and make migratory forays home. In New Zealand itself a natural appetite and flair for opera remains unfulfilled; young audiences have no opportunities to learn the classical repertoire as they may easily do in symphonic and chamber music. For evidence of what heights can be reached one has only to mention the full production of *Meistersinger*, mounted in the Michael Fowler Centre as the centrepiece of the 1990 Wellington International Arts Festival, with Donald McIntyre as Hans Sachs and the New Zealand Symphony Orchestra conducted by Heinz Wallberg.

Notes

[1] Following the international success of Britten's *Peter Grimes* at Sadler's Wells in 1946, dissension within the company showed clearly that future co-operation would not be possible. Britten and Crozier therefore created their own company responsive to their own needs

[2] This orchestra had an exceedingly chequered career and was disbanded as from 31 December 1964

[3] *Comment* 23, vol. 6 no. 2, 1965

[4] *Ring Down the Curtain*, 135. See also list of NZOC productions 191-2, and her account of the events following the amalgamation of the ballet and opera companies that led to the demise of the NZOC, 165ff.

5 Stately galleons: the colonial choral societies and their successors

Choral societies at their best can generate an energy that transforms a musical occasion into one of deep, abiding ritual. They can breed fierce loyalties as partisan as those in politics or sport. Bound together by friendships forged in weekly rehearsals, individual singers lose their identity to become absorbed into the overall conception. The colonial choral society was an awesome sight: tiers of ladies in billowing white, bearded gentlemen in black, beneath a panoply of organ pipes, framed by arum lilies or potted aspidistras.

Colonial choirs also had a strong sense of decorum: while conducting a rehearsal of the Dunedin Choral Society, George West, the renowned local conductor and music emporium owner 'was guilty of the heinous offence of taking off his coat at a practice, one Innes, a member of the committee remonstrating. Such a procedure was *not* done in those days—before the ladies too—and he had no alternative but to resign gracefully.'[1]

The New Zealand choral societies became the pivot of the colonial musical scene. The English choral tradition, which had already established itself in America, Canada, and Australia, proved powerful and durable. Like the choirs that arose from the darkness of mid-nineteenth-century Sheffield, Huddersfield, Leeds, and other such choral bastions, New Zealand choral societies drew hundreds of untrained singers into their ranks. Tutored by the sight-singing systems of Hullah and Curwen, they were led by the Novello scores into the worlds of Handel, Haydn, Mozart, Mendelssohn, and many lesser lights, at a time when it was a composer's first duty to write an oratorio.

The early history of the choral movement in New Zealand has already been traced.[2] The first New Zealand choral societies had arisen a decade or so after settlement: Auckland (1855), Wellington (1860), the Canterbury Vocal Union (1860), and the Dunedin Choral Society (1863). Programmes of the period almost invariably traversed a mixed background. At the opening concert of the Wellington Choral Society's fourth season on 17 December 1863, we find, for instance, an anthem by Dr Crotch, a chorus from *Judas Maccabaeus*, a recitative and air from *Messiah*, followed by glees, a pianoforte solo, part-songs, quartets, and a cello solo. Such selections gradually gave way to complete works, drawn from the current English repertoire. Handelian oratorio had dominated British musical life, until Mendelssohn's *Elijah*, first performed at the 1846 Birmingham Festival, added a new favourite to the repertoire. By the 1860s an English school of oratorio had arisen, led by composers such as Henry Smart (1813-1879) and William Sterndale Bennett (1816-1875). Smart's *The Bride of Dunkerron* (1864) became a favourite of Robert Parker, and was heard as late as 1907 in Wellington by Katherine Mansfield: 'And last night Mr Smith played the trombone in Mr Parker's production . . . I hear, on competent authority, that his part teemed with triple cadenzas—though of course, *you* may not have come across them', she wrote to the Trowell family in London.[3] Sullivan's *The Golden Legend*, acclaimed at the 1880 Leeds Festival, with its echoes of Handel, its demonstrable Christianity, and its mellifluous style, soon found itself indispensable in the repertoire, taking pride of place in Robert Parker's first New Zealand Musical Festival in Wellington (1888). But by far the best loved of all English oratorios was *The Crucifixion* (1887) by John Stainer (1840-1901), an exemplar of late-Victorian musical sentiments, which a hundred years after its first performance is still revived in New Zealand. Coleridge-Taylor's *Scenes from the Song of Hiawatha* (1898) ran it a close second, as did Parry's *Blest Pair of Sirens* (1887).

Deviation from these musical highways might bring an admonitory rap, as when the Auckland Choral Society in 1887 chose to perform Brahms's *Song of Destiny*:

> . . . a dull and funereal dirge . . . to show how repulsive to ordinary musical amateurs are the rhapsodies of a clever follower of Wagner . . . Fortunately for our drooping spirits, *The Bride of Dunkerron* by our own Henry Smart, is a Cantata full of melody, harmony and delicious instrumental combinations . . . Sullivan's *Prodigal Son* and *Light of the World* should also form part of next year's programme . . .[4]

The choral repertoire has since remained surprisingly consistent. Some works, such as those of Parry and Smart, have dropped out; others, such as *Messiah, The Seasons, The Creation* and *Elijah*, continue from decade to decade. So much effort over a long period of time goes into the preparation of a large-scale oratorio that only the well-tried and durable will last the course.

By the turn of the century the choral societies had become institutions, with their phalanxes of loyal followers, as the renowned historian J. C. Beaglehole relates:

> My mother and my aunts sang in the Musical Union, conducted by the great, the revered Mr Robert Parker, the touchstone of the musical art in Wellington. And my grandfather was one of two gentlemen who played the double bass in the orchestra—who supplied the double bass, indeed, in everything that demanded a double bass in Wellington. I understood that he was personally known to Mr Robert Parker and I derived great satisfaction from that circumstance.[5]

Especial interest attached to the first New Zealand performance of Elgar's new work *The Dream of Gerontius* by the Wellington Choral Society under Maughan Barnett in 1910. Baeyertz, in the *Triad*, who had heard Elgar conduct the work in New York, could not yet make up his mind whether it was 'in very truth a great work of art'. He would wait until he heard the visiting Sheffield Choir perform it the following year.[6]

World War I bit deeply into New Zealand musical life, although for a time both the choral and orchestral societies continued with resourcefulness and spirit. In December 1914, for instance, the Australian bass-baritone Peter Dawson sang in *Messiah* for the Royal Choral Society in Wellington. 'To hear Mr Dawson sing, it is akin to getting sparkling Burgundy off the ice in Wagga of a January eve', wrote the *Triad*.[7] But it criticized Robert Parker's Wellington Liedertafel, as it did the same institution in Christchurch, for being 'so thoroughly British. It is so reliable, so respectable, so discreet, and mostly—so dull . . . Dr Bradshaw conducted with his usual frightful agility . . .'[8] By the last year of the war, the loss of male singers and instrumentalists had had a marked effect: the *Triad* chronicles dwindling numbers and their sad musical consequences. In August 1918 Robert Parker chose *Elijah* for his farewell concert, and the following month, shortly before the Armistice, he wrote poignantly to his friend Maughan Barnett, then city organist in Auckland: 'The war, which seems endless, has paralyzed our choral world. I am struggling on to the end of the year with the Society, but it is heart-breaking work.'[9]

Robert Parker (1847-1937) exemplified the type of dedicated English-born organist and choirmaster who laid the foundations of choral and orchestral music in nineteenth-century New Zealand.[10] In 1878 Parker moved to the historic church of St Paul's Pro-Cathedral in Wellington, Frederick Thatcher's masterpiece of colonial architecture, which still exists. This henceforth became his spiritual and musical centre. He took over the Choral Society in the same year, giving the first Wellington performance of *Elijah*, with 120 voices, and a few months later, Rossini's *Stabat Mater* and Smart's *The Bride of Dunkerron*. He formed a boys' choir, properly vested in cassocks and surplices, the first of its kind in the city—soon the men were similarly robed. Parker preferred to use Monk's *Hymns Ancient and Modern*, rather than Purchas's *The New Zealand Hymnal* (1871). A battle of the hymn-books ensued. Many opponents of *Hymns Ancient and Modern* regarded it as so High Church as to open the door to Anglo-Catholicism, even predicting that it would virtually undo all that had been achieved by the Reformation. A parish meeting was held, one of the largest up to that time, where the use of *Hymns Ancient and Modern* was approved without the prophesied grim results.

Robert Parker. *Judith White collection*

Parker's musical tastes showed in his programmes for the New Zealand Music Festivals, which he initiated in 1888 with Sullivan's *Golden Legend*, Mendelssohn's *Elijah*, and Handel's *Zadok the Priest*. The second Festival in 1894 presented Dvořák's *The Spectre's Bride*, Mendelssohn's *Hymn of Praise*, Alfred Hill's *Time's Great Monotone*, and Handel's *Israel in Egypt*. The *Triad* compared it favourably with similar festivals in Birmingham, Leeds, Manchester, and other English provincial towns: 'Too much praise cannot be bestowed upon Mr Robert Parker for his painstaking and effective drilling of the chorus.'[11]

Through his frequent lectures, Parker showed a strong historical sense, lucidity of expression, and a concern for doctrinal changes within the church, especially as they affected music. Basically conservative, his early preferences for such composers as Stainer and Barnby gave way to Bach and Mendelssohn. A Platonist, he thought of music as leading to 'the good, the just and the beautiful'. The lofty idealism of a book popular at the time, H. R. Haweis's *Music and Morals*, attracted him deeply. He was also quick to see the value of what has become known as music therapy. The *Triad* described him as 'gentle and tolerant, with striking charm of manner' and as 'a man incapable of malice'.[12]

During World War I New Zealand lost nearly 17,000 men, the total casualties representing one in seventeen of the population.[13] This had a devastating effect: 'Almost a generation of the best young men were wiped out, and throughout my life I have been conscious of this deprivation', wrote the noted surgeon Sir Douglas Robb.[14] Musical life had virtually to begin again. It is no accident that the 1920s and 1930s were in many respects the most artistically barren in New Zealand's history. The country seemed to have slipped into a cultural cul-de-sac dominated by forces of conservatism and mediocrity. Many aspects of national life suffered in this way, including education.

Yet these decades also saw the rejuvenation of music in schools through the appointment of Douglas Tayler as Supervisor of School Music in 1926, and shortly afterwards (1927-1928) the arrival of a new generation of musicians from England, including Vernon Griffiths, Ernest Jenner, and Horace Hollinrake as lecturers in music at the training colleges. They infused new life into choral music, not only in schools but throughout the community. This period also saw the gradual rebirth of the choral and orchestral societies and the appearance of several new gifted choral conductors. Music proved to have a power, not only of healing, but of eventual regeneration.

Dr V. E. Galway, for example, revived the fortunes of the Dunedin Choral Society when he became its musical director in 1922. The city further benefited from its fine church choirs and the work of musicians such as Sidney Wolf (1859-1922). Notable groups arose elsewhere, such as H. Temple White's Wellington Harmonic Society and Apollo Singers in the 1920s. After a concert with them on 23 November 1935, Percy Grainger wrote: 'I don't know that I can recall *any* choral program of my works, in any city of the world, in which every item was rendered with the unvarying perfection attained . . . H. Temple White carries within him the accumulated skill, tradition, experience and insight of 700 years of British leadership in music.'[15] In 1927 Victor Peters (1890-1973) formed the Harmonic Society in Christchurch, which premièred Constant Lambert's *Rio Grande* in 1934 with Frederick Page as solo pianist, and later, under William Hawkey, tackled Schoenberg, Britten, Penderecki, and others. Peters had exceptional abilities as a choral trainer based on qualities of 'acumen, adaptability and perseverance'.[16]

Stanley Oliver's Schola Cantorum (1936-1950) in Wellington became a noteworthy specialist group, as did Albert Bryant's Dorian Choir (1936) in Auckland. Oliver (1891[?]-1964), an Englishman who had built up an enviable reputation for his choral work in Canada, concentrated on contemporary music, especially that of English composers such as Vaughan Williams, Holst, and Bliss, as well as American compositions. After their first concert on 6 August 1936 under Sir Malcolm Sargent, the conductor concluded: 'Would be Grade A in any city in the world.'[17] Bryant's Dorian Choir of thirty-two trained solo voices gave works of outstanding musical merit which would not otherwise have been presented in Auckland. Besides these finely tuned ensembles, many other types of choir arose, some associated with industries such as the Addington railway workshops and the Kaiapoi woollen mills. New Zealand was undoubtedly emerging as a significant singing nation.

In 1937 Dr J. C. Bradshaw (1876-1950) resigned from his influential position as organist and choirmaster at Christchurch Cathedral, a position he had taken up in 1902. Like Robert Parker, Bradshaw had enjoyed a distinguished career in England. At the age of twenty-five he had graduated as doctor of music at Manchester University, the youngest such in the British Empire. For health reasons, however, he was compelled to emigrate, and in Christchurch he became a mountain climber. At the cathedral he maintained the highest standards as organist and choirmaster, training his choristers with an iron will, as Walter Harris, who sang as a choirboy from 1912 to 1919, recalls:

We had eleven practices and six services a week, and at every practice and service Braddy expected the utmost effort towards perfection. Most of us boys rather disliked and feared him, but we admired him for his skill and unrelenting purpose. 'He isn't a man' we would say, 'He's a musician'. Every service was expected to be near perfect. 'Last evening', Braddy would say at practice the next morning, in his rather high and whiny voice, 'at the end of the creed (unaccompanied), you were half a semitone flat. Flatness is laziness. You'll do half-an-hour's extra practice in the holidays.' The next evening we would try to pitch it up a bit. The following morning he would say, 'Last evening at the end of the creed you were half a semitone sharp. Sharpness is carelessness. Half-an-hour's extra practice in the holidays.' Although holidays were few, he spared neither himself or us.

Time and pitch seemed to be his obsession. There were 24 boys in the choir and four probationers. Each new boy was put in the care of one older, who held his hand to beat the time. At practice we had each to beat with our hands and in services with our toes inside our boots. There was no conductor in church. We were so well trained we didn't need one. The service books and anthems were marked in pencil—*cresc, clim, accel, rit* etc., and pauses with the number of beats above—'One, two, three, four, off'. And we all stopped together. The book boys, six each week, had the job of putting Braddy's markings in every copy.

The organ was not used for the responses or amens. Not even to give the note. We were expected to pitch an A, lead the men in, and give exactly two beats to each note of the Amen. To some, the singing of Bradshaw's choirs was a little too precise.

After many quarrels, the Dean and Chapter, instead of, as usual, climbing down, accepted his resignation. His last service was on a weekday when there are ordinarily not about more than eight in the congregation. The word had got around and the cathedral was full. It was just the ordinary service with no mention of Bradshaw. The choir filed out. The congregation remained for a voluntary. Then, with the most eloquent interpretation I've ever heard of the Bach D minor Toccata and Fugue, Bradshaw expressed his frustration and anger. His large audience were thrilled. In that retiring voluntary, Braddy had had the last word.[18]

Bradshaw did not retire from music but continued his work as Professor of Music at Canterbury University College, where his students included Frederick Page, later to become the first lecturer in music at Victoria University College, and the composer Douglas Lilburn.

Notes

[1] Macandrew, 'Memories', 4

[2] See chapter II, 'Music in the First Settlements'

[3] Mansfield, K. *Collected Letters*, vol. 1, 29. What indeed were 'triple cadenzas'? Could Katherine Mansfield have meant 'triplets'?

[4] *NZ Herald*, 27 August 1887, quoted in Nalden, C. 'The choral tradition in New Zealand' *American Choral Review* VII (December 1964)

[5] Beaglehole, J. C. 'Our music through the years' 13 *Theme* 14-15 (October 1968)

[6] *Triad*, 10 December 1910, 17-18

[7] *Triad*, January 1915, 41

[8] *Triad*, August 1916, 17

[9] Maughan Barnett Scrapbooks, no. 3, ATL, MSS (not catalogued)

[10] Parker's early training included an association with Dr W. H. Monk (1823-1889), compiler of *Hymns Ancient and Modern* (1861), at the new church of St Mathias, Stoke Newington, where daily choral services took place, with the choir leading the congregation

[11] *Triad*, October 1894, 15

[12] Much of Robert Parker's church music forms the basis of the present collection at the Wellington Cathedral, where it is still in use. The scores bear his elegant copperplate signature. For tributes see *MNZ*, February 1937, 13 and obituary in *Evening Post*, 20 February 1937

[13] See Sinclair, K. *History of New Zealand*, 233, and Wicksteed, 25

[14] Robb, D. *Medical Odyssey* (1967) 18, quoted in Sinclair 'Political biography in New Zealand', from Phillips, J. (ed) *Biography* 31

[15] Letter from Grainger to H. Temple White, Auckland, 10 December 1935 (family papers)

[16] Pritchard, 63

[17] Howe, C. 5

[18] Communication to author

Choral Music since 1945

Auckland

In line perhaps with the city's expansive urban growth, the choral movement in Auckland has blossomed since the Second World War, not only in the number of its performing choirs, but also in the kinds of concerts and breadth of repertoire being sung. This trend has undoubtedly been helped by the fact that almost all newly-formed choirs have been moderate in size.

Nevertheless the Choral Society has continued in vigorous fashion. Georg Tintner, appointed director in 1947, raised the choir's standards and in his six-year term introduced such pieces as Bruckner's *Mass in F Minor* and Beethoven's *Missa Solemnis* into the repertoire. Ray Wilson began his directorship of nearly thirty years with Bach's *Ein' Feste Burg* and Beethoven's Ninth for the choir's centenary, continuing through the following decades to intersperse the regular favourites with twentieth century works like Stravinsky's *Les Noces*, Bernstein's *Chichester Psalms* and Honegger's *Joan of Arc at the Stake*.

From 1983 the Society was directed for three years by its long-standing deputy conductor and rehearsal accompanist, William Power. He was succeeded for an even briefer period by the expatriate opera conductor John Matheson, during whose time a highly successful production of the Bernstein Mass was mounted. However the cost of orchestras, large venues, and advertising has begun to throw into question the viability of such ambitious projects, especially when

Georg Tintner. *Carlotta Munz*

the annual *Messiah*, complete with international soloists, can no longer be guaranteed to fill the Town Hall. Prudently, then, the Society has, under its latest conductor Peter Watts, opted for more intimate and even largely unaccompanied concerts. There is still room for the spectacular, though; to mark the opening of the Aotea Centre in 1990, a massive performance of Berlioz's *Te Deum* was staged in conjunction with twelve other North Island choirs—600 voices in all.

Many of the smaller groups existing in 1945, and many that arose subsequently, did not outlast their founding conductor. Claude Laurie's Lyric Harmonists continued for some time, singing a conservative repertoire, but stimulating interest in New Zealand compositions and amassing a large choral library. Another worthwhile collection was built up by Harry Woolley during his work with the Royal Auckland (male voice) Choir and his broadcasting ensemble The Minstrels. Women's groups were also much in evidence, especially the Albyn Choir, conducted by Patricia McLeod for forty years and steeped in the Gaelic tradition of song, a tradition also preserved in Edith Campbell-Black's Auckland Orpheus Choir.

Without a doubt the Dorian Choir (known at various times as the Dorian Singers) continued to be the 'glamour' choral group in Auckland. But if the choir had become a city institution under founder Albert Bryant, followed by twenty years of Harry Luscombe's direction, it took a step towards wider recognition when Peter Godfrey, recently arrived from England to take up the position of musical director at Auckland Cathedral, was appointed conductor in 1960. The membership of the choir was radically overhauled (only seventeen out of fifty remained after his first audition), as was its repertoire. Where the Dorians' programmes had previously been dominated by English music of the nineteenth and early twentieth centuries, Godfrey added both earlier and more contemporary works. Renaissance masses, motets and madrigals became staple fare, and such diverse pieces as Carissimi's *Jephtha* and Vaughan Williams' *Hodie* were given their Auckland premières. The repertoire still had a predominantly English flavour but, influenced by his academic colleagues at the University's School of Music (where he lectured and later held the chair), Godfrey introduced such composers as Ligeti and Penderecki into the choir's programmes, well before similar groups in England were performing their music. Contemporary New Zealand compositions were also featured, and sometimes commissioned.

It is hard to overestimate Peter Godfrey's influence on choral music in Auckland, and indeed in the whole country. His training as a chorister at King's College, Cambridge and later as a choral scholar impressed on him the value of strict choral discipline, and he proceeded to instil into his New Zealand choirs a more rigorous sense of intonation and blend than had previously been the norm. Most of all, he realized the need to place constant challenges in front of amateur groups working at near-professional levels; the success of the Dorian Choir, the Festival Choir and the National Youth Choir in the BBC 'Let the

Peter Godfrey with the
National Youth Choir in
Wellington Cathedral.

People Sing' competition during the 1970s and 1980s showed how well such challenges could be met.

Godfrey's belief in the choral benefits of touring sparked a series of overseas trips by Auckland choirs in that same period. Although there had been earlier choral and madrigal societies at the University under such conductors as Ronald Dellow, Tom Rive and Ronald Tremain, Godfrey formed a new group in 1970, the University of Auckland Festival Choir, in response to an invitation to perform in a university choral festival in New York. The eventual tour in 1972 took the choir through America and across the Atlantic. They were followed to England and Europe in 1975 and again in 1977 by the Dorians, who sang in the BBC Proms and at the Three Choirs Festival. Finally in that era, the Auckland University Singers (successor to the Festival Choir) toured Australia in 1974 and 1980. While these were by no means the first overseas expeditions by New Zealand choirs, they did much to establish an international reputation for the country's choral work.

When in 1983 Peter Godfrey left Auckland to become director of music at Wellington Cathedral, there was an inevitable void. After an unsettled period in which several temporary conductors were used, the Dorian Choir appointed Karen Grylls as director in 1985. Recently returned from post-graduate study in choral conducting in Seattle, Grylls reduced the choir's numbers to 35 and injected an American flavour into its programmes, while retaining the Dorians' familiar performing style and standards. Like Godfrey before her, she also became conductor of the University Singers and the larger all-comers' group, the University Choral Society. In 1989 she succeeded him as musical director of the National Youth Choir.

Groups founded by one-time Dorian members have sprung up in each of the last two decades. The Orlando Singers began in 1972 as a group of friends meeting to sing madrigals, but were soon giving regular concerts and broadcasts. A 12-voice group, the Orlandos function as a small choir rather than an ensemble and specialize in refined singing, mainly of Renaissance music, but of other styles as well. They are currently conducted by Anita Banbury. Viva Voce was formed by past National Youth Choir and Dorian Choir singer, John Rosser, in 1985. Though dedicated to technical excellence, this 25-voice chamber choir concentrates on the attractive presentation of both traditional and lighter a cappella music, basing each of its concerts on a particular theme. Rosser inserts visual and humorous elements into Viva Voce's performances, aiming for a kind of choral theatre in programmes such as 'Strictly for the Birds' and 'Spooky Tunes'.

Church choral music has been in steady decline since the War. The 1950s and 1960s saw some vigorous activity, especially in combined groups like the Auckland United Methodist Choir under Leo Foster and Arthur Reid. But twenty years later only a few scattered parishes of various denominations have a regular church choir, and those often struggle for male voices. A notable exception, though, are the many Samoan, Tongan and other Pacific Island church choirs, which have thrived in their adopted city and even built on already strong traditions of choral singing. The two cathedral choirs have generally prospered, with Douglas Mews exerting a lasting influence on the music at St Patrick's, and the consistently high standards of the Anglican Cathedral being maintained by Peter Godfrey, Anthony Jennings, and James Tibbles.

Just as the first of these Anglican musicians spread his choral energies wider, so have the latter two. James Tibbles formed Cantus Firmus largely from cathedral choir members to sing Renaissance and Baroque music in an authentic style, accompanied where appropriate by original instruments. Normally the group's concerts are held in warm church acoustics; in 1990, however, Cantus Firmus increased its numbers and presented a re-creation of Handel's *Messiah* to 2000 people in the Aotea Centre. Collegium Vocale is a choir in similar mould, though its membership and administration are linked more to the University. Set up in 1988 by Anthony Jennings along with a complementary instrumental group, it has given performances of Bach's *St John Passion* and Handel's *Israel in Egypt*, the latter in conjunction with the other university choirs. The Bach Cantata Society under Ronald Dellow sings its Baroque music in a more modern idiom. Along with its own orchestra, the Society presents a cantata each month, and has done so since its foundation in 1977 by Roger Harris. Dellow, who had earlier established a successful octet, the CAS Singers, took over the directorship in 1978.

A large number of community choirs of varying sizes and aims adds to Auckland's choral diversity. Prominent among these are the Te Atatu Men's and Ladies' Choirs, the North Shore Male Voice Choir, the Shore Singers and the Hundred Voice Chorale, groups which use accompanied partsongs, folksong arrangements, and operatic excerpts as the mainstay of their programmes. Smaller choral societies in the wider metropolitan area which regularly perform the standard oratorio repertoire are the Pakuranga Choral Society, for many years under Hal Marryatt, and the South Auckland Choral Society, who have for over ten years been led by a series of guest conductors through a busy and varied schedule. Auckland also has lively men's and women's barbershop movements; the City of Sails Chorus often entertains at corporate events and has won several local choral competitions, even if judges do not always know how to categorize them, while a chapter of the Sweet Adelines is now well established. Perhaps the newest community choir is the Auckland contingent of Te Roopu Waiata Maori, the New Zealand Maori Choir, formed in 1990. This group is already raising the once low profile of Maori choral music within its own community and in the city at large.

It is a platitude to say that the future of choral music depends on its acceptance by the younger generation, but the perception that choir singing is a game for older players is hard to dispel. Perhaps only four of Auckland's many choirs have a healthy percentage of singers in the twenty- to forty-year age group, and the number of youth choirs is not as large as the population might warrant. The Auckland University Singers has been the city's premier training choir, and has made frequent tours of the North Island as well as travelling overseas. But since its membership was restricted to current or former students, the larger Auckland Youth Choir was founded in 1984 to provide an intermediate stage between school choral singing and the adult choirs. Conducted by Brigid McLafferty, the Youth Choir has steadily increased both its average age and choral standards. Older, and younger, than both of these groups is the Auckland Boys' Choir which has catered for treble voices for over twenty years under the direction of Neil Shroff and Terence Maskell.

The strength of each of these youth groups tends to mask the underlying weaknesses in school choral music. In a city which does not have a strong sense of British heritage, singing is given low priority in most schools; few music departments have choral specialists, and choirs are generally rated a poor second to instrumental ensembles. However some private schools have maintained a choral tradition, as for example Diocesan, Baradene and Dilworth Schools and King's College, while notable exceptions in the state schools include David Hamilton's choirs from Epsom Girls' Grammar, the Waitakere College groups under Stephen Nightingale and Terence Maskell's work at the predominantly Polynesian Aorere College. Significantly, each of these teachers is an experienced chorister. The Primary Schools' Choral Festival recently celebrated its fiftieth anniversary and, fostered by Horace Hollinrake, Bill Barris, Robin Holst, Leonie Lawson, John Willmott and many others, it has gained a huge and deserved following. Nevertheless, when they are not actually preparing for the festival, primary choristers can suffer from the same lack of teacher expertise or interest as their secondary counterparts.

To ensure Auckland's future choral health, choirs have already begun to adapt in two distinct areas. The first movement has been toward greater specialization, in an attempt to reach certain audiences in a more focused way. The second has been for the other, 'general' choirs to market themselves and their programmes in a more appealing fashion, not only to concertgoers but to prospective members as well. The repertoire, while still influenced by English tastes, is wide and growing, but effective presentation is vital to ensure that people continue singing it, and listening to it.

JOHN ROSSER

Wellington

Before the turn of the century, Wellington had a choral society, as well as an amateur opera company and an orchestra. At the end of the twentieth century, the scene is somewhat different. Opera and orchestra are there, but choirs have proliferated. If there is one characteristic of choral music in the capital, it is that in the four decades since World War II, choirs have come and gone with disturbing frequency.

For many years, the Royal Wellington Choral Union was the city's major choir, and many distinguished conductors and soloists performed with it. Over half a century of stability and prestige finally succumbed to falling standards as membership dwindled in the late 1950s. Towards the end, Harry Botham took over as music director, and he attempted to revitalize the choir with schemes to encourage young singers and players to perform, without success. In its best years, however, the Royal Wellington Choral Union is remembered for the fine performance of Elgar's *Dream of Gerontius* and *The Apostles* and other large-scale oratorios, including of course the annual presentation of Handel's *Messiah*. Such was the tradition established for *that* work, that every year, when ticket sales opened at the booking office at the D.I.C. on Lambton Quay, the queue would stretch around the block.

The Wellington Harmonic Society was established by H. Temple White in 1914, and he conducted it for 43 years. Between 1919 and 1927 he also conducted the Choral Union. The Harmonic Society concentrated on madrigals, part-songs, and small-scale choral works, with particular emphasis on the late nineteenth century.

In the 1950s audience interest in this repertoire dwindled, and when H. Temple White retired, the choir went through a difficult period. Attempts were made to broaden its repertoire to include oratorio, but after a few years the choir was disbanded. Conductors after H. Temple While included Peter Averi, Peter Zwartz, and Dobbs Franks.

Wellington's leading choir was undoubtedly the Schola Cantorum, which had a high reputation for the quality of its performances. Conductor Stanley Oliver demanded high standards, and introduced new works which were unfamiliar to Wellington audiences. His departure in 1950 ended an era of superb a capella singing. Unlike the Harmonic Society, which tried to continue after its founder had retired, the Schola Cantorum came to an end when Stanley Oliver was no longer at the helm, but re-emerged with a new image and new members as the Phoenix Choir. Harry Brusey was the conductor, and under his leadership the choir reached a standard which resulted in performances with the National Orchestra, most notably in Honegger's *King David* in 1956. After Harry Brusey stepped down a few years later, the Phoenix Choir had a succession of conductors, including Eric Copperwheat, Stanley Jackson, and Simon Tipping, who was in charge for seven years from 1977, and introduced several innovative works. In recent years conductors have included James Allington, David Dobson and Peter Browne.

After World War II, Malcolm Rickard established a small choir of women's voices, called The English Singers. The repertoire seemed endless, as the group produced concerts and radio programmes with great variety. Occasionally, men's voices were added for some works, such as Walford Davies's *Pied Piper of Hamelin*. Concerts were taken on tour around the provinces, providing a stimulus in areas where music needed a boost after the disruption caused by the war. In the early 1950s, Alex Lindsay took over the group for a short time, and he added Pergolesi's *Stabat Mater* to the repertoire. Owen Jensen then conducted it for a short time before the group was finally disbanded.

The Hutt Valley Orpheus Society developed out of the Hutt Valley Musical Society, an organization which embraced instrumental and vocal activities. The first conductors were Horace Hunt and Len Schwabe, followed by Malcolm Rickard, who was at that time conductor of the Eastboure Lyric Singers. Performances of *Judas Maccabaeus*, Schubert's *Mass in C*, *Tom Jones*, *Merrie England*, and Handel's *Messiah* were given in churches and school halls in the valley. Progress was cautious but steady. It was some time before the choir ventured into Wellington city, but when it did, the impact was dramatic. The Orpheus performed, with the National Orchestra (later the NZSO), the big works usually outside the scope of choral societies, which included Britten's *War Requiem*, Dyson's *Canterbury Pilgrims*, Walton's *Belshazzar's Feast*, and Bach's *St Matthew Passion*. Wellington could now lay claim to a symphonic choir, capable of performing large-scale works with orchestra.

Malcolm Rickard was Musical Director until his retirement in 1983, and he was succeeded by Professor Peter Godfrey, who had come to Wellington at the end of the previous year to become Director of Music at Wellington Cathedral. The choir later changed its name to the Orpheus Choir of Wellington, confirming its position as the Capital's central choir, while continuing to rehearse in Lower Hutt.

The advent of television had a dramatic affect on many amateur choirs. In the early 1960s, such was the magnetic draw of the medium that more than one choir had to change rehearsal nights to avoid clashing with popular serials. This parallelled the 'coffee bar' phenomenon of the 1950s: one enterprising choir, concerned that it would lose members, started its own coffee club and others soon followed, concluding rehearsals with a social hour.

Church choirs made a significant contribution to Wellington's choral scene, despite recruitment problems in some parishes. In 1958, the Presbyterian Church took a lead by promoting a combined choirs festival. The objective was to bring together all the local choirs to learn music which could later be used in parish worship, and the festival became an annual event for several years. The Anglican Church had its long-established annual carol concerts, usually conducted in turn by choirmasters within the diocese. Albert Bryant, Harry Brusey, Ernest Jamieson, Stanley Jackson, Eric Copperwheat and others made a significant contribution to the festive season, and as with the Choral Union performances of *Messiah*, the Anglican carol concerts always had many people queuing for tickets.

Singing has always been a strong feature of the Salvation Army, with the Vivian St. Citadel Songsters and the Wellington South Songsters making a vigorous contribution. In the 1950s and early 1960s they made many commercial recordings. As an adjunct to their choral work, the Army put together two very successful stage musicals, in 1970 and 1972.

The Roman Catholic Church had St Mary of the Angels choir as its model. Directed by Maxwell Fernie, who had returned to New Zealand in 1957 after a prestigious appointment at Westminster Cathedral, the choir developed sixteenth century polyphony to a very high degree of expertise. Maxwell Fernie's success with his church choir led to the creation of another group under his direction. The Schola Polyphonica was formed in 1967, with a small membership of singers whose principal motivation was to sing for the sheer joy of it. Unlike most other choirs, the Schola did not seek publicity, nor was it committed to regular concert performances. Its relatively rare concerts were put on when the choir felt ready, a situation which always whetted the appetites of devotees of choral music.

The pinnacle of Methodist music was at Wesley Church, Taranaki Street. H. Temple White had been organist and choirmaster since 1913, and built up a very fine choir, which Malcolm Rickard continued when he took over the position in 1959. This choir suffered, as did several others in the city, from the decline in interest in traditional church music. In contrast, Wellington's Anglican Cathedral choir went from strength to strength, especially from 1983 under the direction of Professor Peter Godfrey, and this is continuing under the new Director of Music, Philip Walsh, a young English musician appointed in 1989 following Professor Godfrey's retirement.

Singing groups associated with some of the city's clubs and societies provided opportunities for many people who enjoyed group singing. The Tin Hat Club of the R.S.A., and the Scottish, Welsh and Irish societies were examples of organizations who fostered this activity. In the mid 1970s, the Musical Director of the Wellington Gilbert and Sullivan Society, Peter Averi, established the Savoy Singers, to provide a continuing programme of choral work between stage productions.

Any survey of choral singing in the city would be incomplete if it failed to acknowledge the work put in by countless chorus singers for stage productions. The Wellington Operatic Society, the Gilbert and Sullivan Society, and Opera Technique involved many singers in their productions. Grand opera has also required skilled singers since the days of the New Zealand Opera Company, the New Opera Company, and in recent years, the Wellington City Opera Trust. Most recently, the latter organization has moved to establish its chorus on a professional basis, a significant recognition of the importance of a reliable and proficient chorus.

School choirs have waxed and waned. The primary school music festivals of the 1940s and 1950s gave way to more individualistic endeavours, and the secondary schools developed their own particular style, more often than not as the result of the stamina and resourcefulness of the music staff rather than any co-ordinated school music policy. In the last few years, the development of the secondary schools choir festivals and the support given by sponsorship are raising the standard of music and there are signs that there is a renewed enthusiasm for music in schools. Some schools and colleges in the region have maintained a high level of activity for many years. The Dawn Chorus of Tawa College, directed by Shona Murray, is one example of the fresh new approach to school singing.

One problem was the break which occurred when young people left secondary school and lost contact with singing because there were few avenues open to them. Their voices were still developing, a factor which placed barriers to their admittance to the established adult choirs. Shortly after the war, Hugh Reid, then music master at Scots College, tried to do something about it. He set up a youth choir, which flourished for a few years but unfortunately did not survive. Judith Temple White also had great success with her Wellington Junior Choir for a time.

At the university level, there have been opportunities for young singers in the Bach Choir, which reached a good standard under Anthony Jennings, John Hawley, and Roy Tankersley. Elizabeth Salmon conducted the choir for a short time, and currently it is under the care of Vincent James. The University Choir was also active, if in a less public sense. Elizabeth Kerr directed its activities for a time, and in 1990, Philip Walsh conducted a concert performance of the Duruflé *Requiem*. The Wellington Teachers College also provided an outlet for young singers with its choral group. Inspired by Tom Young, who held office from 1936 to 1960, this choir tackled some ambitious programmes, including Britten's *Noyes Fludde* and *St Nicholas*, both of which were conducted

Robert Oliver.

by John Hopkins. After Tom Young's retirement, the choral group continued under a number of conductors, including Laughton Patrick, Wilbur Manins, Barry Nalder, and Judith Temple White.

Possibly the most significant event in choral activities was the establishment of the National Youth Choir in 1979. Largely the brainchild of Guy Jansen and Peter Godfrey, the formation of a choir which drew together the best of the country's young singers was a bold innovation. The outstanding achievements of this choir include an award in the prestigious 'Let the Peoples Sing' competition in 1986, and in 1988 the coveted prize of best choir at the International Youth Festival in Vienna. The effect which the National Youth Choir had on local choirs was tremendous. The quality of singing lifted standards to a new level, and many local choirs reaped the benefits brought about by the influx of young singers who had experienced the disciplined training of a national organization, and who could read quickly and accurately.

In the last decade, a veritable bevy of choirs has appeared, each with a distinctive quality in style and repertoire. Access to a hitherto undreamed-of supply of old and new music, more intense scholarship in music editing, and an insistence on authenticity of style have opened new horizons. Not only is early music of the Renaissance and Baroque periods presented faithfully as the composers intended, but romantic and modern music is performed with a clarity and freshness which has given new life to many discarded compositions.

The Festival Singers, established in 1976 by Guy Jansen, serves a number of functions as a concert choir and an evangelistic singing group. Guy Jansen formed Bel Canto in 1988, drawn from the ranks of some of the city's solo singers, an appropriate title for a chamber choir performing music from a wide repertoire. Cantoris was founded by Andrew Baines in 1971, and he was succeeded a year later by Robert Oliver, a counter-tenor and early music devotee who has done much to re-create authentic performances of such works as *Belshazzar's Feast, Messiah*, and *Samson*. The Tudor Consort (1986), directed by Simon Ravens, specializes in sixteenth century music. Overseas tours by this group have won acclaim, and it is an example of the modern approach to choir work, where integrity of style and historic accuracy are paramount. In 1989 a former member of the Auckland University Singers and the Dorian Choir, Marie Brown, inaugurated the Wellington Youth Choir, an important link between school and adult ensembles.

PETER AVERI

Christchurch

The late 1940s and early 1950s brought both gain and loss to Christchurch's choral activities. Choir memberships rose rapidly with the return of men and women from the services, and time for leisure activities increased once the war effort was over. But developments in cinema, radio, and the recording industry inevitably provided competition, and the community spirit engendered by the war years, which had embraced choral activity, whether as singer or supporter, broke down. The Harmonic Society found it could no longer perform the 'music for all' variety programme and concentrated instead on the major works of the choral repertoire, with particular emphasis on contemporary English music. The Royal Christchurch and the Harmonic competed for a smaller audience of choral enthusiasts, which placed some strain on the available pool of performing and subscribing members, choice of repertoire, concert dates and, not least, financial grants.

Community choral activity was taken up by groups in the suburbs (such as the Risingholme Community Choir, or the South Brighton Choral Society) and the workplace, like the Hays Department Store choir or the Addington (Railway) Workshops male voice choir, which was founded by Vernon Griffiths in 1946 'in an attempt to put music into the lives of workers in industry'. An annual festival of community choirs was inaugurated in 1949 by the Civic Music Council; all those cited above appeared in the very first concert in the Radiant (now the Repertory) Theatre, and were still represented at the 1989 event, continuing to perform the popular repertoire of folk-songs, traditional songs, sea shanties, spirituals, hymns, anthems, and occasional larger-scale pieces.

In the first half of the century the works most frequently performed by the two choral societies were the oratorios *Messiah, Elijah* and *The Creation*. Before the 3YA Orchestra was formed in 1938, they had been accompanied by organ or by *ad hoc* orchestra groups or pianoforte. The post-war era saw the addition or revival of works such as *Israel in Egypt, Judas Maccabaeus* and *The Seasons*, the Brahms and Fauré *Requiem*s and Vaughan-Williams's *Hodie* and *Dona nobis pacem*. Bach's sacred music was particularly favoured: in 1948 the Harmonic gave the city its first complete *Mass in B Minor*, while the Royal Christchurch Musical Society began the tradition of an annual *St Matthew Passion* in April 1954.

Broadcasting work (with the National Orchestra) helped the finances of both choirs, and enabled the rest of the country to hear them. The 1950s and 1960s were busy and successful for both choirs. Beethoven's *Choral Symphony* and *Missa Solemnis*, Howell's *Hymnus Paradisi* and Honegger's *King David* (with the Russian, Nicolai Malko, conducting) were all given by the Royal Musical at this time, whilst the Harmonic performed Elgar's *The Dream of Gerontius* at the Canterbury Centennial Music Festival of 1951, Walton's *Belshazzar's Feast* and Verdi's *Requiem* in the 1950s, and Holst's *The Hymn of Jesus* and Tippett's *A Child of our Time* in the 1960s. In 1964 Walton conducted *Belshazzar's Feast* with the combined Christchurch choirs, in Christchurch and Wellington.

When the Royal Musical accepted an invitation to participate in the 1962 Adelaide Festival, with two Adelaide choirs and the London Philharmonic under Sir Malcolm Sargent, in *Belshazzar's Feast* and Dvořák's *Te Deum* it was the first New Zealand choral society to perform at an overseas festival on a grand scale. In 1964 the Government decided that a Christchurch choir should represent New Zealand at the 1965 Commonwealth Arts Festival in England, and it was the Harmonic who, after some debate, became the city's first choral ambassadors. The Royal Musical Society gave the first performance outside Europe of Britten's *War Requiem*, little more than a year after its composition.

English oratorio aside, the 1960s also saw the introduction of a more varied repertoire from all periods. Works such as Bach's *Singet dem Herren*, and the complete *Christmas Oratorio*, Handel's 'Coronation' Anthems, and Mozart's 'Coronation' Mass, Berlioz' *The Childhood of Christ*, Bruckner's *Mass in E Minor* and Rossini's *Petite Messe Solennelle*, together with Orff's *Carmina Burana*, Schoenberg's *A Survivor from Warsaw*, and the Requiem Mass settings of Cherubini, Dvořák and Berlioz, were all performed for the first time by the Christchurch choirs, singly or jointly, during this decade.

Despite the reputedly fine acoustics of the old Choral Hall and the cosy ambiance of the Civic Theatre, the Christchurch choirs did not enjoy the facilities of a large purpose-built concert auditorium until the Christchurch Town Hall was completed in 1972. The combined choirs gave the the local première of Mahler's Symphony No. 8 in 1973, and in 1975, a decade after the Royal Musical had premièred the work in Wellington and Auckland, Britten's *War Requiem*.

If the new concert hall provided the benefit of more spacious accommodation for large choirs and orchestras, it also set them the challenge of attracting audiences large enough to fill the 2500 seats and offset the by now considerable costs of hiring both the hall and the Civic (subsequently the Christchurch Symphony) Orchestra. The annual *Messiah* (given by each choir in alternate years since 1940) continued to draw the biggest attendance of the concert year, but the golden days when large audiences could be expected to attend a performance of virtually any oratorio had gone. The Christchurch Town Hall, which the choirs had awaited for years, was not always within their means. In the 1980s they opted for a variety of concert venues, the two cathedrals in particular.

Economic factors and changing tastes also caused some reappraisal of activities. The Harmonic Society, for example, introduced the 'Sing Along *Messiah*'. The Royal Musical launched a highly successful series of concert versions of opera with overseas soloists: *Fidelio, Aida, Boris Godunov, Il Trovatore, Carmen*, and *Nabucco* all scored notable successes. The Society also inaugurated a series of popular programmes entitled 'Music for All', featuring Christchurch's champion Skellerup Woolston Brass Band, which included items such as Geoffrey Brand's arrangement of *Zadok the Priest*, selections from *Oklahoma, The Music Man* and *The Sound of Music*, and Kit Powell's *The Pink Panther's Picnic*. The title of the final group of items from a 1979 concert, 'The Royal goes pop' was, on the face of it, a new departure, yet popular music and concert opera had appeared in pre-war programmes. In a sense the wheel had turned full circle and the big choral society had (in part) reverted to its earlier community role.

Perhaps the outstanding achievements of the two choral societies conditioned the city to a 'big is beautiful' mentality; at any rate the small S.A.T.B. chamber choir, giving regular public concerts of repertoire unsuited to larger forces, gained acceptance only slowly. Each decade since the 1960s has seen the emergence of a new chamber choir of differing emphasis, and each was founded by a university musician.

As well as his innovative work with the Christchurch Harmonic Choir in the 1960s, William Hawkey continued to direct the University of Canterbury Madrigal Singers, a chamber choir of between fourteen and twenty voices. The group provided a refreshing injection of sixteenth and seventeenth century madrigals and motets, while retaining English allegiance through its part-song repertoire (Gordon Jacob, E. J. Moeran and Peter Warlock in particular) and explored folk-song arrangements by Brahms, Kodály, Bartók, Hindemith, Stravinsky, Seiber and others. Hawkey also realized the potential of a chamber choir to complement the work of his large choir, and in 1964 he founded the Harmonic Chorale, initially with singers drawn from the 'parent' group. When the Harmonic travelled to England for the Commonwealth Festival, the Chorale gave separate concerts, largely of a cappella repertoire, in Glasgow, Cardiff, Christchurch Priory, St. George's Chapel, Windsor and Westminster Abbey. Over the next decade the Chorale introduced to Christchurch contemporary choral works by Richard Rodney Bennett, Peter Maxwell Davies, Hugo Distler, John Joubert, Elisabeth Lutyens, Krysztof Penderecki and Malcolm Williamson. It also took part three times in the European Broadcasting Union's International Choral Competition 'Let the Peoples Sing'. From 1972 membership of the larger choir was no longer a prerequisite and the sixteen places were open for annual audition. The Chorale continued to flourish until Hawkey's departure for Australia in 1976, not only as part of the Harmonic's subscription series, but in work for radio, television, and recording.

The 1970s saw the emergence of the first choir specifically committed to the performance of music from one period, when Dr Brian Pritchard founded the Christchurch Scuola di Chiesa. Between 1972 and 1979 the Scuola aimed to recapture the scale and sonority of seventeenth and eighteenth century choral and orchestral repertoire (albeit without the support of period instruments). The audiences in the lofty surroundings of the Cathedral of the Blessed Sacrament heard for the first time works like F. X. Brixi's *Missa Pastoralis*, Michael Haydn's *Te Deum* and *Victimae Paschali*, German text versions of Handel's *'Brockes' Passion* and Schütz's *Christ ist erstanden*, as well as music by Antonio Caldara in Pritchard's own editions.

In many ways, Christchurch's chamber choir of the 1980s has absorbed something of the ideals and inclinations of each of its predecessors. The 30-voice Jubilate Singers, founded by Martin Setchell in 1977, continue to explore the whole gamut of chamber choir literature from Renaissance polyphony to works specially commissioned from New Zealand composers. The Jubilate's 'Music for Passiontide' programmes have complemented the Royal's *St Matthew Passion* with Schütz's setting in German, Bach's Palm Sunday cantata 182 *Himmelskönig sei willkommen* and Palestrina's *Stabat Mater dolorosa*. The biennial 'Music for Christmas' programme has similarly provided alternative fare to the annual *Messiah* plus carol concert with performances of Monteverdi's *Christmas Vespers*, Buxtehude's *Das neugebor'ne Kindelein*, Britten's *A Boy was Born* and Schoenberg's *Friede auf Erden*. St Cecilia's Day has been celebrated by the odes of Purcell, Handel and Britten. Setchell aims for attractively packaged programmes which not only satisfy as aesthetic unities but appeal in 'extra-musical' terms.

Male voice choral singing in Christchurch has a long history, exemplified by the Christchurch Male Voice Choir and the Liedertafel (the latter celebrated its centenary in 1985). The leadership of such distinguished and dedicated musicians as Dr Bradshaw, Victor Peters, Keith Newson, and Alec Robson, ensured the development of a disciplined musical unit of some 30 voices. Inevitably, such male exclusiveness has been affected by social changes. The old 'Smoke Concerts', renamed 'Men's Night' concerts, gave way in 1973 to 'Subscribers' Concerts'.

Changing social conditions also affected the women's voice choir, the Liederkränzchen, founded in 1934. By 1970 the repertoire which had been well received a decade earlier was now criticized by the *Press* reviewer as 'insipid'. The Liederkränzchen's successors were the Harmonic Singers (1973 to 1979), yet another offshoot of the Harmonic Society. Under Elizabeth Wemyss's energetic and painstaking supervision they rekindled interest in women's choirs, revitalizing the repertoire by presenting for instance, Brahms's *Lieder und Romanzen*, Op 44, and *Gypsy Songs*, Op 103, Britten's *Ceremony of Carols* and *Missa Brevis*. In 1979 they became the Elizabeth Wemyss Singers, pioneering little-known Debussy and other composers. Her excellent work has been furthered by Nan Anderson's Cecilian Singers, who offer small, intimate 'At Home' style concerts in new venues, such as the Provincial Council Chambers. Significant additions to the repertoire have included Fauré's *Messe Basse*, Poulenc's *Litanies à la vierge noire* and a 1985 *Missa Brevis* by John Ritchie.

The Elizabeth Wemyss Singers in the Basilica, Christchurch.

The two cathedrals have maintained their respective traditions; the Anglican choir of men and boys sing choral services on weekdays as well as Sundays (considerably fewer than in Bradshaw's time!), and the Cathedral of the Blessed Sacrament mixed-voice choir sings plainsong, polyphonic, orchestral and contemporary masses on a cyclic principle, and has instituted an annual, liturgical Good Friday performance of Bach's *St John Passion*. Church and parish choirs have fallen somewhat on hard times but continue to enrich worship at Oxford Terrace (Baptist), Durham Street (Methodist) and St Barnabas (the only remaining parish Choral Evensong). Choral singing in schools has always been strong at primary level, perhaps with the encouragement of the Primary Schools Music Festival each September, and secondary school choirs like the Burnside Chorale and Bel Canto have achieved success in national competitions. The Christchurch

School of Instrumental Music recently added two choirs to its Saturday morning music education programme. The Canterbury branch of the New Zealand Choral Federation organized a successful national conference in 1987 and arranges periodic choral workshops, drawing in choirs from the Canterbury province.

Christchurch has thus largely maintained its 'English choral tradition'. American influence has only slightly impinged upon it; the American pianist and conductor Dobbs Franks stayed briefly as Director of the Harmonic from 1976, and the interest in women's barber-shop quartet singing has given rise to a Christchurch chapter of the 'Sweet Adelines'.

MARTIN SETCHELL

Dunedin

During the war the Dunedin Choral Society continued to give regular performances under Alfred Walmsley, who by 1939 had a well-balanced choir of some eighty-five members, with their own orchestra. They also combined from time to time with the Royal Dunedin Male Choir and the Returned Services Association Choir (another all-male group).

Following Walmsley's move to Invercargill in 1943, the Society appointed the highly-qualified English musician Charles F. Collins as conductor. He increased performances to three a year, confining himself to major works such as Handel's *Samson*, Haydn's *Creation*, and the Brahms *Requiem*. The Society joined forces with the 4YA Orchestra, formed in 1946, and despite changes in name the same arrangement has continued. In 1953 the Society became involved in public controversy over a performance of Dyson's *Canterbury Pilgrims* with the National Orchestra conducted by Warwick Braithwaite, who found the Choir insufficiently prepared and walked out of the final rehearsal. (Collins had taken sudden leave and local musicians had taken sectional rehearsals.) The dispute was fuelled by the damning review in the *Otago Daily Times* of 20 October 1953 by the visiting critic Arthur Jacobs, who lit similar fires under other choral societies elsewhere. Collins returned that year to England.

W. H. Walden-Mills, an English musician, directed the Choral Society through the 1950s, a regime which included a highly praised Bach *St John Passion*. Following his departure in 1959 the Choir underwent some of its hardest times. The 4YA Orchestra was disbanded, leaving the Society with a November performance of *Il Trovatore* accompanied by two pianos. The Society's funds had dwindled through poor audiences to a state where they could no longer afford an orchestra themselves nor continue loss-making concerts. *Messiah* was their only guaranteed financial success, but audiences were reluctant to attend performances accompanied only by the organ.

1961 proved to be a turning point, not only for the Choral Society, but for all such activities in Dunedin. The newly-appointed Professor of Music at the University, Peter Platt, became director of the beleaguered Choral Society and immediately organized a co-operative venture in which two university choirs worked with it. The Otago University Musical Union and its specialist a capella sub-group sang the second choir to the Society's first in Bach's *St Matthew Passion* on 5 August 1961, joined by the newly-formed Dunedin Concert Orchestra, of which Platt was also chief conductor. The warmly favourable review in the *Evening Star* of 7 August described this Dunedin première as 'a typical ambitious choice by Platt that came off through his enthusiasm and inspired leadership'.

For its centenary year of 1963, the Society celebrated its turn of fortune due to good management, healthy audience support and money in the bank, with a wide-ranging programme, starting on 8 April with a repeat of the *St Matthew Passion*. This was followed on 27 June, by Beethoven's Ninth Symphony with the National Orchestra conducted by John Hopkins, then in September of the same year by three works which formed the core of the Dunedin Arts Festival: Haydn's *Creation*, Verdi's Requiem, and Britten's *St Nicholas*. All three featured the Dunedin Concert Orchestra conducted by Peter Platt. Enthusiastic reviews contributed to the Society's resurgence, so that with the end-of-year *Messiah*, the Annual Report showed that the centenary had ended with a profit of four hundred and twenty-seven pounds and twelve pence.

In the next two years Peter Platt and the Choir continued their ambitious path with works such as Berlioz's *Childhood of Christ*, Prokofiev's *Alexander Nevsky*, and on 14 September 1965, the New Zealand première of Orff's *Carmina Burana*, which was also Peter Platt's last appearance as director before taking up the position of Professor of Music at the University of Sydney.

Jack Speirs directed the choir from 1966-73. The Dunedin Concert Orchestra was re-formed on a professional basis with a permanent full-time manager and renamed the Dunedin Civic Orchestra, giving its first concert on 19 February 1966. On 31 January 1967, the Dunedin Choral Society amalgamated with the choir of the Otago University Students Music Union, to form the Schola Cantorum, who at their first concert on 13 June 1967 performed Handel's *Saul* with the Dunedin Civic Orchestra. The *Otago Daily Times* commented the following day: 'The generally younger voices of the University contingent have improved the overall tonal quality, and no doubt the experience of many of the Choral Society members will be a valuable and steadying influence . . .'. Over the next six years Jack Speirs reduced the choir to just over sixty excellently-trained choristers. The repertoire reflected the extremely high standards the choir was now capable of achieving—Monteverdi's *Gloria* and *Beatus Vir*, Caldara's *Mass in C*, Bach's B Minor Mass and *Christmas Oratorio*, Poulenc's *Gloria*, Rawsthorne's *A Canticle of Man* and Stravinsky's *Symphony of Psalms*.

Recently, the choir has been conducted by Peter Warwick (1974-82), Dr Raymond White (1983-6) and Peter Adams (1987-). Under Peter Warwick it grew again to around 120 members and maintained a wide-ranging repertoire of choral/orchestral music. On several occasions during these years the New Zealand Symphony Orchestra joined the Schola Cantorum in works such as Beethoven's Ninth Symphony, and on 17 March 1982 the Verdi Requiem under Dunedin-born John Matheson.

In 1980 an a capella group of thirty singers called the Southern Consort of Voices was formed under the direction of Jack Speirs, their first concert on 6 November including madrigals by Gibbons, Morley, Wilbye, Gesualdo and Marenzio as well as Britten's *Five Flower Songs* and Messiaen's *O Sacrum Convivium*. The choir has continued to present unaccompanied choral music from the sixteenth century to the present day and often performs in the attractive acoustic and setting of the Maori Court in the Otago Museum. The Consort has recorded frequently for Radio New Zealand and has given concerts in regional areas such as Alexandra, Oamaru and Balclutha.

Although the notable St Paul's Cathedral Choir pursued a different course, its activities and directors often overlapped with the other choral organizations in the city. In 1940 Ethelbert Heywood, organist and choirmaster since 1912, retired following a well-disciplined and productive regime. Dr Victor Galway, of the Music Department of Otago University, succeeded him until 1946, when Charles Collins, an outstanding recitalist and a composer, arrived from England to hold the position until 1954, when he returned home to teach and perform. Following Galway's brief resumption of the position, in 1955 Donald Byars began a regime during which St Paul's became one of New Zealand's finest choirs; he retired in 1974. Byars was a gifted improviser on the organ and enlarged the choir's repertoire to include recent British and early French music. He

Choristers from Christchurch Cathedral and St Paul's Cathedral, Dunedin, practising for the Southern Cathedrals' Choir Festival, Christchurch, Labour weekend 1987.

composed works utilizing the resonant acoustic of St Paul's. Donald Cullington, also a gifted organist and pianist, succeeded him from 1975-8, and in the latter year inaugurated the Southern Cathedrals Choir Festival associated with Christchurch and Nelson. As the South Island Anglican cathedrals were the only ones in New Zealand maintaining the tradition of male choirs it was felt that annual meetings with performances would be beneficial. Raymond White, formerly of Nelson Cathedral and principal of the Nelson School of Music, succeeded Collington in 1979. He took the choir to Australia in 1982 and to Europe in 1985, the first New Zealand cathedral choir to tour there, undertaking a wide variety of engagements. The Choir continues to broadcast, record and host visits from international musicians.

PETER ADAMS

The growth of a repertoire of New Zealand choral works by a wide range of composers must also be noted. It began with Hill's cantata *Hinemoa* (1896), and continued after a long gap with Lilburn's *Prodigal Country* (1940), an effective work and the only one he has written in this genre. Carr, Farquhar, McLeod, Body, Blake, Griffiths, Hamilton, the Ritchies (father and son), and many others have all since written attractive and sometimes demanding choral works, several of which the National Youth Choir has sung on its overseas tours.

The establishment of the New Zealand Choral Federation in 1985 has been a major step forward, in giving encouragement to choirs, providing assistance and advice, organizing training programmes, and compiling a most valuable catalogue of the music held in choir libraries all over the country. The Federation has the potential to bring about growth and stability to the choral scene. For the first time in New Zealand, a national voice is speaking on behalf of the thousands of dedicated singers who week by week, up and down the country make their vocal contributions to choirs, sacred and secular.

6 Orchestral patterns: from the nineteenth century to the NZSO

Until the advent of the National Orchestra in 1946 New Zealand lacked any consistent orchestral tradition. In retrospect, however, it is astonishing to discover just how much was achieved. The most stable orchestras were usually associated with string-playing conductors, whose pupils provided a sound core. Fine brass players came from the bands. Conductors in the colonial period were mostly German, Italian, and English; players were a mixture of amateurs and teachers, with a sprinkling of paid professionals. Civic councils occasionally gave support, as they did for bands. But orchestras balanced their books within exceedingly precarious margins, as the records of the Wellington Orchestral Society in the late 1890s show.[1]

While choral societies could boast a plethora of good voices, orchestras, with which they frequently worked, faced a chronic shortage of instrumentalists. Audiences seemed never to tire of the choral war-horses, yet had to be wooed to their orchestral counterparts. High ideals often succumbed to circumstance, as programmes became progressively more popular. Without subsidies of some kind or another, even a semi-professional orchestra could scarcely count on a long life. Two notable opportunities to establish permanent orchestras presented themselves but both foundered. First, the Government-financed Christchurch Exhibition Orchestra of 1906-1907, conducted by Alfred Hill, could have become the first professional orchestra in New Zealand, but was disbanded. Secondly, Verbrugghen's New South Wales State Orchestra, which toured in 1920 and 1922, had been conceived on an Australasian basis, but the New South Wales State Government fell out with its conductor Henri Verbrugghen and the enterprise collapsed.

The principal cities were naturally the most favoured. In Auckland, Karl Schmitt (1834-1900) pioneered orchestral concerts, succeeded by Arthur Towsey (1846-1931), who conducted the Auckland Orchestral Union (founded 1889).[2] Johannes Wielaert (1878-1948), a conscientious, highly temperamental conductor, took the orchestra of the Auckland Orchestral Society (founded 1903) to the Christchurch Exhibition with much success.[3] Colin Muston's Bohemian Orchestra (1914-1936) built up considerable subscription lists, with programmes based on the classical symphonic repertoire.[4] His work continued with the Auckland Symphony Orchestra (1939-1947), a heroic attempt to regain lost ground.[5]

Wellington's orchestral life took root when, following early groups and an *ad hoc* ensemble formed for Robert Parker's *Elijah* in 1878, the Wellington Orchestral Society began in 1882. The original players included a number of

THE ORCHESTRA 1884 OF THE AUCKLAND CHORAL SOCIETY.

Orchestra of the 1884
Auckland Choral Society.
Alexander Turnbull Library

accomplished musicians, some from the 65th regimental band. Conductors
included Angelo Forrest, J. B. Connolly, Otto Schwartz, and Parker. The
ensemble's most distinguished regime was that of the young Alfred Hill from
1892-1896, hailed by Baeyertz of the *Triad* as the best in the colony. Its
complement of around forty players gave four to five concerts a year, accompanied
visiting artists, and supported the capital's musical life in a variety of ways.
The Society possessed a fine library, mostly purchased from Europe. It ran on
a shoestring—in 1892 it had only 114 subscribers and a credit balance of 17/4d.

Hill presented good classical programmes based on his experience as a student
in the violin section of the Leipzig Gewandhaus Orchestra. He experienced
difficulties, however, in convincing his committee that each programme should

contain a symphony, and there were problems too in securing the co-operation of his players, some of whom resented 'this chip of a boy' and made his life miserable. Matters reached a head in 1896 when the visiting eighty-year-old Chevalier de Kontski, 'Concert Pianist to the Emperor of Germany and the Only Living Pupil of Beethoven', requested the use of the orchestra. Hill suspected charlatanism in de Kontski's trick of playing a work or two from under a folded blanket and declined to conduct. The musical storm that enveloped Wellington, 'almost rivalling in intensity that of the Gluckists and Piccinists of bygone days', gives a unique picture of the volatile feelings of the late nineteenth century towards 'overseas' artists and the returning prodigal son.[6] Hill resigned to join the visiting company of the violinist Ovide Musin.

Leon de Mauny. *Spencer Digby*

The Wellington Orchestral Society was succeeded in the early twentieth century by the Municipal Orchestra (conducted by Maughan Barnett) and the Wellington Professional Orchestra (conducted by Leela Bloy), both of which had troubled lives, despite the abilities of their directors.[7] Subsequent influential figures included the Australian pianist John Bishop and the English violinist Leon de Mauny. Bishop, born into a humble family in a small South Australian country town, showed early gifts on the piano and, after study in London and some English professional engagements, became conductor of the Royal Wellington Choral Union from 1928 to 1934. His arrival virtually coincided with the demise of the cinema orchestras, which prompted him in 1929 to gather together a number of musicians to form the Guild of Music Makers, a chamber orchestra of some twenty-five players, which performed a wide range of contemporary and classical works. In 1930 he founded the Wellington Philharmonic Orchestra with seventy-five players, many from the theatres. Bishop engaged visiting artists and on occasions performed piano concertos himself. His influence extended to promoting the Haydn Bi-centenary Festival in 1932 and the Brahms Centenary Festival a year later. He became a leading force in the formation of the Juvenile Concert League, which brought children to orchestral and choral concerts in which his orchestra took part. Bishop was an ardent, energetic, and idealistic young musician, whose subsequent career centred on the Elder Conservatorium and the founding of the Adelaide Festival.[8]

In 1923 Leon de Mauny, with his wife Evelyn (a piano gold medallist from the Guildhall, London, and a fine singer), emigrated to Wellington, where he founded the Wellington Symphony Orchestra in 1928. He was an excellent violinist, but war injuries, including gassing, led to some impairment in one hand. Notable visitors who performed with the Wellington Symphony Orchestra included Sir Malcolm Sargent in 1936, who on a later visit to the Christchurch Festival in the 1960s, recorded his impressions at that time:

> I must say the orchestra was not of the best in quality but it was certainly of the best in spirit, again the beauty of their desires was better than the truthfulness of their utterance. We had a bassoon who happened to be playing

Signor Squarise. *Hocken Library, Dunedin*

on an instrument of high pitch, the rest of the orchestra was of low pitch, but what are a few vibrations amongst friends. The oboe player was fascinating, a charming man who played very beautifully, and he came to me, it was most touching, after a rehearsal: 'Would you mind telling me something?' he said. 'Would you mind telling me if the sound I'm making is anything like an oboe, because I've never heard one'.[9]

In the early part of this century two stable ensembles emerged in the south. The Christchurch Orchestral Society (re-established 1908-1939) was conducted by Benno Scherek, Alfred Bünz,[10] and Angus Gunter.[11] The Christchurch Symphony Orchestra (1916-1920) was conducted by Alfred Worsley, who had studied piano with Egon Petri.

The distinguished cellist Harold Beck, who founded the Laurian Club (1932-1942), created an accomplished string orchestra of about twelve players, the forerunner of the Alex Lindsay and John Ritchie ensembles after World War II. It became a focal point of musical activity, generally giving two enterprising concerts a year, as well as recitals with visiting artists. It was nourished by Beck's own pupils and those of Irene Morris, a gifted string teacher, who led the orchestra for eight years. The founding of the National Orchestra in 1947 deprived the Laurian of five key players and forced it to disband.[12]

Dunedin seemed to have a penchant for pioneering exhibition orchestras, beginning with George West's ensemble of fifty members for the Philharmonic Society in 1865. The 1889 New Zealand and South Seas Exhibition Orchestra was led by Signor Squarise and conducted by Arthur Towsey. This forty-five piece orchestra, drawn from local and Australian sources, and 'a disbanded Spanish troupe from Madrid', presented ten Haydn symphonies and a good selection of classics.[13] It resulted in the founding of the Dunedin Philharmonic Orchestra (1904-1933) by Squarise, the original players being his pupils. Again, orchestral stability and expertise depended upon a regular supply of trained string players. Squarise, an outstanding violinist, had been a bandmaster in the Italian army and had led opera orchestras in Melbourne. His skill as an orchestrator and arranger enabled him to prepare a copious library of scores for his players, which could never have been purchased from the Society's own scanty resources.[14] Towsey later made an important contribution to Auckland orchestral life.

James Coombs (1862-1930), a professional violinist, attracted audiences of over a thousand to the Garrison Hall for popular concerts by his Orchestral Society (1888-1930). Gil Dech, who had directed the Columbia Recording Studios in New South Wales, became conductor of the Dunedin Symphony Orchestra in 1936, and also conducted the 4YA Orchestra.

Music had become an indissoluble part of New Zealand Exhibitions since West's 1865 ensemble in Dunedin. When the Government decided to mark the change from colonial to dominion status with an International Exhibition to be held in Christchurch in 1906-1907, Alfred Hill was asked to form an orchestra. He recruited just over fifty players, some of whom had been in the renowned Melbourne Exhibition of 1880-1881 under the direction of English composer Sir Frederic Cowen, including their leader George Weston.[15] The orchestra soon built up a following, giving two concerts a day, one classical and one popular. Its programmes of symphonies, overtures, incidental music, and concertos, played by New Zealand soloists, aroused much enthusiasm and won excellent reviews. As the orchestra's reputation grew, attendances increased, reaching a peak as the exhibition drew to a close.

At this point the *Triad* turned to assess its influence. Although the orchestra 'could claim no phenomenal mechanical excellence, nor profundity of thought in expression . . . Mr Alfred Hill . . . has unquestionably endeared himself by his ability, tact and *bon homme* [sic] to orchestra and public alike . . . the greatest achievement of the orchestra was the conversion of the public; it was a veritable triumph for instrumental music of the highest type.'[16]

Despite such accolades and despite pressure on the Government, no action was taken to preserve the ensemble. Private sponsors, Mr and Mrs John Prouse of Wellington, financed a national orchestral tour. At the last concert in Wellington, the orchestra played Haydn's 'Farewell' Symphony. Afterwards Alfred Hill likened the snuffing out of the last candle to their disbanding. Forty years elapsed before this hapless decision could be made good.

Notes

[1] See Thomson, J. M., 'A question of authenticity', *TLR*, October 1980, 80-92
[2] Towsey was trained in England and became organist at St Paul's Cathedral, Dunedin in 1865, and later musical director of the New Zealand and South Seas Exhibition of 1889-1890. He organized a fine orchestra for the Auckland Exhibition of 1913-1914
[3] See *NZ Herald*, 22 January 1907; *Triad*, 1 July 1908, 38-40 for a full analysis of the strengths and weaknesses of the orchestra; Wielaert Scrapbook, ATL, MSS F/H 471, Acc. 86-96, no. 1
[4] APL hold a complete set
[5] Muston was a gifted English violinist and an excellent teacher. See Walsh thesis, 24; also 'An appreciation of Colin Muston' (anon) in *Centennial Music Festival Auckland 1940*, 37; and note on his retirement in *Music Ho!*, September 1947, 16
[6] *Triad*, Wellington report, 2 November 1896, 23. See also Thomson 'A question of authenticity'
[7] The *Triad* in May 1913 and 1914 discusses their respective qualities in scathing terms and also the question of orchestral finances
[8] See Hewlett, 31-4, including *Dominion* editorial of 12 January 1934, 'Music in NZ', which warmly assesses Bishop's influence
[9] RNZ Sound Archives, Timaru. There was a chronic shortage of professional oboists at the time
[10] Alfred J. W. M. Bünz (1876-1950), son of a German musician C. F. Bünz, also strongly influenced musical life as a pianist and as a piano teacher. He conducted the Society in the years 1908-1914, 1916-1921, 1935-1939

[11] Gunter took the orchestra to fresh heights with two all-Beethoven concerts and new works, including the first New Zealand performance of the Delius C minor Piano Concerto with Frederick Page as soloist in 1928. See Watson thesis, 154; Page, 42, 47

[12] See Griffiths, T.V., 'The Christchurch Laurian Club', *MNZ*, 10 January 1936, 7; repertoire discussed in Watson thesis, 159

[13] Campbell, M., 50

[14] See Sinton W., 'Entertainment in Dunedin', *Evening Star*, 28 September 1974; Campbell, M., 51

[15] Chapter 5 in *ADM*, gives a full account of the formation and success of the orchestra. Cyril Monk, a former student of Hill's and later founder of the Austral Quartet in Sydney, became sub-leader

[16] *Triad*, May 1907, 35-7

From the National Orchestra to the NZSO 1946-1990

Opinions are still divided as to the contribution of the first conductor Andersen Tyrer (1946-1949), to the development of the National Orchestra. Some players stoutly maintain that he was exactly the right temperament for such an undertaking. Other reacted against his often brusque conducting style and left. His regime began with a controversy that was never silenced, despite his evident achievements and organizational skills. For his position had not been advertised—he was appointed from within, having formed and conducted the Centennial

The National Orchestra under Michael Bowles in the Dunedin Town Hall. *Campbell, Dunedin*

Orchestra, widely seen as a precursor to the National. Large sections of the musical world remained opposed to him. Tyrer's tastes leaned towards the more flamboyant romantics, and amongst contemporaries, to his own countrymen of the English pastoral school. If he alternatively bullied and cajoled his players, he nevertheless held them together in the most arduous years of concentrated travelling and of learning the orchestral repertoire. He established the concept of a national orchestra that over a period would play in almost every city and town throughout the country. During this period guest conductors included Sir Eugene Goossens (1947), Edgar Bainton (1947), Warwick Braithwaite (1947), Franco Ghione (1949) and Manno Wolf—Ferrari (1949), the latter two on tour with a visiting Italian Opera Company in *Barber of Seville, Rigoletto, Il Trovatore* and *Manon*. Braithwaite conducted the first substantial New Zealand composition to be played by the orchestra—Lilburn's *Song of the Antipodes*, (subsequently renamed *Song of the Islands*). Visiting soloists in these early days of air travel included the pianist Alexander Hellman, the cellist Peers Coetmore, performing her husband E. J. Moeran's Concerto, and the young New Zealand pianist Cara Hall.

Tyrer's successor Michael Bowles (1950-1952), inherited an orchestra that still had to prove itself as a national asset and so justify its source of funding. It was also an ensemble of uneven attainments, with its own administrative problems, including a restructuring initiated by the Musicians' Union. By this the original group system in which players dispersed at the end of each year to their home town, was disbanded. Bowles had been principal conductor and director of music for eight years for the Irish Broadcasting Service. He was an Elgarian and his performances of the Second Symphony might have been judged highlights of a regime that brought a further breadth to the repertoire, (such as Sibelius symphonies), introduced subscription and promenade concerts and brought into prominence many New Zealand artists. Guest conductors included Sir Bernard Heinze from Melbourne (1951) and the distinguished Argentinian Juan José Castro (1952), whose vitality and charm lifted the orchestra and audiences to new heights. When Michael Bowles left in 1952, Warwick Braithwaite returned as principal conductor from 1953 until 1954. His eclectic tastes took audiences to the fringes of contemporary music with Bartók's Piano Concerto No 3, Béla Siki being the soloist, and to many feuilletons such as

James Robertson, conductor of the National Orchestra, 1954-57. *Tom Shenahan*

Cowen's *The Butterfly's Ball*. His repertoire remained consistently in the middle ground. Braithwaite's final concert on 20 August 1954 of Beethoven, Sibelius, Haydn and Rachmaninov fairly echoed the tastes of a nevertheless fully professional and at times rollicking conductor.

With the arrival of James Robertson (1954-57) a new era began, epitomized by his favourite word 'exciting'. With considerable operatic experience in England, notably at Sadler's Wells (1946-1954), he dispersed the doldrums that had begun to envelop the orchestra, and set about creating a fresh image. He immersed himself in musical activities throughout New Zealand, gave new opportunities to New Zealand soloists, supported Donald Munro's enterprising New Zealand Opera Company (1954), built up the strength of the orchestra, initiated a systematic programming plan, and defended it against would-be critics and nihilists with ebullient intensity. This was achieved at some cost to himself. His highly volatile temperament at times sent shock waves through the orchestra. Robertson's contribution however, was immense, not only in the refinement of his Mozart and his notable choral performances, but in the precedent he established in commissioning Douglas Lilburn's *A Birthday Offering* for the orchestra's tenth birthday. He had also performed John Antill's now classic *Corroboree* and set up workshops for composers and conductors. By now the orchestra was working at full capacity on a severely testing touring schedule, with some sixty evening concerts each year, twenty for schools, many lunch-hour concerts and broadcasts which included two operas.

By 1958 and the appointment of John Hopkins, not yet thirty and conductor of the BBC Northern in Manchester, the orchestra was ready to take an immense step forward. It had several outstanding players amongst its section leaders,

John Hopkins, conductor of the National Orchestra, 1957-63. *Tom Shenahan*

its position in the community was more assured than ever, and it had assimilated its basic repertory. John Hopkins showed energy and flair in the way he introduced new works including Bartok's Concerto for Orchestra, Stravinsky's *Symphony of Psalms* and *Firebird*, Ginastera's *Pampeana*, and Tippett's *Child of Our Time*. His concerts of contemporary music trained and inspired a new audience: their effect is still felt today. He emphasized the importance of the symphony orchestra both in its own community and in a wider one. He allied himself with the aspirations of New Zealand composers, his premières including Lilburn's Third Symphony, which he commissioned, David Farquhar's First and a host of other works. His zeal communicated itself to audiences, for despite a somewhat reserved Yorkshire temperament, unshowy by nature, his artistic intensity flowed into the music itself.

Igor Stravinsky, conducting the Finale from *Firebird* in the Wellington Town Hall on Saturday 18 November 1961: 'tiny, fragile, an aristocratic spider', a concert which ended with rose petals and a standing ovation. *Tom Shenahan*

New Zealand's musical isolation was almost over. Air travel made more frequent and shorter visits by overseas artists possible. The Czech Philharmonic's 1959 tour startled players and audiences alike, proving such a potent cultural force that the Americans felt obliged to send the following year the Boston Symphony Orchestra under its resident conductor Charles Münch, with the composer Aaron Copland on the Australian part of the tour. By 1963 the number of symphony concerts each year was nearing one hundred, soloists proliferated, both world-famous names and gifted New Zealanders. John Hopkins became a leading force in the establishment of the National Youth Orchestra and the Orchestral Training Scheme which evolved into the Schola Musica.

A visit of an exceptional kind came with the arrival of Igor Stravinsky and his mentor Robert Craft, in 1961. Stravinsky's conducting of the last movement of *The Firebird*, fortunately preserved both on film and tape, tells as much about the playing and spirit of the orchestra as it does of a great musical occasion. Innovative programmes continued to appear: Bartók's *Duke Bluebeard's Castle* (1962) and Britten's *War Requiem* (1963) amongst them. Guest conductors during this period included Karel Ančerl (1961) from the Czech Philharmonic, and the Italian Alceo Galliera (1963) who had time to develop in the players a warm and singing lyricism. In 1963 John Hopkins left to take up the position of Federal Director of Music for the Australian Broadcasting Commission, a position subsequently followed by several others in the Australian hierarchy. He has never relinquished his close links with New Zealand ensembles, players and audiences, and his initial response to the music of New Zealand composers has been deepened and broadened through his work with the NZSO and the Auckland Philharmonia. His regime has been described as the orchestra's 'Golden Age'—a time of fruition and achievement, of a sense of purpose with stimulating challenges. Josef Krips on his 1959 visit summed it up when he described the orchestra as 'potentially great'. It was also a coming of age for the concert managers of the orchestra, from the first tireless 'one-man-bands' of John Proudfoot, James Hartstonge and Maurice Glubb.

Hopkins' successor, Juan Matteucci (d. 1990), the Italian-born conductor of

Brian Priestman. *Tom Shenahan*

the Chilean Philharmonic Orchestra, brought an extrovert Latin approach, successful in many respects, but one which eventually proved limited. The orchestral management thereafter virtually abandoned their policy of appointing a permanent conductor and relied on a principal guest. Many distinguished artists appeared, including Piero Gamba (1969), Walter Susskind (1970), Lawrence Foster (1970) and in 1971 Christopher Seaman, Uri Segal and Edouard van Remoortel. This policy was changed for three years when Brian Priestman, in keen competition with Lawrence Foster, accepted the position of chief conductor for 1973-1975. The structural changes that followed the arrival of the Labour Government of 1972 with Roger Douglas as Minister of Broadcasting implementing the Adam Report, resulted in the abolition of the NZBC and the orchestra being administered by the Concert Section of the new entity, Radio New Zealand. Priestman had lobbied hard for an orchestra he held in the highest regard and which was now for the first time, financed by the Consolidated Fund.

Following administrative changes and improved publicity (again at his urging), Priestman took the orchestra on its first overseas tour to Sydney in 1974 with Kiri te Kanawa and Michael Houstoun as soloists. Works by Edwin Carr, Anthony Watson, John Rimmer and Douglas Lilburn were included in demanding programmes that won highly appreciative reviews as the orchestra moved on to other cities. Priestman had proved a vital, challenging and haranguing force (especially to the players), but following his departure there seemed even less inclination to restore the role of a permanent conductor, and Michie Inoue, who first toured in 1975, was appointed principal guest from 1977-1980.

In 1975 the orchestra became the sole responsibility of Radio New Zealand, a position it held until 1977 when it became an independent yet integral part of the Corporation under its own management, with Peter Nisbet being appointed general manager. Many guest conductors arrived, including on the popular side, the very successful Ron Goodwin. Since then the orchestra has expanded its range of recordings, given notable New Zealand premières, such as Lyell Cresswell's *Salm* (1979), become the centrepiece of Jack Body's Sonic Circuses and made another overseas tour, to Hong Kong in 1980, where it unwittingly became the focal point of local orchestral feuds and attracted biased comment and criticism. In the same year the arrival of Franz Paul Decker foreshadowed his eventual position as principal guest conductor, achieving a warm accord with players and audiences. His last act of Wagner's *Walküre* with the visiting English singer Anne Evans and the New Zealand bass Donald McIntyre in November 1989, proved a highlight of a period which revealed and re-affirmed the heights the orchestra could reach.

What are the special forces that shape New Zealand's oldest and largest symphony orchestra? No single answer can be given, for its character, personality and style are facets of a living organism, dependent not only on the vision of a gifted conductor but on the quality of teaching in schools, institutions and universities, on the private music teacher, as well as on the sustaining capacities of musical life. The original difficulties of developing a symphony orchestra in a remote part of the world have largely disappeared: a new set of problems confronts orchestral management. Should they reconsider and perhaps restore the role of permanent conductor or continue the present system of offering short-term engagements as chief conductor to eminent musicians? This remains one of the most crucial debates as the orchestra enters the 1990s following yet another re-organization, this time under a newly-appointed board of management.

The New Zealand Youth Orchestra

In 1955 when Walter Harris inveigled James Robertson into conducting over one hundred young players at a musical seminar in Wellington, there were high hopes that this would be the precursor of a 'national' youth orchestra. Unfortunately, despite the conductor's enthusiasm, the time was not yet ripe, but when Harris renewed his approach with John Hopkins in 1957, he found both a ready ally and a response from government. Hopkins had particular gifts with young musicians and sponsored a plan for the formation of a national youth orchestra funded for the following ten years from the Broadcasting Account. Administration was to be in the hands of a joint committee of the Education Department and the NZBS, with Hopkins as artistic director.

Over the following five years he achieved extremely high standards, even though players met only for fourteen days during the year, testimony to his dedicated skills and commitment. The orchestra had played works by twenty-three composers, recorded commercially and had been televised. Distinguished local and overseas soloists had appeared with it, in concertos, and it featured in a National Film Unit production.

On Hopkins' departure for Australia in 1965, Ashley Heenan took over. He recommended that regional rehearsals bolstered with a training group precede the main rehearsal period each year, that the size of the orchestra be increased to over one hundred players to ensure that promising young players could be included and to create a reserve. With Symphony Orchestra principals as section coaches and the above new developments, the Youth Orchestra rapidly expanded its activities and influence. Between 1965 and 1974 it introduced thirty-six works by twenty-two composers, with ten young New Zealand musicians as concerto soloists, undertook a North Island tour playing in ten towns and cities, made several television features and records annually. The latter were issued on transcription services and attracted wide attention overseas, culminating in an invitation to participate in the International Festival of Youth Orchestras held at Aberdeen in 1975. This was expanded to include a cultural exchange visit to China and concerts in Hong Kong and Tokyo. This spectacular tour marked the end of a decade. The orchestral patterns in New Zealand had themselves changed with the development of executant courses at universities and of regional orchestras. The symphony orchestra organization now pursued a policy of promotional sponsorship, renaming the ensemble 'The New Zealand Youth Orchestra' and using visiting guest conductors to direct the annual concerts — Hopkins, Tintner, Seaman, Meredith Davies, Sanderling, Lougran, Segal, Salomon, Gamba and Decker are amongst these. In 1985, the orchestra, now sponsored by the New Zealand Post Office, appeared in a festival to mark 'The Year of Youth', with the National Youth Band, the National Youth Choir and the Yamaha National Youth and College Jazz Orchestras, with over 250 young musicians taking part. In 1988 the orchestra visited both Perth and Brisbane for the Australian bi-centennial, directed by its new conductor Michael Vinten, with Michael Houstoun as soloist and presenting several New Zealand works. In 1989 the orchestra became the 'New Zealand Post National Youth Orchestra', continuing to win high praise for its overall excellence.

The New Zealand Symphony Orchestra Trainees and the Schola Musica

Growing from his experiences as outlined above, John Hopkins devised a scheme to form an orchestral training group to provide a bridge between the National Youth Orchestra and the Symphony Orchestra. He was fortunate to find strong support from John Schroder, Director of Broadcasting, Malcolm Rickard, Head of Music, and Jim Collins, Secretary of the Musicians' Union in Wellington. With such dogged forces behind him Hopkins' scheme gained ministerial approval, Ashley Heenan being appointed Musical Director, a position he held for twenty-four years. This unique scheme was the first permanent training orchestra to be established in the world and over the next decades 75% of its members established themselves as professional musicians. Moveover, it recorded commercially more music by New Zealand composers than any other ensemble in the country, and appeared in concert in every major city and town.

After initial experiments, the Schola Musica established itself as a string performing group with its own concert series. Following an acclaimed visit to the Perth 11th International Society of Music Educators' Conference and subsequent concerts in Melbourne and Sydney, the Schola began a series of recordings for Kiwi/Pacific Records, proving a dynamic force in making known compositions by New Zealand composers, particularly the string works of Douglas Lilburn. In 1975, as part of the National Youth Orchestra's Aberdeen visit, they gave performances throughout the tour, and on their return to New Zealand continued to win recognition as a highly professional ensemble in their own right. In 1985 the young conductor/composer Michael Vinten succeeded Ashley Heenan but in the changed economic climate of the then Labour Government with its strict 'user-pays' philosophy, the scheme once described by Owen Jensen as 'Radio New Zealand's most valuable musical investment'[1] was brought to an end by the newly-elected Board of the New Zealand Symphony Orchestra.[2]

Notes

[1] *Evening Post* 3 November 1975
[2] I am indebted to Ashley Heenan for providing detailed information on both the National Youth Orchestra and the Schola Musica, much of which could not unfortunately be included in this necessarily abbreviated summary.

7 *The quest for a conservatorium: Michael Balling at Nelson*

The Nelson Harmonic Society, founded in 1860, had established an unusual tradition of engaging its conductors direct from Germany. When Michael Balling (1866-1925) arrived in October 1893, nobody could have dreamed that they had appointed an exceptional musician, with an insatiable curiosity about the world and its inhabitants, an ability to adapt himself to unpromising circumstances, and the fervour to bring about an artistic transformation.

Balling had been born into a poor Bavarian family in Heidingsfeld, near the baroque city of Würzburg, where he studied the viola with a noted instrumentalist and scholar, Hermann Ritter (1849-1926), who had revived the older, larger viola alta, for which he claimed improved resonance and a more brilliant and powerful tone.[1]

By 1889 five of Ritter's pupils were playing in the Bayreuth orchestra, including Balling, who was already an ardent Wagnerian. As the youngest member he sat in the last desk, but Felix Mottl, the conductor, soon noticed his abilities and moved him to first viola. From here his ascent was rapid. Invitations to the exclusive musical evenings at Wagner's home 'Wahnfried' followed, where Balling met leading musical personalities such as the Wagner proselytizer Hans von Wolzogen, Hans Richter, and Humperdinck. At this stage of his career he decided to go to Nelson.

A Herr Schultz from Hamburg had accepted the conductorship of the combined Orchestral and Harmonic Society orchestras, but he relinquished it in favour of Michael Balling, who was reported as recovering from a nervous breakdown. While visiting Herr Schultz, Balling found him regretting his promise to accept the position, so offered to take his place. Whether he expected the renowned Nelson climate or the long sea voyage to restore his health is unknown. Before leaving Germany, Balling is reported to have visited Bismarck at Friedrichsruhe, a meeting which left an overpowering impression on him. He was held by a gaze he described as 'wild yet piercing'. 'You are going to New Zealand?' asked the aged Chancellor, adding somewhat prosaically: 'I envy you that. Whoever wants to learn can do nothing better than see the world.'[2]

From the time of his arrival Balling seemed amazingly dynamic. Two intelligent local residents with a passion for music became his allies and friends: Frederick Gibbs, Headmaster of the Central School, and J. H. Cock, a shipping agent. Balling was immediately drawn into the Musical Evening Society where he played his favourite instrument, a specially made viola alta. Gibbs noted in his diary that only a man of enormous strength and reach could attempt to hold it.[3]

Michael Balling. *Musical Times, 1 January 1913*

The paucity of musical life in the city shocked Balling. He soon protested publicly and suggested that a school of music be set up:

As a foreigner I am singularly struck by the prominence given to 'sport' of all kinds, even to the extent of legal protection and encouragement within certain bounds, and while Colonial youths go home and take prizes in athletics against all comers our musical students must at great cost proceed to Europe to learn even piano playing efficiently. With so much time and money for sport, we may resolve to reserve a little for higher things such as music. In order to have a growth of musical acquirements and talent, it is absolutely necessary that the young people be completely trained, and even with a city of 7,000 inhabitants surely 3,000 could find 1s.0d. each for a year, which would yield a sum of £150, sufficient to provide and maintain instruments and music, a modest 'school of music' of which I am prepared to undertake the direction and upon which I would expend great pains. The difficulty of such a scheme is only apparent and would disappear if serious attention were given to this subject! For me, a lengthened residence here is only possible if there is some hopeful growth of musical life such as I have indicated and I do not write this letter like a gust of a south-easter from the Cook Strait, merely to raise dust in our midst, but in the hope of finding those who will cooperate earnestly with me in the direction indicated, and I shall indeed be glad to find on my return from a month's holiday, that a determination has been arrived at to give life forthwith to the project.[4]

During his holidays Balling travelled throughout the country giving concerts, usually with the viola alta. On one memorable occasion he ventured into the heavily forested Urewera country, still a Māori stronghold and particularly difficult for a European to penetrate.[5] Not only did they entertain him as a royal visitor but they showered him with valuable gifts. Balling later spoke highly of their music, especially of their pre-European chants. He had witnessed Māori funeral rites and hakas, and on a ceremonial occasion had played viola solos for a chieftain who had presented him with a carved stick.

The most important of these expeditions took place shortly after the publication of the letter. Balling joined Mr Cock, the shipping agent, on a trip to Mount Cook. While weather-bound in their mountain hut, Balling elaborated on his idea of starting a smaller version of a German conservatorium in Nelson. This so appealed to his companion that on their return he immediately arranged a public meeting at which he and the mayor spoke to an enthusiastic audience. If such a school were to be established, Michael Balling promised to stay in Nelson a further two years. This was used as an argument for starting a conservatorium immediately, with a temporary home in the Harmonic Hall until their own premises could be built. About £300 was raised, most of which was spent on buying instruments. Some of these were displayed in local shop windows and aroused keen interest in the project. Balling's other friend Gibbs, who was also deeply involved with the Nelson Institute and Philosophical Society, helped in canvassing for subscriptions and determining the constitution and scale of fees. On 9 June 1894 the Nelson School of Music was declared open.

> Balling dominated the musical scene. The people of Nelson reached new heights of enthusiasm for the serious study of music which perhaps have never been equalled. Soon he was giving lectures to packed audiences on high musical theories though very few of his audience understood him thoroughly as they scarce knew a quaver from a crotchet. The numbers in the Harmonic Society rose and when a concert was given it had to be held in the theatre to accommodate all who wanted to attend instead of the Provincial Hall as previously . . .[6]

Early accounts by his students, which were published in England, had an appropriately quaint tone:

> A New Zealander, Miss Dogtail, taught the pianoforte, and played well; Mr Balling taught all the orchestral instruments and musical history. In his first harmony class there were twenty-three pupils, including a Colonel Bramfield, who had been through the Indian Mutiny and was now over seventy years of age, and a little girl of nine years, daughter of Mrs Houlker, the teacher of singing.[7]

By the end of 1895 Balling was anxious to leave. Although his two years were not yet up, he felt he had been away from Europe long enough. He reported to the Trustees of the School of Music on the standards that had been reached and on the improvements that should take place. Under his direction, the School had given a three-year course, granting certificates at the end of the first and second years, and a diploma at the end of the third. (After his departure the courses were affiliated with the English Associated Board.)

Balling, who had earlier toured with Alfred Hill, made a farewell tour of New Zealand with the English musician and composer Maughan Barnett. He played his viola alta in the remote towns as well as the cities. Their programme usually included the Rubinstein sonata, which in Wanganui was hailed as a work of 'nobility and grandeur' whose opening theme 'aroused the enthusiasm of the audience'.[8]

Nelson felt it was losing its resident genius. Balling and Maughan Barnett gave a Farewell Grand Concert, and Balling was presented with a silver inkstand: 'I have been asked by the pupils of the Nelson School of Music to present you with this piece of silver, which, emblematic of their good wishes and your own music, is solid, sterling and good . . .', said Mr Pitt.[9] 'May pleasure and prosperity be your future lot.' In reply Michael Balling urged his audience to try to make the new School of Music a success. 'Nelson is not a large place', he said, 'and some may say it is a sleepy hollow, but I find it can recognize the good . . . I feel somewhat ashamed at leaving, for my intention had been to remain three years, but circumstances have occurred to alter my plans . . . I am really sorry to leave Nelson.' (applause)

Balling had an outstanding subsequent career. In 1912 he succeeded Richter as conductor of the Hallé Orchestra in Manchester, where the force of his personality impressed and his German origin aroused the opposition of figures such as Thomas Beecham. He strove for proper financial support for the orchestra and proposed a Manchester opera house to be the centre of an English school: 'He was a strong personality in every way and at his first concert had given the impression of a masterful musician.'[10] The outbreak of World War I caught him in Germany, and he was forced to resign his Hallé conductorship. His subsequent career unfolded entirely in his own country, at Darmstadt and as the regular conductor of *The Ring* at Bayreuth. After a performance of *Götterdämmerung* on 17 August 1925, directed under great personal duress, he collapsed, and died on 4 September.

In distant Nelson he was still remembered. His friend Gibbs wrote in the *Nelson Evening Mail* of 25 November 1925:

> . . . he was a big man in every sense of the word. No-one could come into contact with him without being impressed by his forceful personality — as well as by his great musical genius . . . the great stimulus which he gave to the study of music in Nelson persisted down to the present day . . .

The new Nelson School of Music was opened on 4 September 1901 by the Countess of Ranfurly with the customary Grand Concert, including an *Ode* by the third principal, Herr Julius Lemmer. A utilitarian brick building, with excellent acoustics, it could accommodate an audience of over 500, with an orchestra and chorus of 150.

Glass with engraved motif from Wagner's *Tannhauser*, presented by Michael Balling to his student Christiana Kidson. *Marion van Dijk, Margaret Campbell, Nelson*

Memorials of Michael Balling abound. Modest treasures are retained in Nelson, such as musical exercises worked for him and a glass goblet etched with a Wagnerian opera motif, given to one of his pupils.[11] On a larger scale, there are his important Breitkopf and Härtel Wagner editions.[12] 'There was something of the musically baroque in him', wrote Dr Werner Kulz in his Bayreuth tribute, 'with his naturally human modesty and noble simplicity. There was a compulsive way in which he extracted the finest expression from a chorus, which for him came before everything, even before the rectitude of all details . . . He always embraced all great music with his whole personality.'[13]

Notes

[1] Ritter found his model in Antonio Bagatella's *Regole perla construzione di violini*, published in Padua in 1786. The instrument was credited with having clear tones, increased power, and a striking delicacy and richness. It was around eighteen inches in length

[2] This and other incidents in Balling's life are described in Dr Werner Kulz's obituary tribute in the *Bayreuther Festspielführer* (1927)

[3] See Mann, S. 'Frederick Giles Gibbs — His influence on the social history of Nelson 1890-1950' (M.A. thesis), Victoria University of Wellington, and its subsequent publication by the Nelson Historical Society in 1977

[4] Quoted by Mann, 144

[5] In his obituary tribute Dr Kulz describes it as an 'excursion into the jungle'

[6] Mann, 145

[7] Hadden, 259

[8] *Wanganui Chronicle*, 29 October 1895

[9] *Nelson Colonist*, 4 February 1896

[10] Rees, 52

[11] In possession of Margaret Campbell of Nelson, whose mother, Christiana Kidson, was a Balling student

[12] These were almost completed at the time of his death, and include the first publication of the early operas *Die Hochzeit, Die Feen*, and *Liebesverbot*

[13] The subsequent history of the school is outlined in Appendix I. For a fuller account, see Wall, Arnold, comp. *The First Ninety Years of the Nelson School of Music*, and Thomson, J. M. 'From Bayreuth to the Urewera' *TLR* October 1990

IV

The world beyond

1 Visiting artists from the nineteenth century to the present day

Before 1900

During the first decades of settlement touring musicians tended to resemble vaudeville artists who might sing, play the piano, tap dance, and render cornet solos. A number of such figures wandered through colonial New Zealand, enlivening hotel entertainments, social evenings, and dinners. In the decade following the Otago gold discoveries of the 60s, concert artists began to venture forth, such as the Australian-based singer Marie Carandini, whose 'English Opera Company' made the first of several tours in 1863. Offering shortened versions of popular operas linked with a spoken libretto, Madame Carandini immediately established herself as an attractive singer and personality.[1]

Other artists soon followed. On 21 January 1866 Jane Maria Atkinson wrote to Margaret Taylor from Beach Cottage, Taranaki: 'I must tell you of the musical treat we have just had—7 concerts from a Mr and Mrs Heine, he (blind from birth) a really fine violinist playing with great delicacy and feeling. She is a very good pianist with brilliant execution.'[2] Eight years later she writes from Nelson in praise of Arabella Goddard, married to the London music critic J. W. Davison, and one of the first to play late Beethoven in public:

> Such a musical treat as we all had at the beginning of the month is rare in Nelson, the great pianist Mde A. Goddard came here straight from Melbourne and gave two concerts which were crowded. She was nearly buried in splendid bouquets and at the end of the second concert everyone stood up and gave three cheers, a very unusual thing for even great musical favourites I am told . . . One didn't know which most to admire, her amazing power and vigour or her exquisite brilliance and delicacy of touch . . .[3]

Other visitors of the period included the Croatian soprano Ilma de Murska (1876), renowned for her Queen of the Night, with an unusually fine supporting company. Some decided to stay, for instance the flautist John Radcliff, with his wife Rita, a singer, who both settled in Wellington in 1885, making their

Fisk Jubilee Singers, an American concert group of American ex-slaves and the sons and daughters of slaves, who first introduced spirituals to New Zealand from 1874 onwards, making several visits and proving extremely popular, especially with Māori audiences. *Alexander Turnbull Library*

first concert appearance in Handel's *Acis and Galatea*.[4] Radcliff also delivered a celebrated series of lectures: 'From Pan to Pinafore—the pipes of all peoples'. During a tour in 1885, Reményi, the 'gypsy' violinist once associated with Brahms, advised Alfred Hill's father to send his talented son to Leipzig, and Sir Charles Santley, the greatest baritone of his day, sang *Elijah* at the 1889-1890 exhibition in Dunedin. Other visitors included the pianist Kowalski (1892), who loved 'to sparkle', the fine Belgian violinist Ovide Musin (1892, 1896), Camilla Urso-Sapio (1895), Antoinette Trebelli (Dolores) (1896), and perhaps the most flamboyant of all, the 'last surviving pupil of Beethoven', the Chevalier de Kontski, who brought about such a furore in Wellington musical life.[5]

Camilla Urso-Sapio, a notable French violinist. *Author's collection*

The famed Kennedy family, who toured the world singing Scottish songs from 1872 to 1876, arrived in Dunedin at the end of 1873, where their 'Twa Hours at Hame' lasted five weeks. David Kennedy jun. published an entertaining account of their travels.[6] The family roughed it in Central Otago, giving a concert in a barn at Popotunoa, and forded the flooded Waitaki on their way to Canterbury: 'We would advise no one with weak nerves to ford a swollen river in New Zealand', he wrote.[7]

Worse was to come:

> At the great Manawatu Gorge we had a trying adventure . . . Here the coach goes no farther, and each passenger is slung across the mighty chasm, which is 750 feet wide, sitting on a couple of planks suspended from a wire-rope 200 feet above the level of the river. Whether lady or gentleman, you have

to get astride this frail support and hold on by both hands to a small line overhead. It is a perilous aerial flight . . .

All crossed safely until the last two of the family set forth. They had advanced successfully to the half-way point 'when a jerk of the hauling rope whipped off my sister's hat, which swooped down into the white foam of the river, where it floated a black speck far beneath. . . .'[8] What motivated musicians to undertake such risks? 'Moving about becomes after a while a kind of friction that generates a mental and physical electricity of being' was Kennedy's apt answer.[9]

The French soprano, Antoinette Trebelli (Dolores). *Author's collection*

1900-1914

Singers

By the turn of the century travel could still be hazardous, as Paderewski discovered, and often uncomfortable, although recognized 'tourist' routes existed, and were set out in Murray's famous red *Hand-Book* of 1893. Following a successful visit in 1902 by the Australian singer Amy Castles (although Baeyertz attacked her in the *Triad*), Dame Nellie Melba's arrival in Auckland the following year proved a highlight of the era. She made a royal progress up Queen Street in a carriage, men raising their hats as she passed. Tickets cost up to one and a half guineas, but two people often clubbed together to buy them, each hearing half the programme. Bernard Shaw felt she had 'an unspoiled, beautiful voice and perfect intonation' when he heard her Marguerite in an 1894 London performance of Gounod's *Faust*.[10] She was clearly in marvellous form and aroused passionate interest. Her Auckland programmes included the mad scenes from Donizetti's *Lucia di Lammermoor* and from Thomas's adaptation of *Hamlet*: she graciously allowed three encores. The audience included the Premier and the gross takings were £1,400, said to be a record for the colony. Baeyertz in the *Triad* expressed momentary surprise at the lightness of her voice, but realized it had remarkable carrying power, although her singing seemed to appeal to the head and not to the heart. In 1910 he was more critical: 'The tone is liquid as a crystal snow-fed mountain brook—and as cold. The voice is white and colourless.'[11]

At the Australian soprano Ada Crossley's Auckland concert on 5 December 1903, over 200 people filled every nook and cranny of the stage, so high was her reputation, but on her subsequent visit in 1909 it was reported 'Her fall from grace is a spectacle to make angels weep.'[12] The *Triad* could, on the one hand, praise the English tenor Watkin Mill's voice for its range, quality, and mastery of technique and phrasing, and on the other, lambast the French prima donna Blanche Arral, who toured early in 1907, for every fault from her

The Australian soprano Ada Crossley in 1905. *Musical Times, 1 May 1905*

Clara Butt and her husband Kennerley Rumford in Māori costume. *Author's collection*

pronunciation to her figure. Emma Albani, renowned for her interpretation of the great soprano roles of Italian opera, showed signs of age, but nevertheless held audiences by the force of her personality.[13] Her accompanist, the young English composer Haydn Wood, later achieved fame himself for 'Love's Garden of Roses' (1914) and 'Roses of Picardy' (1916). After a meeting with Alfred Hill, 'a Maoriland musician', Madame Albani took some of his songs into her repertoire, including 'The Maori Canoe', which suited her to perfection. She later sang 'Waiata Poi' in the Queen's Hall, London.[14]

Clara Butt and her husband Kennerley Rumford had a brisk encounter with Baeyertz on their first tour in 1908 (see chapter IV, 3). 'The whole programme was a concession to the bourgeois', he wrote.

> A snack of Schumann, a goût of Gluck, a happy handful of Handel—just the formal proportions—and then, having paid tribute to cant and tolerated the 'classic' music, the joy-filled audience paddled in the shallow waters of English drawing room songs . . . Have the artists no sense of responsibility? There is a mission open for them here: a mission to lead the public towards a higher world of music.[15]

This was hardly Clara Butt's style.

Emma Calvé, the French-born soprano, noted for her dramatic ability and strongly realistic interpretations, visited in 1910.[16] Both she and her colleague, Gasparri, were not deterred by the concert stage from displaying their customary operatic gestures: 'It was perfect to the last brilliancy of elaboration; it was artistic to the last shadow of restraint . . . The gestures of Calvé are sometimes exquisite—no less.'[17] Calvé may not have had Melba's technical brilliance, but she had 'emotion, warmth, glow, personality, enthralling verve, soul . . . call it what you will. The heart of a breathing woman tumultuously alive is in her every note. Baeyertz also praised Antonia Dolores (formerly Antoinette Trebelli), who toured in 1911 with the New Zealand baritone John Prouse.[18]

Baeyertz attended John McCormack's one concert in the Wellington Town Hall on 12 January 1912. The singer's gramophone records had led him to conclude that the artist had 'a very pretty tenor voice, but it is far from being a noble voice. It lacks power, roundness, fullness, sonority and variety of tone colour . . .' He later found no reason to alter his opinion: 'His singing is interesting but never very moving . . . he is never perfectly satisfying to the sensitive and cultivated connoisseur of vocalization.'[19] The *NZ Herald*, on the other hand, admired his skilful manipulation of sustained *pianissimo* tones in the head register and the achievement of a *diminuendo* effect when vocalizing in the highest altitudes.[20] Baeyertz implored Rosina Buckman, the associate artist, to 'get to Europe at all hazards'. McCormack, in fact, helped her to do so.[21]

Madame Kirkby Lunn, the popular English contralto, attracted large audiences and good reviews, with a note of approbation from the *Triad*: '. . . on occasion the great dramatic pulse of art at its super-best throbs strong and clear and true'.[22] The French-Canadian tenor Paul Dufault, who arrived in March 1914, proved close to Baeyertz's ideal: 'He believed that every syllable of the singer's speech, every shade of the singer's conception must come to the ears of the audience.'[23]

Instrumentalists

The pianist Ignacy Paderewski in his youth. *Author's collection*

Outstanding visiting pianists included Mark Hambourg, with the flautist John Lemmone, in 1903, and Paderewski the following year. Katherine Mansfield particularly admired Hambourg, as she did the cellist Jean Gérardy, who had toured in 1902. Gérardy had encouraged a public appeal to send the two Trowell brothers from Wellington to study in Frankfurt. Thomas eventually became professor of cello at the Guildhall School of Music in 1924 and joined the staff of the Royal College of Music from 1937. He also had a modest reputation as a composer, especially for his idiomatic salon music for cello and piano. Katherine Mansfield fell in love with Thomas, then transferred her affections to his twin brother Garnet, who became a professional violinist.[24]

Paderewski won acclaim from most critics, although the *Triad* remained cool. He encountered immense difficulties in arranging for after-concert meals, being obliged to negotiate with the workers' union.[25] He made a perilous journey from Rotorua to Napier by coach. 'It was one of the most dangerous trips I can remember. We travelled for hours and hours along an abyss . . . There was not more than a foot between [it and] the carriage. It was a precipice some 2000 feet deep. If one of the horses slipped, we would go down—and for ever.' The party of eight in the large coach included his wife and her maid, his doctor, piano tuner, and valet, plus two other men. When he eventually arrived in Napier, 'it was just like playing in London. The contrast of that audience (everyone in full dress and the ladies décolleté), after that wilderness, the geysers, the precipice and the discomfort caused by nature and by man, was really something extraordinary.'

Teresa Carreño, who toured in 1907, probably made a more powerful impact than any other pianist. Venezuelan by birth, she had earlier been noted for her fiery temperament, but after her marriage in 1892 to Eugen d'Albert, the composer and pianist, her style changed and she became a serious, profound interpreter. Later, on 3 October 1908, Katherine Mansfield heard her at the Bechstein Hall, London: 'What a tremendous genius! I am staggered by her playing, by her tone, which is the last word in tonal beauty and intensity and vitality—No other pianist can so sway me . . .' Carreno returned to New Zealand in 1910, when Baeyertz berated audiences for neglecting her.

The notable but underestimated English pianist, Leonard Borwick, gave three recitals in Wellington in September 1911. The *Triad* found him in many respects 'the most delightful of the several virtuosi who have visited us. For refinement, delicacy, sincerity and sheer beauty of tone, he stands out absolutely alone.'

Teresa Carreno in her youth. *Author's collection*

The Czech violinist Jan Kubelik. *Author's collection*

Borwick showed that an English pianist could hold his own with foreign rivals, his Schumann and Chopin being outstanding.[27]

The period was rich in celebrities: the violinists Jan Kubelik (1908) and Mischa Elman with Percy Kahn (1913), the famed Cherniavsky Trio (1908, 1915, 1924), and two outstanding dancers Adeline Genée (1913) and Maud Allen (1914). Katherine Mansfield saw the latter at the Palace Music Hall in London: 'As she dances, under the changing lights, coming and going to the sound of a thin, heady music which marks the rhythm of her movements like a kind of clinging drapery, she seems to sum up the appeal of everything that is passing, and coloured and to be enjoyed.'[28] Larger ensembles included the Steel-Payne Bellringers (1900, 1905), the Westminster Glee Singers, the Fisk Jubilee Singers, who gave negro spirituals (1905, 1910), the Royal Welsh Male Choir (1909), and the Sheffield Musical Union (1911).[29] The Besses o' the Barn Band set new standards at the Christchurch Exhibition of 1906-1907 and returned in 1910,[30] and the Royal Artillery Band made a fine centre-piece at the Auckland Exhibition of 1914.

Percy Grainger

One visitor at this time stood out particularly. Percy Grainger had first visited New Zealand in 1903 with a touring party accompanying the noted Australian singer Ada Crossley.[31] Invariably they encountered an enthusiastic reception. The visit was also notable for the extraordinary jaunts undertaken by Grainger: he walked from Oamaru to Timaru (56 miles) between 2 p.m. and 6 a.m. the following morning, resting for only half an hour, and from Masterton to Eketahuna (32 miles) directly after a concert, from 11 p.m. until 6 a.m. next day without a rest.[32]

In 1909 he returned for a tour of the main cities with a troup of artists under contract to J. C. Williamson. 'Whenever he was able Grainger went to the Maoris to note down their music and in the North Island he secured the valuable services of Maggie and Pomeri [*sic*], two famous Maori guides', writes Grainger's biographer John Bird.[33] Grainger's interest in the Māori had begun in the last decade of the nineteenth century, when a boarder in his London house, the English botanical artist A. E. Aldis, used to recite Māori chants: 'He would keep the marrow-curdling Maori rhythms hammering away by the hour or so it seemed to me. So that when I heard the Maori speech at Rotorua in 1909 it was like a homecoming for me. I have always adored heroic sounding languages.'[34]

In Otaki he met 'quite a card', A. J. Knocks, who was married to a Māori and had two sons:

> [Knocks] takes phonograph records of every bit of native music he can. 2 years ago Rarotongan natives were brought over to Christchurch (NZ) Exhibition.

Percy Grainger in his youth. *Author's collection*

They sang gloriously. This old man phonographed them. Nobody else did seemingly . . . I came to hear his Maori records, but he made me hear the Rarotongan records & I straightway noted them down in his cobwebby, brokenwindowed, queersmelling house from afternoon early to 5 the next morn. The old man stayed up to 2 o'clock with me, & he & ½ breeds & I had great fun manning the phonograph & chatting and getting on well together & feeding on tea & bread & butter. That old chap is a dear trustful tolerant (though a bit bitter against the whites) kindsouled born artist nature; you don't find that sort in Australia.

Both Knocks and Grainger were pioneers in their fields.[35]

On his final tour in 1935, Grainger left a permanent imprint on New Zealand musical life: he offered a prize for an original composition, which was won by Douglas Lilburn with his tone-poem *Forest* (see chapter VIII, 1).

1918-1939

In the days before commercial flying, steamship voyages still shaped the life-style of virtuosi. A fleet of handsome ships served Australian and New Zealand ports, whose arrivals and departures made for a unique ritual. The musical monarchs who stepped ashore found their reign extended from the first shipboard interviews to the last few words gasped or shouted to the eager reporter at the gangway, whose readers wanted to hear above all, 'We *loved* New Zealand!'

Little more than an impressionistic haze comes from the artists themselves. Newspaper interviews tended to be stereotyped, unless a quarrel broke out within a company, or a hostile hotelier refused an after-concert meal, or no first-class seats appeared on the creaky railway system. Most daily press criticism expired under the weight of its own superlatives; without a Baeyertz (safely in Australia by now), most critics scarcely dared find fault, although *Music in New Zealand* occasionally expressed doubts. Artists' autobiographies usually proved models of reticence and diplomacy, with a flow of anecdotes and purple prose descriptions of the Māori, the scenery, and the adoration accorded them at concerts. They loved to be photographed in Māori costume. Clara Butt omitted to mention the feud with Baeyertz on her 1913 tour, as well as the spectacular row with a member of her company that threatened to split them asunder in 1921. Instead she tells of meeting Rupert Brooke on the ship from Auckland to Tahiti and an idyllic recital she gave there.[36]

With the arrival of the twenty-year old Jascha Heifetz and a retinue of relatives in 1921, the pattern of world tours by great artists resumed. Press publicity was overwhelming. Heifetz had made his London début in the Queen's Hall the year before, and already his name had acquired that aura of technical brilliance and perfection associated with Paganini. He performed in the main cities and smaller towns to full houses and ecstatic reviews, in an atmosphere of such excitement as to obscure the fact that his programmes were packed with brilliant,

The Russian-American violinist Jascha Heifetz. *Author's collection*

showy pieces by Paganini, Wienawski, Sarasate, and Tartini, which had become familiar through recordings. His almost habitual aloofness — he has been described as having 'a chiselled, unsmiling face, even when acknowledging an ovation' — became animated when he told a reporter of his experiences while travelling on New Zealand trains.[37] By the 1930s, visiting artists such as Szigeti, Kubelik, and Hambourg could find one or two orchestras experienced enough to work with, but most often violin concertos were heard in piano arrangements.

Williamson and Fuller also promoted vaudeville, variety, and pantomime shows, which continued to attract audiences despite the growing popularity of the silent film. In 1920, for instance, Wellington had ten cinemas but only two theatres: His Majesty's, home of Fuller's vaudeville, and the Opera House. Nevertheless, huge profits could still be made by both impresario and artist.

Singers

Rosina Buckman in 1921.
Author's collection

In 1921 Clara Butt, by now firmly established in her role as the Empire's most popular singer, returned with Kennerley Rumford to entertain overflowing halls with her 'latest successes', nearly always managing to squeeze in 'Land of Hope and Glory' — 'in response to numerous requests'. The 1922 tour by Rosina Buckman and her husband, tenor Maurice d'Oisly, had special overtones, as it was the first time a New Zealand-born singer of international renown had returned to her own country. Within half an hour of her stepping ashore from the *Ionic*, she found herself the centre of a unique welcoming party in Wellington's Concert Chamber. As she entered with the Mayor, Mr R. R. Wright, she received an ovation. A telegram arrived from the Mayor of Blenheim, her home town, the Prime Minister W. F. Massey made a short speech, and after Rosina had referred to her ever-present great wish 'to come back to my own dear people to see you all again and sing to you', the reception dissolved in emotional fervour. This set the pattern for the tour.

Other visiting singers included Madame Marguerite d'Alvarez, described as 'the world's greatest living contralto' (1922), the Russian Lydia Lipkouska (1923), and the famed Italian soprano Amelita Galli-Curci (1925). She appeared only in Auckland and Wellington, her top ticket prices being a guinea each (the average weekly wage was two guineas). She was believed to have received £1,000 for each concert. Her many acoustic recordings for the Victor Company were already familiar: Desmond Shawe-Taylor has described them as 'being among the best of their kind ever made . . . She remains, along with Caruso, McCormack and Shalyapin, among the supreme gramophone stars of the early period'.[38] Galli-Curci received an overwhelming ovation, the impact of which must have influenced her decision to return in 1932, with undiminished powers but during the great Depression, when her manager struggled to secure audiences, especially in the south.

The great Russian bass Shalyapin also gave concerts only in Auckland and

The Italian soprano
Amelita Galli-Curci.
Alexander Turnbull Library

Wellington. Like many Russian artists he had become an emigré in the 1920s, and like them embarked on extensive world tours, arriving in New Zealand in 1926 with a retinue of ten, and displaying those temperamental extremes associated in the popular eye with the most gifted of artists. An Auckland concert had to be cancelled because the singer had become voiceless 'mainly as the result of having chainsmoked for 12 hours'. The provident manager had also booked the Town Hall for the following night, which left the artist no option but to appear.[39] Earlier in the year Clara Butt and Kennerley Rumford had made their fourth and last visit.

Toti dal Monte, the celebrated Italian soprano, then with the Chicago Opera, toured in August 1926 with the baritone Augusto Beuf, the Australian pianist William James (later to be Head of Music of the Australian Broadcasting Corporation), and the flautist Stanley Baines. Then at the height of her powers, she gave complete programmes of operatic arias and duets with simplicity and charm. She was one of the last of the Italian divas to perform a style of programme which Adelina Patti had made her own.

In 1927 the notable Scottish tenor and teacher Joseph Hislop made his first tour, with Isidor Goodman as his accompanist, returning in 1931. In the same year the second New Zealand-born singer to have achieved overseas recognition swept through the country, the soprano Frances Alda (1883-1952), who as Frances Davies, had been born into an affluent Christchurch family.[40] Her voice had a pure lyrical quality, technically almost perfect, ideally suited to roles such as Gilda, Violetta, Desdemona, Manon, Louise, Mimi and Cio-Cio-San. She had previously toured Australia, apparently with mixed success, attributed chiefly to the jealousy of Melba, twenty years her senior. In Auckland she publicly announced that she had quarrelled with her pianist Max Rabinowitsch, who had accompanied Shalyapin, and she heaped praise on her new accompanist, the Aucklander Cyril Towsey. She was especially outspoken in her home city of Christchurch where she described the Australians as unmusical, their minds running on 'tin hares, horse-racing and football'.[41] Her concerts brought immense admiration and praise. Her own country stirred her feelings: 'I felt a surge of pride that I was of the same blood as the men and women who had created this.' She visited a Māori village: 'One of the Maori songs haunted me for days. Finally I wrote it down. When the first of my series of radio broadcasts began, I used a bar of that song to introduce each of my weekly programs on the air.' She ran these with great success for many years in New York.[42]

Although the 1920s proved to be vintage years for visits by great singers, notable artists toured in later years. The Australian Peter Dawson visited in 1931 with the pianist Mark Hambourg, and the Australian-born baritone John Brownlee, protégé of Melba, stayed for three months in 1933 and spoke warmly of the talents of Mary Pratt, who became a well-known New Zealand singer. In 1935 the English contralto Muriel Brunskill sang Elgar's *Sea Pictures* with the Dunedin orchestra, conducted by Alfred Walmsley. In 1936 the light opera star Gladys Moncrieff, an artist indissolubly associated with *The Maid of the Mountains*, won a popular following. The same year brought a very different artist to the country: the great Wagnerian singer, Australian-born Florence Austral, with Browning Mummery as tenor. The American tenor Richard Crooks and the Russian tenor Chostiakoff also toured. The handsome profile of the American baritone Lawrence Tibbett was already familiar through his films *New Moon, Metropolitan* and *Under Your Spell*, assuring full houses on his 1938 tour. The Russian bass Alexander Kipnis thrilled audiences the same year with his aria from Musorgsky's *Boris Godunov*. Almost the last of the travellers proved also one of the most illustrious — Lotte Lehmann, who arrived in June 1939, had been driven from Austria by the Nazi occupation the preceding year.

Impresarios had survived the Depression years only by lowering their prices — reserved seats in 1933 cost six shillings and four shillings; others sold at two and even one, around the same price as in the 1920s. Artists often had to compromise, not only by accepting lower fees, but also by widening their range. By 1935, when an upward turn in fortunes was about to begin, a new impresario had entered the field, the National Broadcasting Service, which in 1935 organized a further tour by Percy Grainger and his wife Ella. Grainger arrived as 'guest conductor, solo pianist, organist, ukelele player, composer etc': the 'etc' covered those bizarre activities for which he was renowned. On 21 November 1935, as guest conductor for the Wellington Symphony Orchestra, he played the piano in his 'Lord Peter's Stable Boy', 'Blithe Bells' (aluminium marimba: Ella Grainger), his 'Clog Dance', and 'Handel in the Strand'.[43]

Two nights later, on 23 November 1935, he presented a programme of his own music with the Wellington Harmonic Society and the Wellington Apollo Singers. One of the works was his sea shanty 'Shallow Brown', for which he summoned all the ukeleles and guitars that could be mustered, to be strummed by local musicians who also tried out the giant chimes and marimbas under Ella's direction.

Pianists

Visiting pianists also enriched the country's musical life and provided inspiration for piano teachers and their pupils. The Russian Mischa Levitski arrived with five pianos (1921, 1931); Jascha Spivakovsky, later to be part of the famed Spivakovsky-Kurtz Trio, toured in 1922; and the Polish pianist André Skalski, who had succeeded Henri Verbrugghen as conductor of the New South Wales State Orchestra, in 1923.[44]

There followed some of the world's finest artists. Moiseiwitsch, whose passion for gambling also created headlines, made the first of four tours in 1923. In 1926 Wilhelm Backhaus arrived with his own piano and his famous piano stool, which was fitted with a spirit level to make it adjustable to any stage. Paderewski returned in 1927, his stature now considerably enhanced as the former Prime Minister of Poland. His regal manners—in press advertisements he asked his audience to be seated by ten to eight—were reflected in the behaviour of his audiences. Frederick Page recalls his appearance in Christchurch:

> . . . when Paderewski walked on to the stage, the whole audience stood up in his honour as a tribute to a former premier of Poland—the poor man was taken aback. But we did hear him play the 'Moonlight', Schubert's Impromptu, Schumann's *Carnaval*, two of the Liszt Rhapsodies in the most high romantic style. There was a hint of gold about every note. Also, when on stage with a group of pieces, he modulated from the key of the previous piece to that of the next in the most extraordinary manner. These tiny improvisations were like a composition lesson.[45]

The pianist Eileen Joyce in the early 1930s. *Peter Downes collection*

'It was worth travelling the length and breadth of the country to hear him play a Chopin Mazurka with its subtle rubato rhythm and mood changes', said Ernest Empson, who found that on his 1927 visit 'his Bach and Beethoven had deeper mystical significance'.[46]

Paderewski was followed in 1927 by Ignacy Friedman (1882-1948), another gifted Polish pianist and composer who settled in Sydney in 1940; by the young Shura Cherkassky (1928); by Mark Hambourg (1931); and by Paul Vinogradoff and Moiseiwitsch again (1932). In 1933, during the depth of the Depression, Andersen Tyrer, an English pianist, arrived, who was later to play an influential

The young Yehudi Menuhin. *Peter Downes collection*

part in New Zealand musical life; and a virtuoso Australian boy pianist called Philip Hargrave. Pouishnov came in 1934, Eileen Joyce in 1936, and in 1938 the refugee Viennese pianists Diny and Paul Schramm.

The Schramms were in a special category. Paul Schramm (1892-1953),[47] a child prodigy and European concert hall virtuoso, had made a successful tour in 1937 for the National Broadcasting Service. The following year he settled in Wellington with his wife Diny, also a gifted pianist, and began teaching and performing. 'Diny looked so striking with her black frock and Belgian lace collar', recalled Tom Young, lecturer in music at the Wellington Training College. 'They played Bach's "Sheep may safely graze"—I was amazed at the tone; her technique was so glossy, so bell-like. It was the best two-piano playing ever heard in Wellington.'[48]

Violinists

The Australian violinist Daisy Kennedy toured in 1920, and the stars who followed, especially Heifetz (1921), had the compelling magnetism and appeal of the singers and pianists. Daniel Lubowski, a 'wonder-boy' aged twelve, played with a small orchestra conducted by his father in 1921, and Toscha Seidel, described as 'great' after his New York début three years earlier, came in 1922. Kreisler, with his three famous violins, limited himself to the main centres in 1925, when the seat prices were doubled; in 1927 he returned for a shorter time. The Russian-born Efrem Zimbalist (1927), who had a reputation for 'modern' works, gave disappointing programmes and his concerts were poorly attended, perhaps because his visit clashed with that of Paderewski. Jan Kubelik brought his Hindu valet and two Stradivarii with him in 1930; and in 1931 an exotic Croatian, Zlato Balokovič, arrived in his own yacht *The Northern Light* and became known as 'the sailor virtuoso'. In 1932 Szigeti played with the Wellington Symphony Orchestra, and in 1935 the boy prodigy Yehudi Menuhin visited New Zealand as part of his first world tour.

The Austrian violinist and composer Fritz Kreisler. *Author's collection*

Other artists

Larger ensembles also toured, such as Henri Verbrugghen's New South Wales State Orchestra in 1920 and 1922,[49] soloists of the Sistine Choir (1925), several opera companies, the Don Cossack Choir, and Anna Pavlova and her ballet company in 1926. The Grenadier Guards' Band (1934) revived memories of the earlier Besses o' the Barn Band at the Christchurch Exhibition of 1906-1907; the musical *White Horse Inn* enjoyed widespread acclaim in the same year. The Vienna Boys' Choir (1935) was followed by the Budapest Quartet and the Monte Carlo Russian Ballet (1937). As a final artistic gesture in the face of the disasters about to overwhelm Europe, the Covent Garden Russian Ballet made a triumphal tour in 1939, conducted by Antal Dorati.[50]

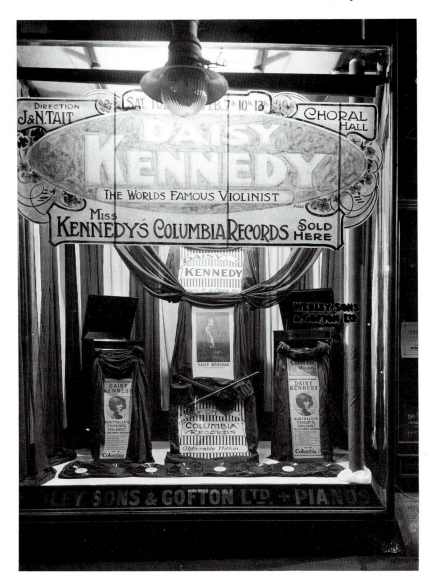

Display window in the
Christchurch musical firm
of Webley Sons & Gofton
Ltd for Daisy Kennedy's
1920 tour. *Alexander
Turnbull Library*

In 1934 *Music in New Zealand* published Mary Martin's 'All things considered',
an assessment of the advantages and disadvantages of visiting artists:

> Here, in New Zealand, in this remote corner of the earth, the appearance of
> a world-famous artist—a Levitsky, a Kreisler or a Pouishnov—causes a great
> stir in the community. We welcome them not only on account of their
> outstanding ability as performers and exponents of music, but because, coming
> fresh as they do from the art centres of Europe, they link us up with the great
> world beyond. Through them we expect to keep in touch with the latest
> developments in our art or at least that they should help us to a greater

understanding of modern and contemporary music. Unfortunately, we often expect more than we get and have to be content with a few crumbs accidentally dropped.[51]

She reminded readers of the importance of New Zealand musicians, praising local conductors and the courageous church organist, 'forging his way through a barbwire entanglement of prejudice, ignorance and popular taste to raise the standard of church music'. She applauded the work of the conscientious private teacher, and those in schools: '. . . to these and to a host of unclassified labourers whose work passes unhonoured and unsung, we look to lay the foundation of a sound musical culture in New Zealand rather than to the visits of world-famous artists'. But New Zealand needed both—the visiting artist as well as the finest work of its own musicians.

After World War II the pattern changed. Artists arrived by air, made rapid tours, and had gone almost before their personalities had time to make an impact. New Zealand's sense of isolation gradually faded and disappeared, and with it, inevitably, a little of that magic so well conveyed by the pianist Ernest Empson: 'Their impressions stay vividly with us for all time, providing us with standards, giving us courage and sometimes consolation, but always inspiration . . .'.[52]

Visiting Artists Since 1946

The formation of the Wellington Chamber Music Society in 1945 and the National Orchestra the following year, brought about extensive changes in the pattern of visiting artists. With the establishment of its Concert Section, broadcasting had gradually assumed a more active role as impresario, engaging the overseas singers associated with the centennial for instance, but the orchestra now offered new possibilities. For some time broadcasting arranged both orchestral and solo tours but gradually such events as the piano or vocal recital tended to fall out of favour, a process accelerated with the coming of television. The chamber music societies initiated their own imaginative concert schedules, working always in the closest co-operation with broadcasting, including the sharing of artists. In 1950 they became the Music Federation of New Zealand, continuing to make the best use of their close links with similar organizations elsewhere, notably Musica Viva of Australia. A few individual promoters managed to bring out artists, notably D. D. O'Connor, whose tour of the Boyd Neel Orchestra in association with the British Council in 1947 had proved such a triumph, and R. J. Kerridge who toured the pianist Julius Katchen in 1955.

For the artists themselves, world tours on ocean liners yielded to the age of the jet. Through Australia, New Zealand was now linked to the world's principal artistic circuits. Very few major musical figures have failed to make at least one visit to this country since the war. Festivals in Auckland, Wellington and Christchurch have provided a new incentive, master-classes have proliferated and that sense of isolation which persisted even through the 1950s and beyond, no longer exists. More recently, the music departments of the universities have played their own part in initiating visits, especially by overseas composers. A complete listing of the artists engaged by the Broadcasting Service, now Radio New Zealand, is given in Joy Tonks' *The New Zealand Symphony Orchestra* (1986) and of those by the Music Federation in the present author's *Into a New Key* (1985). These books make superfluous a detailed description of the kind required for the earlier years, when no such record had previously existed. They trace the highlights of successive years, with an atmosphere of increasing momentum. The electrifying impact of the Boyd Neel Orchestra and the personality of Lili Kraus, which roused poets such as Denis Glover to a fervour, could never be repeated, but the tours of Solomon, Isaac Stern, the return of the New Zealand virtuoso pianist Richard Farrell and the arrival of Victoria de los Angeles, were early post-war highlights. Since then it has been a continuing roll call of the celebrated and distinguished, not only by press reviews and archives recorded for us, but by the photographic gallery of the artists themselves which imparts to the staircases and corridors of the aged building housing the Concert Section, something of that spirit of immortality bound up with the quintessence of music itself.

Notes

[1] See chapter II, 2
[2] Letter to Margaret Taylor, Richmond-Atkinson, vol. 2, 203. See also early photograph in Main, *Auckland*, 55
[3] Letter to Ann Elizabeth Richmond, vol. 2, 387
[4] New Zealand Industrial Exhibition, 8 September 1885. In 1870 Radcliff designed a flute bearing his name, taken up by many professional flautists, notably the celebrated John Amadio, whom the author heard play on it at a ship's concert in 1961
[5] See chapter III, 6
[6] Kennedy, preface
[7] Ibid., 192-3
[8] Ibid., 295-6
[9] Ibid., 308
[10] *Shaw's Music*, vol. III, 232-3
[11] *Triad*, October 1910, 7
[12] *Triad*, 1 March 1909, 41, quoted in Murray thesis, 88
[13] See Murray thesis, 89
[14] Thomson, *ADM*, 7-8, 10
[15] *Triad*, 1 February 1908, 35-6
[16] *Triad*, October 1910, 5-6
[17] Ibid., 7-8
[18] *Triad*, April 1911, 12-14
[19] *Triad*, February 1912, 3-4
[20] See Murray thesis, 96
[21] *Triad*, 10 January 1913, 57

22 *Triad*, 10 January 1913, 9
23 *Triad*, 10 March 1914, 141, quoted in Murray thesis, 97
24 See Mansfield, *Collected Letters*, vol. 1, 24, 57ff.
25 Paderewski, 341ff.
26 Mansfield, *Collected Letters*, vol. 1, 64-5
27 *Triad*, October 1911, 50-1
28 *Collected Letters*, vol. 1, 61-2
29 See chapter V, 2
30 See chapter III, 2
31 The company also included Jacques Jacobs (violin), W. A. Peterkin (bass-baritone), and Benno Scherek (accompanist and tour manager)
32 Bird, 85
33 Bird, 128. For Maggie Papakura's subsequent career see chapter VI
34 Bird, 16
35 'The incunabula of instantaneous ethnomusicological sound recordings, 1890-1910: a preliminary list', in Kassler and Stubington (eds) *Problems and Solutions: Occasional Essays in Musicology presented to Alice M. Moyle.* Sydney (1984) 322-55
36 See Ponder, 250
37 See Boris Schwarz in *New Grove*, vol. 8, 435. Julia Millen's RNZ talks, 'Star Spangled Years', give fuller details of tours between the wars. I gratefully acknowledge their help in writing this section
38 *New Grove*, vol. 7, 126
39 Millen, RNZ scripts, nos. 2, 4
40 See Millen, nos. 1, 7; Alda, 24; Pleasants, 272ff.
41 Millen, nos. 1, 8
42 Alda 274-5. Biographical information from *Evening Post* obituary, 10 September 1952; *Evening Post*, 18 December 1954; Millen, nos. 1, 7ff. See also Adrienne Simpson 'This country may well be proud of her.' *MNZ* April 1982 36ff.
43 The programme also included John Alden Carpenter's Concertino, *To a Nordic Princess*, composed for and played at Grainger's marriage to Ella Viola Strom at the Hollywood Bowl in California on 9 August 1928, and Tchaikovsky's Piano Concerto No. 1
44 The *Triad* quoted his successful NZ tours as examples of a superior musical culture: Skalski had found himself the centre of innumerable controversies in Sydney
45 Page, 45
46 RNZ Sound Archives, Timaru, recorded 3 April 1960
47 See Appendix: Music in Education
48 Interview with author, 1977
49 See chapter V, 3
50 See John Gray's account of the Budapest Quartet tour, with vocal interludes by Mary Pratt, in Thomson *Into a New Key*, 21
51 Martin, M. 'All Things Considered', *MNZ*, 10 August 1934
52 RNZ Sound Archives, Timaru

2 'Round the world on wings of song': the Sheffield Choir 1911

The spirit of Edwardian music-making—and the spirit of Empire—coincided in the spectacular world tour by Sir Henry Coward's Sheffield Musical Union in 1911. Coward had acquired his musical skills through the tonic sol-fa system, and had formed his own association which had developed into the Sheffield Musical Union, one of Britain's most illustrious choirs. In 1911, Coronation year, 200 songsters travelled more than 40,000 miles through three continents with a message of 'Reciprocity'.

The tour was organized with panache and military precision. Ten days before embarking, each member of the choir was given a 'Book of Instructions' of seventy-six pages, with a map of the world showing every place to be visited and the name of each steamboat. The allotted berth of each member was specified, together with names of hotels, hosts, and hostesses. Coloured labels for each part of their luggage were supplied—first sopranos light red, second sopranos dark red, first contraltos light yellow, second contraltos dark yellow, etc. There was information on rehearsals, usually limited to one a week, getting on and off the concert platform—'*place aux dames* on all occasions please gentlemen'—and 'An infallible method of preventing sea and other sicknesses caused by oscillation'. Each member received an official badge which proclaimed that he or she was one of 'the elect of the earth', with an assurance that return fares had been paid and they would not be 'left stranded on a distant shore'. Five golden sovereigns for each singer were to cover incidental expenses.

Before their departure, a Grand Final Concert-Rehearsal was held in the Albert Hall, Sheffield, on Saturday 11 March to 'set the seal of preparedness on the choir for the responsible task of upholding the honour of the Homeland throughout our "far-flung Empire"'. Each ticket-holder could request a piece from the choir's repertoire of some 160 works. Before this marathon they adjourned to the Cutler's Hall 'to partake of a banquet generously provided by the ever-genial and greatly esteemed Master Cutler . . . Fortified in the body by the banquet and exalted in spirit by the many rhetorical bouquets which had been handed to us, we returned to the Albert Hall, braced up for running the gauntlet of 2,000 critics who knew "all the tricks of the game". . .'[1]

When the choir arrived at the Princess Dock in Liverpool and saw their ship RMS *Victorian* lying before them, they burst spontaneously into song with 'Now my heart upbounds' from Elgar's *Bavarian Highlands*. Having sung their way across North America and enjoyed tumultuous receptions in Sydney, they boarded the tiny 4000-ton *Wimmera* (their own *Zealandia* having broken down). After the return of two drunken stowaways to a shore boat, they ran into a cyclonic

The Sheffield Choir arrives in Montreal in 1908 on their first American tour. *Author's collection*

Sir Henry Coward, conductor and founder of the Sheffield Musical Union. *Author's collection*

storm, the worst the captain had known for twenty years. As the tempest increased, the captain gathered as many as were still able to walk into the saloon to sing 'Eternal father strong to save', and after a short prayer, committed them all to the hands of God. Around midnight the cyclone burst upon them, the ship's head was put to the wind, and she was allowed to drift. 'Meanwhile the roaring waves, which rose higher and higher still, burst through all the barriers, destroyed a porthole, flooded every cabin, lifted portmanteaux, handbags, hats, clothes etc., from their moorings, and sent them swish-swashing from one end of the cabin to the other . . . The boat deck and bridge deck were washed away, the ironwork being twisted as though it were paper . . . The captain himself said it was a case of "touch and go", and it was a good thing we were all too ill to realize the danger we were in . . .'[2] The *Wimmera* hurricane proved the most traumatic episode of the whole tour.[3]

A crowd of people had been waiting for the choir on Auckland wharf on Sunday afternoon, but on hearing news of the storm, returned next morning to give them a rapturous welcome and disperse them to their billets. That same night, in a large wool shed ('by permission of the Customs'), they sang Elgar's *Dream of Gerontius* to 'an enthralled audience of about 4,000'. The Auckland Town Hall was not yet completed. Although Maughan Barnett had previously performed the work with the Wellington Professional Orchestra and Choral Society in 1910, it was still virtually unknown. The Sheffield Choir's performance revealed it as a masterpiece. C. N. Baeyertz, however, felt unable to decide whether it was indeed a great work of art.[4] On Wednesday they sang their miscellany of 'Empire Music', and the following night, after a performance of *Elijah*, caught the 11.30 p.m. night train to Wellington, which gave them more surprises. With visions of American Pullmans uppermost in their minds, they found they were expected to sit bolt upright in narrow compartments for most of the journey. Only two sleeping carriages were attached, and Sir Henry Coward himself, fetched up in the luggage van, was 'reposing' on the case of a double bass. By 2.30 p.m. the next day they had reached Palmerston North, where they lunched in the A & P Association Hall. After a journey that had lasted eighteen hours, they eventually arrived in Wellington. That same evening they sang *Gerontius* again to an audience of over 3,000, in the presence of the Governor, Lord Islington. Next day they returned to Palmerston North and found the whole town *en fête* — 'Five concerts in two days and three evenings, under such conditions, was a great feat', wrote Coward laconically.

Gerontius was clearly the highlight: 'such wonderful choral singing has never before been heard under the Southern Cross'. The Bach Motet for unaccompanied double chorus, 'Sing ye to the Lord', showed the choir at its most impressive: 'They finished, as they began, in perfect time and intonation. The effect on the vast audience was electrical. It lifted them off their feet so to speak.' Dr Harris's *Pan* was 'pretty but it is also patchy and disjointed. It is ephemeral and lacking in distinction.' The *Free Lance* had carried a full-page caricature of Dr Harris as the modern Pied Piper, leading an entourage of local celebrities, a feather in his cap bearing the words 'Musical Reciprocity'. The Coronation Empire Programme found little favour — Sullivan's *The Golden Legend* would have made more sense. *Elijah* passed muster, but only just, for the inclusion of 200 local voices was clearly a sad mistake.

After the Wellington concerts the choir boarded the *Mararoa* for Lyttelton. The ship was so crowded that the men had to go into the hold: 'The mere mention of the word "hold" sent a thrill of horror through them', but they found it to be clean and airy and better than many of the bunks. Dr Charles Harris, sponsor of the tour, felt obliged to offer anyone who felt aggrieved one gold sovereign — about a hundred changed hands.

In Christchurch they received a particularly warm welcome: Dr Bradshaw invited them to his weekly organ recital, and slides of New Zealand were shown in Her Majesty's Theatre. The choir repeated *Gerontius* in the Drill Hall, and at their last concert, joined by the local choir, they sang *Elijah* in an unheated hall. The singers wore overcoats and cloaks, while the audience wrapped themselves in rugs with hot water bottles: 'What we lost in artistic finish, was counterbalanced by power and vitality.' As they passed through Timaru by train, *en route* to Dunedin, they stopped for morning tea in a large marquee erected by the Corporation. A great crowd had assembled, filling the hillside, the railway station, and every position of vantage — 'we sang four bright pieces right off the reel and sent the crowd into the seventh heaven'.

At Dunedin railway station a huge gathering welcomed them vociferously. The Town Hall had burnt down, so they gave their concerts in the Tramway Shed: the cars were removed each night, the raised tramlines and sunken repair wells covered with wooden flooring, and seats, chairs, and forms carried in

The 1911 souvenir programme. *Author's collection*

by specially hired labourers at enormous cost. The Festival Orchestra (prepared by Johann Wielaert and Maughan Barnett), which had accompanied them on their journeys from Auckland, was now about to leave them. The choir boarded a ship for Bluff and Invercargill, and as they left the wharf the orchestra burst into the demon theme from *Gerontius*, ending 'with a truly demoniacal "Ha! Ha!"'[5]

The Sheffield choir set new standards of choral singing through its discipline, ensemble, and tonal qualities. Perhaps its greatest effect was on the choirs of Christchurch.[6] It also made *Gerontius* a living reality. But the *Triad* did not let the management off lightly. In an article headed 'Brilliant work and deplorable mistakes', it slated an administration which imposed such appalling travelling burdens on its singers:

> the choir must have been in some degree jaded on its every appearance in Wellington . . . If any theatrical manager worked his people so, there would be a public scandal. These gentle Sheffield folk may be meek enough to tolerate anything, if only they are permitted to sing to a house of a thousand guineas: but Australians would not stand that sort of driving for a day.[7]

Yet the singing was 'superb':

> It must have been a revelation in choral singing to those whose experience has been entirely of New Zealand choruses . . . The sopranos sang as one soprano, the altos as one alto; and so with the tenors and basses. And that, of course, is the acme of effective part singing . . . This choir is almost perfect in tone-quality and balance, the things that make for excellence in choral singing.[8]

But the worst criticism was reserved for the entrepreneurial perfidies of Dr Harris, who had already been been taken to task by the *New Zealand Times* and *Evening Post* for foisting on the public his own 'reminiscent and tawdry' music. 'The endurance of those martyrs of Sheffield is remarkable. They sang like larks.'

The final word might lie with the anonymous 'Footlights' in the *Free Lance*:

> This visit will be productive of lasting results in our musical evolution as a people. It has brought home to us, as no other previous other event ever did, the glorious potentialities of choral music and our own crude deficiencies and shortcomings. It has set up a lofty standard for our emulation. It has created a strong desire to impose and enlarge our musical resources.[9]

Notes

1 Coward, 16-17
2 Ibid., 129-30
3 The ship itself had a tragic end: in June 1918 it hit a mine planted by the German raider *Wolf* outside Auckland. It sank with the loss of twenty-seven lives, including the captain, chief officer, and chief steward
4 *Triad*, December 1910, 17-18
5 Coward, 144. See whole chapter on Australasia
6 A throaty acoustic recording of their 'Hallelujah' Chorus from *Messiah* is held in the RNZ Archives at Timaru; later electrical recordings of the early 1930s give an excellent impression of their power
7 *Triad*, 10 August 1911, 9-12, probably the best assessment of the choir on this tour
8 Baeyertz criticized the pronunciation of the soloists, the inclusion of local voices in the choir, and the conducting of Coward, especially his tempi. His criticisms were subsequently reinforced by Julius Lemmer, Balling's successor at the Nelson School of Music
9 *Free Lance*, July 1911

3 Henri Verbrugghen and the New South Wales State Orchestra 1920 and 1922

In 1910 the Sheffield Choir brought international choral standards to New Zealand. Ten years later the New South Wales State Orchestra, founded and conducted by a fiery, highly articulate, Belgian-born, Glasgow-baptized, and London-famed violinist, Henri Verbrugghen, proved to be one of the outstanding ensembles of its time, unequalled until Sir Eugene Goossens' regime with the Sydney Symphony Orchestra in the 1950s. Before Verbrugghen became director of the new Conservatorium in Sydney in 1915, he had won renown as a violinist, his achievements including the first British performance of Sibelius's Violin Concerto.

Verbrugghen also conducted the Glasgow Choral Union, and founded the Quartet which played under his name. His Beethoven Festival of 1914 with the London Symphony Orchestra, followed by the three B's (Bach-Beethoven-Brahms) the following year, established his prowess as a conductor. 'He is a little, dark, vivacious man, overflowing with music and energy', wrote the French soprano Antonio Dolores.[1] A classicist in his musical tastes and a perfectionist, he persuaded the NSW State Government to bring out the members of his Quartet, and on this foundation he created his orchestra, at first on an amateur basis, then fully professional. With it he repeated his London Beethoven festival, and after successful tours to Melbourne and Adelaide, he looked towards New Zealand.

He engaged the New Zealand musician H. Gladstone Hill to find guarantors, set up a committee, and arrange an advance subscription scheme, so that most concerts were sold out before the tour started. Five hundred guarantors put up £10,000, a sum which was never called upon. Gladstone Hill cabled to Sydney: 'Enthusiasm unbounded'. With Verbrugghen as principal conductor, Alfred Hill as deputy (as well as a member of the viola section), and Madame Goossens-Viceroy as soloist, an extensive tour was planned.

Nearly 100 players arrived in Auckland, by far the largest number of instrumentalists to have been heard there. The high spirits of the orchestra not only reflected their artistic confidence, but the fact that they had made a profit of over £2500 that year, a virtually unheard of state of affairs, for most European and American orchestras depended upon patrons and guarantors.

The tour opened in the Auckland Town Hall with Beethoven's Overture *Leonora No. 3* and Tchaikovsky's Sixth Symphony (a Verbrugghen favourite for such occasions). The *Star* on 8 January 1920 commented on 'the bright

Henri Verbrugghen
conducting the New South
Wales State Orchestra in
Martin Place, Sydney,
during World War One.
Mitchell Library, Sydney

penetrating tone and rich quality . . . the clean simultaneous attack . . . the marvellous vigour and precision'. The orchestra was at the top of its form: 'One of the most remarkable and finished concerts ever held in the Dominion.' The *Herald* wrote of new standards being set: 'For once in a way Parnassus was reached in a programme which swayed many emotions before a memorable evening was brought to a conclusion.'[2]

Thus it continued: in Hamilton the following night the concert was described as '. . . the greatest event in the musical history of the town', and after the reception Verbrugghen announced that 'New Zealand is going to kill me with kindness'. Alfred Hill wrote to his daughter Isolde in Sydney: 'I have never heard them play better. Mr Verbrugghen has also excelled himself.'[3] The orchestra proceeded on its triumphal tour, giving over thirty concerts, with several performances by the Verbrugghen Quartet. One of these took place before a Māori audience in a meeting-house between Napier and Hastings, where men, women, and children sat cross-legged on the floor and the members of the orchestra listened from outside through the windows.[4]

Verbrugghen himself wished to make his orchestra 'Australasian' in concept and practice. This theme found expression in several New Zealand editorials, such as that of the Christchurch *Press* of 3 February 1920, which urged those in responsible musical positions to confer with Verbrugghen and form a deputation to wait on the Prime Minister. It noted that with the formation of a Conservatorium, Sydney now offered opportunities lacking in New Zealand and also that in 1907 the Christchurch Exhibition Orchestra had been disbanded and not been retained: 'Opportunity knocks again at our door, and should not this time be denied.'

The tour brought in a gross profit of £11,894.2.6 which, after the deduction of expenses, yielded a net amount of £111.13.8. This money was lodged in a trust account in Wellington for 'the encouragement of music in New Zealand'.[5]

Before the second tour of 1922, the future of both Verbrugghen and his orchestra was called into question, as the NSW State Government quarrelled bitterly with their conductor over the question of fees, holding that his conductorship was part of his Conservatorium directorate. The orchestra had by now become a national Australian institution, as its Prospectus of 16 May 1921 announced: 'Great orchestras are educational institutions. Ours is a great orchestra.' The Government nevertheless prevaricated, and the struggle assumed epic proportions as an inspired artist pitted himself against a cautious, unimaginative state bureaucracy. Verbrugghen's health suffered, but despite medical advice he decided to keep faith with his backers and audiences and took the orchestra once more to New Zealand, believing that the change of scene and the bracing climate would carry him through.

He had brought a slightly smaller ensemble than before, but he felt it had greater musical stature. The orchestra played in Wellington for *seven* nights: 'A SUPERB BAND / HENRY VERBRUGGHEN ACCLAIMED' wrote the *Dominion* of 23 January 1922. The orchestra is 'a combination which creates in everyone . . . a feeling of joyous exhilaration, born of the spirit of exaltation in which the music is interpreted and played'. The Wagner evening was described as 'a revelation'.[6] On 24 January they played Alfred Hill's *Tangi* and Verbrugghen's orchestration of *Waiata Poi*. The Wellington Artillery Band created another sensation when it took part in the Tchaikovsky's *1812 Overture*. 'There is a spell and an enchantment in Verbrugghen's baton', concluded the *Dominion*.[7] Popular concerts packed the halls, whereas Wagner and Elgar nights saw many empty chairs. Nevertheless, it was another triumphal progress. After a *Messiah* with the Royal Christchurch Musical Society, the tour ended with a popular concert in the Christchurch King Edward Barracks, when 5000 seats were offered at low prices—many had to stand. Verbrugghen was presented with a warm travelling rug, and Alfred Hill, on behalf of the players, gave him a diamond tie-pin in the form of the Southern Cross. Verbrugghen, in reply, said: 'The Orchestra is unique in the world.'[8]

The tour ended with a deficit of £2,019.9.6, small enough, but an amount quickly noted by the NSW State Government, which still owed Verbrugghen £720 for thirty-six concerts at £20 each. After further acrimonious exchanges, Verbrugghen resigned from Sydney and accepted the conductorship of the

Minneapolis Symphony Orchestra. His beloved NSW State Orchestra was eventually disbanded. 'Exit Verbrugghen', wrote A. L. Kelly in the *Triad* of 10 January 1923: '. . . he showed himself over and over again a big man; an unselfish man; a man of vision and courage; a civilised man.' His tours had provided a touchstone of what an orchestra might be.

Notes

1 *Sydney Morning Herald*, 3 July 1915
2 *NZ Herald*, 8 January 1920
3 See relevant chapters in Thomson, *ADM*
4 The orchestra visited Auckland, Hamilton, New Plymouth, Hawera, Wanganui, Palmerston North, Hastings, Napier, Wellington, Christchurch, Timaru, Dunedin, and Invercargill
5 In the late 1950s the original sum, with accumulated interest, was handed over to the Music Department of Victoria University of Wellington to provide awards for students
6 *Dominion*, 24 January 1922
7 *Dominion*, 30 January 1922
8 *Lyttelton Times*, 15 February 1922

V

Musical media

1 Silent film music

Ten months after the first public screening of moving pictures by the Lumière Brothers in Paris, Messrs L. H. Lohr and Edwin Geach presented a short programme of films on 13 October 1896 at the Auckland Opera House. During the following decade, movies, as they came to be called, increased in popularity. New Zealand audiences saw rush-hour scenes on London Bridge, traffic on Broadway, the 1896 Derby, the Melbourne Cup, and Queen Victoria's Diamond Jubilee. Boer War scenes aroused patriotic fervour, and crowds flocked to see a film of Queen Victoria's funeral in 1901, as they had in London.

An early film poster.
Alexander Turnbull Library

In the earliest silent films, music might be provided by a pianist, a small ensemble, or a full orchestra, depending on the nature of the programme and the resources of the entrepreneur. Music not only gave depth and a context to the action, but also covered the noise of the projection machine. Early films were very short, being interspersed between music and 'acts'.[1] T. J. West's picture shows in 1905 featured the Brescians, an orchestral group with singers, dressed in Italian peasant costumes. Henry Hayward (1866-1945), later to achieve fame as an entrepreneur, acted as the Brescians' Advance Manager. His brother, Rudall Hayward, who became the outstanding film-maker of the early part of the century, sang baritone. Their programme, 'of immaculate refinement', contained 'nothing base or suggestive, nothing blood-curdling or vulgar', just 'the world day by day', 'the unseen world', 'the earth's beauty spots', and 'comedy pictures' with 'refined fun'.

By 1914 Hayward's Pictures had fully established themselves, and the flautist Signor A. P. Truda led a Wellington orchestra which accompanied such epics as *The Last Days of Pompeii*. Many kinds of music were re-scored, adapted, and then classified by genre in catalogues, so that Schubert's 'Unfinished' Symphony might appear as a 'light, flowing agitato' and Beethoven overtures might be suitable for tree-felling, aeroplane dives, or cannibal island escapes. Signor Truda's orchestra played such works as Suppé's Overture *Raymond* and Brahms' Hungarian Dance No. 2 as an Entr'acte. Max Reinhardt's film *Miracle* had a grand augmented orchestra and a choir of trained voices to perform Humperdinck's music. Both Haywards and Fullers, in intense rivalry, established a chain of cinemas throughout New Zealand. In 1914 they combined as New

The Regent Theatre in
Wellington, 1926.
Alexander Turnbull Library

Zealand Picture Supplies Ltd and Fuller-Hayward Theatres, with sixty theatres
valued at £350,000.[2]

In the 1920s cinema orchestras enjoyed their heyday. Edith Lang and George
West's *Musical Accompaniment of Moving Pictures* shows how skilled musicians
had become.[3] A typical Lang and West synopsis might run: 'Rose feels that
these letters are too sacred for the eyes of the outside world (*Massenet's Élégie
leading into an agitated strain*); Rose realizes how repulsive her present husband
is to her and how much she still loves her lost hero (*Suggest the inner struggle
of Rose by treating main love motive in minor mode, breaking it up in short phrases
which successively rise in pitch and finally lead into a calmer transition*); . . . her health
gradually fails and they decide to send her to England to recuperate (*Suggestion
of the Hindu theme leading into 'Home Sweet Home'*); Rose returns to England
to the home of her first husband (*'I Hear You Calling Me'*) . . .'

Musical cue-sheets arrived only a few days before the film. Many a silent
film musician must have welcomed Lang and West's advice: 'Tuck your music
under your arm and walk into the orchestra pit with a firm tread and a confident
heart. There is no time now for any misgivings . . .' The English-born musician
L. D. Austin began his antipodean career in Australia, playing the piano for
an outdoor cinema at Manly, near Sydney. When a southerly bluster blew up
and the music ascended into the air, the orchestra stopped playing, but Austin
continued. This gift for improvization led to an offer in New Zealand as pianist
in 'A Grand Symphony Orchestra', consisting of cornet, violin, and piano, which
played at the old skating-rink at Vivian Street in Wellington. Here, on crowded
nights, the screen was placed in the middle of the rink and patrons sat on both

Programme, printed on silk
for the opening of the
King's Theatre, Wellington
on 16 March 1910.
Alexander Turnbull Library

SOUVENIR PROGRAMME.

"Her Eyes are Homes of Silent Prayer."

THE KING'S THEATRE,

WEDNESDAY, 16th MARCH, 1910.

The orchestra of the Paramount Theatre in Wellington. *Alexander Turnbull Library*

sides, those on the wrong side holding up mirrors to the screen to reverse the image. Austin's career reached its peak as Musical Director of the De Luxe Theatre (later the Embassy), which opened in Wellington in 1924 with Cecil B. De Mille's *The Ten Commandments*.[4] The De Luxe had 'simply wonderful' acoustics—'you'd have sworn there was an orchestra of 30 or 40'. The repertoire of the thirteen or so players included Wagner's *Siegfried Idyll* and the March from *Tannhäuser*. The 'Mighty Wurlitzer Organ', which succeeded the orchestra, survived at least until the 1940s, rising dramatically from the depths. It was fully equipped with all the devices of the time, including a tremulous *vox humana*.[5]

H. Gladstone Hill took over the Wellington Paramount Orchestra in 1927, when the management made a bold attempt to increase patronage by providing musical programmes of the highest quality. The orchestra of nineteen, billed as 'the largest picture theatre orchestra in the Dominion', played for a trial period. 'It was an entertainment de-luxe', wrote Gladstone Hill, 'but it was not what the public wanted'. In February 1928 it was disbanded.[6]

In Auckland several cinemas, such as the Tivoli, Lyric, and Everybody's, had orchestras. Henry Shirley, a pioneer cinema pianist, played at the Britannia:

. . . there was no way of seeing the film before arranging the music. In fact, the evening programme was sometimes held up awaiting the arrival of the next can of film from some cinema on the other side of town showing the same feature. My solution to the problem was to lay out four or five piles of music on the top of the piano, each one suitable for a different 'mood'. It was quite a trick to read the music at sight, follow the picture and conduct when needed with the right hand. If there was a quick scene change from say, children playing to a 'baddie' lurking round the corner, I had to grab a number from the 'suspense' pile, throw left and right a violin and trumpet part and try to keep some sort of sound coming from the piano until we were ready to start together again. With a musical vocabulary of only a handful of chords, I eventually worked out formulas that would carry me through a three-hour programme of assorted love and hate, humour and horror. It was one way of learning composition.[7]

A. J. Bünz left the Christchurch Orchestral Society in 1921 to conduct the Crystal Palace 'Symphony Orchestra', which, with Howard Moody's 'Liberty Quality Orchestra', Everybody's 'Select Orchestra' under W. J. Bellingham, and 'The Grand Theatre Orchestra', won respectful reviews. 'For one winter in the 1920s, my grandfather took me every Wednesday night to the Grand, irrespective of the film, to hear the piano quartet', recalled Walter Harris. 'I suppose this was the first chamber music I ever heard live.'[8] Harris remembers one artist in particular, Howard Moody:

I used to go to the Liberty especially to hear him and marvelled at his ingenuity. He usually had a glass of beer at his right, watched the screen and let his hands wander, sometimes brilliantly over the keys. It was said that he was sacked after a screening (with a number of beers), of the life of Christ. At the resurrection he joyfully played 'For he's a jolly good fellow' to the anger of dismal Christians.[9]

'Within 15 years a whole new branch of musicmaking was born, reached a splendid maturity and suddenly died', writes Henry Shirley. 'Thousands of musicians were needed in a hurry so music teaching flourished. Everything connected with the production of music (composing, arranging, publishing and retailing) enjoyed a boom. Nobody doubted that it would last forever.' All over New Zealand local pianists found themselves becoming celebrities.[10]

In the 1920s orchestral players received from 25 shillings to 45 shillings a week: the cinema syndicates themselves became very prosperous. After complaints, the Arbitration Court fixed a Musicians' Award. Cinema proprietors gradually based their payments on merit rather than statute. L. D. Austin's salary during the final phase of the silent film orchestra reached four figures — 'but there were several others, chiefly foreign importations, who flew much higher'.[11]

At the end of 1927 Al Jolson uttered his historic words 'You ain't heard nothin' yet!' and proceeded to sing 'Mammy', in the first important sound film, *The Jazz Singer*, which spelled out, however crudely, the death of the silent film and the dispersal of the musicians associated with it. Effective sound films followed. Alfred Hitchcock's *Blackmail* (1929) introduced synchronized music, and by 1931, in Selznick's *Symphony of Six Million*, Max Steiner had scored the complete film.

The dissolution of the cinema orchestras constituted a major disaster for musicians. Hundreds lost their positions in the midst of the world Depression. Musicians formed tea-room ensembles, played on the cross-Tasman ships, or changed their jobs.[12]

Today a new and younger audience flocks to hear old-time silent film pianists and their contemporary counterparts. Classics of the silent cinema have been revived and the music re-recorded. The New Zealand Film Archive has engaged a resident composer, a position held by Dorothy Buchanan in the 1980s. 'The silent film at its best had by 1928 attained singular completeness as a human experience', wrote the cinema historian Richard Griffiths. 'To walk into a darkened theatre, to focus upon a bright rectangle of moving light, to listen somewhat below the level of consciousness to music which was no longer good or bad in itself but merely in relation to what was on the screen . . . this was an experience complete and unique . . .'[13]

Notes

[1] Hayward, Bruce W. and Selwyn, 2. Early in the century J. C. Williamson's 'Bio-Tableau' showed the Russo-Japanese War or 'A Day with the Hop Pickers in Kent'.

[2] Henry Hayward arrived in New Zealand at the age of thirty-nine to manage West's pictures and the Brescians, a family company who performed opera, comic opera, etc.

[3] Lang, E. and West, G. *Musical Accompaniment of Moving Pictures, a practical manual for pianists and organists.* Boston 1920

[4] For anecdotes concerning this, see Thomson, J. M. 'Music in the dark', *NZL*, 22 February 1957, 7; also Austin, L. D. 'Reminiscences of the silent cinema', *MNZ*, 10 January, 1932, 171-4; and broadcast scripts 'Flickering Shadows', RNZ

[5] It eventually went to Hutt Valley High School, 'but without some of its gadgets'; W. B. Harris, letter to author from London, 21 February 1987

[6] Gladstone Hill, 'Autobiography', MS Papers 1723, ATL

[7] Shirley, 56-7

[8] Letter to author, 21 February 1987; also *Lyttelton Times*, 3 March 1924; and see Frederick Page's account of Christchurch cinema orchestras in *A Musician's Journal*

[9] Letter to author, 21 February 1987

[10] Such as Miss Spanhake at the Lyric Theatre, Helensville

[11] Austin, 'Reminiscences'

[12] In 1957 the author interviewed Archie Jerome, formerly musical director of the King's Theatre in Wellington, who was then running a floral shop. His music scores were kept tidily at the back

[13] Robinson, D. 'Rediscovering the age of the golden silents'. *The Times*, London, 26 November 1982

2 The rise of the gramophone and player piano

The gramophone

'. . . imagine me today carrying the Graphophone—three packets of records, and the cylinder home in the tram—It was worth the carrying though—when I heard the Beethoven Serenade.'[1] Thus wrote Katherine Mansfield in 1907 to the Trowell family in London, of her first experience of a machine by then firmly established throughout the world. The graphophone was the invention of Alexander Graham Bell and his assistant Charles Tainter, working in Washington. It had to compete for public approval with Thomas Alva Edison's 'perfected phonograph', developed a little earlier.[2] Edison's invention had aroused great excitement in New Zealand. In 1879, two years after he had first demonstrated its prototype, the *Lyttelton Times* announced: 'Sudden disappearance of 2,000 citizens. Where! Why, to hear Edison's wonderful phonograph speak, sing, laugh, whistle and play Levy's cornet solos.'[3] On 17 March 1891 the *Evening Post* advertised

Graphophone advertised for seven guineas in the *NZ Illustrated Magazine, October 1903*

> the brilliant and unequivocal success of Mr Edison's latest phonograph which is nightly attracting crowded and delighted audiences. Tonight at 8 o'clock, Professor Douglas Archibald, MA, Oxon, will deliver an intensely interesting lecture, illustrated by limelight views, and exhibit the incredible capabilities of Edison's astounding talking machine . . . By means of the Phonograph, human speech may be preserved for ever, and the voices of the living and the dead will mingle in futurity.[4]

Meanwhile a third contender for the public purse had arrived in an invention of Emile Berliner (1851-1929), a German from Hanover who had emigrated to the USA and taught himself enough of acoustics and electricity to invent a microphone. His 'gramophone' differed from the wax cylinders previously employed in that it used a flat disc, which gradually increased in size from seven inches to twelve by 1903, the speed of its rotation becoming standardized at 78 r.p.m. around 1918. These three systems struggled for supremacy. By 1902 three American companies marketed talking machines: Edison's supplied only cylinder instruments, the Victor Talking Machine Company only disc instruments, and the Columbia Phonograph Company supplied both. Peripatetic lecturers extolled the virtues of one system over another and arranged programmes of vocal and instrumental music to drive home their message. On 9 December 1903 P. H. Bohanna, Sydney agent for the Gramophone Company of London, wrote from Dunedin to his office: 'You can scarcely imagine the keen competition there is in everything over here . . .'[5]

W. Golledge of Nelson demonstrates his tin foil phonograph. *William Main collection*

Balting's Phonograph
Parlour, Hardy Street,
Nelson. *F. N. Jones,*
Alexander Turnbull Library

This early 'acoustic' period of recording lasted from 1877 until 1925, when electrical techniques took over. Artists sang and played into large horns to funnel the sound energy to the diaphragm/needle assembly at the other end. Recording sessions became fraught with difficulties as musicians moved backwards and forwards to bring themselves within range. Some instruments failed to register — tubas might replace string basses, for instance.

Records began to arrive. In 1905 the Talkeries of Wellington advertised that 15,000 had just been delivered: in November they demonstrated them at a 'Talkeries All Star Concert'.[6] By 1907 a considerable repertoire had been recorded, much of it stemming from the efforts of the Gramophone Company, founded in 1898 in London and inspired by Emile Berliner. In December 1908 the Talkeries had records of Melba, Tetrazzini, Caruso, and Lauder, and in the same year afternoon concerts demonstrated their prowess. In 1909 Beggs of Wellington installed a Phono Studio suitable for hearing great singers on record.[7] Early recording artists became well known throughout New Zealand; this familiarity was vital for the impresario planning a tour. In May 1911 the Dresden Piano Company advertised gramophones ranging in price from £4 to £50. By 1912 one could have bought Tetrazzini on a pink label for 12s 6d singing 'Home Sweet Home', with 'individual touches, the suave cantabile, and the original finish to the shake'.[8] Melba appeared on her own exclusive lilac label.

Recording companies were set up in Australia. In 1925 Mr Manson of the Gramophone Company of England established a factory at Erskineville in New South Wales, and the following year the first Australian-pressed records were

Edison Standard
Phonograph c. 1906, with
a two-minute gold-
moulded record and dust-
cleaning brush. *William
Main collection*

produced—the Empire Day address to boys and girls by King George V and
Queen Mary, with a speech on Sportsmanship by the Prince of Wales. Manson
had earlier recorded Prime Minister Massey at Hayes, Middlesex, on 'The British
Empire'; Peter Dawson sang 'God defend New Zealand' on the reverse. A copy
was lodged with the British Museum, where it remained untouched until 1925.[9]

Most homes now possessed a gramophone. An advertisement in the *Evening
Post* of 22 May 1926 stated that during the month 3,064 gramophones had
been sold. HMV instruments ranged from a portable at £11 to a cabinet model
for £67. Recitals demonstrated the qualities of the latest recording innovations.[10]
Developments took a decisive step forward on 14 October 1926 when the
Columbia Gramophone Company opened a recording studio at Homebush,
NSW, directed by Gil Dech, who worked closely with the Australian light
opera singer, Gladys Moncrieff.[11] The first Columbia records appeared around
Christmas.[12] In 1930 Beggs advertised a new HMV gramophone with an
International Horn, and in March 1931 HMV issued a recording of Gladys

Popular portable wind-up gramophone of the 1930s. *Alexander Turnbull Library*

Watkins, Wellington's first carillonist, playing 'Annie Laurie' and 'The Bells of St Mary's'. These she recorded in Hyde Park, London, where the new bells were exhibited before being sent out to New Zealand. The carillon itself was opened on Anzac Day the following year.

Pioneer recordings by New Zealand composers and artists included those of Alfred Hill for HMV on a London visit in 1926: 'Waiata Poi,' *Tangi*, the lake music from *Hinemoa*, and 'Waiata Maori,' with the Mayfair Orchestra.[13] New Zealand performers were invited to Columbia's Homebush studios, notably Robert Lane (Tex Morton) from Nelson, whose later hits included 'Just Plain Folk', 'If You Please Miss, Give Me Heaven', and 'The Stockman's Last Bed'. Although popular music composers subsequently succeeded in having their music recorded by a variety of means, including forming their own companies, the serious composer remained out in the cold until the establishment of Kiwi/Pacific records under the direction of Tony Vercoe. Since then they have recorded much of Lilburn's music, beginning with *Landfall in Unknown Seas* in 1959 and including early works and electronic music. Without Kiwi/Pacific records, Tony Vercoe, and sponsoring bodies, especially the Composers' Foundation, New Zealand music would have been locked into a frustrating isolation. Kiwi/Pacific in 1989 added 'International' to its title and under new direction embarked on a policy of issuing compact discs. In 1990 the Auckland Philharmonia issued its first CDs, two of which were of New Zealand compositions.

The player piano

On 7 November 1900 Paderewski wrote to the Orchestrelle Company of London: 'Gentlemen — I desire to order another Pianola for use in my residence. Will you kindly select an instrument in rosewood and have packed with it rolls of music and shipping via the steamer.' It would have cost him £65.[14] Early models of the player piano, perfected in 1897, had a separate pedalling device attached to the piano, but later ones incorporated the mechanism within the case. By pedalling a series of bellows, the player drew in air through the holes in the paper roll; hand levers below the keyboard controlled speed and dynamics, the latter also affected by pressure in pedalling. The player-piano, with collapsible pedals, regulating keyboard, and stack of rolls, had a fond place in many New Zealand homes.

From this basic system there developed a more sensitive technique of recording a live pianist on a roll and registering his own interpretation: Grieg, Saint-Saëns, Paderewski, Rachmaninov, Carreño, Rubinstein, Victor Herbert, George Gershwin, Percy Grainger, and others recorded thus. Stravinsky composed his Etude, op. 7 no. 1 especially for the pianola. Several companies specialized in this type of player piano, the best known being the Welte 'Mignon' from Germany, the Aeolian Company's 'Duo-Art', and the American Piano Company's

'Ampico'. Each operated on different systems so that their rolls were not interchangeable. Dealers often pitted the player piano against a live performer, both set behind screens. The audience was then invited to distinguish one from the other, something it often found difficult, if not impossible, to do. Of a Wellington Themodist Pianola Recital on 21 October 1909, Baeyertz of the *Triad* wrote: 'It has always puzzled me that there are not more pianolas in this country. I think it is safe to say that only a musician could have been sure (if the pianola had been kept out of sight) that the accompaniments were being played by a machine . . .'[15]

In the 1920s there developed the phenomenon of the battle of the rolls in which both sides (by then Duo-Art and Ampico) employed every technique they knew, from elaborate graphs of their exclusive recording artists to appeals to the artistic tastes of the time. Pianos appeared in a variety of styles, with curved, straight, and carved legs; purchasers were offered 'the piano case as a work of art'. The Sheridan style ultimately proved one of the most popular. A host of subsidiary attachments enticed buyers to store rolls in cabinets indistinguishable from those which already housed the family glass. In the 1920s a new mechanism could be fitted to make a roll re-wind and repeat itself indefinitely. Outsize rolls made 'Dancing to the Ampico' a practical party attraction. Instrumentalists could play the solo part to a roll of Brahms' Violin Concerto, and suitable works were offered to singers and others. Percy Scholes prepared his 'Audiographic Music' for electric piano and magic lantern; with an epidiascope attached (offered free to institutions), one could play the roll, project the scenes, and read the commentary aloud. Symphonies were recorded as piano duets under a separate conductor. Duo-Art brought out the Aeolian organ, capable of being installed in a discreet recess above the stairs or in a special room. Nearer to home, an Australian-made instrument, the Meltona, established itself in New Zealand. Rolls were cut by the artists themselves.

The player piano reached a peak of popularity around 1923, when over 200,000 were made. Thereafter it gradually declined in popularity, yielding its place to the gramophone and to the latest invention, the wireless.

Notes

[1] Mansfield, *Collected Letters*, vol. 1, 28-9

[2] The phonograph repertoire included some notable early recordings, such as Brahms playing his Hungarian Dance No. 1 on the piano. See Chew, V. K. *Talking Machines* for an excellent account of their history

[3] *Lyttelton Times*, 9 June 1879. In his Autobiography, Gladstone Hill mentions an Edison phonograph heard by Sir George Grey and Professor Archibald on 10 February 1891, describing it as the first

[4] *Evening Post*, 17 March 1891

[5] Bruce Anderson MSS, including letters from P. H. Bohanna, who also wrote of the small coastal steamers on which 'one gets pitched around . . . This is acknowledged to be the roughest coast in the world.' ATL

6   Anderson, B. *Story*, 1, a full account of the development of recordings and the growth of a New Zealand industry

7   Anderson MSS, ATL

8   Quoted in Pearsall, R. *Edwardian Popular Music*, 137

9   Anderson MSS, 16 ATL

10   In the *Dominion* of 22 May 1926 the No. 4 Sound Box was described as 'possibly the most famous . . . ever made'. Two recitals of No. 4 took place in the Town Hall Concert Chamber

11   Dech later conducted the 4YA Orchestra in Dunedin, where he had a teaching studio

12   The widespread appeal of records is shown by T. L. Buick's book *The Romance of the Gramophone* (Wellington 1927), a general history without specific references to New Zealand conditions

13   Anderson MSS, 31

14   Quoted in Pearsall, *Edwardian Popular Music*, 126. The Pianola was the player piano made by the Aeolian Corporation

15   *Triad*, November 1909, 5. The artists were Mr Alex Law (pianola), Mrs Arthur Mead (singer), Mr F. R. Johnston (cello)

3 The growth of broadcasting

The Radio Broadcasting Company of New Zealand 1925-1932

When Clive Drummond, later to become a national figure as an announcer, heard 'Come into the Garden Maud' on a gramophone record broadcast from Dunedin, he 'nearly went through the roof . . . All the sound you ever heard was morse and static, but to hear a voice—well!'[1] The recording came from Professor Robert Jack's experimental studio at the University of Otago which broadcast on 17 November 1921 the first radio programme to be transmitted in New Zealand. It included the popular song 'Hello, my Dearie', one of several records supplied by a local music store. Broadcasts took place for two hours on Wednesdays and Saturdays each week until Christmas Eve, and were heard as far north as Hamilton. Dr Robert Jack, Professor of Physics at the University, saw the social possibilities of what was then called wireless telephony. On an overseas visit in 1921 he had brought back the basic components for a radio transmitter, mostly gathered cheaply from surplus war stores. His pioneering team of supporters included John Sutherland and Edgar Finlayson.[2]

In February 1922, Charles Forrest's International Electric Company began broadcasting in Wellington from 2YB's studio in Courtenay Place on Mondays and Fridays from 7.30 p.m. until 9 p.m. Forrest owned a shop which sold radio parts and wanted to stimulate a market. Early entertainers included the singers Mrs Violet Gyles and Mr Tony Wood (who also managed a picture theatre in Courtenay Place). The song 'Yes, We Have No Bananas', promoted by Charles Begg and Co., became a broadcast hit. 2YB's musical equipment consisted of a piano (succeeded by a pianola), a spring-wound gramophone, and a carbon microphone which occasionally stopped working without showing it was 'dead'. A member of the popular Tutschka's Orchestra, the leading local band, recalled how the announcer before and after every item would ask listeners to phone the studio if they had heard them playing: one call came from Wanganui. By the end of 1922 three stations operated in Dunedin, one in Auckland, and one in Christchurch.

The Government gazetted the first regulations concerning the use of broadcasting licences in January 1923, and by the end of the year there were 2000 licensed receivers. In 1925 William Goodfellow, managing director of the New Zealand Cooperative Dairy Company, and A. R. Harris, an electrical engineer, formed the Radio Broadcasting Company of New Zealand. In return for the receipt of 5/6th of listeners' licence fees and 9/10ths of radio dealers' fees, which were collected annually by the Government, it undertook to erect 500-watt stations in Auckland and Christchurch within six months and two

Irine Ainsley, a 1YA artist in the 1920s and 30s. *Peter Downes collection*

The 2YA Orchestrina, which Aunt Daisy often engaged to play in her programmes of classical music. The conductor is the flautist A. P. Truda. *S. P. Andrew. Peter Downes collection*

more in Wellington and Dunedin, when requested to do so by the Minister of Telegraphs. Stations were required to broadcast for not less than twelve hours a week and the programmes had to restrict themselves to 'matter of educative, informative or entertaining character'.[3]

The RBC's first official transmission took place from Dunedin in time to cover the opening ceremonies of the New Zealand and South Seas Exhibition 1925-1926. It included the Argyll and Sutherland Highlanders' Band and the combined Wellington and Dunedin choral societies, followed later by two concert performances of *Il Trovatore* and relays from the Exhibition Cabaret.[4]

Heralded by the eight o'clock chimes of the Wellington General Post Office clock, followed by Bandmaster Goffin's 'Red Shield March', played by the Salvation Army Citadel Silver Band, station 2YA Wellington came on the air on 16 July 1927. The programme included solo songs, instrumental items by the Ellwood Trio, band selections, and a flute solo by A. P. Truda. There followed on 23 July the first issue of the weekly *Radio Record*, a programme journal which ran until 1939. Music advisers were appointed to the YA stations; the adviser for Wellington was H. Temple White, a noted choral conductor and educationalist. Station accompanists were also engaged.[5]

In September 1927 W. J. Bellingham became the first director of music, a position he held briefly, but long enough to set out guidelines: 'Do not underrate the capacity of the audience to appreciate good music, well played. I believe in a varied programme with a major proportion of standard works. The essential feature is that what is done, whether it be a foxtrot or symphony, must be well done . . ."[6] At each station Bellingham formed permanent instrumental groups (trios, quartets, etc.) who received modest remuneration.[7] The budget for artists' fees jumped from just over £300 in the first year to £4,000 in the second, and the RBC made the claim, as valid now as it was then, that it was 'already the greatest employer of concert talent in New Zealand'.[8]

With their primitive equipment and slender economic resources, early programme organizers had an unenviable task. To encourage and raise the standards of local talent, concert programmes had been limited to 25% of recorded music from gramophone record or pianola. At first, records were broadcast by placing the microphone near the sound-box of an acoustic gramophone, until an electric pick-up was introduced in 1928 which carried the sound directly from the record surface. Complete operas, symphonies, and chamber works could now be transmitted. Programmes improved, and the old days of using 'local artists' of disparate and diverse abilities disappeared, although it still proved extremely difficult to entice visiting overseas artists into the studio, as their fees were usually prohibitive.[9] An hour of 'Dinner music' from 6 p.m. began at 2YA in April 1929, with a five-minute silence every quarter of an hour. Without the silences, it remains on the Concert Programme to this day.

Norman Kerr, 1YA announcer, with the standard microphone of the 1930s. *Peter Downes collection*

Public advisory committees in music, drama, religion, and children's programmes arose. Concert orchestras broadcast, such as the ten-member 2YA Orchestra, which Mrs F. Basham ('Aunt Daisy') often employed in her classical music programmes on Sunday and Monday evenings.[10] In January 1930, 2YA made history with its relay of a public concert from Wanganui featuring the Queen Alexandra Band. It broadcast on 2 May the first concert by the newly formed Wellington Symphony Orchestra under Leon de Mauny.[11]

Radio changed many aspects of New Zealand life. Despite poor reception, often caused by the mountainous terrain, it helped dispel isolation and became a prime source of news and information. By welding itself into a single controlling body rather than a series of separate commercial stations it set a pattern that, however distantly modelled on the BBC, substantially shaped the future. However, the lack of a consistent musical policy brought criticism from prominent musicians such as the conductor John Bishop, who asked it to show 'more courage and daring'.[12] He wanted educational programmes similar to Sir Walford Davies' influential BBC series, 'Music and the ordinary listener'. Bishop also asked the RBC to employ more of the country's fine musicians, and to broadcast more major symphonic scores to compensate for the fact that the studio orchestras rarely exceeded ten players. The company responded by appointing Karl Atkinson as supervisor of recorded music in 1931, whose special musical programmes had a wide and beneficial influence.[13] Sixty thousand people now held licences in a population of one and a half million.

Mrs Amy Woodward, a Wellington singer who broadcast regularly from 2YA in the 1920s and 30s. *Peter Downes collection*

The New Zealand Broadcasting Board 1932-1936

The coalition Government, formed at the height of the Depression in 1931, set up the New Zealand Broadcasting Board, which assumed control the following year. It increased the power of the main stations and extended broadcasting hours. It appointed an advisory council to represent the interests of listeners, but this consisted of Government nominees and had little influence. The Board's programmes have been described as 'unenterprising, prosaic and monotonous', and the members themselves as 'conservative businessmen whose personal taste would have been for entertainment that was safe and comfortably familiar'.[14] The Broadcasting Board regarded the BBC as a model to be followed and its own role as that of political, social, and moral censor. It vetted gramophone records and had no hesitation in returning to England those considered unsuitable. In 1934, the Board permitted Bernard Shaw to broadcast unscripted, as he had requested, although one of his plays had previously been turned down. In the same year the Board rejected the offer of the Russian pianist Pouishnov to give a free recital.

Audience research of a somewhat basic kind was conducted by the Board, which showed that band music had the greatest appeal, followed by light orchestral items. Concerts took twelfth place, with opera and oratorio, classical and chamber music in fourteenth and fifteenth places respectively.[15] The Board, influenced by its General Manager Charles Harris, nevertheless engaged a number of celebrities, such as Szigeti, Chostiakoff, Gladys Moncrieff, Percy Grainger, Malcolm Sargent, Eileen Joyce, and Stella Power. It undoubtedly encouraged local artists too.[16] From June 1932 a concert orchestra of around eighteen players was attached to 2YA, conducted by Leon de Mauny. It gave three studio performances weekly, including an hourly classical recital and selections from musical comedies.[17] Complete recordings of grand opera were presented on Sunday evenings, and more musical masterworks given in their entirety. By 1934, each of the four cities enjoyed seventeen hours of broadcasting a day. Serious music occupied 17.26% of programme time, light music 42.88%.[18] The Board continued to broadcast 'Community Singing', which had begun in the late 1920s but reached its peak in the Depression.[19] Charity concerts also attracted full houses, and included overseas guests as well as local artists.[20] Overall, the Board had proved an unsatisfactory compromise. Early in 1936, a Labour Government swept in with a large majority and abolished it.[21]

The New Zealand Broadcasting Service 1936-1947

Labour formed a new organization, the National Broadcasting Service, and in August 1936 appointed Professor James Shelley (1884-1961) from Canterbury University College as director. 'I consider radio to be the greatest invention for the raising of democratic culture since the invention of printing', he had written in his application.[22] The Prime Minister, Michael Joseph Savage, took over the portfolio for broadcasting and C. G. Scrimgeour was appointed controller of the National Commercial Broadcasting Service, set up by the Act in 1937. The commercial network soon became extremely profitable: its style of presentation established a racy image of broadcasting in New Zealand. The ZB stations contained advertising during the week but not on Sundays, a freedom they used to promote music and operas. Scrimgeour encouraged local talent and local programmes. Their 'Personality Quests' discovered such artists as baritone Stewart Harvey (1936) and bass Inia te Wiata (1937).

James Shelley, a phenomenon in New Zealand cultural life, was above all things a passionate actor. He had founded the Canterbury Repertory Theatre, for which he became set designer, lighting director, and principal player. He also became a proficient painter and art critic on the *Lyttelton Times*, a designer of a banknote, and the maker of a gramophone stylus. A fine orator, he had a charisma that strongly affected people: he assumed the mantle of an autocratic Prospero. In later generations' eyes he was the Lord Reith of New Zealand.

At the official opening in 1937 of the new sixty-kilowatt transmitter for 2YA Wellington, Shelley announced plans for a great national broadcasting centre to include a conservatorium of music and the cultural arts.[23] Dr James Hight (1870-1958), Rector of Canterbury University College, wrote to the Prime Minister suggesting Shelley visit Australia and discuss the idea of a conservatorium in Sydney and Melbourne.[24] It seemed that the concept of a conservatorium and broadcasting were to be associated from the beginning.

Professor James Shelley.
Alexander Turnbull Library

Letters poured in, including some from Europe, where a group of musicians, including Lili Kraus, wished to emigrate and form a colony of friends.[25] Shelley was forced to reconsider the implications of his plan, but war broke out before it could be taken further.

As a precursor of a more ambitious symphonic project, Shelley set up the NBS String Orchestra in 1939, to be directed by the eminent English violinist Maurice Clare (1914-1987). Clare was born in Dundee, had been taught music by his father, who accompanied him in itinerant street performances and in prosperous local houses. He won scholarships, studied in Prague with Ševčik, and was being groomed by Beecham to lead the London Philharmonic when he inexplicably set sail for New Zealand, arriving in Auckland in early 1939. Shelley, delighted by his playing, arranged a six-week tour of the main cities with Noel Newson as accompanist, whom Clare described as 'of exceptional talent, and great sensitivity'.[26] Shelley then invited Clare to form an orchestra as a basis for the musical needs of the country's forthcoming centennial celebrations: 'My brief was to create the smallest possible group and I decided the minimum was 13 string players.' He auditioned throughout the country and selected an ensemble of excellent musicians led by Vincent Aspey: 'A most gifted violinist and a very skilful handler of human beings. He had natural diplomatic gifts and a brilliant sense of fun and humour.' The orchestra soon became 'quite a little jewel of its sort'.

After the performances by the Centennial Symphony Orchestra, the string ensemble was retained. In 1941 Clare resigned to take up farming for several years in Darfield, to teach violin, and to pursue a concert career.[27]

Shelley imprinted his personality on music both inside and outside the studio. Following his earlier Canterbury enthusiasms for adult education, he established Mobile Recording Unit No. 1 (with producer Leo Fowler), which at the end of the war toured the backblocks for several years collecting material from Māori and school choirs, local soloists, and bands.[28] In his Annual Report of 1946-1947 he advocated using radio 'as a local institution to serve as an instrument for developing the cultural life, artistic endeavour and civic consciousness of towns and districts'.[29] He followed this blueprint by setting up local stations over a period of years.

On his retirement in 1949, Oliver Duff wrote in the *Listener*:

> As clearly as the BBC today is what Lord Reith made it, with all his limitations and faults, the NZBS will long remain what Professor Shelley has made it, in spite of everything in him and in it that has gone wrong . . . The strain on him has been overwhelming; but his mark is now on the Service and on New Zealand, and the vulgarity that is in us all will never quite erase it.[30]

The Rise of the Concert Programme

In 1952 John Schroder created the four YC stations as vehicles for serious music and spoken materials only, each centre providing its own programmes, most of which were drawn from local sources. Schroder cast his net wide and encouraged a diversity of entertainment, the only criterion being that each genre was to be of the highest possible quality. This was the nucleus of the Concert Programme. With the coming of wide band lines in 1963, individual stations were linked to form the YC network, originating from Wellington, but with important contributions from other stations. When broadcasting was restructured in 1975 the name was changed to the Concert Programme, a new transmitter being added in Hawkes Bay in 1977. In 1981 4ZG Gore joined the network.

The Concert Programme benefits especially from its long-standing links with the Transcription Service of the BBC, and to a lesser extent from its world-wide contacts, so that it is able to give outstanding musical coverage, music making up approximately 75% of its programmes. It also interprets the

Broadcasting Act as empowering Radio New Zealand with the responsibility of encouraging the development of New Zealand performers and composers. It also actively commissions new works. The same responsibility exists in the spoken word, for poetry, literature and drama.

The whole New Zealand musical fabric is deeply dependent upon the professional initiative and enthusiasm of the Concert Programme, choirs, orchestras, ensembles, individual artists and composers. This responsibility is discharged with a panache comparable to that of the finest of such world networks. Nevertheless, this has not stopped the Concert Programme from a degree of criticism peculiar to an egalitarian society such as New Zealand where any suggestion of élitism fires prejudices and disdain. Indeed, one might say that the Concert Programme came under that same kind of harassment that once plagued the National Orchestra in its first decade. Without the Concert Programme, the initiatives of the New Zealand Symphony Orchestra, the Music Federation, major festivals, university recitals, competitions, regional orchestras, individual artists and speakers would be severely restricted. Even so, its achievements far transcend the extent of its funding.

Helen Young.

Since 1983 seven FM transmitters have been added to the Network in Auckland, Waikato, Hawkes Bay, Manawatu, Wellington, Nelson and Christchurch. In 1989 two further transmitters in Dunedin and Southland joined it. The four original YC/AM stations became linked to a Radio New Zealand Commercial Sports Network so that the Concert Programme was transmitted in FM only. In December 1988 the Government restructured the Broadcasting Corporation of New Zealand into two separate State Owned Enterprises of radio and television, each with a separate board appointed by the Government. TVNZ has produced a number of operas and arts programmes and televised concerts to make what it considers the most effective use of the miniscule time and funding allotted music. The New Zealand Symphony Orchestra with its own board, receives direct funding from the government and is no longer part of the Broadcasting organisation. The *New Zealand Listener*, which frequently had an ambivalent attitude towards the Concert Programme, became a separate company. In 1990 the Manager of the Concert Programme Helen Young, who had battled spiritedly for its ideals, retired, and the former General Manager of the Auckland Philharmonia, the composer Christopher Blake, succeeded her. His long experience in orchestral and opera management particularly fitted him for the position, but the maintenance of the *status quo* and the development of the Concert Programme into an even more significant force with more generous funding is a national necessity.

Notes

[1] Downes and Harcourt, 10. For earlier events see Hall, chapters 1-3

[2] Hall, J. H., 7ff.

[3] Quoted in Burdon, 92

[4] A special Festival Choir was formed and the first direct trans-Tasman broadcast took place with Neil McBeath's song 'Canberra'. Downes and Harcourt, 24ff.

[5] Miss Aileen Warren in Christchurch, Ernest Drake in Dunedin, Cyril Towsey in Auckland, and Gordon Short in Wellington

[6] Hall, 24

[7] Downes and Harcourt, 38-9

[8] Hall, 23

[9] Hall, 26

[10] Conducted by George Ellwood and led by Miss Ava Symons. George Ellwood conducted the 3YA Orchestra and at 1YA Dorothy Singer conducted from the piano

[11] Collins, 29

[12] Bishop, 'Broadcasting—a Retrospect'. *MNZ*, April 1931, 6-8

[13] Hall described Atkinson as 'one of the stalwarts of broadcast entertainment', 31

[14] Downes and Harcourt, 89

[15] Hall, 63-4

[16] Collins, 47

[17] Hall, 64

[18] Hall, 68

[19] Those held in the Wellington Town Hall featured Owen Pritchard (programme organizer at 2YA) and Albert Russel as song leaders and soloists, and Frank Crowther, a familiar and much loved pianist

[20] Collins, 76-7

[21] The independent weekly *Tomorrow*, founded and edited by Kennaway Henderson, contains lively accounts of the transgressions and bias of the Broadcasting Board

[22] Hall, 87

[23] *Evening Post*, 26 January 1937. See Burdon, 307

[24] 'As Professor Heinz of Melbourne said, there is in New Zealand a unique opportunity to profit by the mistakes and defects of the Australian institutions as well as by their more successful features.' Hight to Rt Hon. M. J. Savage, MP, Prime Minister, 23 March 1937. National Archives, I.A. 1/10/6

[25] Undated letter from Condliffe to Shelley, acknowledged 17 March 1938. National Archives, I.A. BC. ALPHA K.45/30

[26] Tape by Clare, recorded London 26 June 1985, in author's possession

[27] See chapter VI, 5; also RNZ documentary tribute to Clare, broadcast 23 December 1988, RNZ Archive, ATL Archive of NZ Music

[28] Downes and Harcourt, 133

[29] Quoted in *Voices*, 142

[30] *NZL* editorial, 'Professor Shelley', 4

4 *Music journals*

Baeyertz and the Triad

For over thirty years a monthly journal of the arts called the *Triad* provided trenchant and sometimes scurrilous commentary on Australian and New Zealand music. Rudolph Emil Baeyertz (1865-1943), the son of a Melbourne bank manager, and a fine linguist with a phenomenal memory, 'was consumed with the apostolic fire of communication' when he left the *Otago Daily Times* to be a 'knight berserk', rather than 'a squire inconspicuous amid the security of a host':[1]

R. E. Baeyertz, editor of the *Triad*, as he appeared in his own journal on 1 October 1907. *Alexander Turnbull Library*

> So I dashed out of the ranks and started the *Triad*. It was a bold venture, for the *Triad* was a musical and literary monthly for Dunedin and I was to live on the fruits of it. Few men have ever fluttered a pennon in a forlorner hope. . .[2]

Baeyertz approached music as a teacher of singing and languages who considered criticism both a science and an art. 'He learnt how to pick faulty intonation', writes his son, 'he committed to memory the how and wherefore of artistry—literary, vocal, instrumental, painting, criticism—all their salient points . . .' Baeyertz himself could not sing or whistle a note, but his wife was an amateur singer and pianist.[3] When he attended concerts he made 'microscopical notes on the programme—words mispronounced, quality of voice and so on', elaborating from these to produce his criticism. His son described his appearance as 'majestic, with his massive head and intellectual brow. He stood fully six feet and built in proportion. Buoyant is a good description of his whole vibrant personality. He acquired friends as most of us breathe. Few men in New Zealand could have had more, or many more enemies too, perhaps.' Baeyertz believed 'The critic should judge always as though he heard the artist for the first time in his life, in some city in which he was a stranger. . . He is to judge the artist as a craftsman judges a machine, by comparison with the best of its kind . . . Criticism that is merely destructive is at once useless and inhuman.'[4] He modelled himself on the New York critic W. J. Henderson (1855-1937), whose witty and informed writing ranged widely and with whom he shared an interest in singing.[5]

The first issue of April 1893 contained sixteen pages and sold for sixpence, promising reliable reports of music in Australasia with international coverage of the new styles. In due course Schoenberg's name appeared. 'Music in New Zealand' described events in the principal cities, a feature he maintained punctiliously. He spared nothing, from the state of the chairs in the hall, to programme notes and the enunciation of church choirs.

The journal's motto appeared on each cover: *Didicis se fideliter artes emollit mores* ('To devote oneself faithfully to the arts softens the manners'). Baeyertz himself aspired to this ideal but was seldom softened: his trenchant yet illuminating praise could descend into irritated comment or bouncy assertion, which his other editorial self would have eliminated had it been written by an outsider. The second issue opened with an article on Mozart and offered a music supplement—Schumann's *Träumerei*. By 1896 an Auckland edition had appeared and local musical events were reported in greater detail. By 2 October 1899 there were twelve editions throughout New Zealand.

The *Triad* had several electrifying quarrels—with Clara Butt in 1908, and again in 1910 and 1913,[6] when the argument was rather with her husband and co-artist Kennerley Rumford.[7] He chastised Amy Castles[8] and he crossed swords with Maughan Barnett over the value of competitions.[9] But his associate editor, the Australian journalist Frank Morton, brought about the most infamous dispute: '. . . while John [Fuller sen.] had a shrill and tuneful enough little pipe years ago, it is now not much more musical than a pig's whistle'.[10] In the notorious court case which followed, the presiding judge, Mr Justice Edwards, had more sympathy for the *Triad* than the singer and found against him. In the issue of 10 March 1915, a jubilant Baeyertz stated: 'The *Triad* is the most courageous, conscientious, and candid magazine in the Dominion. It is unique in its style and its function.' Nobody could dispute that. In 1915 Baeyertz transferred his editorial offices to Sydney, which he now considered to be the Australasian centre.[11] He still published a separate New Zealand edition, but the focus of the journal had shifted.[12]

Child of the singularly creative 1890s, the *Triad* documented music with unsurpassed flair. Baeyertz strove vigorously for causes he believed in, such as the provision of an orchestra of fifty-six players for the Christchurch Exhibition, holding that the proposed strength of thirty was 'only fit to play at such functions as a fancy fair for the benefit of decayed muffin men'.[13] There has been nobody quite like him since.

Music journals since the Triad

Six years after the demise of the *Triad* in 1925, the first New Zealand journal devoted entirely to music appeared, sponsored by an idealistic musician and patron of the arts, Harry Tombs. Tombs had studied the violin as a boy under C. F. Bünz (1844-1923) and as a student in Leipzig with Hans Sitt (1850-1922), the Austro-Bohemian violinist who had played in the famed Brodsky Quartet and had also taught Alfred Hill. Tombs had already launched and subsidized an important journal, *Art in New Zealand* (1928-1944), and under his own imprint had published a number of significant books, including several school music courses compiled by Ernest Jenner.

Music in New Zealand made its début in April 1931, with T. Vernon Griffiths

Harry H. Tombs, patron of *Music in New Zealand*, playing chamber music with his friends, Phyllis and Gwen Sealy. Pen, ink and wash by Barc (1891-1972), Psudonym for Helen Crabb. Location of original unknown. *Alexander Turnbull Library*

as honorary editor. Griffiths wished to cover 'progressive musical activities everywhere'. He appealed to all musicians to make the journal 'more truly representative of your ideals, of your work and your status'. A steady stream of educational and teaching material appeared, but knowledgeable and well-written music criticism, free from parochialism, proved especially difficult to find, as did regular reports of regional activities. Nevertheless, despite what may now seem an innate conservatism, the journal fulfilled an important function, offering a forum for issues of the day, such as the role of the broadcasting authorities in disseminating music and the role of city councils. Review sections covered recent overseas publications, with perspicacious notices by Frederick Page.[14] New Zealanders studying abroad sent back informative articles.

On 10 March 1937 the editor announced that the journal was to cease publication. Over the past six years Harry H. Tombs had valiantly borne all deficits: Griffiths had earlier described him as 'A New Zealand Belyayev' (after the great Russian patriot, musicologist, and publisher).[15] Griffiths hoped that the time would come 'when an increase in wealth of ideas and intensity of activity will justify the publication of a musical periodical which will actually accomplish what *Music in New Zealand* tried to do. *In magnis et voluisse sat est* ("In great enterprises, to have attempted is enough").'[16]

In 1939 the *New Zealand Listener*, the journal of the National Broadcasting Service, edited by Oliver Duff (1884-1967), fulfilled Griffith's hopes for a successor. Although dealing with all the arts, it immediately showed its allegiance to music. The *Radio Record* (1927-1932) had first provided topical information

november 1941

music ho

*owen jensen's
music news-letter*

First issue of Owen
Jensen's *Music Ho!*, 1941

on radio programmes, with interviews and technical features, but was succeeded by the *New Zealand Radio Record*. The *New Zealand Listener* might have become a tame combination of house journal, Government news-sheet, and programme propagandist. Instead it fused the best of the British *Listener* and *Radio Times* to make a publication of unusual range, energy, and discrimination.

Oliver Duff, editor for the first ten years, shaped it into 'a militant journal with a cultural mission'.[17] His 300-word editorials set a tone of intelligent and provocative discourse that brought within its pages the dominant interests of the country, in so far as they could be articulated, from the life and culture of the Māori, to the farmer and his land, the schoolteacher, the churchgoer, the young poet, and writer.[18] Its first music critic 'Marsyas' (Antony Alpers) established a line of committed writers, which subsequently included Bruce Mason, Frederick Page, and Elizabeth Kerr. Although Duff strongly supported the involvement of broadcasting with the arts, he remained suspicious of the motives of the commercial division, despite their cultural features each Sunday. Not unexpectedly, he incurred their enmity.

Owen Jensen's spirited *Music Ho!* (1941-1948) began as a cyclostyled journal during the war years, presenting important articles on composers, performers, music publishing, and criticism. It reviewed early Lilburn compositions, defended Lili Kraus from the savage attacks of the critic L. D. Austin, and had a constructive approach to New Zealand music derived from the forthright personality of its founder. Later, *Third Stream* in 1968 made a bold attempt to establish an almost luxurious music journal, covering electronic music as well as rock and pop. It succeeded in producing four lively issues before economic circumstances forced it to fold. In 1979, *Canzona*, the journal of the Composers' Association of New Zealand, began publication, concentrating at first on issues likely to appeal to composers. Its outlook subsequently broadened, with beneficial results, such as its 1980 *Festschrift* in honour of Douglas Lilburn. *Concert Pitch*, published by the New Zealand Symphony Orchestra, first appeared in the same year, and concentrated on orchestral personalities and programmes. Adrienne Simpson's quarterly *Early Music New Zealand* (1985) contained scholarly articles reflecting its title as well as original New Zealand material. Sadly, financial considerations forced it to close in 1989. William Dart's quarterly *Music New Zealand* (1988) has high visual standards and has opened up a wide range of stimulating topics from rock to classical.

Musical journals reflect a culture's musical life. They are the life-blood of any effective dialogue about music and the arts. Lively musical discourse is essential to help form and fashion taste and values, to guide and provoke opinion, to introduce and assess international trends, and above all to provide that stimulus which has animated the best journals of the past.

Notes

1. See typescript 'Baeyertz and his "Triad"', Hocken Library, MI 464B by R. E. Baeyertz. See also Seaman, G. 'Early Music Periodicals in New Zealand'. *Continuo*, June 1976, 4-14
2. *Triad*, fifteenth birthday issue, 1 April 1908
3. R. E. Baeyertz typescript, as are subsequent quotations, except where noted
4. *Triad*, 1 April 1908
5. Mulgan, A. *Great Days*, 124. Henderson served with the *New York Times* 1887-1902, and the *New York Sun* 1902-1937
6. See issues of 1 February 1908, 2 March 1908, and 10 January 1910
7. See issue of 10 November 1913
8. See issue of 10 March 1911
9. See issue of 10 May 1913
10. *Triad*, 10 September 1913
11. *Triad*, vol. 23 no. 7 (NZ); vol. 1 no. 1 (Australia)
12. By 1921 the *Triad* had world-wide distribution. In 1925 Baeyertz resigned his editorship, and the last issue of the old journal appeared in June 1927. Its place was taken by the *New Triad*, edited by the poet Hugh McRae and Ernest Watt
13. Quoted in Mulgan, *Great Days*, 127, from a letter in the *NZ Times* (date unknown)
14. See Page's account of the *Evening Post* newsboys' cries. Lilburn quotes one in the second movement of his Symphony No. 2, *MNZ*, 10 July 1935, 7
15. *MNZ*, 10 March 1933, 7-9
16. Vol. 6, no. 12, 1-2
17. Mulgan, *Great Days*, 130-1
18. See *NZL*, 'Portrait of an Editor', 10 June 1949, 8

VI

The New Zealand performer

1 Introduction

The first group of gifted New Zealand-born performers emerged in the late nineteenth century. Several musicians ventured forth to Europe, invariably as a private initiative, frequently supported by a benefit concert arranged in their home town; amongst them Alfred Hill and Sydney Francis Hoben, both of whom studied the violin at Leipzig. Hill became a pupil of Hans Sitt and played in the Leipzig Gewandhaus Orchestra for several years, but although he continued to perform professionally after his return to New Zealand, his energies had by then turned to composition. Hoben became a music teacher and critic on the *Lyttelton Times*.

In 1903 the Trowell brothers, Arnold and Garnet, cellist and violinist respectively, went overseas to study as the result of encouragement from the visiting cellist Jean Gérardy and a public subscription raised in Wellington. Gérardy similarly helped the Ellwood family (Polly, piano, Harry, violin, and George, cello) to study in Europe. They returned to New Zealand at the outbreak of World War One to play a leading part in musical life. George might readily have had a soloist's career but became Director of Music and conductor for the Durban Broadcasting Service, dying in tragic circumstances in 1941.

The establishment of scholarships by the Associated Board of the two Royal Schools of Music in 1906 forged a link between New Zealand and London. There followed a succession of notable award winners, many of whom returned to work in New Zealand, such as Mary Martin, Zillah Castle, Janetta McStay and Ritchie Hanna. The pianists Colin Horsley (1937) and Peter Cooper (1938) went on to make their careers in Europe. Apart from teaching privately, at schools or institutes of higher learning, there was not yet any fabric of concert life to sustain a home-based professional career.

Arnold Trowell

2 Singers

New Zealand may not have quite as spectacular a vocal tradition as Australia but it is nevertheless longer and more illustrious than is generally supposed. Noteworthy amongst early singers was the baritone John Prouse (1856-1930), who sang in the First New Zealand Music Festival in 1888, and for whom

Alfred Hill wrote *Time's Great Monotone*, an elaborate setting of a ballad by Arthur Adams for baritone, choir and orchestra (1894). In the early 1890s Prouse travelled to England, where he studied with William Ganz. He also had lessons with Charles Santley, who helped launch his professional career at the Crystal Palace and elsewhere in London. Following his return to New Zealand in 1892 he gave many concerts and toured with Antonia Dolores. Back in Britain in 1903, he became a supporting artist to several celebrated musicians, such as the violinist Jan Kubelik and the pianist Wilhelm Backhaus. In June 1905 he made several test pressings for the Gramophone Company which show a well-produced light baritone voice, with meticulous phrasing and diction. He eventually settled in New Zealand, where he resumed concert and oratorio work. He and his wife maintained a vigorous musical salon in Wellington, becoming considerable patrons of music. In 1907, for instance, they financed a tour of Alfred Hill's Christchurch Exhibition orchestra. Prouse gave early broadcast recitals shortly before his death in August 1930. Many able singers of this period elected to remain in New Zealand to become regular soloists with local choral societies. Amongst these was Elizabeth Parsons (1846-1924), prominent in Wellington's musical life from the age of fifteen.

A group of fine Māori singers made their mark from the middle of the nineteenth century onwards, many of them associated with concert parties. The most celebrated of these, Princess Te Rangi Pai (1868-1916), had a highly successful professional life, and was especially identified with her own lullaby, 'Hine e Hine'. In 1903 she was a soloist with the Hinemoa band on its overseas tour, with the tenor Chief Rangiuia. Similarly, Princess Iwa made her name in the concert hall. Born Evaline Jane Skerrett on Stewart Island in 1890,[1] her voice was first noted when she won second place for sacred solo and third place for contralto solo in the Dunedin Eisteddfod.[2] She was subsequently 'lead singer' in Maggie Papakura's Maori Concert Party on their tour of Melbourne, Sydney and London, in 1910-11, which was sponsored by Sydney businessmen. Iwa received favourable notices from the critics both in Australia and London. The *Standard* compared her to Clara Butt,[3] while the *Daily Telegraph* wrote: 'Iwa is the possessor of an exceedingly sweet and powerful voice, which she uses in the most natural and easy style'.[4] When the concert party returned to New Zealand she and nineteen other party members elected to remain in London. After World War One, during which she sang in the ANZAC Concert Party, she became a vaudeville singer introducing 'traditional Maori melodies' to music hall audiences at the London Palladium.[5] It is believed that she subsequently married an Englishman and did not return to New Zealand.

The tradition of fine Maori singers has continued this century, most notably in the careers of Inia Te Wiata and Kiri Te Kanawa. Inia Te Wiata (1915-71) from his youth possessed an extemely fine bass voice, becoming a member of the Rev. A. J. Seamer's Methodist Waiata Maori Choir at the age of seventeen

Kiri te Kanawa

and touring Australia with them. He was also one of Princess Te Puea's select traditional carvers, a potential profession he forsook to pursue a career as a singer, winning a government scholarship in 1947. He studied in London at Trinity College and at the Joan Cross Opera School, and in 1950 created the part of John Bunyan in Vaughan Williams' *Pilgrim's Progress* at Covent Garden. Britten wrote the part of Dansker, the grizzled old seaman in *Billy Budd* (1951), especially for him. He sang regularly with Covent Garden until 1953. He then spent several years in musicals, returning to the Garden in 1957. His repertoire included the Speaker and Sarastro in *The Magic Flute*, Count Ribbing in *A Masked Ball*, Colline, the monk in *Don Carlos*, Schwarz in *Die Meistersinger von Nürnberg*, and Don Alfonso in *Così fan Tutte* (for Scottish Opera). He played the leading role in the New Zealand Opera Company's 1965 production of *Porgy and Bess* with great authority and warmth. However, his early love of carving never deserted him, as his fifty-two feet tall pouihi which stands in the entrance to New Zealand House in London demonstrates. At his memorial service in St Martin-in-the-Fields, London, on 22 July 1971, the Maori Choir took part as well as principals and chorus members from the Royal Opera House, when the following tribute was paid him: 'His high quality as a man, his courage, his tremendous ability, his good humour, his warm and friendly nature together with his love of people made him a personality far too rarely encountered.'[6]

Kiri Te Kanawa (b. 1944), began singing lessons in her teens with Sister (later Dame) Mary Leo, the distinguished Auckland nun who also taught Malvina Major and Heather Begg. After winning various prizes, including the Melbourne *Sun* aria competition, she went to the London Opera Centre in 1966 on an Arts Council grant, later studying with Vera Rozsa, who encouraged the soprano rather than mezzo side of her voice. In 1969 she made her operatic debut in Wellington as Carmen with the New Zealand Opera Company and first appeared at Covent Garden the same year as a Flower Maiden in *Parsifal*. Her performance as the Countess in *The Marriage of Figaro* at the Garden in December 1971 launched her on an international career, which she sustained through a number of outstanding interpretations such as that of Amelia in Verdi's *Simon Boccanegra* at the Garden in 1973. The following year, at extremely short notice, she sang Desdemona in *Othello* at the Metropolitan Opera in New York to universal acclaim, where in 1975 her Donna Elvira in *Don Giovanni* provided yet another triumph. Subsequent leading parts have included those of the title role in Strauss's *Arabella*, and Rosalinde in *Die Fledermaus*, conducted by Zubin Mehta at Covent Garden and televised worldwide. She sang at Ayers Rock as part of the Australian bicentenary celebrations in 1989 and in 1990 gave outdoor performances for New Zealand's sesquicentenary with the New Zealand Symphony Orchestra under John Hopkins, attended by vast audiences. She has a rich, warm voice, an attractive and charming stage presence, and is one of the great lyric sopranos of her generation.

The first two New Zealand-born singers of European ancestry to achieve international renown were Frances Alda (1879-1952) and Rosina Buckman (1881-1948). Alda was born in Christchurch, the daughter of David Davis and Leonora Simonsen. Davis was a talented violinist who had played for the Simonsen Opera Company on their 1876 New Zealand tour, during which he married the Simonsen's eldest daughter. The marriage dissolved, and Leonora died in 1884 at the age of twenty-five. Frances Alda was brought up by her mother's family in Melbourne. She soon showed vocal talent, eventually becoming a pupil of Marchesi in Paris. She sang for three seasons in Brussels where her roles included Marguerite in *Faust* and Mimi in *La Bohème*, which were to become favourites. She made her debut as Gilda at the Metropolitan New York in December 1908, marrying the new manager Giulio Gatti-Casazzas in 1910.

Rosina Buckman

She became renowned for her Desdemona, Manon Lescaut, Nanetta in Verdi's *Falstaff*, and particularly for her Mimi, which she sang with Caruso and Gigli. She was a distinguished recording artist. In 1927 she undertook a triumphal tour of Australia and New Zealand. By the time she retired from the Metropolitan in 1930 she had made over one hundred recordings: 'She is probably the most consistently satisfying lyric soprano on pre-electrical records', wrote the critic J. B. Steane.[7] The Australian writer A. L. Kelly has summed up her qualities: 'Frances Alda is not an emotional singer or a stirring actress, but she knows the stage thoroughly, and uses her beautiful voice with fine taste and absolutely sound musicianship.'[8]

Rosina Buckman (1881-1948) became one of the greatest Isoldes of her age, an outstanding Aida and Butterfly, a touching Mimi and a high-spirited Mrs Waters in Ethel Smythe's opera *The Boatswain's Mate*. Born into a musical family in Blenheim, her vocal talents were soon recognized, especially by James Grace, choirmaster of the Broad Street Methodist choir in Palmerston North, who arranged tuition for her in Birmingham, first as a pupil of Dr C.S. Heap, then, in 1900, at Professor George Breedon's Birmingham and Midland School of Music, where she quickly won a high reputation. In 1903 she became seriously ill and returned to New Zealand, where her potentialities were realized as La Zara in Alfred Hill's *A Moorish Maid* (1905). She repeated this success in Sydney in 1906, gained much varied operatic experience and, in 1910, sang Suzuki in the Williamson Grand Opera Company's *Madama Butterfly*, where her dramatic temperament attracted favourable comment. In 1911 she took part in Melba's Grand Opera season, which also starred John McCormack. Melba showed a rare generosity in the encouragement she offered a younger artist—her more usual pattern was to have them removed. Rosina Buckman sang Musetta, Suzuki, Nurse Gertrud in Gounod's *Romeo and Juliet* and Martha in *Faust*. In 1912 she toured New Zealand with John McCormack, who encouraged her to return to Europe.

She first appeared at Covent Garden as a Flower Maiden in *Parsifal* in 1914,

Donald McIntyre

later that year singing Musetta to Melba's Mimi. In 1915 Beecham invited her to become principal dramatic soprano in The Beecham Opera Company, where she performed a series of notable roles: Mimi, Butterfly, Mrs Waters, Isolde and Aida. Neville Cardus wrote of her Cio-Cio San: 'Her evocation of this part is quite marvellous . . . her art elevated and purified Puccini's score of all sentimentality.'[9] Ernest Newman described her Isolde as: 'the most perfectly finished study that this splendid artist has ever given us'.[10] In 1919 she married the tenor Maurice d'Oisly, a lyrical singer with a gift for acting, who had sung Pinkerton to her Butterfly in 1915.

By now she had built up a parallel reputation in the concert hall, appearing with such artists as Tetrazzini, Clara Butt, Kreisler and Heifetz. In 1922 she and Maurice d'Oisly returned to New Zealand for an extensive tour, preceded by a generous proclamation from Melba: 'Rosina Buckman today represents the fulfilled dreams of thousands of young singers . . . Great in opera, magnificent in concert work, Australians will be delighted and charmed with her . . . I know no-one better fitted to carry on the great and noble tradition of music, and New Zealand may well be proud of its Queen of Song.'[11] New Zealand turned out *en masse* to fête both artists. Rosina Buckman made her last appearance at Covent Garden as Aida and Mrs Waters in 1923, and with members of the original Beecham company in a Benefit for Madame Albani in 1925. She appeared as a soloist in the Proms, and in the 1930s began teaching at the Royal Academy of Music in London.

After her death in 1948, the tenor Percy Heming, a former colleague from the Beecham Company, wrote: 'Her voice was a lyric and dramatic soprano of great beauty and warmth, capable of all the finest shades of colour, from the youthful ardour of the first act of *Butterfly* to the terrible curses of Isolde . . . Those of us who worked with her were constantly impressed by her sincerity and integrity as an artist.'[12]

Amongst subsequent singers the tenor Ernest McKinley, a star of the Kiwi Concert Party of World War One, author of *Ways and By-Ways of a Singing Kiwi* (1939), became well-known in the 1930s through his Australian recordings. Mary Pratt, an outstanding Dunedin contralto, pursued a distinguished career within New Zealand. Oscar Natzka [born Natzke] (1912-51), one of the world's outstanding basses, sang at Covent Garden and the Metropolitan, New York. It was Andersen Tyrer, as a Trinity College examiner, who cabled London in 1934 to seek a scholarship for 'the finest voice he had heard',[13] which Natzka won. He began his studies the following year with Albert Garcia, helped also by a fund from well-wishers. He was a noble Sarastro in *The Magic Flute*, and made the leading operatic bass roles in the repertoire his own. Gifted with a commanding presence (he was over six feet tall), he had risen, through extraordinary exertions and devotion, from his lowly job as an Auckland blacksmith's striker at the age of fifteen to a position of international eminence.

This pattern of gifted New Zealand singers has continued to the present day

Oscar Natzka, Wellington, 1949. *W. Walker, Alexander Turnbull Library*

with a proliferation of talents which are to be found in opera houses throughout the world. Donald McIntyre (b 1934), for instance, like Oscar Natzka, is a great bass, encompassing all the major roles and achieving the distinction of singing Wotan at Bayreuth in the complete *Ring* cycle (1967). His Hans Sachs in the Wellington Festival *Die Meistersinger* of 1990, was a noble interpretation. Malvina Major (b 1943) achieved early recognition through her Matilde in Rossini's *Elisabetta regina d'Inghilterra* at the 1968 Camden Festival and went on to win acclaim through such roles as Rosina in *The Barber of Seville* at the Salzburg Festival (1968/9). In 1969 she returned to New Zealand to marry a Taranaki farmer, exchanging an international career for family life and frequent appearances within New Zealand in opera, oratorio and in concerts. In 1985 she courageously decided to resume her international career and undertook a gruelling auditioning tour to America and Europe which restored her to stardom, at first through her Arminda in Mozart's *La Finta Giardiniera* at the Théâtre de la Monnaie in Brussels, then subsequently with Donna Anna in Mozart's *Don Giovanni*, as a principal role with leading European companies and the Australian Opera. Her first Lucia in the Wellington City Opera's 1988 *Lucia di Lammermoor* showed outstanding qualities. She has a warm voice of coloratura agility and a musical intelligence to match.

Malvina Major

Earlier, Denis Dowling (b. 1910) began a longstanding association with Sadler's Wells in 1948 as principal baritone, continuing to sing for the English National Opera, during which time he performed some seventy roles. Brian Drake (b. 1925) had a distinguished career as a baritone with the English Opera Group, Covent Garden and the Welsh National Opera, taking part in such works as Vaughan Williams's *The Pilgrim's Progress*, Britten's *Bully Budd* and the church operas. Heather Begg (b. 1932) became principal mezzo-soprano with the Carl Rosa Opera Company, taking up the same position with Sadler's Wells following guest appearances with the Royal Opera and the English Opera Group. She won acclaim as a character-mezzo and more than this for her performance on the double bass as Lady Jane in *Patience* at the Wells in 1970. She subsequently became a principal with the Australian opera. Noel Mangin (b. 1932), a notable bass, began at Sadler's Wells, joined Hamburg Opera from 1966-76 and since then has worked as a freelance, making his Glyndebourne debut as Sarastro in 1963, followed by leading roles at Covent Garden and for New Zealand and Australian Opera. In addition to such artists as these working in grand opera, Peter Baillie (b. 1933) became a leading tenor with the Vienna Volksoper from the mid-60s onwards, graduating to such character roles as Albert in Britten's *Albert Herring*, Wenzel in *The Bartered Bride* and Monostatos in *The Magic Flute*. Having returning to New Zealand, he undertakes opera, oratorio and concert engagements. Add to this list the innumerable others active as singers, conductors, directors, designers and teachers, and the vessel of New Zealand opera can be seen to be fully equipped: it needs now some new Maecenas to underwrite its re-launching.

3 Instrumentalists

Amongst musicians active in Wellington in the 1890s, the flautist John Amadeo (1890-1964) showed exceptional talents, playing orchestral concertos from an early age. He settled in Australia when he was about eleven, toured with an Italian opera company, then accompanied divas such as Melba, Calvé and Tetrazzini, subsequently pursuing an international career which included his becoming a highly successful recording artist.[14] One of the first to distinguish herself as a pianist was Vera Moore (b. 1896), who studied with Leonard Borwick, a pupil of Clara Schumann. He passed on to her his love of Debussy and Ravel. She later settled in France in the village of Monfort-l'Amaury near Paris. Frederick Page, having heard her play in Christchurch in the early 1920s, described her as 'a great artist'.[15]

Esther Fisher, pianist, pursued a concert career in London, having studied with Bernard Page, the leading Wellington city organist, with Isidore Philipp at the Paris Conservatoire, and with Arthur Schnabel in Berlin. She made a successful début at the Wigmore Hall in 1924. For some time associated with the notable viola player Lionel Tertis, she later became a professor at the Royal College of Music. Noel Newson (1911-44), one of New Zealand's finest pianists, had special gifts as an accompanist. He studied in Christchurch with Miss F. Tindale and Ernest Empson and for a brief period at the Royal College of Music, London. He frequently accompanied visiting artists for the NBS, such as Alexander Kipnis, Essie Ackland, Dorothy Helmrich and the English singers engaged for the Centennial Music Festival. He worked closely with Maurice Clare, a leading English musician of the period, with whom he gave his last public performance before his early death. In 1945 Lilburn wrote *Elegy* for two voices and strings in his memory. Owen Jensen in *Music Ho!* described him as having 'refinement, painstaking care and sensitive feeling for the details of nuance'.[16] Maurice Till (b. 1926) also developed outstanding abilities as an accompanist and has toured with artists of the stature of Victoria de los Angeles and Elizabeth Schwarzkopf besides pursuing a successful career as soloist and teacher.

As the twentieth century progressed, a steady flow of talented artists left to study overseas, many of them returning to work in New Zealand, so that by 1946, when the National Orchestra was founded and the chamber music societies began their activities, they could draw on a pool of experienced musicians. These included the leader of the newly-formed National Orchestra, Vincent Aspey (1909-87), a distinguished soloist and a phenomenon in musical life. As a boy he had played for silent films in Huntly, his outstanding talent taking him in his teens to the Sydney Conservatorium; he later led Australian broadcasting orchestras, the 1YA Studio Orchestra and the NBS Strings. His innate modesty and individual sense of humour defused many potentially explosive situations within the orchestra.

Vincent Aspey. *Tom Shenahan*

Janetta McStay (b. 1919) at an early age found two remarkable music teachers in Invercargill, Mona Rankin and May O'Byrne, both of whom had 'the inestimable ability to make a child love music'.[17] At the age of fifteen she began playing in local trios and quartets, gained her LRSM and a scholarship to the Royal Academy of Music, London. Marooned in England during the war, she joined the music division of ENSA, the entertainment branch of the armed services, and gave hundreds of concerts for them in Britain and Europe. After the war she specialized in Spanish piano music. She returned to New Zealand in 1954, where she proved outstanding in chamber music, showed considerable energy and drive as a soloist and became a gifted teacher. The violinist Alex Lindsay (1919-74), after study at the Royal College, pursued an orchestral career in the London Philharmonic, later founding and conducting his own Alex Lindsay String Orchestra, which played a vital role in the promotion of New Zealand music in the 1950s and 60s. His leader for many years, Ritchie Hanna, had a distinguished orchestral career, latterly with ABC orchestras in Australia. Several New Zealanders have occupied leading positions in British orchestras, such as John McCaw, principal clarinet in the London Philharmonic and the Philharmonia; Harold Beck, principal cello of the Hallé and London Symphony, and his brother Haydn, leader of the Monte Carlo Orchestra; and Gordon Webb, who moved from a career as principal trumpet in London orchestras and as a soloist to perform and teach in Australia. Murray Khouri and Mark Walton, clarinets, have held leading London orchestral positions. Ross Pople, a distinguished cellist, led the Menuhin Orchestra for several years, and in the late 1980s founded his own London Festival Orchestra which specializes in concerts in British cathedrals. The flautist Marya Martin studied with Jean-Pierre Rampal and James Galway, won prestigious competitions and now pursues the career of a soloist in America and Europe. Grant Cooper, trumpet, after a highly successful orchestral career became professor of trumpet in America. In Australia, John Robertson was an exceptional first trumpet in the Sydney Symphony Orchestra.

Colin Horsley (b. 1920) established himself as a leading pianist in Britain, having studied piano with Gordon McBeth in Wanganui before winning a scholarship to the Royal College of Music, London. While still a student he made his London début at the 1942 Promenade Concerts in Bach's Concerto for Three Pianos. In 1943 Sir John Barbirolli invited him to play in Manchester with the Hallé Orchestra which launched him as a soloist. His wide repertoire included much contemporary British music, particularly that of Lennox Berkeley and Humphrey Searle. He has also championed works by Douglas Lilburn. His exceptional technique and energetic interpretations have always been a feature of his playing. Colin Tilney wrote in *The Times* of his performance of the Ravel G major Piano Concerto at the 1959 Proms that he 'realised its pathos and fantastic wit in a rare and moving display of pianism'.[18] Tessa Birnie (b. 1934) studied with Paul Schramm in Wellington, later with Yvonne Lefébure in Paris

Janetta McStay

Alex Lindsay

Colin Horsley

Richard Farrell. *Collection of Peter Downes*

and Karl Ulrich Schnabel in Como. Besides pioneering contemporary New Zealand music she has specialized in Schubert and Haydn, and in recording and performing Beethoven at the lower pitch of his day. She was awarded the Beethoven Medallion and in 1984 the Order of Australia. The pianist Peter Cooper (b. 1918), who first appeared at the Wigmore Hall in 1946, studied under Eric Grant at the Royal Academy of Music and subsequently with Ignaz Friedman and Edwin Fischer. His many performances of contemporary New Zealand works have included Douglas Lilburn's Chaconne, which he premièred. Richard Farrell, (1926-58), one of the most gifted of New Zealand pianists, left for New York in 1947, where he studied at the Juilliard School under Olga Samaroff. He made his début at Carnegie Hall in 1948, winning exceptional notices. He later undertook several tours with the National Orchestra. His solo repertoire included contemporary works, such as Copland's 1941 Sonata, although he became most renowned as an interpreter of the great romantic concertos. His tragic death in a car accident in 1958 ended a career which began as a child prodigy and had already achieved a rare acclaim.[19]

The violinist Alan Loveday (b. 1928) showed early promise: he was taught by his father from the age of two, and gave his first concert performance two years later. Public subscriptions helped him to study overseas with Albert Sammons from 1939 onwards, and he made his first London appearance in 1947. He tended to specialize in romantics such as Tchaikovsky and Paganini, in whose D major Concerto he played the composer's own bravura interpolations along with Sauret's cadenza in the opening *Allegro*. He became leader and co-leader of several important chamber orchestras. In the 1970s he began playing eighteenth century music on an authentic instrument. He has consistently shown an admirable technique and a sure sense of style allied to natural musicianship.

Other pianists who have made reputations in Britain and Europe include Georgina Zellan-Smith, a regular broadcaster for the BBC and professor at the Royal Academy, and David Bollard, an artist of immense integrity, who later settled in Australia and became a member of the Australian Ensemble. Richard Mapp, who studied with Maurice Till and later with Maurice Green at the Royal Academy, has become a highly successful concert artist. David James, a graduate of the University of Auckland, where he studied with Janetta McStay, has won international prizes, appeared at the Lincoln Center both as soloist and in chamber music, and now lives in New York. Christopher Beckett has based his career in Paris. In 1990 the pianist Margaret Lion organized a concert of New Zealand music at St John's Church, Smith Square, London, which recalled the valuable work of the tenor Andrew Gold who founded the New Zealand Music Society after World War Two. The Society was revived in the late 1960s by Murray Khouri and J. M. Thomson; it disbanded in 1973. Margaret Nielsen (b. 1933) is a leading exponent of contemporary New Zealand piano music, having a special affinity with the works of Lilburn.

New Zealand musical life has benefited profoundly from the influence and

Maurice Till

stimulus of refugee musicians, such as the cellists Marie Vandewart and Greta Ostova, the violinist Erika Schorss, and the pianists Diny and Paul Schramm. Such artists frequently became the nucleus of ensembles closely associated with the various chamber music societies. Dorothy Davies (1899-1987), who had studied at the Sydney Conservatorium, with Arthur Alexander at the Royal College of Music, London, and later with Schnabel and Therese Behr, returned to New Zealand in 1940 and quickly became a powerful influence in national musical life through her broadcasts, concerts, and master classes. She specialized in Bach and the eighteenth and nineteenth century repertoire and worked frequently with the refugee musicians mentioned above. During the same period Ruth Pearl, an English violinist, made an enduring contribution to New Zealand musical life through her devoted leadership of a variety of orchestral ensembles and her participation in chamber music.

Gillian Weir (b. 1941), harpsichordist and organist, achieved fame when she won the St Alban's International Organ Playing Competition in 1964 and made her début at the Royal Festival Hall the following year. After her performance of Poulenc's Organ Concerto at the opening night of the 1965 Proms her career expanded rapidly, with a succession of widely-acclaimed international tours. Her technical virtuosity is matched by the profundity of her musicianship. She has devoted much of her life to contemporary music, especially that of Messiaen. Her keen intellect is as much at home in the intricacies of organ design as it is in the subtleties of interpretation. In 1983 she received an Honorary Doctorate of Letters from Victoria University of Wellington.

Gillian Weir

From its earliest years the symphony orchestra made a point of offering opportunities to New Zealand artists, amongst whom featured the pianists Cara Hall and David Galbraith, a brilliant interpreter. However, despite the support offered by the Government bursary system and by the increasingly significant role of the NZSO and the Music Federation, the New Zealand artist still has to show considerable skill, resilience and ingenuity in sustaining a New Zealand-based professional career. Diedre Irons, a Canadian-born pianist, has succeeded in this, with many overseas links, especially in association with the violinist Miha Pogacnik. She became a regular soloist for the Canadian Broadcasting Corporation and in 1966 studied with Rudolph Serkin and Horzowski at the Curtis Institute of Philadelphia, where, after graduation, she taught for seven years, at the same time pursuing an active career as a performer. She settled in New Zealand in 1977, since which time she has become a leading musical personality. Michael Houstoun, a pianist of formidable technique and natural gifts, studied with Maurice Till, came third in the Van Cliburn international competition in Texas and has since established himself as an international artist of increasing integrity and potential. Amongst chamber music ensembles the Gagliano Trio (John and Allen Chisholm and Brian Shillito) won recognition in their overseas tours, such as to China in 1983. The Zelanian Ensemble (Uwe Grodd, Deborah Rawson, Donald Maurice and Rae de Lisle) perform works

Michael Houstoun

New Zealand String
Quartet. *Music Federation*

for unusual combinations of instruments, commission many New Zealand compositions and have toured extensively in New Zealand and overseas. The New Zealand String Quartet (Wilma Smith, Douglas Beilman, Gillian Ansell and Josephine Young), formed in 1987, quickly established a high reputation: it has been awarded overseas residencies and made an Australian tour for Musica Viva in 1990.

4 Conductors

Warwick Braithwaite

Warwick Braithwaite (1896-1971), became the first New Zealand conductor of international stature. Following study at the Royal Academy of Music, he joined the touring O'Mara Opera Company in 1919 and thereafter made opera the centre of his life, pursuing an active career in Britain at Sadler's Wells, Covent Garden (1950-53) and with the Australian National Opera (1954-5). He identified himself with the Welsh National Opera as musical director (1956-60), then rejoined Sadler's Wells, retiring in 1968. John Matheson (b. 1928), has been influential and active at Covent Garden (1955-60), Sadler's Wells (1961-71) and in several principal German houses. He gained recognition for his dramatic interpretations of Verdi and has shown a particular interest in French nineteenth century opera. Ashley Lawrence (1934-90) became chief conductor of ballet at Covent Garden, an art in which he excelled: he had also worked with Kenneth MacMillan in West Berlin, with John Cranko in Stuttgart, and at the Paris Opera.

In New Zealand, the European refugee Georg Tintner (b. 1917) re-invigorated the Auckland String Players from 1940 onwards and subsequently conducted in Australia, Canada, and for the English National Opera in London. William Southgate (b. 1941) has pursued an active conducting career in New Zealand and initiated exchange visits with Finland, in association with the impresario Haydn Rawstrom. Although conducting opportunities within New Zealand still remain limited (1990), the future may well see stronger links with Australia and Asian countries such as Singapore and Japan.

Notes

1 For further details see Registrar-General files — Evaline Jane Skerrett — 4309
2 Unsourced newspaper cutting, T. E. Donne scrapbook, ATL
3 Dennan, 54
4 Ibid
5 The *British Australasian*, undated, T. E. Donne scrapbook
6 Order of Memorial Service, ii
7 J. B. Steane, quoted in *The Grand Tradition* (London 1974), 127. See also Adrienne Simpson, '"This country may well be proud of her": Frances Alda's 1927 Tour of New Zealand', *MNZ*, Spring 1989, 36-41, [61]

[8] Quoted in Simpson, op cit. A. L. Kelly, 'A Music Critic Circles the Earth', *Triad*, 1 June 1926, 11

[9] Neville Cardus, *Sir Thomas Beecham*, London, 1961, 93

[10] *Birmingham Post*, 15 May 1917

[11] Document in possession of author

[12] *Royal Academy of Music Magazine*, n143, May 1949, 43-4

[13] Recounted many times, eg *NZL* 23 November 1951

[14] See, for instance, Arthur C. Payne's 'Stars of the Record World', *Gramophone and Talking Machine News*, April 1924, 122-4

[15] See 'One Moment of Magic', *NZL*, 15 November 1975, 34, and Page, F., *A Musician's Journal*, 45-6

[16] *Music Ho!.*, April, 1944, 6.

[17] Communication to author

[18] *The Times*, 23 August 1959

[19] See *The Times* obituary, 28 May 1958 and Warwick Braithwaite's appreciation in the same paper, 2 June 1958. Douglas Terry, Classical Artists and Repertoire Manager of Pye Records Ltd, wrote a tribute in the *Gramophone*, July 1958, 49

VII

Meeting of the two cultures: Māori and European music

The innate musicality of the Māori had impressed Europeans from the time of Cook onwards, although traditional waiata were felt to be somewhat monotonous. Haka, dances, canoe songs—all made a striking impression. Once the missionaries began their activities they soon found they could win more hearts and souls through music, especially the singing of hymns, than by almost any other means. As early as 1827, 400 copies of a book containing hymns in Māori had been printed in Sydney by Mr R. Davis, and thereafter numerous publications appeared. An arrangement of morning and evening prayers with the litany and forty-two hymns was published in 1839 in an edition of 7000 copies, with a further printing of 20,000 the following year.[1] The 'Old Hundredth', sung by Samuel Marsden during his Christmas Day service at the Bay of Islands in 1814, may have been the first hymn the Māori had ever heard, but in no time they had taken enthusiastically to singing them night and morning.[2] Hymn singing became an integral part of Church Missionary Society services. Mrs Selwyn noted other skills at Waimate in 1842: 'It is a most pleasant sight to see these people at church, and to hear them repeat the responses. Such perfect time do they keep, so completely in unison are their voices that the sound is as the measured tread of a large body of men . . .'[3]

At the same time, the Māori had began incorporating elements of Christian services into their own rituals. Margaret Orbell describes the process in her *Songs of the First Maori Christians*:

> After the acceptance of Christianity the tangihanga [funeral meeting] ceremony continued, with some modifications, and waiata tangi were still sung; though eventually there were fewer new songs, and a greater reliance upon the old ones. Some of the traditional subject-matter had disappeared now that there were no more heroic deaths in battle to mourn, and no more enemies to be cursed and threatened with revenge. And as time went on there were fewer references to the figures in the myths, for in most cases the younger people no longer understood their significance and their roles in the poetry. But new material came from Christianity, all the more readily because the two systems of thought and belief were in some ways not dissimilar. Both were much concerned with death and the fate of the soul . . .[4]

Hone Nukunuku playing the kōauau to young listeners. James McDonald took this photograph on his 1923 ethnological expedition at Waiapu. *National Museum, Wellington*

Traditional waiata began to widen its scope to include new and urgent matters such as the loss of land and the spiritual deprivation it brought. Te Kooti's 'Waiata Tohutohu' was a prophetic song written to instil courage into the Tuhoe in their stand against the Europeans.[5] Later, Puhiwaahine, famed as a composer of songs such as 'Ka Eke Ki Wairaka', sang it as a protest against the sittings of the Native Land Court.[6] Te Whiti o Rongomai, the prophet of Parihaka, composed traditional songs, haka and poi, to help and encourage his followers in their peaceful stance against further appropriations of land following the wars of the 1860s.

A variety of musical forms were used during the wars, when many Māori reacted against European culture, including music, and sought to identify themselves more strongly with their ancient traditions as embodied in the waiata. Yet the followers of Te Ua, the prophet of the Pai mārire or Hau-Hau Māori movement, active first in Taranaki and then elsewhere, borrowed from the Pākehā religion: 'the surviving Pai marire karakia are cast in a mould very much like that of the chants and prayers that Te Ua himself had used as a Wesleyan assistant monitor before the outbreak of fighting in the 1860s', writes Paul Clark.[7] These were not necessarily efficacious: 'We get no benefit from our Hau-Hau karakia', wrote a chief to the Reverend Robert Maunsell: 'it is like a person trying to cross the river in a large square box. There is neither head nor stern and when we try to steer we cannot get it to move rightly.'[8] This theme is developed by Barry Mitcalfe: 'The Maori, displaced in his own land, and lacking the substance of European power, took its forms. He thought these . . . would give him the power of the European . . .'[9]

The first Māori soloists emerged in the later nineteenth century, drawing on the European repertoire as well as their own. The first concert parties to tour overseas won great renown. Māori musicians began to explore European music more boldly. They learned European instruments and appropriated them; in 1901, for example, they carried a piano on to the marae to accompany a haka at the royal welcoming celebrations for the Duke and Duchess of Cornwall and York.

European scholars, collectors, and anthropologists adopted at first a more intellectual approach, content to classify rather than perform, although many 'Māori' melodies had already served as the basis of Victorian ballads. At first Europeans concentrated on the texts of songs, thinking of them as 'Māori poetry', whereas in fact they were always indissolubly related to the music. Prominent among early collectors was Sir George Grey, who, during his first governorship from 1845 to 1853, published five books drawing upon the stories, songs, and proverbs he had gathered.[10] In the Preface to the 1853 edition of his collection *Poems, traditions and chaunts of the Maoris: Ko nga Moteatea . . .*, he explains that he has tried to show the way the country appeared before Christianity took hold, when 'so ancient and highly figurative was the language in which they [the songs] were composed, that already large portions of them are nearly or quite unintelligible to many of their best instructed young men'.[11] This historic work contains over 533 songs in all categories, described by A. G. Bagnall in his *National Bibliography* as 'one of the great gifts of Maoritanga to New Zealand culture'. Later, James Davies, former scholar of Trinity College, Cambridge, wrote an appendix to Grey's *Polynesian Mythology* (1855) entitled 'On the native songs of New Zealand',[12] comparing Māori music to that of the ancient Greeks which he thought it resembled. Grey describes the difficulties he experienced in notating the music and how the singers did not always repeat the musical phrases 'with precisely the *same* modulation'.[13]

Three other smaller collections were published in the 1850s. Edward Shortland's *Traditions and Superstitions of the New Zealanders* (1854) contained nine songs with translations, historical notes, and useful information on song types. In 1855 the missionary Richard Taylor included the texts of eight songs in chapter 10 of his *Te Ika a Maui*. In the same year, Charles Davis's *Maori Mementos* included the text of fifty-four songs, as well as a series of addresses presented by the Māori people to Sir George Grey.

In 1864 John McGregor, while guarding prisoners of war taken at Rangiriri and confined to a prison ship moored in Auckland harbour, asked if they would write down their love songs, promising publication if they did. His *Maori Songs, as written by the Maori of Waikato*, appeared twenty-nine years later in 1893. He had gathered over 400 songs.[14] The Māori scholar John White (1826-1891) collected many karakia in his six volume *Ancient History of the Maori* (1887-1890).

White's interest in Māori culture developed during his fifteen years at Hokianga, before he became government interpreter in 1852.[15] Towards the end of the nineteenth century a notable group, including the ethnographer Elsdon Best (1856-1931), the free-thinker, socialist, public servant, and scholar James Tregear (1846-1931), and the young composer Alfred Hill (1870-1960), explored Māori music. Then in 1892 the Polynesian Society was founded, largely through the influence of Percy Smith (1840-1922), an English-born surveyor and ethnologist, who edited their influential *Journal* for the following thirty years. Hill's extensive use of Māori material in songs, string quartets, orchestral works, and opera, is detailed elsewhere (see chapter VII, 3). Hill retained a lifelong affection for the Māori people and their culture, but his approach to collecting was not followed up. 'It may have seemed that New Zealand was set on a bi-cultural path in music that could have yielded a unique national style and an awareness, spreading outward, of Oceanic and Asian musics', wrote Alan Thomas. 'In fact the reverse was the case.'[16]

Māori girl playing the jew's harp. *William Main collection*

Best's *Games and Pastimes of the Maori* (1925) included sections on Māori songs, singing, and instruments. Best's major achievement proved to be his recording of the traditions of the Tuhoe of the Urewera, still relatively intact.[17] Johannes C. Andersen (1873-1962), a Dane who had emigrated with his family at the age of two, became part of this group. His *Maori Music* (1934) is a compilation of what was known about Polynesian music at the time, as reported in missionary, travel, and other accounts. A dedicated ornithologist, he notates and gives background information on many bird-calls in his pioneering *Birdsong and New Zealand Song Birds* (1926), speculating on their effect on the Māori (and Pākehā'): 'There are instances of birds singing short phrases reminiscent of phrases in our own music; the four opening notes of 'Scenes that are brightest' have been heard from a tui, not only the sequence of the notes but their values too.'[18]

An outstanding Māori became active at this time. Sir Apirana Ngata, with Sir Peter Buck and others, stimulated a cultural revival and encouraged research. Ngata (1874-1950) was a member of the Young Maori Party, a movement that had grown from the Te Aute College Old Boys' Association after the land wars of the 1860s, when the Maori population was dramatically declining. His three-volume work *Nga Moteatea* (1928)[19] is an extensive collection of songs, with notes giving the provenance of waiata and the significance of allusions in the text. He had collected these over a period of forty years, in many instances from his own recordings.

The enthusiasm of the Māori for bands led them to form numerous ensembles containing an astonishing diversity of instruments, some of them modelled on the Salvation Army. Others demonstrated notable polish and skill: the famed drum and fife band at Parihaka, which at the time of Sir Peter Buck's visit in 1897 consisted of about thirty players, and the excellent Arawa Silver Band of 1910. In the latter part of the nineteenth century the Salvation Army, notably through the activities of Brigadier Ernest Holloway and his wife, penetrated

The fife and drum band at Parihaka. *Collis, National Museum, Wellington*

the fastnesses of the North Island, including the Wanganui River, Taranaki, and the King Country, where they taught many Māori to play such instruments as the cornet and tuba, side drum, autoharp, harmonica, the 'fairy bells', and musical glasses.[20] The first Maori songbook compiled by the Army was *Te Pukapuka Waiata mo nga hoia o Te Ope Whakaora* (1890): 'Our new Maori song book is greatly prized and we have a singing lesson every meeting. It would do you good to hear the brown-skinned, bright-eyed, white-teethed boys. They sing with a vengeance and are learning the new songs well.'[21] Salvationist Māori contingents visited England.[22]

1 Waiata ā ringa

Around the turn of the century a new form of Māori music came into being, the Waiata ā ringa, or action song: 'a vital, exhilarating, resonant, thriving and integral part of Maori life today', wrote Wiremu Parker in 1984. 'Action songs represent the Maori's own unique and distinctive cultural and racial expression. They provide a source of new diction and vitality to meet the fresh and changing experiences in the new life-style, in work, play and leisure, in new-found tastes, loyalties, affections and disaffections.'[23] Action songs can be adaptations and extensions of overseas melodies, such as 'Blue Eyes', the waltz tune behind Paraire Tomoana's 1916 song 'E Pari Ra', a tribute and lament for Māori soldiers of World War I. Similarly, 'You're a Flower from a Lovely Bouquet' is absorbed in Apirana Ngata's action song of the early 1920s, 'He Putiputi Koe i Katohia'. The co-operative dairy farmers amongst the Ngati Porou took to their hearts Ngata's 'Cream Song', written to encourage them in their struggle for economic independence.[24] 'In the Mood' was rearranged by Tuini Ngawai as a tribute to the Māori Victoria Cross winner 2nd Lieutenant Te Moana-nui-a-Kiwa Ngarimu, becoming a lament with hymnal affinities, 'E Te Hokowhitu a Tu'.[25] Ngawai's 'Arohaina Mai', with its echoes of Gershwin's 'Love Walked In', bade farewell to the men of the Ngāti Porou. Tuini Ngawai (1910-1965) has a special place in the regeneration of Māoridom. Born on the East Coast, she showed an early gift for writing songs and in 1939 joined Walter Smith's Choir, which then broadcast regularly in Auckland. In the same year she founded the Hokowhitu-ā-Tuu concert party, organized to farewell local soldiers departing overseas. Smith gave her a grounding in composition, and in return she wrote Māori words for a number of the choir's works. 'Te Reo' ('The Voice'), 'Arohaina Mai', and a host of entertaining and satirical songs drawn from her experience as an expert shearer, have become celebrated. While the tune was often derived from the hit parade or from an old-timer,[26] the words were crucial to her, and she disdained both mixed metaphor and cliché.[27] Other leading figures include Kumeroa Ngoi Pewhairangi (1922-1985), an author and craftswoman active in the 1970s and 1980s, whose 'Poi-e', sung by the Patea Māori Club, fused action song with the latest electro-acoustic dance rhythms to create an international hit; and Ngoingoi Pewhairangi, a prolific songwriter from the Ngāti Porou. Jennifer Shennan has concluded that the action song is 'effectively the national dance of New Zealand'.[28]

Scholars working in the field of Māori music today are greatly indebted to the outstanding work of Margaret Orbell and Mervyn McLean, whose *Traditional Songs of the Maori* (1975) is the first to include both texts and music. Fifty songs representative of the most common types have been transcribed by McLean, with translations and annotations by Orbell. McLean estimates that the 5,000 or so existing song texts are probably only a small fraction of the repertoire that once existed, 'but this is a substantial oral literature by any standards and New Zealand may count itself fortunate that so many texts have survived'.[29] In addition to an extensive literary output, McLean established the Archive of Pacific Music at the University of Auckland in 1970[30] Barry Mitcalfe's work in this field also won recognition. His *The Singing Word* (1974), although criticized by Māori scholars for linguistic inconsistencies, is imbued with sympathy for the subject, notably in its spirited introduction and in the chapter entitled 'The singing word'.[31]

Maggie Papakura's concert party before it left New Zealand for Sydney in 1910 and London the following year. Maggie is in the second row up, third from the left. *The Bath House, Rotorua's Art and History Museum, Rotorua*

2 *Māori concert groups and solo artists*

While changes occurred within Māori music, it came to have quite another impact on the western world through the emergence of concert groups and soloists. An early instance was that of Haggerty's ragbag touring 'concert party' in 1863, which became confused with that of the Methodist Māori converts taken to Britain by William Jenkins the same year to commemorate the Mission's jubilee and to demonstrate 'good works'. Jenkins lectured on New Zealand; the chiefs sang and performed hakas.[32]

More successful expeditions followed, as outstanding Māori singers arose, characterized by the spectacular career of Princess Te Rangi Pai (1868-1916), the wife of John Howie and daughter of Herewaka and Colonel T. W. Porter, a Māori war veteran. She received lessons from Charles Santley and from a Mr Partridge in London, and pursued an active professional life in the early 1900s. Her lullaby 'Hine e Hine' became a particular favourite with audiences.

Vigorous displays of Māori dancing and music had characterized events such as the royal tour of the Duke and Duchess of Cornwall and York in 1901, and the 1906-1907 Christchurch Exhibition. They continued to be featured at Rotorua, which rapidly developed as an international tourist resort in the latter part of the nineteenth century. Makereti or Maggie Papakura (1870-1930), as she was known, was born in Whakarewarewa of the Arawa tribe. She organized a group of accomplished performers whom she took to the Māori village at Clontarf in Sydney in 1910. Forty of them went on to London for Coronation year, 1911,[33] winning triumphant receptions from the British Press and public. The artefacts they took with them, including a house and pataka (store house), aroused great interest.[34] Maggie Papakura became one of the best-known Rotorua guides, working with her gifted sister Bella, a composer and choreographer, and the Reverend Frederick Bennett. She subsequently married an Englishman, settled near Oxford, and wrote her classic introduction to Māori culture, *The Old Time Maori*.

Princess Iwa, (*floreat* 1910) billed as 'the famous Maori contralto', who formed part of Maggie Papakura's party both in Australia and London, thereafter pursued a singing career, appearing in Boosey Ballad concerts, Harrison provincial tours, the Albert Hall, and the Palace Theatre.[35] During World War I she sang in the ANZAC Concert Party, where her repertoire included 'Kamati Kamati' and 'Hoki, Hoki Tonu Mai', a canoe song.

The tradition of notable Rotorua guides continued with Guide Rangi (1896-1970), whose family belonged to the Ringatu religion, founded by the Māori rebel and patriot Te Kooti. The religion was based largely on the Old Testament, mixed with Māori religious beliefs and customs. 'Our days always began with the singing of hymns and with prayer', she told her biographer

Princess Iwa. *Alexander Turnbull Library*

Rangitiaria Dennan. 'The singing was always spontaneous and hearty and very beautiful.'[36] At the time when she travelled overseas in Maggie Papakura's concert party, she felt Rotorua to be 'almost the last stronghold of the poi dance'.[37]

Princess Te Puea's concert party, Te Pou o Mangatawhiri (TPM), and the Band, a sub-group whose instruments included violins, guitars, and mandolins, and who played 'non-Māori music', were active in the 1920s. Te Puea 'borrowed as many Maori costumes as she could, sewed others herself, and bought a second-hand set of blazers and white trousers' for the Band, wrote Michael King. In 1923, with swags on their backs, they began touring, walking vast distances until the soles of their shoes were worn off and their shirts were disintegrating. In over three months they had saved £900, which went to Te Puea's community at Turangawaewae. They had developed a fine ensemble spirit and aroused fresh interest in Māori music and action songs.[38]

This pattern continued in a variety of ensembles, some connected with broadcasting, some with the church, such as the Waiata Maori Choir formed by the Reverend A. J. Seamer of the Methodist Maori Mission. One member and soloist of this choir was Inia te Wiata, soon to have a distinguished overseas career.[39] 'In the Waikato, the Methodists were especially successful because they did not attempt to reform Maori values, but were prepared to adapt church ritual to suit Maori tastes', writes Donna Awatere.[40] This was typified by A. J. Seamer, who, through a lasting relationship with Te Puea, took part in the communal life of the marae, including Pai marire services.

3 *Recording Māori music*

Pioneering attempts to record Māori music on wax cylinders probably began in the late nineteenth century and continued during the following decade. Alfred Hill believed that he was instrumental in James McDonald and James Cowan's undertaking a recording expedition in the King Country.[41] Immeasurable difficulties were experienced in using such equipment effectively.[42] The earliest recordings held by the Archive of Maori and Pacific Music are those of A. J. Knocks and his friend Percy Grainger. Systematic recordings on wax dictaphone cylinders began in 1919 at a large meeting in Gisborne to welcome home members of the Māori Battalion after World War I.[43] 'New Zealand has the great good fortune to possess a virtually continuous profile of recorded traditional Maori music from 1909 right through to the present day', concludes Mervyn McLean.[44]

The commercial possibilities in making recordings of Māori music led the Parlophone company of Australia and the Columbia Gramophone Company of England to record Dean Waretini and Ana Hato, a guide, at Rotorua during the 1927 visit of the Duke and Duchess of York, later to become King George VI and Queen Elizabeth. The contralto Ana Hato (*c.* 1906-1953), began as a penny diver; by the age of seventeen she was regarded as one of the best Māori singers in Rotorua.[45] In 1930 Columbia records sent the composer, arranger, and conductor Gil Dech to Rotorua to record the famous Rotorua Maori Choir. Māori artists and choirs became a central part of the tiny New Zealand recording industry.

During the 1920s and 1930s Māori music became heavily westernized. After hearing a Rotorua concert party in 1939, Alfred Hill concluded that 'much of what was precious in Maori music was being rapidly lost'.[46] Later that year he again lamented the neglect of Māori music: 'They are becoming Hawaiian, complete with guitar, ukelele and Maori words set to a Hawaiian tune. . . .'[47] He proposed an annual competition to cover games, dances, songs, and all forms of Māori art. Donna Awatere has confirmed this decline, despite the efforts of Māori such as Guide Rangi: 'Many waiata were merely Maori words put to popular songs. These new waiata along with poi and haka became the basis for haka party groups. Spiritually meaningful haka invoking nga mana atua (literally, the power of the gods) became, along with much empty grimacing, the matter of frivolous entertainment.'[48]

In recent years, Māori performing arts groups have sprung into being who have benefited from the renaissance of Māori culture, embodying its approach and findings in their own performances.

Ana Hato (c. 1906-53).
*The Bath House, Rotorua's
Art and History Museum*

4 *The two cultures today*

Over the last two decades many New Zealand composers have responded to the Māori inheritance, embodying many different approaches, from the romantic and pictorial to the authentic and interpretative. A need to be properly sensitive to the other culture must be uppermost in composers' minds.[49] Lilburn's *Summer Voices* (1968), an electro-acoustic work influenced by the well-known Māori oriori (lullaby) 'Po! Po!', shows such qualities. Earlier, his sound images to Alistair Campbell's poem 'The Return' (1965) had shown sensitivity to the musical qualities of the Māori language. Jenny McLeod's spectacular theatre piece *Earth and Sky* (1968) drew on childhood memories of the Māori. Later she was attracted by their ancient creation poetry: 'The power of the poetry and the extraordinarily fresh, direct, truthful performance that children are capable of, gave *Earth and Sky* its unusual impact I feel, more than any musical contribution made by me.'[50] 'It is marked by the masterly use of spoken word, speech intonation and chant which set the Maori text of creation in a way which is both evocative of Maori traditions and accessible to contemporary audiences', wrote Thomas.[51] Ross Harris's interest in Māori themes culminated in the opera *Waituhi* (1984) to a libretto by Witi Ihimaera which dealt with contemporary issues such as land, and contrasted the power of the local marae with the attraction of the city. The composer set it in a traditional operatic framework interspersed with haka, poi, action song, and waiata.[52] Douglas Mews' 'Love Song of Rangi-Pouri' is a setting of one of the songs in McLean and Orbell's *Traditional Songs of the Maori*, for a conventional four-part choir with a male soloist assigned the original chant.[53] Gillian Whitehead has written many delicately textured works with Māori associations, which stem from her Māori ancestry.

At Wellington's 1984 Asia Pacific Festival, the internationally respected Vietnamese musician Tran van Khe summed up the problem: 'Acculturation works or is beneficial when elements borrowed are compatible with the original tradition.'[54]

Witi Ihimaera, well placed to understand both cultures, commented in his 1982 Turnbull lecture that 'The singing word, as Barry Mitcalfe characterised waiata, does not have the power to sing out across generations and the empty spaces as it once had. Yet, by far, the oral literature forms the basis for the underground movement which is the Maori people. Its voice may not be strong but it still survives despite the political and cultural imperialism of the majority in New Zealand.'[55] As Mitcalfe had earlier written: 'Out of the spindly manuka, a new forest is springing.'[56] Both Māori and European artists traditionally see beyond such connotations of 'cultural imperialism', even if political and commercial interests lag behind. Seven years later, Witi Ihimaera suggests there may well be new developments:

Group of young Māori
playing European musical
instruments in an outdoor
setting. *Alexander Turnbull
Library*

Perhaps the most convenient definition of Maori music is that 'It is Maori if
Maori people say it is'. The positive side of this is that Maori people are thus
able to assimilate western musical influences and turn these into forms which
are acceptable to them as an expression of their identity. So, apart from the
traditional forms of waiata, which continues to be composed, we also have
the contemporary waiata-a-ringa, or action song with movements . . . while
some of the tunes may sound suspiciously Gershwin-esque, the lyrics are what
is important here: in virtually every case, the lyrics express the joys of being
Maori and of upholding Maori culture. In this respect, the direction of modern
Maori music is often determined by its accepted and most popular exponents.
Tuini Ngawai, Bill Kerekere, Ngoi Pewhairangi, Mauka Jones, Peter Sharples,
Sir Kingi Ihaka, Kohine Ponika, Dalvanius Prime and Sydney Melbourne,
among others, have all brought western influences into Maori music and made
their music 'Maori' . . . But the negative side of the definition is that while
it enables Maori composers to range widely through many modern forms, it
has often led to a lack of concentration on development of Maori music from
the centre—from Maori culture itself . . . Maori composers need to go back
to the roots of their music and develop a genre more appropriate to Maori
culture, even if it means sacrificing their 'popular' standing among the
community. They need to tune their ears to tradition, to take heed of the
centre and, if they can, become less susceptible to the influences coming in
from the rim. Perhaps, above all, we need a Maori equivalent of Janáček, or
Lilburn, or Britten to develop for us a tradition which might set the standard
for the development of a truly unique Maori sound, and which takes its compass
point from its very own magnetic lodestone, the pounamu ngakau, the
greenstone landscapes of the heart.[57]

Notes

1 McLean, 'Analysis', 148

2 See McLean, 'Towards a typology of musical change', 36

3 Letter dated 6 September 1842, quoted in Annabell thesis, 'Music in Auckland', 146. The compass of the response 'O Lord, Open thou our lips . . .', for instance, closely resembled that of a Māori waiata

4 *Landfall*, March 1984, 70ff. See also her excellent introduction to *Maori Poetry*

5 McLean and Orbell, 37

6 Ibid., 55

7 Clark, P., 93

8 Quoted in Morell, *Anglican Church*, 84

9 Mitcalfe, *Maori Poetry*, 110

10 See Orbell, M., 'Aotearoa's written history'. *NZL*, 23 February 1985

11 Quoted in McLean, 'Preservation', 21

12 Grey, *Polynesian Mythology*, 239-40. Davies published transcriptions of the opening lines of four songs from Grey's *Ko Nga Moteatea*

13 This first attempt to notate Māori music was not followed up in a scholarly way until McLean's notations began to appear in the Māori journal *Te Ao Hou* from 1964 to 1966

14 Published in Auckland by John Henry Field, printer. Supplements published 1898 (no. 1), 1903 (no. 2), 1905 (no. 3), 1909 (no. 4) by Champtaloup and Cooper, Auckland. See Orbell, *NZL*, 23 February 1985

15 Bagnall writes: 'It was a bold project for the time in which the courage and persistence of the author and the tolerance of the Crown were not matched by adequate liaison with informants, critical standards of scholarship and, not least, printing skills.' *NZNB*, 1/2, 116-17

16 'Pacific awareness in New Zealand composition' in Norman (ed.) *Aspects of New Zealand Composition 1950-80. Canzona*, vol. 3, November 1981

17 *Tuhoe, the Children of the Mist* (2 vols., Polynesian Society Memoir, New Plymouth, 1925). Vol. 1 contains numerous song texts and translations. See Bagnall's sympathetic tribute to Best in *ENZ*, vol. 1, 199

18 Andersen, *Maori Music*, 412. Samuel Butler in the 1860s felt that 'the birds in New Zealand approached the diatonic scale more nearly than European birds do', quoted in Andersen, 413

19 Later revised and expanded by Pei Te Hurinui Jones (1959, 1961, 1970)

20 Brigadier Ivy Cresswell, 'Canoe on the river', *War Cry*, from 3 April 1971 in 38 weekly parts

21 'Captain Bain at Otaki', *War Cry*, 10 July 1971

22 *War Cry*, 4 September 1971, 4. A visit to London in 1849 is mentioned

23 Wiremu Parker in Foreword to Jennifer Shennan's *The Maori Action Song*, vii

24 Shennan, J. 19ff.

25 See George Bryant's 'A kiwi fighting for the highest prize', *Dominion*, 29 December 1988, 10, a vivid account of Ngarimu's exploits in the Middle East, 1943

26 'Tuini Ngawai, her life and songs', Gisborne, 1985; 'Whaikoorero ceremonial farewells to the dead', Continuing Education Unit of RNZ, University of Waikato, Hamilton 1981

27 See Mitcalfe, 87

28 Ibid., xi

29 McLean, 'Preservation', 23

30 See McLean, *Annotated Bibliography*, 1977, and *Supplement*, 1981

31 For reviews see Awatere, D., *JPS*, vol. 84, no. 4, 510-19; Orbell, M., *Landfall*, vol. 29, no. 1, 86-91

32 James Smetham's painting *Maori Chiefs in Wesley's House* (1863), Hocken Library, shows the Rev. Jenkins with his flock. Leonard Bell (Bell, 50-1) believes it gives a disarmingly harmonious picture of good relationships, a view disputed by Thora Parker, Chs 3 and 4

33 Dick Papakura led the Arawa Silver Band, whose members were also part of the haka troupe. See Maggie Papakura's letter to Alfred Hill from Clontarf in Thomson, *ADM*, 120, and Makereti

34 Makereti, vii. After a year in Britain, part of it on the music-hall circuit as entertainers, twenty of the group remained in London under the management of Rangiuia, a highly successful Māori singer from the East Coast. See T. E. Donne Scrapbook, and MS Papers 1387, ATL

35 She had earlier studied singing from a European singing teacher in Invercargill

36 Dennan, 23

37 Dennan, 50

38 See fuller account in Michael King's authoritative biography *Te Puea*, 116ff.

39 See biography by Wiata, B. Te

40 Awatere, 84

41 Thomson, *ADM*, 189

42 See McLean, 'Sound archiving as an aid to musical conservation in the Pacific', *Continuo*, vol. 4, no. 1, 1974, and McLean, 'Preservation of the indigenous musical heritage of NZ', *Continuo*, July and November 1981

43 The recording team from the Dominion Museum was led by Elsdon Best, accompanied by Johannes C. Andersen, James McDonald, and H. Balneavis. See McLean, 'Preservation', 27

44 McLean, 'Preservation', 29

45 For details of her career and strenuous efforts to raise funds for the armed forces, see Dennan, 90

46 Interview in *Radio Record*, 3 March 1939, 12

47 *NZL*, 11 August 1939

48 Awatere, 87

49 Many European New Zealand composers have worked in this genre

50 Communication to author

51 'Pacific awareness', in *Aspects of New Zealand Composition*, November 1981, 29

52 See chapter IX, 2

53 Some scholars consider this one of the most successful fusions of Māori and western idiom. It was sung by the Dorian Singers on their 1975 European tour

54 Quoted by Thomson, J. M. in 'New Zealand', *Musical Times*, May 1985

55 'Maori life and literature: a sensory perception', Turnbull Winter Lectures 1981. Wellington (1982) 49

56 Mitcalfe, 157

57 Communication to author, 1986

Part Two

Growth of a Composing Tradition

Douglas Lilburn and Allen
Curnow at a performance
of *Landfall in Unknown
Seas*, Victoria University of
Wellington. *New Zealand
Listener*

VIII

Forerunners

1 *Preamble*

When Douglas Lilburn spoke to the students at the first Cambridge Summer School of Music in January 1946, his talk, 'A Search for Tradition', was given from a unique standpoint. He could not only evaluate the heritage of the musical past, but with a new generation of young composers in his audience, adumbrate a future.[1] With hindsight, it seems no coincidence that he should address himself to the central issues of New Zealand music on this occasion. Nobody had done so before. There had been, it is true, a number of prophetic utterances: for example, when Alfred Hill left Wellington to study in Leipzig, the *New Zealand Times* of 15 March 1892 declared him to be 'among the first of what we believe will be a long line of musicians destined to rise in this colony . . .' Many pious hopes had also been expressed in the pages of the *Triad, Music in New Zealand*, and elsewhere.

Lilburn pleaded the necessity 'of having a music of our own, a living tradition of music created in this country, a music that will satisfy those parts of our being that cannot be satisfied by music of other nations'. He made it clear that he did not hark back to nationalistic music, as had arisen, for example, in Bohemia, Russia, or Spain. His was a practical exhortation: 'I find myself wanting to remind you that our cultural problems have to be worked out in the totally new context of these islands we live in, a context that has an infinite potential richness we've hardly drawn on yet.'

Such a context included 'qualities of colour and line and distance, and the clarity of light that plays over us'—the visual artist in the musician. New Zealand music should communicate an awareness of these qualities—'and in some way bring us into harmony with them . . . Physically and materially perhaps we are, but in a spiritual sense we still behave in many ways as though we were strangers in the land.'

Any tradition of music that developed in New Zealand 'should give us that feeling of our proper identity that I've been speaking of, to remove from our conscience that uneasy thought that we are simply living on the spiritual capital of an older world, or that we're unfortunate exiles from the real world of music that goes on overseas'. Only those who have developed a tradition of their own can enter fully into those of others.

Lilburn also touched on the nature of the tradition inherited by the young New Zealand composer, who, by comparison with his counterparts in England and Europe, might seem poverty-stricken but who 'in another sense is immensely rich, because being heir to no particular tradition he inherits the whole world's music'.

In its inheritance of Polynesian music through the Māori people the country possessed a unique historical repository, but one that in 1946 was more like a locked bank vault of treasures than a viable living organism. Pre-European Māori music seemed virtually inaccesible to the Pākehā and had limited currency even amongst the Māori people. The generation of Pākehā pioneers who used Māori culture to weave it into a European texture, such as Alfred Hill, had not yet been succeeded by those who were to create impressive oral archives. Māori music was in a transitional state, westernized, served up to tourists, or used by both Māori and Pākehā popular entertainers. Lilburn could not see it as the basis for 'the founding of a national music', a concept which had previously engaged the attention of the young Alfred Hill when he wished to set up an institution for the study of Māori music in Rotorua early in the century. Nevertheless, 'the Maoris have shown themselves much more able and willing to absorb our culture than we to absorb theirs'.

Deprived of a valid folk-song tradition, unlikely to find fruitful stimulus in living Māori music, the young composer 'having no local tradition to guide him must seek one out for himself'. Lilburn placed particular stress on certain aspects of music:

> . . . this environment of ours is shaping us into characteristic rhythms of living . . . everything about us, the patterns of our landscape and seacoasts, the changing of our seasons, and the flow of light and colour about us . . . show patterns of movement or characteristic rhythms. And these things in a subtle way affect our manner of living . . . It is this factor of our new and unique environment in New Zealand, and the change of outlook it is producing in us, that will mark our departure-point from the older traditions of music. Whatever disadvantages we labour under in a small and isolated country, we have the advantage of being able to come closer to those fundamental and rather simple things that are the fountainhead of any art, and we have the opportunity, if we care to take it, of seeing these things with a freshness of vision. Out of them I believe that with faith and hard work we can make something of value to ourselves, and that the effort involved in doing so is infinitely worth while.

Notes

[1]   Lilburn, *A Search for Tradition*

2 *Early colonial composers and their publications*

The musical publications of the colonial period revive memories of the voyage out, of ballroom quadrilles, waltzes, galops, and polkas, of the presence of British regimental bands. They summon the sports field as well as the drawing-room. Visiting artists who fancied themselves as composers might dash off a ballad in praise of a particular city or town, no doubt celebrating full houses as well as adulation, and reaping extra rewards from sales of the music (quickly produced by the local printer) in the concert hall foyer. Many of these publications are elegant examples of the skills of the time. Some were printed in Leipzig or Berlin by the finest European engravers. Others look homespun and amateurish by comparison, set in crude music type and printed on local steam presses. The titles reflect these predilections: 'The Huia Waltz', 'Colonial Mazurka', or Angelo Forrest's 'Porangi Polka'.[1] 'On the Ball' became the official song of New Zealand rugby.[2] Music of the period utilized all the techniques currently available: engraving on copper plate, music type, and lithography. Itinerant music engravers produced work of high quality throughout the nineteenth century in New Zealand, but nearly all of their tools of trade, such as punches and copper plates, have vanished.[3]

Luscombe Searelle, *Melbourne Bulletin*, 15 May 1885. *La Trobe collection, State Library of Victoria*

Publishers included the prosperous music emporia of George West and Charles Begg in Dunedin, the Dresden Piano Company of Wellington (renamed the Bristol during World War I), and Arthur Eady of Auckland.[4] Alfred Hill's 'Waiata Poi', written in the early years of this century, kept John McIndoe's Dunedin presses busy, meeting the demand for New Zealand's first international best-seller. Between 1879 and 1900 over fifty different publications appeared, reflecting changing tastes, passions, and crazes. Cycling, which swept the world in the early years of this century, was one such:

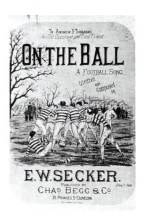

> Our little bykes are trim and neat;
> Their tyres are firm and strong,
> Their lamps send forth a brilliant light,
> Their bells ring fast and long . . .[5]

One song stands out in this period: John Woods' 'God Defend New Zealand'. Many countries have acquired their national anthems through competitions: New Zealand was no exception. In 1876 John Joseph Woods (1849-1934) won a contest for 'The Best National Air' to accompany the poet Thomas Bracken's 'National Hymn'. In 1878 'God Defend New Zealand' was published as the National Anthem, later restyled to National Song. The Premier, Richard Seddon, presented a copy to Queen Victoria in 1897 when the second edition appeared,

although formal status as the National Song was not accorded until 1939. It was recognized as one of New Zealand's two Anthems (along with 'God Save the Queen') in 1977.[6]

Woods came to New Zealand from Tasmania and earned his living as a clerk with the Tuapeka County Council at Lawrence in southern Otago. He played a number of instruments, especially the violin, and for many years conducted the Roman Catholic church choir.

Thomas Bracken (1843-1898) had already penned the words of a possible national anthem, and dedicated his verses to Governor Normanby:

God of Nations, at Thy feet
In the bonds of love we meet,
Hear our voices we entreat,
God Defend our Freeland.

The weekly Dunedin newspaper, the *Saturday Advertiser*, then offered a prize of ten guineas for the best setting of Bracken's words, stating that 'National songs, ballads and hymns have a tendency to elevate the character of a people and keep alive the fire of patriotism in their breasts.' The judges consisted of 'three competent gentlemen living in Melbourne', Messrs Zelman, Zeplin, and Siede.[7]

Joseph Woods entered the competition under the *non de plume* of 'Orpheus Lawrence', a title which stuck. In the face of keen national competition, he is reported to have won the prize unanimously. The first public performance appears to be that given by the Lydia Howarde Troupe in a sacred concert on Christmas Night 1876 at the Queen's Theatre, Dunedin, when 'it was rendered as a chorus with the Artillery Band accompaniment and evoked very loud applause . . . The music is simple, pleasing and expressive and is sure to become very popular.'[8]

In March 1878 Sir George Grey, then Prime Minister, heard it sung by 800 children in a wool store when he visited Lawrence. On his arrival with the official party, over 300 people welcomed the train: 'The band under the indefatigable bandmaster (Mr Corrison) was also in attendance and struck up "See the conquering hero comes" directly the train ceased motion.'[9] The children sang three verses of the new anthem — 'the words and singing touched his heart'. An avid collector, Sir George soon solicited the original manuscript from the composer, who obligingly sent a holograph copy.[10] At the personal request of Sir George, Thomas H. Smith, retired judge of the Native Land Court, translated 'God Defend New Zealand' into Māori.[11] Woods, who gained the sole rights to print and publish the work from Bracken, promoted it tirelessly, particularly its use in schools. After a record fifty-five years of meritorious service, the faithful clerk and part-time composer was eventually awarded the freedom of Tuapeka County. A blue plaque now graces his former Lawrence home.

New Zealand has learned to live with the difficult intervals and rhetorical sentiments of its national song and has not yet felt obliged to plan a successor as Australia attempted to do in 1973, when it held an inconclusive competition to replace the unofficial 'Waltzing Matilda' with a more fitting anthem than 'Advance Australia Fair'.[12]

Since Woods' day there have been a number of arrangements for a variety of forces, and in recent years the song has suffered near-mortal mutilation on television. Yet when it received a measured and sonorous rendering by the Dresden Staatskapelle at Wellington's Michael Fowler Centre in 1986, it seemed to acquire a new dimension. New Zealand's national song could be considered a sober Victorian hymn.

A different vein is found in the publications of several talented English musicians who emigrated to New Zealand, often for health reasons, in the nineteenth century. Imbued with the English choirmaster and organist tradition, they held influential positions in city churches, and found that their music was of interest to publishers in England, where the principal market lay. A leading exponent of this rather neglected aspect of New Zealand musical life was Thomas Tallis Trimnell (1827-1897), originally a chorister in the Cathedral Choir, Bristol, and later an organist and brass band conductor, who came to Auckland from Sheffield in 1886. He was a prolific composer, and some of his works, such as an Evening Service in C and an anthem 'Thou'lt keep him in perfect peace', were published by Novello.[13] Alfred Hill admired his improvising abilities, and described him as a good conductor.[14]

Maughan Barnett (1867-1938), an excellent pianist and a gifted organist, is probably the most considerable talent of this generation, with the widest range. He moved beyond the choral tradition to become a popular city organist in Wellington and Auckland, as well as an orchestral conductor.[15] He wrote church music and occasionally for orchestra (Concert Overture in E minor, for example). His salon work, 'Valse Caprice' for piano, has an assured and agreeable style. He maintained a deep interest in the piano, writing *A Short Course of Pianoforte Technique*.[16] His prominent public position led him to compose two Odes, one for the opening of the Canterbury Jubilee Industrial Exhibition of 1900,[17] the other for the laying of the foundation stone of the Town Hall, Wellington by the Duke of Cornwall and York in 1901.[18]

Robert Parker (1846-1937) played a leading part in establishing the high professional level of Wellington's musical life over a considerable period, and is consequently best known as a teacher and conductor. He wrote occasional compositions in the English choral tradition.[19]

From this group, Alfred Hill soon emerged as the composer on whom many pinned their hopes for a truly New Zealand music. His first publication, 'The Organist', a sentimental ballad with a cover designed by his artist sister Mabel, showing an elderly man seated at the organ, appeared in 1886 when he was sixteen. On his return to Wellington from Leipzig, he soon showed the extent of his abilities.

Notes

[1] See Lodge, M. 'Publishing pianissimo'. *NZL*, 4 August 1984, 40-1

[2] Words and music written and composed *c.* 1880 by 'Forward' (E. W. Secker), a noted singer and talented musician, and dedicated to A. D. Thomson, a leading Wanganui player of his day

[3] In 1987 the author encountered a Wellington taxi driver who described a set of engraving punches still in the family's possession

[4] See, for instance, West's 1872 catalogue, 140 pp., Hocken Library

[5] 'Our Bykes and We', music by C. Algar and words by A. Booth. See Elizabeth Nichol's survey of NZ music registered for copyright 1879-1900, *TLR*, October 1984, 85-97

[6] For an entertaining account of the origins of national anthems and songs, see New Grove, vol. 13, 'National Anthems'

[7] See advertisement in the *Saturday Advertiser*, 1 July 1876; entry for J. J. Woods in *DNZB* (1940); and Annabell, 'NZ's cultural and economic development'

[8] *Saturday Advertiser*, 29 December 1876. An earlier performance is noted in ATL MS 355 (undated), at a ball given in aid of the Lawrence Hospital, in an arrangement for the local band

[9] *Tuapeka Times*, 13 March 1878

[10] The original manuscript now resides in the Grey Collection in the Auckland Public Library. See also MS Papers 355, J. J. Woods, ATL

[11] It was published in the *Saturday Advertiser*, 26 October 1878

[12] Professor John Steele of Otago University has pointed out that the 'difficult' intervals are surprisingly prophetic of Elgar, instancing the 'Nimrod' variation in *Enigma*. See Heenan, A. D., 'New Zealand's National Song', October 1990

[13] Trimnell was organist at Chesterfield Parish Church for twenty-four years, spent a number of years at Sheffield, and moved to Wellington from Auckland in 1890

[14] The author met his son, also Tallis Trimnell, in Wellington in the late 1950s, and was shown a silver trophy cup presented to his father for choral conducting at the Crystal Palace

[15] Maughan Barnett, born in Leamington, Warwickshire, a pupil of Gustav Ernst and Frank Spinney, emigrated for health reasons to Hobart in 1890. He became organist at Napier Cathedral in 1893; organist at St John's, Wellington, in 1895, where he was also conductor of the Choral and Orchestral Society; and city organist in Auckland in 1912.

[16] Published in London by Reynolds & Co (1904)

[17] Words by O. T. J. Alpers, printed at the office of the *Lyttelton Times* (1900)

[18] Words by S. Clarke Johnson, printed by Turnbull & Palmer, Wellington (1901)

[19] See chapter III, 5

3 Alfred Hill: the first professional composer

Alfred Hill, a gifted violinist who trained at the Leipzig Conservatorium, became the first fully professional New Zealand composer. He wrote over 500 compositions, covering many genres from romantic opera to orchestral works, string quartets, and songs. He also pioneered the use of Māori material in western composition, and enjoyed lifelong friendships with notable Māori personalities such as Bella and Maggie Papakura, the famed guides of Rotorua. Although his musical language and style remained that of late classical romanticism, his vein of lyricism and nostalgia, his skilful writing for strings, his use of orchestral colour, and the theatrical flair of the most telling arias from his operas assure him of a permanent place in the repertoire and an honoured one in the tradition.[1]

Alfred Hill as cornet player in the Wellington Garrison Band at the age of eight.
Alexander Turnbull Library

The Hill family of hat-makers emigrated from Bristol to Melbourne, where Alfred was born, but moved to Auckland when he was two, later making their base in Wellington. They formed their own small orchestras, sang while at work in their Lambton Quay hat shop, toured a Christy Minstrel show called 'Hill's Brigands', and had within the family a fine tenor in Edwin and an accomplished flautist in Charles, who taught the Australian virtuoso John Amadio. Alfred's sister Mabel, a contemporary of Frances Hodgkins, became an acknowledged painter. Alfred also had cornet and violin lessons from visiting musicians in the touring opera orchestras, and rudimentary, frustrating instruction in composition. His father, an excellent violinist who had played on the Australian gold-fields, recognized his son's gifts, and on the advice of the visiting violin virtuoso Reményi, sent him to the Leipzig Conservatorium, where he soon gained a place in the first violins of the Gewandhaus Orchestra under Carl Reinecke, their resident conductor. He played under guests such as Brahms, Tchaikovsky, and Richard Strauss, and heard many notable soloists including Clara Schumann, Joachim, and Ysaÿe. He studied violin with Hans Sitt (1850-1922), whose many-sided life as composer, conductor, and teacher strongly influenced him. The techniques imparted by his composition teacher Gustav Schreck (1849-1918) remained the basis of his own work throughout his life. He won the coveted Helbig Prize, and his 'Scotch' Sonata for violin and piano was praised by the *Leipziger Zeitung*.

He returned home to conduct the Wellington Orchestral Society (1892-1896), making it the finest in the country, with well-balanced programmes based on those of Leipzig. He also taught and composed. He suffered criticism from inside and outside the orchestra, which culminated in a sensational scandal when he refused to conduct for a visiting virtuoso, the Chevalier de Kontski (see chapter III, 6). Hill's firm artistic stand and subsequent resignation aroused

The stage of the City Hall, Auckland, decorated for the first performances of *Hinemoa*, 1-4 March 1897, when the composer conducted and Ovide Musin led the orchestra. This photograph is pasted into the front of the conducting score of the work. *Alexander Turnbull Library*

considerable controversy. He joined the visiting violinist Ovide Musin's ensemble, travelling as far as Sydney, where the company disbanded. Thereafter he moved between the countries, pursuing the career of composer, conductor, and teacher. He applied (unsuccessfully) for the professorship in music at Auckland University College in 1900.[2]

Hill's New Zealand works include the cantata *Hinemoa* (1896) for soloists, chorus, and orchestra, to a libretto by the writer Arthur Adams (1872-1936). Based on a traditional Māori legend, it was the first European work to set Māori melodies in a western harmonic context. It won high praise from all sections of the community and established Hill's reputation. Perhaps the most valued comment came from the Māori scholar Edward Tregear who wrote: 'I could not have believed that any European music could have so well interpreted the genius of the Maori feeling.'[3] There followed other works embodying Māori themes such as *Tangi*, a Māori lament, 'Maori' Symphony, the cantata *Tawhaki*, and the song 'Waiata Poi' and its successor 'Waiata Maori', both of which introduced countless overseas audiences to Māori music for the first time. Hill might have made a career in London as a composer of romantic opera on the strength of his *Tapu* (1902) and *A Moorish Maid* (1905). 'See O'er the Mountains' from the latter, 'quite reaches the plane of grand opera', wrote C. N. Baeyertz, editor of the *Triad*.[4] Rosina Buckman's brilliant portrayal of the leading role La Zara launched her on an international career. Illness, however, prevented Hill from taking up these opportunities.[5]

Hill formed and conducted New Zealand's first fully professional orchestra at the Christchurch Exhibition of 1906-1907, when he wrote his *Exhibition Ode* (which included military band) to words by J. C. Anderson.[6] After an

Alfred Hill in 1926, pencil drawing by his sister Mabel. *Elizabeth Mason collection*

unsuccessful attempt to establish an institute for the study of Māori music at Rotorua in 1910, he resumed teaching and composing in Sydney where a variety of operatic and musical enterprises occupied him, including the formation of the Australian Opera League in 1913-1914 with his own *Pierrette* and Fritz Hart's *Giovanni*. In 1915 Henri Verbrugghen appointed him first Professor of Composition at the newly formed New South Wales Conservatorium of Music. Henceforth his connections with New Zealand gradually weakened. He wrote the music for two films, one at Lake Taupo in 1930, at the behest of an American producer, Alexander Marky, who decamped with the film and Hill's music; and *Rewi's Last Stand*[7] in 1938, for Rudolph Hayward, doyen of New Zealand film pioneers. He returned occasionally to visit his family and take part in concerts.

Hill has been aptly described by the Sydney critic Lindsay Browne as 'one of music's *petit maîtres*; a craftsman who seeks for perfection of style in works of smallish aspiration', who has an 'unequivocal love of long-drawn, spacious melody of pensive richness', such as is found in his Viola Concerto, one of his best orchestral works.[8] Many of the sententious elements in his music are simply the current coinage of the poets and writers of the time, of the richly entwined melodies of the late Victorians. Nevertheless, his best string quartets, such as No. 2 ('Maori') and No. 11, largely escape this (although even here judicious cutting might prove beneficial).

Hill had a strong influence on Australian composers (notably John Antill and Roy Agnew) but little on those of New Zealand: '. . . he was a forerunner working in this country about fifty years earlier than the first main group of professional composers', writes Lilburn. 'They, and their younger colleagues, might well salute him for the courage and tenacious energy with which he

Mirrie Solomon Hill, Alfred's second wife, pencil drawing by Mabel Hill, 1926. *Alexander Turnbull Library*

battled against difficult circumstance. As a composer he was simply practical in writing for current taste in a remote colony. As a general musician he was distinguished in his time and place . . .'[9]

Hill's life covered the period of New Zealand's most intense operatic activities, the emergence of a high late-Victorian culture in the principal cities in the 1890s, the first professional orchestra at the 1906-1907 Christchurch Exhibition, and the first sustained attempts to study Māori music. 'Keep singing your Maori songs', he told the children of Whangamarino school, near Rotorua, in 1952. 'Keep on learning your crafts—your weaving and your carving. The Maori culture should never be forgotten.'[10] Early Hill compositions, including *Hinemoa*, the two 'Maori' string quartets, and the tone poems on Māori themes, are examples of early New Zealand music and stand in a similar relationship to the cultural tradition as do the poems of his colleague Arthur Adams and the Māori scholar Edward Tregear. It is nineteenth century in substance, a last flowering of romantic feelings and rhetoric, yet with individual touches of charm and manner. He energetically encouraged colonial musical life and significantly shaped a performing tradition. Above all, he gave meaning to the word 'composer'.

Notes

[1] Thomson, *ADM* gives a full biographical account of Hill's life

[2] For details, see Thomson, J. M. 'A question of authenticity', 80-92

[3] See Thomson, *ADM*, 62, and Alfred Hill Papers, MSS 528 Uncatalogued Papers 1854-1960, Mitchell Library, Sydney

[4] *New Zealand Times*, 9 September 1905

[5] Jeremy Commons, an authority on opera of the period, recently arranged a recital of songs from Hill's operas, setting them alongside those of his European contemporaries. Hill's melodic qualities and sense of form ensured that they more than held their own

[6] See chapter III, 6

[7] A copy is held by the New Zealand Film Archive

[8] Lindsay Browne in the *Sydney Morning Herald*, 18 December 1950

[9] Thomson, *ADM*, Introduction

[10] *New Zealand Herald*, 19 July 1952

Overture Aotearoa

DOUGLAS LILBURN
(1940)

IX

Douglas Lilburn

'My mother, Rosamund Lilburn, perhaps on her 85th birthday.' *Lilburn collection*

1 From Drysdale to Canterbury University College

Douglas Gordon Lilburn was the youngest son of Robert and Rosamund Louisa Lilburn who farmed the Drysdale Station in the upper Turakina Valley, eighteen miles from the nearest township of Hunterville in the North Island. He was born on 2 November 1915 at Mrs Tripe's Maternity Home in Wanganui: 'I came into the world lazy, was held up by the heels and slapped before I'd breathe.'[1] His parents, of predominantly Scottish ancestry, were aged 49 and 42 respectively.

After Robert's retirement, when their son was around seven, his parents made a grand tour of Europe, leaving the boy in the care of his beloved eldest brother Jack and his wife Edith (Howie). Childhood at Drysdale was secure, rich in experience and mainly idyllic. His parents returned two years later, almost like 'elderly strangers'—their absence abroad had left indelible marks of estrangement. When they retired to Wanganui, Lilburn attended the Friends School, 'an enlightened Quaker Institute where learning was imaginative joy'.

Instead of following family tradition and going on to Wanganui Collegiate, he was unexpectedly sent to Frank Milner's bastion of high imperialism, Waitaki Boys' High School at Oamaru in the South Island. Modelling himself on Sanderson of Oundle, in England, Milner built Waitaki's reputation on scholastic achievement and discipline. Flamboyantly and unashamedly imperialistic—the British Empire might have come into existence especially for him—his regime was welcomed by some boys and detested by others. For the fourteen-year-old Lilburn, 'an intellectual with specs and physically retarded . . . an unwelcome stranger from the north', it was a circle of Dante's *Inferno*. His intellectual and musical gifts brought swift response—during his first week he was caned for using a piano out of hours.

Nevertheless, his resolution to become a composer took shape. Given an essay on an imperialistic theme as a holiday task, he handed in instead a Sonata in C, 'bravely called Opus 1, still extant in some crazy manuscript'. Milner, known as 'The Man', caught him with pen and ink on top of the piano in the Hall

Robert Lilburn, father of the composer, in the Wanganui garden, c. 1937. *Lilburn collection*

Drysdale in the early 1930s, looking up the Pohunui Valley: 'The magnificent stand of bush across the river was still intact'. *Lilburn collection*

of Memories, where Kipling's 'Recessional' resounded each morning. Taken aback at finding a boy 'composing', he cautioned him against using ink on his treasured grand. Lilburn learned how to avoid aggressors and how to survive: 'I'd think the total experience a salutary one in that it taught me to recognize the world the way it is.' He discovered what became an enduring love for the South Island. But the transition from a previously sheltered existence 'was too harsh and sudden and left traumatic scars'.

At Drysdale, c. 1919. Douglas Lilburn at the wheel with his brothers Bob and Ewan and sister Janet. *Lilburn collection*

Lilburn had no aptitude for farming, but remembering his literary activities, the family felt he might make a journalist, so in 1934 he enrolled for both BA and Diploma of Journalism at Canterbury University College. The lectures on 'Principles and Practice' from a city editor quickly cured him of any desire to become a professional. He had already started classes in the Music Department, where he gained high marks, and thereafter he committed himself to music under the uncommonly strict surveillance of Dr J. C. Bradshaw (1876-1950), organist and choirmaster of the Cathedral, founder of the Male Voice Choir, and conductor of the Royal Christchurch Musical Society (see chapter III, 5). Bradshaw's remorseless concern for 'the rules' usually inhibited his students, although they admired his *Matthew Passion* and his organ recitals. Bradshaw offered Lilburn £40 a year to join the cathedral choir as a bass singer but this was rejected: 'I was antagonistic to notions of the Establishment and unwilling to give up freedom of time, especially at weekends when I enjoyed walks on the hills and wild parties.'[2]

Lilburn's Christchurch years coincided with those of a fresh wave of New Zealand poets, including Allen Curnow and Denis Glover, and with those of liberal thinkers such as Tom Shand (later Minister of Labour), and Priestley Thompson (ex-head of the Department of Forestry). Although he once summed up Christchurch as 'politics, pubs and piecarts', the outlook and views of the poets and artists greatly affected him, far more than Dr Bradshaw's Kitson harmony books and strict classes on orchestration and ear-training. He wrote species counterpoint but never heard or studied Palestrina. He wrote fugues in triple counterpoint but never analysed one by Bach: 'We studied orchestration in the abstract and were never encouraged to compose anything whatsoever.'[3] He completed requirements for a Diploma in Journalism, a B.A., and B. Mus., except that in the latter he did not submit his exercise in composition. None of these degrees was actually conferred, leading to a lifelong myth that Lilburn 'possessed no academic qualifications'.[4]

Besides Dr Bradshaw's music-making, Christchurch offered choral and piano recitals, and concerts by the Harmonic Society founded in 1927 by Victor Peters, an accomplished musician who built a choir of international standards (see chapter III, 5). He heard his first Sibelius symphonies and other contemporary works on friends' gramophones and listened regularly to the programmes of the 3YA orchestra. In piano lessons from Ernest Empson (1880-1970), a Godowsky pupil who taught many New Zealand pianists of note, he gained a technical foundation hitherto lacking.

During his 1935 visit, the pianist and composer Percy Grainger said in a broadcast that New Zealand composers would soon 'bring some quite strange and special beauty into music through the influence of the New Zealand scenery . . .' Grainger offered £25 for an orchestral work which would 'present typical New Zealand cultural and emotional characteristics . . .'[5]

Lilburn entered the competition, submitting the tone poem *Forest*, which was written after an Easter holiday walking in the Mount Peel Settlement. The work brought more than a flicker to Dr Bradshaw's face: 'his interest set me wondering whether he had not been a little bored himself with Kitson exercises year in year out'.[6] *Forest* won the first prize of £25, the anonymous judge commenting that a particular passage was 'quite a marvel of both counterpoint and orchestration' and concluding that it was 'A thoughtfully unified work whose contrasts are well ordered and whose climaxes are invariably broad and mighty and well worth while.'[7] The predominant influence on *Forest* was that of Sibelius:

> [I] have tried in my work to capture some of the elemental magic that pervades our remote mountains and forests. Sibelius, I have the very highest regard for, and prefer his atmosphere and powerful construction next to the great humanity of Beethoven and Bach . . . I think now that my people can be persuaded to send me to England to study further, and you can realise what that means to me.[8]

Forest was performed on 25 May 1937 by Leon de Mauny and the Wellington Symphony Orchestra in the city's Town Hall. 'He has given the world something quite fresh and new in his interpretation of the moods of the forest', wrote the critic of the *Dominion* next day. 'Mr Lilburn has something individual in his musical make-up.' Lilburn decided to study with Vaughan Williams, doyen of English composers, at the Royal College of Music in London.

Notes

[1] Lilburn wrote a series of autobiographical notes at the request of Janet Paul and myself. Unattributed quotations are drawn from these manuscripts, which are held by the composer

[2] Later he felt he had been crass to have rejected an offer that might have given him a needed discipline

[3] See Page, 40-1, 50-2, for colourful descriptions of studying under Bradshaw

[4] See confirming letter from Dr James Hight, 17 May 1937, Lilburn papers. For his B.A. Lilburn studied History III, Philosophy II, first-year English, French, Economics, and Music

[5] See Harvey, D. R. 'Douglas Lilburn and Percy Grainger'. *TLR*, October 1986, 155-62

[6] Lilburn, *A Search for Tradition*, 17

[7] *NZ Radio Record*, 9 October 1936

[8] Letter from Wanganui, 1 January 1937, to Percy Grainger, Grainger Museum, Melbourne, quoted in Harvey, 'Douglas Lilburn and Percy Grainger'. *TLR*, October 1986, 155-62

2 London, Vaughan Williams, and the return home

In London the young composer installed himself in a room at 10 Earl's Court Square, with a Broadwood purchased for £30 and a restricted view on to a neighbouring back wall. In September 1937 he enrolled at the Royal College of Music and began lessons with Vaughan Williams, whose confidence he soon won:

> He was an incredible personality. He wasn't clever. He didn't tell one a lot about technical things at all, but I could learn that from elsewhere. But he did convey the essence of a personality and this thing about integrity—he liked to say 'Cut out all the bits you like best'. You know this is paradox, but it conveys the message 'Don't be clever, don't be silly, don't try to impress— search for what is valid in your intuition, your understanding, and go from that'.[1]

He proved to be the outstanding influence of those College years; a lifelong friendship and mutual respect developed.

The expertise and musical experience of his fellow students at first bewildered him. He felt himself to be out of sympathy with most of them and began to seek out New Zealand expatriates: the writers Robin Hyde, D'Arcy Cresswell, and James Courage—'anyone sharing my dichotomy'. 'I was as baffled by myself as by London, made play with left-wing politics, worked hard, was socially hapless and very lonely, realized that I was an alien and that my salvation, if any, lay 12,000 miles away.' The New Zealand violinist Alex Lindsay described the College under the direction of George Dyson as 'a high-class music factory with mass production problems where any student of outstanding ability had to kick out sometimes or be submerged'.[2]

Lilburn found much of London's music unexpectedly conservative but some experiences stood out—the Busch Quartet playing late Beethoven and the Schubert and Mozart Quintets. There were brilliant orchestral occasions: Toscanini conducted the BBC Symphony Orchestra twice, his Beethoven Ninth raising critics' eyebrows for its exceptionally fast tempi and inexorable rhythms. In early 1938 the Berlin Philharmonic visited with Furtwängler. The International Society for Contemporary Music Festival was held from 12 to 24 June, and included Webern's *Das Augenlicht*, which caused a sensation. He heard Bartók and his wife perform the Sonata for Two Pianos and Percussion, and was 'mightily impressed'. Beecham gave a Sibelius Festival with his London Philharmonic at the end of October. On 4 November 1938 Nadia Boulanger conducted Stravinsky's *Dumbarton Oaks* with the BBCSO, and on 16 November

Lilburn as a student in London in 1940, with the published score of his *Overture Aotearoa. Lilburn collection*

Britten played his Piano Concerto, conducted by Boult, which Lilburn heard and disliked.[3]

Vaughan Williams' faith showed tangible results when in 1939 Lilburn won the Hubert Parry Prize for Composition, the Cobbett composition prize for his Phantasy for String Quartet based on the old air *Western Wynde*, and the Foli Scholarship. Fellow New Zealanders who won awards included the singer Denis Dowling, the pianist Colin Horsley, and Alex Lindsay.

Shortly after the declaration of war on 3 September 1939, as the air-raid sirens wailed over London, Lilburn was busy composing *Prodigal Country*, settings of New Zealand poems for baritone, chorus, and orchestra, which he was to enter for the Centennial Music Competition. He helped fill sandbags, volunteered as an ARP warden, and was drafted (twice) but failed because of his eyesight. He resolved, if possible, to serve with the Medical Corps of the Zealand forces. At Christmas that year he visited D'Arcy Cresswell: 'I heard him read his poem *Forest* and realized where I belonged.'

His prize-winning *Phantasy Quartet* was performed at the College on 28 February 1940 in a concert given by the Contemporary Music Society. From Christchurch Frederick Page, then teaching music, wrote to Lilburn for the score and parts: 'The Cobbett Quartet may not rouse much enthusiasm', replied the composer, 'though I think it one of the best things I have done . . . a very restrained work, and you may find it more bleak than your own Port Hills'.[4] In Christchurch—'reluctantly emerging from a Coleridge-Taylor chrysalis'—Frederick Page had difficulty in cajoling players to work on an unknown quartet, but the première eventually took place in the Radiant Hall.[5]

Meanwhile Lilburn learned of a Centennial matinée for New Zealand forces to be held in His Majesty's Theatre, Haymarket and wrote to the New Zealand-born conductor Warwick Braithwaite at Sadler's Wells Theatre, offering an overture for the occasion. Braithwaite replied cautiously: 'Could you possibly guarantee that the overture would be suitable, or even a success or even playable?'[6] On Monday 15 April 1940 the audience in His Majesty's heard the opening chords of a work whose mood and shimmering atmosphere marked the arrival of a new voice in New Zealand music. *Aotearoa* (the title was Braithwaite's), with its images of a sea-spumed coast, was subsequently recorded by the BBCSO under Boult and made available on their transcription service. After an Empire Day broadcast in 1942, W. R. Anderson wrote in the *Musical Times* of its 'excellently sonorous scoring', attributing its modal character to the influence of Vaughan Williams: 'An exhilarating air is that of his country, which many of us would like to breathe.'[7] Ironically, its first live performance in New Zealand did not occur until 23 June 1959, when it was played by the National Orchestra under John Hopkins.

The remainder of the programme represented an extraordinary constellation of New Zealand talents as the writer James Courage reported:

> The N.Z. concert was all I had feared and worse—some of it much *much* worse. I can't begin to tell you what it was like. Oddly enough, it started off extremely well, with Gordon's overture [Lilburn's middle name], which was a good simple sound piece of work, and was well played save that there were not enough string-players to give the full effect he must have intended. After that the fare was mixed feeding, to say the least. Dr Merton Hodge (dramatist) made a quite inaudible speech about the famous men of N.Z. Then came a young N.Z. pianist—from Wanganui, I believe—a lad of about nineteen—with a truly amazing technique: he tore through a couple of Chopin Etudes like a racehorse on the home-farm. (His name is Colin something) [Colin Horsley]. Sir Hugh Walpole then gave quite a competent speech containing several terrific double-entendres which the audience were not slow to take up. Next, Low drew about four cartoons (quite a good turn, this—supreme mastery in fact). After that, however, several very odd things began to happen: the old brigade began to take over: Rosina Buckman appeared in a sort of nightgown and panted a few words of apology for not being able to sing: Shayle Gardner appeared looking like the shade of Henry Irving, literally from the grave, and fired off Othello's defence at us—Stella Murry [*sic*] appeared in a crimson dress, carrying a bouquet of roses that looked as though they had died of fright and sang some wildly-inappropriate song. (D'Arcy [Cresswell] and I were by this time in a state of coma with suppressed laughter). But the real climax of embarrassment was reached when a troop of (presumably) soldiers, in Maori undress, gave a haka: their leader was a very fat full-blooded Maori who sprang about the stage with such vim that the grass skirt he was wearing suddenly slipped completely off, revealing a tremendous paunch punctuated by a navel the size of a plug-hole. God alone knows what the Duchess of Kent, who was sitting in a box quite close to us, thought of it all! (The Maori had to rush off and re-robe himself) . . . Anyway, all this gives you, for good or ill, some idea of what you have missed.[8]

Douglas Lilburn
conducting at the
Cambridge Summer School
of Music, 1946.

On learning that his sister Louisa's ex-army husband Bill Britton had volunteered again, leaving her to manage the farm, Lilburn felt it was time to return to New Zealand. Having been rejected for service on account of his eyesight, he believed that in wartime he might be most usefully employed on their farm.

In later life he was asked if he had seriously contemplated remaining in Britain: 'Yes, I may have considered it', he replied, 'but even apart from the war I was very conscious before I ever went to England of Ian Milner, son of the Rector at Waitaki, saying, "I write with spleen from another ruined summer [in England]; one remains a colonial speaking the same language". I took note of that.'[9]

Lilburn arrived in a wintry downpour on the Wellington wharves to find himself famous: 'Enter the man who won the laurels. Douglas Lilburn returns unexpectedly from England.'[10] He had won three out of four of the musical prizes awarded by the Government as part of the Centennial celebrations. The *Drysdale Overture*, written in 1937, won the orchestral class — it had been given a rehearsal performance by the first orchestra of the Royal College in 1938. His *Festival Overture*, written in 1939, won second prize in the same class, having been performed by the College Orchestra under Dyson in 1939. *Prodigal Country* won first prize in the choral class. The judge Andersen Tyrer found that the *Drysdale Overture* had musical ability of 'a refined order', the *Festival Overture* had 'commendable sincerity of purpose', and *Prodigal Country* showed 'fine work and judgment with never a stodgy line'.[11] Its text included words from Robin Hyde's poem 'Journey from New Zealand':

> I too am sold into strangeness,
> Yet in my heart can only dissolve, re-form
> The circling shapes of New Zealand things.

Apart from a perfunctory broadcast in 1940 the work lay unperformed until Sir Charles Groves recorded it for Radio New Zealand in 1987, when it made a powerful impression. In 1988 Sir David Willcocks gave the first public performance in Wellington.

The £170 prize money might have shown Lilburn's sceptical family that music could also make money, but when he began working on his sister's Taihape farm he felt strongly that in their eyes 'I was still no good as a farmer—that if I had been any good as a musician I wouldn't have come home'.[12] For a year he milked cows, kept an eye on some 800 ewes, did odd jobs, cut firewood, and when necessary killed sheep, an assignment that subsequently haunted him, the total experience proving 'tough and rough' but with 'compensating health and enjoyment'. In 1941, no longer required on the farm, he accepted Professor Shelley's invitation to follow Maurice Clare as guest conductor of the NBS Strings, holding the position for three months. He then returned to Christchurch to freelance: 'I enjoyed a marvellous context of friends and a large freedom and got on with my composing.' They proved 'six of the best and most fruitful and formative years of my life'.

He took students, made arrangements for broadcasting, with occasional conducting, and wrote criticism for the *Press* in 1943-1944. From Maurice Clare he learned more of instrumental technique than he ever had at the Royal College.[13] His circle of friends included Denis Glover and Leo Bensemann at the Caxton Press, the painter Rita Angus, and the poet Allen Curnow. He absorbed early Stravinsky and went to the concerts of the Harmonic Society under Victor Peters.

In 1941 the historian J. C. Beaglehole invited Allen Curnow to commemorate the tercentenary of Tasman's arrival in New Zealand. Curnow sought Lilburn's collaboration to provide the musical framework to a poem for narrator and strings. *Landfall in Unknown Seas* was conducted by Andersen Tyrer with the NBS Strings and broadcast on 13 December 1942, exactly 300 years after Tasman's discovery. It later established itself in the repertoire of the Alex Lindsay String Orchestra. Curnow conceived of his poem in three 'movements':

> First, a kind of recitative, setting the historical scene, and the setting forth of the voyages into the unknown—likening them too, to the ancient Polynesian voyagers. Second, a dramatic lyric, in rapid, short metre and strict pattern, recounting the Landfall in New Zealand, the bloody clash with the islanders, and Tasman's departure. Third, a lyric meditation, harmonising the vision and action of the first two parts, and offering a possible meaning for the whole to our own age and nation.[14]

Allegro for Strings (1942), page 16. *Alexander Turnbull Library*

He described the collaboration as 'one of those rare and happy circumstances'. During 1942 Lilburn's other works included the Allegro for Strings, two concert overtures for strings, and an *a cappella* Magnificat and Nunc Dimittis for the Christchurch Cathedral Choir. His own language and tone of voice, first revealed in *Aotearoa* and *Prodigal Country*, developed greater strengths.

In 1943 he began writing theatre music for Ngaio Marsh's accomplished Canterbury University College Dramatic Society. The first concert devoted entirely to Lilburn's works took place in Canterbury College Hall on 29 September that year, promoted by Frederick Page.

It opened with the Allegro for Strings, followed by *Landfall in Unknown Seas*, Five Bagatelles for piano played by Noel Newson, and a first performance of the Sinfonia for Strings. The 3YA Orchestra, led by Vivien Dixon, a fine English-born violinist, was conducted by the composer. In the *Press* the following day, Frederick Page commented on 'a quite remarkable concert' and identified some of the Lilburn fingerprints: 'an insistent rhythmic phrase, a shift to a telling bass note, a way of coming to a passage in a high register, that seems to let sunshine and clear air pour through it. These high keen sounds are typical, they may even point to the fact that he is a New Zealander . . .' In the *Listener* of 15 October 1943, 'Marsyas' (Antony Alpers) wrote: 'There seems no doubt that Mr Lilburn is one of the new discoverers.'

Following a prize-winning Prelude and Fugue for organ and an *Elegy* for two women's voices and strings, commemorating the death at 33 of Noel Newson, the culminating work of his early years was *A Song of the Antipodes*, later renamed *A Song of Islands*, 'derived from notions of Psalms and Whitman poems (both with connotations of praise) and of our antipodean circumstance'.[15] It was first performed by Warwick Braithwaite and the National Orchestra the following year, when it was recognized as a further affirmation of his personal style: 'There's my threefold statement', wrote the composer later. 'First, the Overture, intuitively in 1940, second, *Landfall*, explicit with the poem in 1942, and third, *A Song of Islands*, a considered song of praise, in 1946.'[16]

Owen Jensen invited Lilburn to take the first composers' class at Cambridge in 1947, a historic gathering which brought together musicians who were to become leading figures over the next decades. Jensen summed up Lilburn's influence:

> He did not embark on any formal teaching, or elaborate on the technique of composition. He did not, indeed, attempt in any way to impose his own ideas. Anything in the way of a cult he would have found distasteful. He encouraged and helped. Almost every composer now well known in New Zealand worked with Lilburn in those early Cambridge music schools. The Composers' Groups included Robert Burch, Edwin Carr, David Farquhar, Dorothea Franchi, Larry Pruden and Ronald Tremain. Each of these has achieved distinction as a composer. But none has become a neo-Lilburn or even derived his style from the same source as Lilburn. Each has developed an individuality. Each stands on his own feet, a composer in his own right.[17]

In March 1947 Frederick Page offered Lilburn a part-time position in the new Music Department of Victoria University College at £250 a year: 'Winds of change had to be recognized and all musical opportunity seemed centred in Wellington while the Christchurch context shrank.' His arrival in the capital coincided with the first concerts of the National Orchestra, ushering in a new regime of state patronage of music.

Notes

[1] Harris and Norman, 21. Lilburn's other teachers included R. O. Morris, Gordon Jacob, and the pianist Kendall Taylor
[2] Harris and Norman 28
[3] Lilburn to Frederick Page, 12 May 1940, Page Papers, ATL
[4] Lilburn to Page, 12 May 1940, ibid
[5] Page, 'A New Zealand Composer'. *Comment*, June 1980, 5-6
[6] Braithwaite to Lilburn, 5 March 1940, in possession of Lilburn
[7] Quoted in *Music Ho!*, December 1942, 2
[8] James Courage to Frederick Page, 14. 17 April, 1940, Page Papers, ATL
[9] Harris and Norman, 21
[10] *NZL*, 16 August 1940
[11] Ibid, 29
[12] Ibid, 19
[13] See *Canzona*, Autumn 1988, 11
[14] Sleeve-note by Curnow to Kiwi/Pacific recording SLD-79
[15] Letter to author, 12 August 1976
[16] Sleeve-note, Kiwi/Pacific recording SLD-79
[17] See *NZL*, 29 October 1965

3 *Wellington: from* Diversions *to the* Third Symphony

When Frederick Page came to the red-brick Gothic of Victoria University College's Hunter Building to form a Music Department, he thought he had been sent to 'an institution for bad girls'.[1] The College stood high on a hill, near a sturdy wooden cable-car, on which students who sat outside would be lashed by southerly gales as the car trundled up its steep incline. It looked out over a superb seascape to a rim of hills on the horizon and the distant peaks of the Tararuas.

Victoria's strength, however, lay within. 'The College has always been the home of what one may call, for want of a better phrase, the "social conscience"', wrote Dr J. C. Beaglehole, on the occasion of its fiftieth birthday in 1949.[2] 'The social conscience has made students critical, has made them compassionate, has made them rebellious and non-conformist. It has led them to nourish all sorts of heresies, just as it has led them into wars and into Christian missions and into all sorts of mad devotions and impossible loyalties . . . Pride or shame, there sits the College on its hill, its old clay patch . . .' In this radical intellectual climate, Frederick Page and Douglas Lilburn fashioned a unique Music Department.

The Boyd Neel Orchestra performed *Diversions for String Orchestra* on 9 July 1947 in the Wellington Town Hall: 'A work of high merit, orchestrated with deftness and facility of imagination, with a freedom of form and expression that conveyed originality in musical thought', wrote the *Dominion* of 10 July. Boyd Neel, originally a medical doctor, had invited Australian and New Zealand composers to send him compositions. From the flood that descended on him only one 'was of a high standard': Lilburn's *Diversions*.[3] The Lilburn work comprised five short pieces, light music in the best sense and free in form.[4] The orchestra was brought to New Zealand by the impresario, Dan O'Connor.

Boyd Neel played *Diversions* at the Chelsea Town Hall, his London base, on 14 February 1949, which *The Times* next day described as 'bubbling with spontaneous ideas and written with resourcefulness'. Oxford University Press subsequently published it.[5] At the 1965 Commonwealth Festival of the Arts in Liverpool *The Times* again found it 'full of melodic invention lightly spiced with rhythmic intricacies, much in the style of Jacques Ibert', the last movement 'brimming over with high spirits wittily expressed'.[6]

In addition to the National Orchestra, the New Zealand Ballet Company, and (soon) the New Zealand Opera Company, Wellington had its own group of poets, whose meetings Lilburn began to attend: 'Although he was a composer and we were poets, we came to regard him as a mentor', wrote Alistair Campbell.

'Driftwood' from *Elegy*, page 9. *Alexander Turnbull Library*

'We went to him with our poems and our ideas, and although we did not always see eye to eye with him, we respected him for the honesty and forthrightness of his opinions.'[7] Subsequently Lilburn set Campbell's fine sequence *Elegy*, written to commemorate the death of Roy M. Dickson, killed in a climbing accident on 1 January 1947 at the age of 20, which opens with an evocation of a storm in the Hollyford Valley.

John Steele, a student at the time, now Professor of Music at the University of Otago, recalled Lilburn's presence:

We absorbed his reverence for the music of Vaughan Williams and eagerly awaited new compositions from the master's hands . . . The first performances of some of Douglas's own works were red-letter days: I heard the premieres of the Violin Sonata, Piano Sonata and the First Symphony. I have never felt before or since a comparable feeling of "being in" at the creation of new art that I was sure then as now will have a vital place in our history.[8]

Second Symphony, page 11. Alexander Turnbull Library

The First Symphony, written in 1949 and performed by the National Orchestra in May 1951, was an extended lyrical and meditative work in A minor. It comprised just three movements, *Allegro non troppo, Andante con moto*, and an *Allegro*, with no scherzo. 'The Symphony . . . sums up every revelation— melody (and what lovely melody!, almost a lost art in present day composition), harmonic perception, growing rhythmic feeling, and over all the expression of mood', wrote the pianist Dorothy Davies in *Landfall*.[9] It has latterly won sympathetic performances from John Hopkins and Sir Charles Groves.

The Second Symphony (1951) received a first (inadequate) performance as a studio broadcast in 1953, and a worthy one under Georg Tintner, the Austrian-born conductor,[10] in December 1954. Owen Jensen found it 'completely original, individual, remembering only itself and the general trend of Lilburn's music over the years . . . music of distinction'.[11] Later, John Hopkins took the work into his repertoire, as did several other conductors, including Alex Lindsay, Ashley Heenan (who made the first recording), and William Southgate.

The work is in four closely related movements. Ashley Heenan wrote of the first recording:

> Twenty-five years after its composition, this symphony, with its subtle allusions to the [*Evening*] *Post* boy's call (II), the oppressiveness and pride of West Coast weather and landscape (III), the opening up of the mountain skyline (IV), or more generally the sweep of the horizons around us (I), has the power to arouse in New Zealanders an indefinable feeling of identity with their country.[12]

The *New York Times* discerned 'a uniquely personal atmosphere of airy athleticism'.[13]

For the tenth birthday of the National Orchestra in October 1956, its conductor James Robertson invited Lilburn to write a work using full orchestral resources, triple woodwind, saxophone, piano, and plenty of percussion, leaving him free to choose the music's form. The resultant *A Birthday Offering* somewhat resembled an overture, with a lengthy introduction to present various sections of the orchestra. The composer said of it:

> But I can see no evidence of sonata form . . . the music is rather in concertante style with a good deal of solo work, and as wide a range of colour and mood as I can manage . . . The style also gave me new problems of composition. To solve these I have used a form which is in vogue today, as much as it was in the 16th century. At the opening of the work a solo horn summons the orchestra with a theme of four notes. Everything that follows melodically and harmonically derives from these . . . The central section of the work owes something to one of Denis Glover's *Sings Harry* lyrics. Have I set out to uncork a bottle of champagne? Certainly not, but I hope the music may please those who like to taste a New Zealand wine.[14]

Later in the year Lilburn and the composer Ashley Heenan visited Sydney to discuss with APRA (Australasian Performing Right Association) the role the New Zealand composer might play in an organization which until then had been primarily orientated towards Australia. A Music Advisory Committee was formed, with New Zealand members to advise the APRA Board in Sydney.[15] Heenan and Lilburn visited Alfred Hill, now 86. Lilburn found much of Hill's music, although cast in the idiom of an older generation, 'as fresh, honest, spontaneous and beautiful as when it was written'.[16]

When the Government proposed a revision of relevant laws through its

Copyright Committee Report in 1958, Lilburn led a national campaign against a bizarre document that would have made New Zealand a pariah among western countries.[17] He addressed meetings of composers in national centres, from which a deputation presented a case to the Minister of Justice, Mr Mason. Writers and other artists did likewise. Lilburn challenged the Committee's passive view that New Zealand was a consumer country in music, and quoted the growing number of performances of its own works and the greatly increased earnings of its composers.[18] The Report was scrapped and Acts passed in line with international legislation.

As if to back up Lilburn's assertion that 'we are just beginning to make headway here', the National Orchestra under John Hopkins made its first recording of popular classics in July 1959, which included the *Festival Overture*.

'Song of Allegiance' from *Three Songs for Baritone and Viola. Alexander Turnbull Library*

Soon afterwards Kiwi (now Kiwi/Pacific) Records recorded *Landfall in Unknown Seas* and the song sequence to Denis Glover's poems *Sings Harry*, written in 1953 and later published by the University of Otago Press. In his annual report to the journal of the Composers' Guild of Great Britain in October 1959, Lilburn quoted from the cycle:

Sing all things harsh or sweet upon
These islands in the Pacific sun . . .

He continued to develop his theme that 'we come from Europe but we waken to a consciousness of being in this Pacific world . . .', likening the best of Alfred Hill's music to 'the freshness and clarity of a school of early New Zealand

Symphony No. 3, page 64. fMS Papers 2483. Folder 105. *Alexander Turnbull Library*

Douglas Lilburn receiving the Order of New Zealand from the Governor-General, Sir Paul Reeves, in 1988.

Lilburn at 22 Ascot Terrace, Wellington, in the early 1960s. *Lilburn collection*

watercolour painters'. For him the attraction of Māori singing lay largely in 'the charm of its timbre and melodic inflections and the suppleness of its rhythm . . .', qualities which did not readily lend themselves to instrumental transcription.[19]

In 1962 John Hopkins premièred Lilburn's last work in the traditional European style, his Third Symphony, written the year before. The composer later described it as 'a harsh, didactic personalized piece of searching rhetoric', though at the time all he vouchsafed his audience was his description of it as 'a brief work in one movement of five main sections'.[20] It puzzled both audience and critics, who found difficulty in relating it to its predecessor. Roger Savage gave a cogent response:

> Though a short work, quite unpadded, it seems a long one; not because it is ever dull, but because keeping up with the arguments of such an intelligence in such an uncongenial mood is something of a strain. A short work—but the most distinguished New Zealand music I have yet heard.[21]

Following its publication by Faber Music in 1969 (the first New Zealand symphony to appear thus in Britain), Elaine Padmore wrote in *Music and Letters*: 'Lilburn has a fine ear for sonorities: he scores economically, delighting in thin clear textures.'[22]

The Third Symphony marked the end of Lilburn's commitment to instrumental writing: 'my last exercise in the European tradition—I turned then to the new world of electronic music'.

Notes

1. Page, 90
2. *NZL*, 13 May 1949
3. Neel, 124. Max Hinrichsen, Lilburn's London publisher, had prepared the ground by sending Boyd Neel several of the composer's string works
4. *NZL*, 25 July 1947. See also interview with Harvey Blanks, *Evening Post*, 6 October 1947; and Ward, P. and Panter, M. 'The Boyd Neel Orchestra's tour of Australia and NZ'. *RCM Magazine*, vol. 44 no. 1, 1948; and Simpson, A., 'Boyd Neel and after: a tale of two orchestras', *EMNZ*, Autumn 1990, 36 ff.
5. They pulped it without reference to the composer in the 1970s!
6. *The Times*, 4 October 1965
7. *NZL*, 29 October 1965, reprinted in *Canzona*, January and July 1980
8. Lilburn, *Canzona*, 56
9. *Landfall*, September 1951, 230-1
10. Georg Tintner (b. Vienna, 1917) sang in the Vienna Boys' Choir and studied conducting under Joseph Marx and Felix Weingartner. He arrived in New Zealand in 1940, when he began working with the Auckland Choral Society
11. *NZL*, 7 January 1955
12. Ashley Heenan, sleeve-note, Kiwi/Pacific SLD-48
13. *New York Times*, 11 December 1983. In 1931 Frederick Page described the cries of the *Evening Post* newsboys in *MNZ*, July 1935. *R Crescendo* n. 20, August 1988, 7-8
14. *NZL*, 19 October 1956, 6-7
15. See Lilburn report on formation of NZ Advisory Council, *APRA Bulletin*, November 1959, 1-2
16. Thomson, J. M. 'Vigour in Australian Music'. *NZL*, 7 December 1956
17. See *APRA Bulletin*, November 1959, in which the likely effect of the proposed New Zealand legislation is summarized
18. See Mahoney, D. 'NZ Composers to Fight for Copyright'. *Auckland Star*, 11 December 1959
19. 'New Zealand', *The Composer*, October 1959
20. *NZL*, 27 July 1962
21. *NZL*, 17 August 1962
22. *Music and Letters*, April 1970, 215. It appeared with a handsome blue cover designed by Shirley Tucker. Copying and production were supervised by Roderick Biss, a fellow New Zealander, then Production Manager of Faber Music

4 *The electronic world*

Lilburn remained true to his word. An NZBC commission to realize incidental sounds for an anonymous script *The Pitcher and the Well* provided the stimulus to explore a new musical spectrum, but one which had always attracted him. In 1963 his journey began with a visit to Myron Schaeffer in the electronic music studios of Toronto, followed by visits to Columbia and Princeton Universities, the BBC Radiophonic Workshop, and the English composer Daphne Oram, herself a pioneer in the field. In a Wiltshire barn, near the home of a former student Peter Crowe and his wife Jenny, he began working with basic equipment, making use of old farm implements around him: 'For me that was an extraordinary week of searching into some new conception of sound.'[1]

A further three months in Toronto gave him sufficient skills to set up a Wellington studio.[2] In 1965 he realized an electronic sound image to Alistair Campbell's fine poem 'The Return', a portrayal of the drowned Dionysus in a Polynesian setting.

The Victoria University Electronic Music Studio (VUW/EMS) opened in October 1966 — 'a small "classical" studio, a pioneering enterprise some years ahead of Australian and English universities'.[3] From now on it welcomed visiting composers from overseas, local ones for training periods, and it began student classes: 'the compositional exercise with traditional equipment was hard and laborious, with long hours spent in editing sounds with a razor-blade, synchronising and blending tapes to make a composition.'[4] *Poem in Time of War* (1967) expressed his own feelings about the Vietnam conflict, based on a sung oriental poem of 'poignant simplicity'. The studio began earning revenue through numerous commissions, such as music for Richard Campion's production of James Ritchie's *He Mana Toa* for the Maori Theatre Trust (1967), and through work for film, radio and television.

With the support of Professor D. F. McKenzie, a distinguished scholar and practitioner of printing, who had established the Wai-te-ata Press in a garage near the University, Lilburn in 1967 published a series of composers' autograph scores.[5] Printed by photolithography, they were assembled in evenings and weekends with voluntary (and involuntary) labour. A second series appeared in 1969 and a third in 1972. By now Price Milburn Music, directed by Roderick Biss and Peter Zwartz, had begun commercial publication of elegantly designed scores with funding from APRA, the first venture of its kind in New Zealand. Sadly, this proved short-lived, leaving the Wai-te-ata Press publications still with a role to play: in 1982 and subsequently, further series appeared under the direction of Jack Body. The founding of the music publishing side of the Press illustrated Lilburn's ingenuity, commercial acumen, and native wit.

Lilburn in the EMS/VUW
studio, c. 1975. *Lilburn
collection*

In the ensuing years he kept himself abreast and sometimes ahead of international development in electronic music. He composed *Summer Voices* (1969), whose origins lay in a recording by East Coast schoolchildren of the chant 'Po Po', a traditional lullaby describing how the kumara was brought to New Zealand. '. . . I found that rhythms of the chant could be printed onto electronic sounds, suggesting ghostly voices whispering through the dry grass and a chorus of cicadas, and other impressions of half-heard sounds in the summer air.' In 1969 he revisited Toronto, where Gustav Ciamaga was now in charge, assisted by the brilliant Hugh le Caine. His *Five Toronto Pieces*, composed in five weeks, showed a more aggressive, brittle, and acerbic sound spectrum. He took account of work in Michael Koenig's Utrecht studio and in London. At a concert of electronic music in the Royal Festival Hall, which included the American pioneer Milton Babbitt, his two worlds met when he encountered his old friend Georg Tintner, who had given such a sensitive performance of his Second Symphony. Tintner was in anguish over the sounds he had just heard: 'Can Douglas *really* believe in it?'[6] Lilburn did believe, and took with him the emerging generation of New Zealand composers, initiating them into the mysteries of the studio. Some later won international recognition.[7]

Meanwhile Lilburn's own mastery of the medium proceeded steadily, perhaps reaching its apotheosis in *Three Inscapes* (1972). This took as its starting point the poet Gerard Manley Hopkins' definition of an 'inscape' as an inner pattern or essence of a natural configuration of shapes and colours. Its central statement is probably Lilburn's most significant achievement in electro-acoustic music.

His subsequent works include the ballet *Welcome Stranger* (1974), commissioned by the New Zealand Ballet Company, but in practice greatly changed from

Three Sea Changes, first
page of the third.
Alexander Turnbull Library

his original concept; *Carousel* (1976), created 'for no purpose at all—just to
make happy'; and in complete contrast *Winterset* (1976), with its 'nostalgic
memories of a superb and searing American film produced in the harsh thirties'.
Triptych (1977) 'is a zany piece, a through-the-looking glass piece', with its
three shapes growing out of each other, the last having strong rhythmic patterns
and a motivic rhythm reminiscent of Bach's Brandenburg Concertos. *Of Time
and Nostalgia* (1977) 'tries to explain this conundrum: we, and those we know,
seem to exist simultaneously in many different strata of time, from our present

to varying degrees of our past. The experience often makes for tension and conflict, and these in turn may result in nostalgia.' The synthesized sound is of 'a wider range than usual'. The composer retuned to the natural world in one of his last electro-acoustic works, *Soundscape with Lake and River* (1979), in which the different expanses of water provide pivots, 'making what might seem transitions from afternoon to evening, from night to morning. The work owes something to the spaciousness, the distant small sounds, the slowly changing horizons, the moods and colours of Lake Taupo.'

From 1970 Lilburn held a personal chair in music while directing the Studio. In 1978 the Composers' Association of New Zealand (CANZ) presented him with their Citation for services to New Zealand music. Since his retirement in 1980 he has been actively associated with the Archive of New Zealand Music at the Alexander Turnbull Library which he had been instrumental in setting up in 1974. (His proposal had been immediately adopted by CANZ with the aim of being 'its first practical achievement'.[8]) He recently set up the Lilburn Trust, in association with the Archive, to further the growth and development of New Zealand music. In 1988 he was awarded the rare honour of the Order of New Zealand.

In the ceremony conferring on him the distinction of an Honorary Doctorate in 1969, Professor Alan Horsman of the English Department of the University of Otago said: 'The emergence of a professional composer like Lilburn is part of the process by which New Zealand has ceased to be a place of exile and has become, for us who live here, a centre in its own right.'

Notes

[1] Lilburn to Crowe, 22 August 1963, quoted in *Canzona*, January 1980, 67-8
[2] See Lilburn's 'EMS/VUW: A personal note' for an entertaining account of establishing the studio (published as a brochure accompanying the recording of 'NZ Electronic Music', Kiwi/Pacific SLD 44/46, 6)
[3] Ibid., 7
[4] Ibid.
[5] The first composers were Body, Farquhar, Lilburn, McLeod, Pruden, Ritchie, Tremain, and Whitehead
[6] Verbal communication with author
[7] Jack Body's *Musik Dari Jalan*, for instance, won the Bourges Competition in 1976, and works by John Rimmer, Dennis Smalley, and Kim Dyett were also successful abroad
[8] David Farquhar in *Canzona*, July 1980, 87

X

The expanding tradition: composers since Lilburn

1 The first post-war generation: Carr, Pruden, Tremain and others

It might be assumed that no composers existed between the time of Alfred Hill and the emergence of Douglas Lilburn. The programmes of the British Music Society, which had its own composition groups, and those of the radio stations, with their concert orchestras, show a variety of names, most of whom were amateurs. The relatively few professionals included Gil Dech, an influential conductor, arranger, and composer who settled in Dunedin, and H. C. Luscombe of Auckland, an accomplished musician who taught at the Auckland Teachers' Training College. Others were Dorothy Shepherd, Henry Shirley, an advocate for New Zealand music, and Max Saunders, who went to London before the war and became a leading composer and arranger for the BBC. The Broadcasting Service charitably gave performances to a number of others to encourage 'local talent'. 'In the past we had the days of "the New Zealand composer"', wrote Ashley Heenan. 'If there was to be a radio broadcast, everyone was cushioned for the shock. The biggest advance we ever had was the day when an overture of Lilburn's appeared in the programme with only his name alongside it.'[1]

Among university composers, Vernon Griffith's compositions proved to be the most substantial. A pupil of Stanford, much of his large output satisfied the practical needs of schools, through his part in the *Dominion Song Books*, orchestral exercises for King Edward Technical College at Dunedin, and the Christchurch Teachers' College music classes. His many devotional works include the cantatas *Peace and War, Ode of Thanksgiving*, and *Song of Joy*, three masses and organ pieces, written for the Catholic liturgy, a number of which were published in New Zealand and London. Victor Galway, at the University of Otago, had a similarly practical bent: his secular and sacred works found ready performance in Dunedin and beyond, and some were published by Oxford

University Press in London. The original assumption remains, however: this was an interim period before New Zealand composition began to find its own proper course.

Members of the first composers' class at Cambridge in 1947 formed the nucleus of a group still influential in New Zealand musical life. Some, such as David Farquhar and Ronald Tremain, have university careers, whereas Edwin Carr and Larry Pruden freelanced, Robert Burch became an orchestral player, and others tried a variety of occupations in a search for a balance between composing and the need to earn a living. Common to almost all was their meeting again several years later in Benjamin Frankel's class at the Guildhall School of Music in London.[2]

The emergence of such a group coincided with a radical change in the structure of New Zealand musical life. For the first time direct state patronage became available, thus fulfilling Prime Minister Peter Fraser's pledge to the arts. The profits from the commercial side of broadcasting helped underpin the newly formed National Orchestra, which gave its first concert under Andersen Tyrer on 6 March 1947. The role of Fraser in supporting the orchestra cannot be overstated. His committee secretary, Gerald O'Brien, later chairman, has written of:

> the virulence of opposition to the orchestra at the time of its foundation . . . Fraser fought hard to establish [it] against both grossly opportunist political opposition and the usual philistine hostility . . . Far from New Zealand not being able to afford these things [orchestra and ballet], Fraser argued strongly that we could never be a nation without the dimension of the arts, a viewpoint in which he was consistently supported by the Waterside Workers' Union inside the Labour movement whose view was that man's spirit must have parallel development with his physical requirements.[3]

The Guild of New Zealand Composers, the first such professional organization, was established in Auckland in 1947, following a visit from Frank Hutchens, a New Zealander who taught piano at the New South Wales Conservatorium. Henry Shirley, pianist and composer, assisted by Dorothea Franchi, brought an incorporated society into being, with Thomas Rive as the first president and Ronald Dellow the first secretary. The Guild's aim was to foster higher standards of composition and promote concerts of New Zealand music. It even tried to obtain a quota for them.[4] From 1947 until 1953 the Guild promoted a variety of concerts in Auckland, mainly of piano, string, and vocal works, as the formation of the National Orchestra had deprived the city of many of its best players. It felt most strongly that it had to break the genteel image that had hitherto surrounded New Zealand music.[5]

At Victoria University, Page performed (and broadcast) contemporary and New Zealand music, organizing a celebrated series of university lunch-hour concerts. He and Francis Rosner, a European-born violinist, founded the New Zealand Branch of the International Society for Contemporary Music in 1949. From then until the Society disbanded in 1966, it performed sixty-nine works by New Zealand composers, a little over 16% of its repertoire.[6] Ronald Tremain founded an Auckland Society for Contemporary Music in 1961, which ran until 1969 with high standards and an enterprising repertoire. This could be seen as a continuation of the work begun by the Guild. A Christchurch Society for Contemporary Music (brought into being by the enthusiasm of David Sell, John Jennings, and John Cousins of the university staff), operated successfully from 1968 to 1975, presenting works by several resident composers. Although these groups, like similar societies elsewhere, tended to find themselves playing to audiences already acquainted with contemporary music, they nevertheless had an important function.

The mood of this post-war era was typified by the electrifying concerts of the 1947 Boyd Neel tour, organized by the New Zealand impresario Dan O'Connor. Stimulated by the visitors and their repertoire, Alex Lindsay formed his own orchestra in 1948, undergoing considerable financial hardship to do so. It remained in existence for twenty-one years, and commissioned a number of works. A similar group began in the north, when Owen Jensen founded the Auckland String Players in 1940. It was continued by Ramsay Howie until 1948, then revived by Georg Tintner in 1951. In 1958 John Ritchie formed his own string orchestra in Christchurch.

When the Government started a music bursary system in 1948, students at first went mainly to England, a pattern questioned by Dorothea Turner in her review of the year's activities in 1950: 'The choice made by these scholars [American Fulbright scholars who chose a wide variety of countries to study in] . . . should make us question England as almost the only training ground for our own students, and our main source of contemporary music and performers.' She also felt New Zealand urgently needed more first-rate string teachers, a dozen or so Steinways, another full-time orchestra, and the repeal of the Sunday Observance Act of 1780, which had been done away with in England in 1932 but which still crippled activities in New Zealand.[7] Broadcasting continued to play its vital part, and the existence of the orchestra allowed ensemble groups to form, which in turn set off commissions such as that offered to Lilburn in 1957 by the New Zealand Wind Quintet.

The sense of a new beginning expressed itself in a literary quarterly, *Landfall*, launched in March 1947 by Charles Brasch. The opening editorial set forth its task:

> What counts is not a country's material resources, but the use to which they are put. And that is determined by the spiritual resources of its people. We speak a European tongue; we think thoughts that are European, if with a difference; but we look out on the Pacific.[8]

The Caxton Press in Christchurch, under Leo Bensemann and Denis Glover, provided literary evidence of Brasch's words in a series of finely printed books, principally of the poets, but including Lilburn's Four Preludes for piano. Similar presses included those of Bob Lowry in Auckland and later the Pegasus Press in Christchurch. Blackwood and Janet Paul began publishing in Hamilton, with an enterprising list of New Zealand writers. A new generation of talented poets had emerged, including James K. Baxter and Alistair Campbell. In art, Colin McCahon began his solitary ascent, as New Zealand painters, scattered by the war years, returned to work in the country's oldest artistic tradition.

Several young architects fresh from the Auckland school, known as 'The Group', began publishing a critical journal *Design Review*, which brought a fresh approach to New Zealand architecture and design.[9] An Architectural Centre came into being in Wellington, which promoted enlightened town-planning ideas and held regular exhibitions. The uncompromising views of the Austrian refugee architect Ernst Plischke (b. 1903), as well as several of his buildings, brought stimulus and controversy.[10]

The New Zealand singer Donald Munro, who had recently returned after a successful English career, formed an opera company in 1954, on a mere hint of financial security. Their performances of chamber works such as Pergolesi's *La Serva Padrona* and Mozart's *Bastien and Bastienne* are still remembered. The New Zealand Opera Company, the first of its kind, could best be compared to Britten's English Opera Group in the scale and scope of its activities.

The National Orchestra was learning its repertoire under Andersen Tyrer, giving concerts with such choirs as the Auckland Choral Society and the Schola Cantorum in Wellington, which under Stanley Oliver had won a world-wide reputation.[11] In 1954, Warwick Braithwaite, then a guest conductor, said: 'A real miracle has taken place before your eyes during the past eight years . . . the National Orchestra. To have built an orchestra of such excellence in New Zealand is an almost incredible achievement . . .'[12] The orchestra's touring schedule remained one of the heaviest in the world, with almost continuous travelling of over 16,000 km a year, in an effort to fulfil its policy of flying the musical flag in even the smallest town. Players often had to sit up all night on the Wellington-Auckland express, undergo a 400 km bus ride over mountain passes, or pitch and toss at sea in a stiff southerly as they journeyed between the islands. 'The orchestra is perhaps on the young side: but what youthful players lack in experience can be made up for, when there is sufficient rehearsal, by technical ability and enthusiasm', wrote James Robertson, who retrieved their fortunes when he became permanent conductor in 1954.[13] The orchestra not only showed dramatic improvement, as it had done under guest conductors such as de Castro and Braithwaite, but took on a lively public image. When John Hopkins succeeded James Robertson in 1957, the orchestra greatly enlarged its repertoire of New Zealand compositions. At the same time the Music

Larry Pruden. *In possession of Mrs Penny Pruden*

Federation of New Zealand entered a new phase of activity under Fred Turnovsky, then Arthur Hilton.[14]

The pattern of New Zealand's musical life had irrevocably changed. A tenuous, hard-won performing tradition, built up since the colonial period, had survived two World Wars and now entered a new stage. With this more secure and more stimulating performing ambience came a wave of professional composers.

They emerged from a variety of backgrounds. Ronald Tremain (b. 1923) grew up in the small town of Feilding, a farming centre, in a Salvation Army family. His father had been a music student at Trinity College, London. At Christchurch he was influenced by Page, Lilburn, Jenner, and his piano teacher Lillian Harper. Later he attended the Royal College of Music, where, following in Lilburn's footsteps, he won the Cobbett Prize for a string quartet. From 1957 to 1967 he taught many young composers at the University of Auckland, including Gillian Whitehead, Jack Body, and John Rimmer.

Tremain is a natural composer for the voice, and his *Four Medieval Lyrics* for mezzo-soprano and string trio stands out, though there are fine moments in his earlier settings of Vaughan, Traherne, and Herrick, *Three Mystical Songs* (1951). Both the *Allegro for Strings* (1958) and *Five Epigrams for Strings* (1964) repay attention, as do his more recent rhythmical experiments in *Music for Violin and Strings*, part of his movement away from the cerebral ideas of 'the agonising 50s' to the freedom of choice of the 1980s.

Larry Pruden (1925-1982), from a Methodist New Plymouth background, began his composing career after gaining self-confidence at the first composer's class of the 1947 Cambridge Music School. Largely self-taught, he went on to study with Benjamin Frankel at the London Guildhall School of Music. He wrote several colourful and highly approachable works, mostly connected with specific places, such as *Harbour Nocturne* (1956) and *Lambton Quay* (1957), sound images of aspects of Wellington. Other works in this vein include *Westland: A Back-Country Overture* (1960-1961), *Taranaki* (1976), *Akaroa* (1974), and *Haast Highway* (1975) for brass band. His earlier *Dances of Brittany* for strings (1956) reflected a lifelong feeling for French culture, being one of his most performed works, though it is in his heartfelt String Trio (1954) and *Soliloquy for Strings* (1952) that the essence of his musical personality is revealed.

Edwin Carr in the 1950s. *Carlotta Munz*

Edwin Carr (b. 1926) also studied at the Guildhall with Frankel, who encouraged him to develop his melodic talent and introduced him to serialism: 'This brought me to a purely personal way of handling it in which I have written most of my music since 1961.' Equally important was Frankel's 'insistence on perfection of musical craft at the same time as the unfolding of a personally expressive style'. Carr's early overture *Mardi Gras* (1950) remains vibrant, and his love of the directness and economy of Stravinsky shows in his *Blake Cantata* (1952) for children's choir and small orchestra. His First Symphony (1981), written in memory of Stravinsky, has a sustained central movement framed by sharply etched material. In his Symphony No. 2 'The Exile' (1984), the three movements express phases of the life of an exile, in this instance the notable German Jewish poet, Karl Wolfskehl, who became a refugee in New Zealand at the end of his life. His Symphony No. 3 (1988) had an unusually reflective slow movement, but maintained that ease of communication that is such a feature of his work. A prolific and energetic composer, devoted to ballet, he is also a fine pianist, and has written two Piano Concertos, the second (1987) reflecting a lifetime's devotion to the patterns, arabesques, and delicacy of French music, notably Debussy. Works that are now established in the repertoire include his Sonata for Piano (1955), *Nightmusic* (1958), a Scherzo for Orchestra, and a Sonata for unaccompanied violin (1961). His opera based on Dostoevsky's *The Idiot*, entitled *Nastasya* (1969-1972), has so far had only radio performance.

David Farquhar conducting his one-act opera *Shadow*, at Victoria University of Wellington in 1988. *John Casey*

Paradoxes exist in the works of David Farquhar (b. 1928), whose professionalism and skills, evident from an early age, have placed him at the forefront of New Zealand composition. On the one hand his *Ring Round the Moon* (1953, rep. 1957), an orchestral suite compiled from music for Anouilh's play of the same name, shows a penchant for Schubert and Stravinsky waltzes, and enjoys widespread popularity. Yet his Symphony No. 2 (1983) seemed relatively inaccessible to audiences, as have some of his more hermetic piano pieces. At Arthur Broadhurst's St Peter's School at Cambridge, he gained a musical education difficult to parallel elsewhere at the time, studying singing, piano, organ, and the cello. At the age of eleven he began writing songs and piano pieces with a natural fluency that soon attracted the attention of Gordon McBeth, an enlightened teacher at Wanganui Collegiate School, and then of Lilburn, with whom he had informal lessons in Christchurch. Early influences were Schubert, Bartók, and Britten; the latter's song cycle *Les Illuminations*, for instance, resulted in his setting of Blake songs (1947-1949). His large output includes his prizewinning *Partita* for piano (1957), a First Symphony (1959) more traditional in scope than his Second, and the dark-hued *Three Scots Ballads* (1964). His opera for children, *A Unicorn for Christmas* (1962), rose above a saccharine story to suggest theatrical gifts which he has found difficulty in realizing in New Zealand. Nevertheless, writing for voices continues to attract him, as in *The Score* (1969), a collection of twenty school songs.

From the 1970s onwards he became involved with working out a variety of resonance effects, as in several piano works, *5 Scenes* for guitar (1971), and *Bells in their Seasons* (1974), a choral symphony for double choir and orchestra. Eastern and western influences blend in his *Duet* (1972) for guitar and sitar, and the gamelan pieces *Ostinato* (1975) and *Palindrome* (1979). His *Concerto for Six* (1987), written for John Rimmer's Karlheinz Company, admirably projects a cool, stylish craftsmanship.

Dorothea Franchi (b. 1920) has had distinguished professional careers as both harpist and composer. Her romantic Viola Rhapsody (1950) won the Tertis Prize at the Royal College of Music. In 1953 she became pianist and musical director for the newly formed New Zealand Ballet Company under Paul Gnatt,

Dorothea Franchi conducting her ballet suite from *Do-Wack-a-Do*, 12 February 1965. *Dominion*

writing *Do-Wack-a-Do* in 1968, revived by the Royal New Zealand Ballet in 1988. A self-confessed neo-romantic, very fond of Bach, of pianistic composers, and of Bartók, Stravinsky, Sibelius, and Mussorgsky, she is a spirited original, with an unquenchable enthusiasm for music.

The professional career of Ashley Heenan (b. 1925) in the New Zealand broadcasting services from 1943 onwards has nevertheless led him to devote much of his life to enhancing the status of New Zealand composers and to performing and recording their music. He directed the National Youth Orchestra from 1965 to 1975 and was founding director (1961-1985) of the Schola Musica, the training group for the New Zealand Symphony Orchestra. His music covers many genres, including arrangements, and shows a deep interest in Polynesian and Māori music, as in the film score *Moana Roa* (1951) and *A Maori Suite* (1966). He wrote orchestral music for James K. Baxter's radio play *Jack Winter's Dream* (1958), staged at the Wellington International Festival of the Arts in 1988.

Robert Burch (b. 1929), also a member of the Cambridge and Guildhall classes, was strongly influenced by the clarity of Frankel's teaching. Dennis Brain persuaded him to take up the horn and he pursued this career in the symphony orchestra. He has written several chamber works of quality, including *Capriccio for Saxophone Quartet* (1965), a deft, flowing piece in contrasting moods, *Essay* for cello and piano in memory of Shostakovich (1975), and *Serenade* (1965), a wind quintet. He feels that tonality still has much to say.

Although pursuing an academic career, John Ritchie (b. 1921), Professor of Music at the University of Canterbury, was strongly influenced by his mentor

Vernon Griffiths towards community music-making. His extensive orchestral, brass band, and choral experience included conducting the Addington Railway Workshops Choir and founding a string orchestra under his own name. A clarinet player, Ritchie wrote a Concertino for clarinet and strings (1957) which has a firm place in the repertoire. His wide range includes *Four Zhivago Songs* (1977), *Aquarius* (1982), a second suite for string orchestra, and a sonorous Partita for Wind Octet (1970).

Ashley Heenan

Dorothy Freed (b. 1919) became a professional librarian, specializing in musical interests. She won the 1958 NZBC/APRA Song Award, the Philip Neill memorial prize for composition in 1959, and in 1980 the APRA award for outstanding services to music. She has written many songs, instrumental music, and incidental music for radio and theatre. Her library work has included much pioneer cataloguing of resources, making music more freely available to performing groups throughout New Zealand.

These composers have held senior positions in New Zealand musical life, have taught younger musicians, and promoted their music. Their styles are as various as their influences and achievements. Through them music and composition have become a stronger force.

Notes

[1] Heenan, A. 'Music in a cold climate', *NZL.* 1 November 1968
[2] This recalled Nadia Boulanger's salon in Paris of the 1920s and 1930s, attended by many Americans
[3] Letter from Gerald O'Brien, *Concert Pitch*, Issue 23, January-May 1987, 19
[4] See Shirley, 172, for a lively description of the response
[5] Norman thesis, 711. During the nine years of its existence the Guild had a total of fifty-four members, reaching a high point of twenty-seven in 1953
[6] See Norman thesis, 716ff. and Page, 'Contemporary music in New Zealand'. *Landfall*, June 1956, 146-7
[7] Turner, D. 'Music in 1950'. *Landfall*, December 1950, 332-6
[8] *Landfall*, March 1947, 3ff.
[9] This included a well-deserved attack on the proposed design of the Wellington Cathedral which would have demolished old St Paul's, immolating parts of it in a concrete monolith
[10] See his *Design and Living*
[11] It went into recess in 1955, being replaced by the Phoenix Choir. The Royal and the Harmonic remained active, occasionally visiting other cities
[12] *NZL*, 20 August 1954
[13] Robertson, James, 'Music Scene in New Zealand'. *Concert-Goers' Annual*, ed. Evan Senior, London, 1958, 139
[14] For a full account of the development of the Music Federation see Thomson, J. M., *Into a New Key*

2 New influences: from Darmstadt and Messiaen to minimalism

Jenny McLeod. *Kenneth Quinn*

The young composers of the 1960s looked towards Europe and America rather than Britain. Donaueschingen and Darmstadt had arisen as centres of the new music, with Boulez, Stockhausen, Messiaen, Berio, Maderna, Nono, Cage, and others as resident teachers. In 1958 Frederick Page, prompted by the composer and musicologist Richard Hoffman, visited both. Exhilarated by what he heard, he made invaluable contacts with composers such as Boulez, and through broadcasts, concerts, and lectures, energetically promulgated their music.[1]

Jenny McLeod (b. 1941), first studied with Messiaen in Paris: 'There I found a very unique, wonderful human being, and a fabulous musical mind. Messiaen awoke my own musical intellect enormously, set me thinking in new ways about colour, resonance, pattern, mode, rhythm and the properties of organic forms.' After a flirtation with the strict procedures inculcated by Stockhausen's Cologne classes in *For Seven* (1966), she returned to New Zealand and became absorbed by ancient Māori creation poetry. In her *Earth and Sky* (1968), she created an exuberant theatre piece that brought together a whole community, to be followed in 1971 by *Under the Sun*, in rock idiom. Her recent film scores, choral and orchestral works reaffirm the spontaneity, lyricism, and sense of celebration that lie at the heart of her music.

Messiaen also attracted Robin Maconie (b. 1942) as a student, and he also studied with Stockhausen. Maconie has subsequently worked mainly outside New Zealand as an experimenter, as in *Touché*, in which he created a special environment for listening to electro-acoustic music. His keen musical mind found an outlet in London journals: 'I used the conservative *Daily Telegraph* to promote avant-garde music and *The Times Educational Supplement* to attack humbug.' In his book *Stockhausen* (1976, rep. 1988), a standard work, he shows that even the most difficult new music can be defended as rational and coherent.

Robin Maconie. *Jenny Scown, Times, Hamilton, New Zealand*

Annea Lockwood (b. 1939), encouraged in her early works by Vernon Griffiths and John Ritchie in Canterbury, must have astonished her mentors by becoming the most innovatory composer of all. After study in Cologne, where 'Koenig's very precise organisational mind provided fine teaching of structural aspects, and working in the CEM studios opened up all those alternative fields of sound sources', she found Cage's influence 'a final catalyst', and pioneered many occasions, such as a series of glass concerts in the mid-60s: '. . . partly theatre, and partly a rather ascetic minimalist piece, a little ahead of their period in their minimal insistence on one sound at a time'. Following her experiments with old pianos, entitled the Piano Transplants (including a ceremonial piano burning), she settled in America where she explored environmental sounds, which linked with her childhood experiences of the Southern Alps around Arthur's Pass in Canterbury: 'In this respect I feel myself most strongly a New Zealand composer.' She is described in Slonimsky's *Baker's Biographical Dictionary* as 'composeress of the militant avant-garde'.

Not all composers followed this golden road. Barry Anderson (1935-1987) found his true métier in London and pioneered electro-acoustic music through the West Square Electronic Music Studio (1971), forming his own concert ensemble in 1975. He worked on the integral computer-generated sound elements in Harrison Birtwistle's opera *The Mask of Orpheus* (1986), described as 'some of the most exciting electronic music composition to have come from IRCAM'.[2] His fiftieth birthday celebratory concert in London included his own *Fanfare* (1983), only eighty-four seconds long, his realization of Stockhausen's *Solo* in a version for voice and multiple tape delays, *Colla Voce*, commissioned by Jane Manning for voice, with virtuoso vocal writing, and *Piano Piece 2* (1969), 'gritty and atonal, showing sympathies with the post-Webern school'.[3] His *Mask* (1976, rep. 1985) is an ambitious piece for flutes, story-teller, two percussionists, and a large screen replica of a north-western American Indian mask realized in its primary colours. Although his life centred on London and Europe, Barry Anderson always cherished his New Zealand roots. He died in Paris following a première of his *ARC* at IRCAM.

Barry Anderson

Gillian Whitehead (b. 1941) also found her direction in Britain. She studied with Peter Maxwell Davies in London, having been attracted by his ideas on analysis and composition in lectures he delivered in Sydney (where her early *Missa Brevis* had been praised for its imaginative qualities). She began a series of works on Māori themes, harking back to her Māori ancestry, such as *Pakuru* (1967), a setting of a Māori love poem by Hone Tuwhare, and *Whakatau-ki*

Gillian Whitehead with the 'Golden square' behind her in the lecture room of the Music School, Victoria University of Wellington, 1989. *John Casey*

(1970), based on Māori sayings vividly describing the seasonal cycle. Her first chamber opera, *Tristan and Iseult* (1978), was followed by *The King of the Other Country* (1984), to a text by the poet Fleur Adcock, with whom she collaborated in several works, notably *Hotspur* (1980) for soprano and chamber ensemble. In composing she has made constant but not exclusive use of her own version of 'the magic square' which Maxwell Davies and others employed, earlier suggested by Bartók. She has always thought of music as a totality of form, rhythm, and melody, with a quality of wholeness, as opposed to breaking it down into its constituent elements, or accentuating one against the whole. At the age of seventeen she had written to her mother: 'I want to be a composer. The kind of music I want to write has something of the structure of Dufay, the orchestration of Webern and a kind of Debussian approach to harmony.' Each of these is indeed embodied in her music, which is redolent with the influences of natural sounds—'birds, the sound of wind from nothing, the sound of rain and the great sense of space and the changing light'.

Kit Powell (b. 1937), having completed a science degree, attended the Cambridge Summer Schools of Music and subsequently created a particular role for himself, compounded of Swiss-New Zealand experience. He studied with Petrassi at Siena, visited Darmstadt, where Earle Browne's *Available Forms*, with its ideas of clusters, chance procedures, open forms, live electronics, and parameters, stimulated his own work. His *Palindrome* (1972) for five orchestras led to his forming an experimental group of young percussionists (*Stone Poem* (1976), *Ever Circling Light* (1980)), and a series of works in collaboration with the poet Michael Harlow. The latest of these, *Les Episodes*, was successfully performed at the 1987 Sonic Circus. Found and home-made instruments, theatrical elements, and the use of chance permeate his music, perhaps best summed up in his music-theatre *Piece of 4* (1981). Since moving to Switzerland he has developed an increasing interest in computer music.

John Rimmer (b. 1939) studied with Ronald Tremain and participated in the Cambridge Summer Schools. A period of study with John Weinzweig of Toronto, 'a marvellous composer and wonderful teacher', orientated him especially towards electro-acoustic music, an interest reinforced by regular meetings with Lilburn from 1969 to 1978. His technical expertise, enthusiasm, and flair for organizing performing groups such as the Karlheinz Company, has made his work at the University of Auckland of particular importance. His music is characterized by natural sounds of sea, waves, water, birds, and wind as in *Where Sea Meets Sky* (1975), impressions of a trans-Tasman flight. Electronic music has affected the shape and substance of his instrumental music, as has the work of New Zealand painters like Don Binney and Michael Smither, and poets such as Ian Wedde. His *Composition* series, begun in 1968, sets out to integrate vocal, instrumental, and electronic sounds in works of diverse mood for horn, wind quintet, percussion, piano, and soprano, etc.[4] He has also attempted this synthesis in *Visions 1* (1975) (choir and tape), and *Tides* (1981)

John Rimmer. *Kenneth Quinn*

(horn and tape). His *The Ring of Fire* (1976) and *Meeting Place* show him moving from a European concept of sound to one in which environmental influences have an important place. Rhythm, space, and timbre are vital factors in his music.

The range of influences and styles of these composers, more diverse than those of the previous generation, is further shown by Ian McDonald (b. 1937), who also paints and sculpts, writes poetry, manifestos, scripts, and lyrics, and talks about electronic music. His works cover a wide range of media, notably theatre, radio, television, and film. In his *Makara* (1968), the sound material is developed from a single stroke on a china plate. 'Music communicates', he writes. 'It is a mediator. This definition embraces all known music including that of birds, the sea and urban collectivities.' Michael Smither (b. 1939), a painter with a highly developed sense of colour and form, has published piano pieces which examine the relationships between music and artistic forms, shapes, and colours, his most valuable contribution in this field being his invention of a chart in 1981 relating sound to light in a harmonic way. Yorkshire-born Jack Spiers (b. 1939), who teaches at the University of Otago, combines European and New Zealand worlds, as in his *Three Poems of Janet Frame* (1972) for tenor and twelve instrumentalists. A skilled conductor, he has commissioned a number of works for his Dunedin Civic Orchestra—'in a way, my conducting is part of my composing'. Gary Daverne (b. 1939) spans both the classical and pop and rock worlds. He directs the Auckland Symphony Orchestra (which he founded in 1975) as well as the Mandrill Recording Studios, which has gold and silver awards to its credit.

Anthony Watson (1933-1973), the first Mozart Fellow at Dunedin in 1971/2, had a tragically short life but nevertheless left powerful music, notably his three string quartets and *Preludes and Allegro for strings* (1960), written for Alex Lindsay and marked by an acerbic dissonant quality that unexpectedly yields to lyricism.

By the end of the 1960s the influence of Darmstadt and Donaueschingen had waned, although the cerebral, minutely structured style, establishing parameters for every aspect of a musical composition including pitch, which it had especially encouraged, still held some attraction. Many New Zealand composers of this generation absorbed what it had to teach them, then moved in different directions. The Electronic Music Studio at Victoria University attracted many; some remained more orientated towards traditional performance media. Jack Body (b. 1944) was one who successfully moved between both. He studied with Mauricio Kagel (b. 1931), the exponent of expressionism, surrealism, and dadaism. This Kagel period encouraged a dedication to happenings, which found fullest expression in his famed series of Sonic Circuses, culminating in that of 1987, an explosive affirmation of a multitude of talents.

Body continued his studies in electronic music, notably under Koenig at Utrecht, who influenced his *23 Pages* (1971) for large orchestra. Two years as guest lecturer at Yogyakarta in Indonesia profoundly affected him: 'It has

Jack Body. *John Casey*

given me a taste of another world of sensibility and awareness and made me understand that all knowledge and understanding is only relative.' The unique character of Indonesian sounds is reflected in his *Musik dari Jalan* (Street Music), an electro-acoustic work which won first prize at the Bourges Festival in 1976. Asian and Pacific music have inspired works such as *Melodies for Orchestra* and *Five Melodies for Piano* (both 1983), his virtuosic piano duet *Three Rhythmics* (1986), and *Three Transcriptions* (1987), a string quartet. Minimalism, strongly linked to repetitive rhythmic patterns, shows its influence, along with that of Penderecki, in the glissandi and string clusters of *Little Elegies* (1984-1985), written for the NZSO, marking in an unexpectedly serious style the twenty-fifth anniversary of television in New Zealand.

Lyell Cresswell (b. 1944), whose international reputation is based on a series of impressive works, lives in Edinburgh. He is unequivocal on his earliest influences: 'I cannot imagine that I'd have taken to writing music without the example of my uncle Ray, who wrote Salvation Army music.' His extensive studies have included periods at the Toronto electronic music studios, the Institute of Sonology in Utrecht, and a computer music course at the Massachusetts Institute of Technology at Cambridge, Mass. His music has fallen into three periods. The first (1965-1970) grew from string quartet pieces in the style of Bartók to reach a climax with his first orchestral work, the Violin Concerto (1970). In the second experimental period (*c.* 1971-1975), his works ranged from the black comedy of the *Threnody for Mrs S—, who was drowned at her baptism* to the social realism of *A Music for Skinheads*, a period of 'searching for a true means of expression'.

In the third period, one of consolidation, from 1976 onwards, he has sometimes used folk music as the basis of a work—'part of a search for some common ground between myself and the audience'. His *O! for Orchestra*—the title is from William Booth's words for a popular Salvation Army song, 'O Boundless Salvation'—is central to his work. It contains 'cries of joy and sorrow, of anguish and hope, and of supplication and glorification'. Notable recent works include his *To Aspro Pano Sto Aspro—'White on White'*, settings of six short, neo-imagist, modern Greek poems, his vast Third String Quartet, *The Silver Pipes of Ur* (1981) for wind quartet, and his Cello Concerto (1984), a work of power, breadth, and feeling which won recognition at the 1988 Paris Rostrum. A highlight of Sonic Circus '87 was the performance of the last two movements of his forty-five minute *A Modern Ecstasy* by the New Zealand Symphony Orchestra, conducted by Francisco Feliciano. The complete work was played by the BBC Scottish Symphony Orchestra under Jerzy Maksymiuk on 6 May 1989 when critics acclaimed it.

Denis Smalley (b. 1946), who directs the electro-acoustic music studio at the University of East Anglia in Norwich and composes almost entirely in this medium, has won international recognition for his works. Committed from his earliest days to the avant-garde (his youthful playing of Messiaen and Ligeti

Denis Smalley, *Arts Council of Great Birtain*

Lyell Cresswell in Edinburgh, 1989. *Doug Simpson, Edinburgh*

on the organ outraged conservative Christchurch critics), he studied with Messiaen himself in Paris, an ambience he found 'very Byzantine'. He was the first student to complete the diploma of the Groupe de Recherches Musicales, and began composing seriously. The tape medium is his principal means of large-scale expression: 'the place where all thoughts, instrumental, vocal and purely electro-acoustic may meet on an ambitious scale—my symphony orchestra if you like'. His *Pentes* (1974) develops the sound of Northumbrian pipes, *Pulses of Time* (1979) those of the clavichord, *Tides* (1985) uses computer manipulation of water sounds, and *Wind Chimes* (1987) computer manipulations of the sounds of a set of pottery chimes discovered on his 1986 visit to Nelson. It was first performed at the Electric Weekend in the Queen Elizabeth Hall, London in September 1987, when Robert Maycock of the *Independent* described it as '. . . music of great beauty and range and a virtuoso use of space, moving rapidly around in complex patterns that constitute one of the medium's greatest excitements.'[5]

John Cousins (b. 1943) has followed his own path single-mindedly, with his own kind of integrity. As his works (and views) question commonly held beliefs about the relationship of the individual to music, art, and society, the critical controversies aroused by some of his electro-acoustic and performance/installation works seem inevitable. Nearly all of his output is

John Cousins

Ross Harris. *John Casey*

characterized by a personal or autobiographical aspect. Works like *Christmasmusic* (1974), *Parade* (1983), and *Tense Test* (1986) are closer to sonic parables or allegories than to purely musical forms. In the performance installations he constructs various functional visual environments and then interacts with these through the use of ritual, narrative, and most importantly, physical confrontation and integration, as in *Sleep Exposure* (1979), *Soundings* (1982), *Birthday* (1983), and *Membrane* (1984), featured at the 1984 Edinburgh Festival. He regards his work in performance installations and electro-acoustic music as 'gestural, freeing, open rather than closed forms', embodying what he had learned from his own teaching and from working with the Canadian dancer/choreographer Mary Fulkerson. His life has been a search for his own creative identity: 'Eclecticism is only useful when one has one's own creative spirit intact.'

Ross Harris (b. 1945) succeeded Douglas Lilburn as director of the Victoria University Electronic Music Studio in 1980. His most ambitious work to date is his opera *Waituhi* (1984), with a libretto by Witi Ihimaera. Harris used the traditional operatic framework of arias, duets, ensemble pieces, and choruses, interspersing them with haka, poi, action song, and waiata. He combined aspects of traditional Māori chant with contemporary Māori and European harmonic idioms, both atonal and electronic. Most of the singers were untrained Māori. His earlier settings of Māori texts include *Kia Mau te Rongo* (1983) ('Live in Peace'), written for synthesizer drone and choir in from four to twenty-four parts, with Māori words drawn from the Māori Bible, I Corinthians 13, 'Love is patient and kind'. He is continuing his collaboration with Ihimaera. Other works include an engaging *Games Affair* (1974), originally written for a children's TV film, *Shadow Music* (1977), *Skymning* (1978), composed in Stockholm, a haunting *Echo* (1979) for trumpet and tape delay, and an instrumental Quintet (1980). His recent music reveals a search for a vernacular and a desire to escape from the entrenched position of the avant-garde, a direction supported by his formation in 1982 of a live electronic music ensemble, Free Radicals, with Jonathan Besser and Gerry Meister, to explore aspects of rock, jazz, and electro-acoustic music. Besser has evolved his own distinctive synthesis of these styles and media in a variety of enterprising works.

International success came to Philip Dadson (b. 1946), sound artist, composer, and teacher of sculpture and Inter-media, with his formation of the outstanding music/performance ensemble From Scratch, which in his own words 'has a distinctive sound, look and character', with its invented 'percussion stations' and intriguing instruments which give concerts a physical intensity, part ritual, part sculpture. 'The best performance art music I've ever seen', wrote Marina Vaizey of their 1984 Edinburgh Festival season.[6] The performers on this occasion were Wayne Laird, Don McGlashan, and Philip Dadson. Recent works include *Drum/Sing* and *Pacific 3, 2, 1, ZERO*, a protest against nuclear testing and waste-dumping in Oceania. The ensemble evolved from Dadson's experience in Cornelius Cardew's original Scratch Orchestra in London.

Noel Sanders (b. 1948), who has an A.M. from Harvard, must be one of very few composers to have specialized in linguistics. Now in the Communications Department at the New South Wales Institute of Technology in Sydney, he lectures and writes on the role of music in present-day society, in a trenchant, highly individualistic manner. His works include the piano solo *Flame Tree* (1975), *Erlking* for small ensemble, successfully performed in 1985 by the Australian ensemble Flederman, and *Marram* (1980, rep. 1987), a terse, well-knitted piece, which won recognition at the 1987 Sonic Circus. In 1989 Sanders was the first composer-in-residence of the Music Federation of New Zealand, working with the New Zealand String Quartet. A concern for social issues suffuses the music of Christopher Blake (b. 1949), though landscape and place also arouse an immediate response. In his powerful *Till human voices wake us* (1986), he chose passages from *We Will Not Cease*, Archibald Baxter's classic memoir of his bitter experiences as a conscientious objector in World War I, while the title of Blake's work arises from Ian Hamilton's account of similar trials in World War II. Amongst women composers, Dorothy Buchanan (b. 1945) writes prolifically, influenced above all by the landscape. She has deeply involved herself with film music, much of it for silent films held by the New Zealand Film Archive, where she is resident composer. She held the position of first Composer in Schools. Gillian Bibby (b. 1945) studied piano and composition in Berlin, composition with Stockhausen in Cologne, and worked with Kagel and Pousseur. Her music is often experimental, diverse in its allegiances, and forcefully direct.

Noel Sanders. *Brett Robertson*

Christopher Blake. *Express Photo Studio, Auckland*

The careers of most of the youngest generation of composers, those at present in their thirties, are still in the making, though the gifts of Christopher Norton (b. 1953) have already taken him far. His flourishing *Microjazz* tutors circulate throughout the world, incorporating elements of jazz, pop, and rock. An accomplished pianist, he graduated M.Phil from York University. He has settled in England, where he also writes educational and gospel music. His stage musical *Daniel*, which includes a punk animal song and a rock symphony of psalms, was described by Wilfrid Mellers as 'an absolute masterpiece'.

David Griffiths (b. 1950) teaches singing at the University of Otago, and has a special affinity for voices: 'I love their richness, colour and intensity and their correctly directed use.' He is a prolific writer, and his evocative choral works include a number for worship. David Hamilton (b. 1955), influenced by George Crumb, Philip Glass, and Steve Reich, has written a prize-winning Double Percussion Concerto (1979), many choral works, such as his *Te Deum* (1986), and pieces for a variety of media, including *Canticle* (1981), *Nix Olympica* (1985), and *Kaleidoscope* (1987). He is Head of Music at Epsom Girls' Grammar School.

Dorothy Buchanan

Other active and aspiring composers include Chloe Moon (b. 1952), who spent four years as a member of the Camerata Quartet in Christchurch. She studied violin at Ghent, and showed her skill in writing for strings in *Shadows*

John Elmsly

Philip Norman

(1979). John Elmsly (b. 1952), a graduate in mathematics and music, and an accomplished flautist, studied at Brussels, Ghent, and Liège, and combines electro-acoustic works with traditional media, as in his *Ritual Auras* (1982). He teaches at Auckland University. Philip Norman (b. 1953), whose *Bibliography of New Zealand Compositions* (1982) is an indispensable research tool, has written ten musicals, notably *Footrot Flats* (1983), and *Love off the Shelf* (1985-1986), also several ballets, including *Terrible Tom* (1985), and *Te Maia and the Sea-Devil* (1987) for silicon chip duet of keyboard and drum synthesizers. Chris Cree Brown (b. 1953) is active in electro-acoustic and mixed-media work. One of his installation pieces included an imaginative Aeolian harp, which he tried to persuade Wellington City Council to build. His *Neap Tides* (1983) won the Wellington Youth Orchestra's Young Composers' Contest. Martin Lodge (b. 1954) combines composition with writing about music. He has composed a virtuoso trumpet study, *Gyres* (1981), and a wind quintet, *Divisions*. Nigel Keay (b. 1955), a string player, had his Quartet for piano, violin, viola, and cello (1985) published by the University of Otago Press while he was Mozart Fellow. Kenneth Young (b. 1955), tuba player in the NZSO, feels there is no greater joy in an orchestra than 'sitting on the bottom of a Bruckner chorale on the tuba . . . you feel as if you're supporting the whole section'.[7] His works include a Concerto for tuba and orchestra (1977), a brass quintet (1981), performed in over 200 schools with the NZ Brass Quintet, *Sinfonietta* (1985), a symphony, as well as pieces for piano, cello, and other instruments, commissioned by the Music Federation. Kim Dyett (b. 1956) won a prize in the Italian Luigi Russolo competition for electro-acoustic music, followed by a scholarship to study electronic music in Stockholm, and in 1987 an award at Bourges for his *Wallpaper Music*. Michael Vinten (b. 1956), conductor of the Schola Musica in succession to Ashley Heenan, has written a short opera, *I Sing to Thee Through Open Windows*. His *Ritual Songs* won the 1985 Wellington Youth Orchestra/Commercial Union Young Composer Competition.

As Anthony Ritchie (b. 1960), a fluent young musician with an affinity for the music of Bartók and Eastern Europe, stressed in *Canzona* (March 1987), New Zealand composers must strive to create fresh fields of work within their

Nigel Keay

own society. The present upsurge of activity, coupled with a responsive critical sense and an awareness of other musical cultures, bodes well for the future vitality of New Zealand music.

Notes

1 See Page, *A Musician's Journal*. Quotations from composers, unless otherwise annotated, are from communications to the author
2 The *New Yorker*, quoted in Stephen Montague's obituary tribute, the *Independent*, London, 30 May 1987
3 Stephen Montague in *Classical Music*, 12 October 1985, 13
4 See Elizabeth Kerr's evaluation 'Composition Series: problems and possibilities in live electronic music'. *Canzona*, March 1987, 11-18
5 *Independent*, 15 September 1987
6 *Sunday Times*, 19 August 1984. See also Cordelia Oliver in the *Guardian*, 9 September 1984, and Edward Gage in the *Scotsman*, 20 August 1984
7 Quoted in *NZL*, 12 October 1985, 128

A boys' fife band with harmonium, at Glendining Home, Dunedin, possibly c. 1920, or earlier.
Glendining Homes collection, Dunedin

Appendix 1: Music in education

The music teacher

From the first settlement until 1956, when Dr Charles Nalden set up the first executants' diploma course at the University of Auckland, private music teachers and the nuns of the Catholic Church shouldered the task of training musicians in New Zealand. There had been many attempts to set up a conservatorium on European lines, notably that of Michael Balling in Nelson in 1893 (see chapter III, 7), but each had foundered, usually for economic reasons and for those of regional pride. The Government had little interest in music, and the educational authorities had other priorities. As late as 1937, Mary Martin could deplore the country's plight in the pages of *Music in New Zealand*: 'Until music has a place in our general educational scheme we cannot hope to have a discriminating public; we cannot hope to raise the standard of orchestral playing and choir singing, nor can we hope to attract talented musicians from overseas to come and settle here.'[1] The following account of music in education not only bears out such judgements but shows what a sustained (and continuing) struggle it has been.

Nineteenth-century music teachers arrived with a variety of credentials. Some had diplomas from the English schools, some from the conservatoria of Germany. Others were pupils of celebrated teachers, such as H. M. Lund (1847-1932), for instance, who became the distinguished critic of the *Press* in 1905. He had known Brahms, von Bülow, and Wagner, and had often heard Liszt and Rubinstein play. Their personalities were as various as their origins. Even in the smallest towns, from the middle of the century onwards, the local music teacher brought an exotic touch to a community otherwise mainly concerned with commerce, agricultural, or pastoral pursuits. Most became the backbone of a struggling musical culture, nurtured their talented pupils, often played in local orchestras and bands, conducted choirs and orchestras, and spread their talents widely. Many are vividly recalled by their former pupils as dominant musical influences in their lives. Frederick Page remembers Miss Henderson of Lyttelton in the years before World War I, one of six piano teachers in a town of less than 4,000:

> Miss Henderson had a background of well-made Scottish rosewood furniture, good books, again a decent house, scrupulously looked after. The lives of these teachers were not easy. First pupils came at 6.30 a.m. and were taught until 8.45 a.m., a few would be crammed in at mid-day and then the main work would start at 3 p.m. and continue until 7 and 8 p.m. It was a gruelling task as fees were only twenty-five shillings a school term at the most. Lessons were made up for illnesses, Miss Henderson also visited homes when it was not convenient for pupils to come to her and tramped from one end of Lyttelton

to the other. She ended her days in penury, a fact which I think shameful to our society and to our education system.[2]

Margaret Clark recalls Madame Elsie Betts-Vincent of Wellington, a brilliant graduate from the Royal Academy in London: 'She had a passion for everything French (including hand-made hats), for cricket, Chinese food, books in general and the products of Bloomsbury in particular . . . She lent books, gave concert tickets, and taught her pupils the disciplines of music as well as its joys.'[3] Such impressive figures included European musicians who sought refuge in New Zealand before and during World War II. Diny and Paul Schramm, famed duo-pianists as well as soloists, installed an upright piano on a trailer and made extensive schools tours, charging sixpence for programmes that ranged from the classics to Debussy and jazz.

Teaching organizations

However individualistic music teachers might wish to be, they still found advantages in forming regional societies to protect their interests—by 1907 several existed throughout New Zealand.[4] Attempts to amalgamate these separate groups soon ran into difficulties, especially in reaching agreement over the qualifications for registration. In 1924, at a conference of music teachers in Wellington,[5] the New Zealand Society of Professional Teachers of Music was formed.[6] In 1925, a second dominion conference discussed the implementation of a Bill for the registration of music teachers, and made recommendations on school music, which led directly to the appointment of E. Douglas Tayler as Supervisor of School Music to the Education Department the following year. But the 1928 Bill, which eventually became law on 1 January 1929 as The Music Teachers' Registration Act, was a compromise and lacked some of the proposals of its original advocates. It provided for the creation of the Music Teachers' Registration Board.[7]

On 29 January 1937, the ninety-year-old Robert Parker, after a lifetime's distinguished work, resigned his presidency of the Society.[8] S. K. Phillips, an organist, choirmaster, and singing teacher, who had conducted the Kiwi Concert Troupe in 1918 in France and had served on the New Zealand Broadcasting Board in the 1930s, succeeded him. Phillips was the first New Zealander to gain a Mus. D. degree. In 1945 he retired, to be followed by Stanley Oliver, an organist and choral director who had arrived from Canada in 1934. He became conductor of the Royal Wellington Choral Union and founded the enterprising Schola Cantorum in 1936. Under the protection of the Act, improvement in the economic position of music teachers gradually took place: the Registration Board also spoke out publicly for teachers in their private capacities, in schools, and in their professional relationships such as those with broadcasting.

English examinations have always dominated New Zealand music teaching: 'Proportionate to its population [New Zealand is] the best client of the Associated Board and Trinity College', writes David Sell.[9]

No history of the achievements and role of the private music teacher in New Zealand has yet been written. Glimpses of their influence appear in testimonials from their pupils and, on occasion, in books. Yet their importance remains today as crucial as ever.

Music in schools

Early and provincial period 1819-1876

Music found a place in hardly any of the early fee-paying schools, where only three subjects were taught: religion, industrial training, and the English language.[10] During the era of provincial governments (1853-1877), some public schools taught singing, success depending on the abilities of the teachers. Although one ex-pupil recalled that they had only one song ('Ring the Bell Watchman'), in the province of Otago an appointment might hinge on an ability to teach singing efficiently.[11]

Inspectors of Native Schools during the provincial period often commented on the fondness of Māori children for singing and their enjoyment of English hymns. In 1878, the Reverend James Stack, Inspector of Native Schools, recommended the provision of a manual to help teachers, and describes one school where part-singing was taught and multiplication and other tables were sung: 'Mr Masters, the master is an enthusiast, restless and excitable to a degree which to a visitor is distressing, yet no schoolmaster is more successful, and that in the face of all difficulties.'[12] Some Native Schools used harmoniums bought with a Government subsidy: pupils were soon taught such hymns as 'Shall We Gather at the River' and 'There is a Happy Land'.[13]

Some of the newly established secondary schools offered music; Nelson College was probably the first in 1856. Music then consisted largely of singing traditional songs and hymns by rote, with teachers passing on the songs they had themselves learned at school; little equipment or material was supplied.

The Education Act of 1877 and 'Vocal Music' 1877-1899

The 1877 Education Act made vocal music in schools compulsory, but progress was slow, as no material or specialist help was provided by the Department of Education. Many felt diffident about teaching singing. The inspectors, dissatisfied with progress, did not include it in the list of necessary pass subjects in 1885. However, at the training colleges set up in the four main centres, students were required to pass an examination in music for certification, a requirement relaxed in later years, although the work of Cranwell in Auckland and Robert Parker in Wellington, for instance, continued to stimulate teaching in voice production, sight-singing, and general music theory. The earlier establishment of the position of organist and choirmaster at Christchurch Cathedral in 1879 had a deep influence on musical life through its development of a full cathedral choir and later the cathedral Grammar School.[14] Some inspectors and school committees helped teachers by providing copies of songs, and by 1899 most of the larger Wellington schools had a piano bought out of funds raised by parents.[15] The 1877 Act had aimed at giving New Zealand children an education similar to that obtainable in English and Scottish primary schools, although it was clear that this goal was far from being realized.

Nor was the picture more favourable in secondary schools. During the decade 1890-1900, music was taught in only eleven out of twenty-five schools, ranging from lessons in tonic sol-fa to the beginning of orchestral work, with an academic course in music at Napier Girls' High School.[16]

'Vocal Music'—an unsupervised but compulsory subject 1900-1925

The 1904 Education Act made singing compulsory in primary schools and in the same year a syllabus of school music was published. Music had suffered, along with other cultural pursuits, in the depression years of the 1880s, but by 1900 and the social reforms of Seddon's Liberal Government, growth was resumed, though on a very small scale in music. The limited practical aims of most colonial employers, who asked only for the ability to read, write, and count, influenced educational policy, although during the Inspector-Generalship of George Hogben (1853-1920) many enterprising experiments took place. His new primary school syllabus of 1904 revolutionized the system.

As before, music depended almost entirely on the enthusiasm and availability of teachers, and inevitably activities declined during World War I. Although music was now compulsory in primary schools, at the secondary level it depended, as it still does, on the initiative and interest of the headmaster. Schools began obtaining musical instruments: pianos were common, and pupils could afford fairly simple instruments such as a two-octave flute priced at 6s 9d. From 1924 onwards a liberal subsidy from the Education Department allowed schools to purchase gramophones and records—though the latter had to be approved first by the Senior Inspector! Concerts for schools began: in 1924 the pianist Hagen Holenbergh played at Marsden and Nga Tawa. Inspectors called for 'the proper treatment of children's voices', along with the need for more aural training.

Teachers asked for a textbook on music to aid progression from class to class, the appointment of 'musical directors' for schools, and a more effective musical training for student teachers.

The Douglas Tayler regime 1926-1931

Prompted by the recommendations of the Society of Musicians, Wellington, and other lobbying organizations, notably the New Zealand Society of Professional Teachers of Music, the New Zealand Government asked the British composer and organist Sir Walford Davies to select a suitable person for the position of 'Supervisor of School Music'. In April 1926 Mr E. Douglas Tayler, FRCO, ARCM (1886-1932), a fine organist and pianist, took up these duties, becoming, as he styled himself, 'Supervisor of Musical Education'. Tayler worked hard and enthusiastically to cultivate the barren fields he had inherited. In response to his advocacy, full-time lecturers in music were appointed at each of the four training colleges. These were talented musicians who were selected in England: Horace Hollinrake went to Auckland and Vernon Griffiths to Christchurch in 1927, Ernest Jenner to Wellington and J. Crossley Clitheroe to Dunedin in 1928. The excellent results achieved by Griffiths, Hollinrake, and Jenner (Clitheroe did not remain long in New Zealand) led David Sell in 1974 to ask whether their influence had not in fact been too effective, in that they 'set New Zealand music education on a path which, even at that time was not 100% relevant to a society which had already established its own cultural identity to a considerable degree, and was most in need of the stimulus of more varied influences'.[17]

In 1928 Tayler's *A Scheme of School Music Related to Human Life* went to every school, and contained a detailed syllabus of instruction in singing, speech, rhythmical movement, and the use of the gramophone. Tayler held that music was 'a social, not a solitary art, and we should employ it for giving pleasure one to another'.[18] His articles in the *Education Gazette* also encouraged children to write original music. In 1928 he prepared a *Syllabus of Instruction in School Music*, but despite his strenuous efforts, by 1931 only limited progress had been made.[19] At the height of the Depression, when strong pressures were exerted for economies, Tayler was asked to resign. He did so in June 1931, after service of only just over five years: 'too short a time for even this outstanding music educator to work a major musical miracle', wrote Guy Jansen.[20]

Departmental interest was shown in the Atmore Report of 1930, which advocated a broader curriculum for secondary schools. Stimulus came from the increasing use of pianos and gramophones, and from the *Dominion Song Book* (1930-1952), the first of which had been compiled by Tayler, with subsequent editions by Hollinrake, Vernon Griffiths, Ernest Jenner, and others. Conservative in style, these moulded the taste of several generations of New Zealand children, with their arrangements of Māori and British songs, extracts from the classics, and pieces by their compilers.[21]

Jansen believes the Tayler era to be 'a distinct watershed in the history of music education in this country'. 'Tayler accurately pinpointed the basic

E. Douglas Tayler's idealistic educational scheme for school music, 1927

weaknesses of school music . . . within a few months of arriving here and many of them have never been corrected.'[22] During his era, massed schools concerts and festivals sprang up, school music broadcasts began, and Tayler encouraged Vernon Griffiths' 1929 scheme for out-of-hours music classes in Christchurch: by the following year around 1500 children had enrolled to study piano, strings, and wind. Although Tayler's views, like those of his English colleagues, were remote from contemporary European developments, being firmly based on current English educational practice with its bias towards the ideas expressed in Walford Davies' *The Pursuit of Music*, his *A Scheme of School Music* was 'more comprehensive than appears to have been the case in England at that time'.[23] Both Thomas and Jansen believe Tayler's aims are still valid, a view echoed by Owen Jensen's description of him as 'brilliantly imaginative'.[24]

The Griffiths-Jenner era 1932-1944

The 'post-Tayler era', which ranged from the Depression years to World War II, saw the increasing influence of Griffiths' and Jenner's views on music education. They emphasized the need for music to be an enjoyable activity which involved children's active participation as performers, listeners, and creators. For most children of this time 'music was singing', as W. L. Renwick, Director of Education (1987) described his primary school experience in Auckland. 'I do not recall ever seeing a musical instrument other than a piano. Nor can I recall anyone in any of my classes going to a private music teacher. Certainly there were no private music teachers in the suburbs I lived in.'[25] Ernest Jenner applied his knowledge of the tonic sol-fa system and the Paris-Chévé tone name system to his own original and successful ideas on the teaching of sight-singing in primary schools. Vernon Griffiths paralleled this work at the secondary level. When the Christchurch Training College closed during the Depression, he became head of music at Dunedin Technical School (later King Edward Technical College), where in seven years he built up an orchestra, military band, and choirs that included almost every pupil in the school.[26] He made many arrangements of choral music, with particular emphasis on the adolescent male voice. The success of this work, although questioned in certain fundamentals by fellow academics, led directly to his appointment as Professor of Music at Canterbury University College in 1942, succeeding Dr J. C. Bradshaw.[27] Despite Jenner's and Griffiths' evident achievements, there was no official attempt to build on their work, a situation which may well have reflected the lack of interest in music in the higher echelons of the Education Department of that time. Individual teachers, however, followed their example: Robert Perks in his work at Christchurch Technical College, Len White at Papanui Technical College, and Rudolph McLay, a former teaching colleague of Griffiths, at Hutt Valley Memorial Technical College, Petone. At Nelson College, from the late 1940s onwards, Ralph Lilly won for senior orchestral players virtually equal status to those in the First Fifteen.

Although the emphasis of this chapter has lain principally on the state educational system, outstanding work took place in various Catholic and independent schools, including Christ's College (Robert Field-Dodgson), St Andrews, Christchurch (Clifton Cook), King's College, Auckland (L. C. M. Saunders), and at Māori schools such as Queen Victoria and Te Aute, Hastings. In many communities, especially smaller ones, the Catholic nuns had a particularly beneficial influence.[28]

The Thomas Report and the new status of music 1945-1957

The increased use of music broadcasts to schools devised by Tom Young, Keith Newson, and others, the expansion of the Music Festival movement (such as Hollinrake's Auckland primary music festivals), and the sudden growth of interest in classroom instruments, especially percussion and recorder, gave more children access to music than before. But despite Prime Minister Peter Fraser's statement that every child had the right to an education 'to the fullest extent of his powers' (1939), the educational system denied thousands of schoolchildren the right to this in music. There seemed to have been little development since Tayler. A revised syllabus, *Music in the Primary School* (1945), and the Thomas Report (1944), were both designed to help encourage music-making, the development of the ear, and the expressive use of music.

In certain practical areas much progress had been made, such as Nancy Martin's work with recorder players and the publication of her book, written expressly for New Zealand schools. The tradition at King Edward Technical College continued, Tom J. Young's music broadcasts won esteem, and Walter B. Harris initiated new ideas as unofficial music adviser while attached to the National Film Library. Young built up a first-rate broadcast choir in the 1940s, and Harris planned a series of National Secondary Schools Orchestral Courses. These began as a pilot scheme in 1953 with Saturday morning classes for a variety of instruments at Hutt Valley Memorial Technical College, to be developed over a fifteen-year period by Walden-Mills. The scheme expanded to other parts of the country, taking strong root in Christchurch. In 1955 the Christchurch School of Instrumental Music was founded by Robert Perks. It widened its scope to include secondary school students and has subsequently done notable work.[29]

In 1958 W. Walden-Mills, formerly bandmaster, conductor, and music organizer in Norfolk, England, and latterly Director of Music at King Edward Technical College, arrived in Wellington to take up his appointment as Adviser on School Music. He concentrated on the training of in-service teachers in music, and at a refresher course in 1960 the School Music Association was formed with his support. It became a powerful body during its short life, but was wound up in 1972. Its influence proved similar to that of the Society of Professional Musicians in the 1924-1928 period. Under its first President, Ralph Lilly, it presented a unified front in working with the Department of Education. It pressed for the establishment of a pool of orchestral instruments in each Educational Board, to be allied with the provision of free out-of-hours instrumental tuition for primary children and the appointment of a music adviser to each Education Board district from 1963. The Department set up the instrumental pool, and following the appointment of Walden-Mills, established District Advisers in Wellington and Auckland. By the beginning of 1964, all ten Education Board districts in the country were similarly covered. The music advisers proved extremely important.[30]

In 1959 the National Youth Orchestra was formed under the impetus of John Hopkins, then conductor of the National Orchestra, and with the enthusiastic support of Walter B. Harris, who had already enlarged the scope of schools concerts. This became the highest goal of school instrumentalists and encouraged better playing standards with the help of principals of the National Orchestra, who acted as tutors. In that same year the first appointment of a post-primary lecturer in music was made. Recorders, at the height of their popularity in the 1950s, were joined by guitars and other classroom instruments in the 1960s. National youth bands were assembled from time to time as an offshoot of an adult national band. In 1966 Walden Mills organized the first National Secondary Schools Choral Course. It was partly as a result of leading such courses after 1975 that Jansen, now Education Officer, Music, in the Department, founded the National Youth Choir in 1979. In 1977 free vocal tuition to small groups in school time was added to the work of secondary itinerant and part-time tutors. In 1982 a National Youth Jazz Orchestra and the Yamaha High School Jazz Orchestra appeared under the auspices of the New Zealand Jazz Foundation.

In-service courses continued, followed by the publication of the *Primary School Handbook for Music* and another music syllabus based on earlier documents. In 1966 a full MusB course in Music Education was established at Canterbury University by David Sell. It was changed in the early 1980s to provide academic studies at senior undergraduate and postgraduate level.

Recent developments

In 1968 Dr Malcolm Tait of Hamilton Teachers' College published, on a limited scale, his highly critical survey of music education in New Zealand, which had been commissioned by the Queen Elizabeth II Arts Council and the New Zealand Council of Educational Research.[31] It was published privately by the Waikato Society of Registered Music Teachers in 1970. The appointment of William Renwick as Director General of Primary Schools in 1975 saw the initiation of the Composer in Schools project for secondary schools the following year, with Dorothy Buchanan as its first recipient, working in the Christchurch area. She was succeeded by Christopher Norton in Wellington, and others throughout New Zealand. This invaluable project was abruptly suspended in 1982 by Mervyn Wellington, then Minister of Education, following the tradition of nineteenth-century die-hards who saw music as a 'luxury'. It was reinstated in 1985 under a joint arrangement between the Department and the QEII Arts Council.[32] A series of radio programmes, 'The Young Idea' (1975-1977), devised by Allan Thomas and collected from throughout New Zealand, showed a wealth of talent and the diversity of activity in students' creative music-making. A. H. & A. W. Reed, in *Sound and Sense* and their *Soundscape* series, initiated teaching publications by New Zealand authors, a direction followed later by Price Milburn under Peter Zwartz and Roderick Biss, who published a variety of useful New Zealand material.[33] Of equal significance has been the Westpac Schools Music Contest, which began in 1965 under the auspices of the Music Federation of New Zealand, an inspiration of its President Arthur Hilton. Secondary school composers, vocal and instrumental groups compete annually in Wellington at a National Final after selection from district contests. These stimulating occasions have consistently brought forward high qualities of musicianship. Many fine artists have emerged, such as Michael Houstoun, John and Alan Chisholm, and Brian Shillito.[34] Performance departments of the Wellington Polytechnic now train singers as well as orchestral players not easily placed in the Orchestral Trainees scheme (renamed the Schola Musica), which was founded by John Hopkins in 1961 and directed for many years by Ashley Heenan, succeeded by Michael Vinten. The Schola Musica was suspended in 1989, and the following year it became affiliated to the Polytechnic.

In 1983 the New Zealand Society for Music Education was formed, twelve years after the demise of the old School Music Association, thus giving national scope to what had previously been local societies. Their 'Music 83' conference in Wellington was followed by others at two-yearly intervals; the papers of the 1985 conference were published as the Society's first year-book. New Zealand has been closely associated with the International Society of Music Education through Frank Callaway and John Ritchie, who was Secretary-General for several years, and the involvement of music educators in the various conferences. David Sell's *Bibliographical Index 1955-1983* was published under their auspices.

Pilot schemes for secondary school music courses were set up in 1978 and were one of the factors leading to a comprehensive review of music education from early childhood to Form 7, authorized by the Minister of Education in August 1984. Guy Jansen, Chairperson of the representative National Syllabus Committee, believes it is radical in dealing with issues of racial equality and the accessibility of music to all students. He believes that it brings practical music-making to the centre of the stage, 'at *every* level of schooling, supported by work in a few other essential areas such as creativity and appreciation. It legitimates all kinds of music in the curriculum while stressing New Zealand compositions. It also sets goals of excellence in choice of repertoire and performance and in its aim highlights the need for monitoring *individual* aesthetic growth and fulfilment.'[35] At the time of writing (1988), this bold new direction in music education awaits the support of the Government and the whole musical community to ensure its effective implementation. Despite the various administrative changes and initiatives, the quality of music in any school still depends on the enthusiasm, ability, and persistence of the individual teacher, both those in schools and those who teach privately. But there still remains much basic work to be done before the 'music-as-a-Cinderella-subject' syndrome is finally laid to rest.

Adult education

The first memorable initiative in music by the Workers' Educational Association, founded in 1915, was the 'box scheme'. It was the brain-child in the 1920s of that tireless innovator James Shelley, then Chairman of the Schools' Music Association, which he had founded in co-operation with the public spirited teacher, R. B. Owen. A box containing lecture notes, textbooks, prints, and records was dispatched to a study group, who kept it a week before sending it on. The first topic in the series of twenty was 'The nineteenth century in art, music and literature'. In 1928 the Canterbury boxes went north to Auckland and the scheme gradually spread throughout the country. Shelley gained the support of the Carnegie Corporation for sets of records, some of which became the nucleus of university classes. He designed an inexpensive portable cabinet gramophone which could be moved on castors from classroom to classroom. It stood about four feet six inches high, the top portion holding the 78 r.p.m. turntable, the middle part the speaker, and the bottom a space for records—'I can still see its stiff winding handle and its huge horn', wrote Dr C. E. Beeby.[36] More spectacularly, in 1930 he gained a grant of £500 for five years for Canterbury College to begin an experiment of fitting up a car as a library, with facilities for showing slides and playing records as well as accommodating the travelling tutor. From this grew the travelling library scheme.[37]

Subsequent highlights of Adult Education's musical enterprises have included notably, the setting up of the Cambridge Summer School of Music in 1946 under the direction of Owen Jensen, Community Arts Service music tutor. No other single organization has done as much to integrate and stimulate New Zealand musical life in so many fields. Music schools on special topics were subsequently held elsewhere on such special topics as chamber and choral music, recorder playing, and church music.[38] Comparable to the achievements of the Cambridge Music School have been the concerts and opera tours organized after the war by the Auckland-based Community Arts Service (CAS), under the auspices of the first WEA National Council. These included tours by Donald Munro's enterprising New Zealand Opera Company and Poul Gnatt's pioneering New Zealand Ballet Company.[39]

The contributions to music of the original Workers' Education Association and the succeeding adult and continuing education organizations have been profound. They continue to be effective and innovatory, with resources at times so slender they seem almost invisible.

Music in universities

Auckland

Music found a foothold in the New Zealand university system in 1888, when the Council of Auckland University College, founded five years earlier, appointed Carl Gustav Schmitt (1834-1900) as their first Professor of Music for £100 plus fees, demoting him the following year to 'lecturer' at the same salary. Schmitt ignored the snub. A fine violinist, born and educated in Germany, he was one of many German musicians who travelled the world in the late nineteenth century to enrich colonial music life.[40] His conducting was described as 'masterly' and his 'kind and genial manner endeared him to the members of the [Choral] Society and to his many pupils'.[41] Support for the new School of Music came from the Amateur Opera Club, which provided twelve exhibitions in music from 1890 to 1892 to a total value of 200 guineas, and from the Governor's wife, the Countess of Onslow, who offered two silver medals as prizes. The School grew slowly, being unkindly described in the *New Zealand Graphic* of 1894 as 'a white elephant', for it had attracted only twenty students the previous years, all of them women. Schmitt weathered these storms, to the gratitude of his successors, who would otherwise have had to begin the whole enterprise all over again.

Professor Carl Gustav Schmitt, first professor of music, Auckland University College, 1888-1900. *Charles Nalden*

The dominant influence on university music in New Zealand was British. The first English professors of music were academic, orthodox, and strict, though some had more engaging personal qualities. Schmitt's successor, Dr William Edwin Thomas (1867-1946), appointed by a London committee, was an Oxford graduate who had held several conducting posts, had been an examiner for the Royal College of Music, and also composed—in a leaden Victorian style. Contenders for the position had included the young Alfred Hill, who wished 'to make a further study of the Maori melodies, rhythms and colouring, with the idea of embodying it in future Compositions'.[42] Not until over fifty years later did a New Zealander succeed to a similar position, when Frederick Page, who began as lecturer in music at Wellington, eventually became Professor.

Thomas secured significant changes in the requirements for a music degree by pointing out that since the establishment of the University of New Zealand,

Professor William Edwin
Thomas, Auckland,
1900-34. *Charles Nalden*

only two students had taken the Bachelor of Music degree, both from
Canterbury. In 1907 the first graduates emerged from Auckland—Edith Marion
Webb and Horace George Hunt. Within three years he had brought the Faculty
of Music into line with the other disciplines.[43] Thomas's overall syllabus, although
modified later by Hollinrake, remained the basis for the Music Department's
diploma and degree courses until after 1950. The School worked in spartan
conditions: it did not obtain a piano until 1901 and had no music library until
the following year, when Council authorized Thomas to purchase books to
the value of £4.15.0.[44] In 1910 Thomas warmly welcomed a scheme to establish
a conservatorium in Auckland, but this failed, seemingly on economic grounds.
Likewise Thomas also saw the gradual decline and ultimate collapse of his much-
cherished Associateship and Fellowship Diploma courses which had set out 'with
such fair promise' in May and November 1902.[45] Thomas, like Schmitt,
conducted the Choral Society, and was described as 'a scholarly gentleman of
outstanding ability'.[46]

Owen Jensen recalls life for a music student at that time:

> We were nurtured on an unpalatable diet of Ebenezer Prout, his *Harmony* and
> his *Counterpoint* and Higgs on *Fugue*. For exercises, Dr Thomas asked us to
> write chants and double-chants. I must have written hundreds in my time . . .
> We did not have tutorials, just the weekly lecture, your reading of Prout if
> you could bear it, the exercises and the denouement at the next class . . . But
> there was no denying the warmth of his personality, and his kindly if remote
> manner.

Professor Horace
Hollinrake, Auckland,
(1935-55). *Roger Hollinrake*

Following Thomas's retirement in 1933, Horace Hollinrake (1902-1955), then
lecturer in music at Auckland Teachers' Training College, became attached to
the university for two days a week. He quickly revived a Department that
had started to become moribund by organizing a free course on musical
appreciation. He was offered the professorship in 1935, but maintained a back-
breaking double load of lectures at the university and the training college until
1939. It was not until 1945 that he gained a full-time lecturer in Thomas Rive.
The parsimony of the University Council towards its Music Department is
doubly evident when comparison is made with the facilities and salaries then
available in Christchurch and Dunedin. Nevertheless, Hollinrake initiated the
B.Mus. and Honours course, and similarly the M.A. He attempted to persuade
the University of New Zealand to introduce a four-year 'Specialized Course
in Music Education', to train graduates for post-primary school work and adult
education, an enlightened scheme tailored to the country's practical needs. Despite
unanimous support from the other heads of music departments, it was turned
down by a benighted Senate. At the time of his premature death he was seeking
to establish an Executant Diploma Course, which subsequently came into being
as the Conservatorium of Music under his successor, Charles Nalden.

Besides his conducting abilities and administrative flair, Hollinrake became an excellent pioneer broadcaster. He associated himself closely with the Centennial music celebrations, with its orchestra, and its successor, the National Orchestra. As his son Roger noted, he had 'a kind of musical equivalent of green fingers'.[47]

Charles Nalden (b. 1908), who took over the conductorship of the Auckland Youth Orchestra, founded by Gordon Cole, campaigned so successfully for the concept of an executant training school that he brought the Executant Diploma Course into being in 1956 with five students. Numbers soon swelled, so that by the time of Nalden's retirement in 1973 there were fourteen permanent teaching staff. He could testify to having witnessed 'a veritable transformation within our Music Department': the slavish following of English university training had been replaced by a more open style.[48]

Peter Godfrey (b. 1922), a distinguished English organist and choral director, succeeded Nalden in 1974. His gifts in choral training raised the University Singers and the Dorian Choir to new heights, and his direction of the National Youth Choir brought them international acclaim. He resigned in 1982, to become organist and choirmaster of Wellington Cathedral and thus devote more time to his first love, choral music. In 1989 he undertook to spend six months of each year training a professional Melbourne choir. Heath Lees, a Glasgow-trained musicologist, became the next Professor. In its award-winning new building (1986), the School of Music has two composers on its staff: John Rimmer, who directs the electro-acoustic music studio and the contemporary performance group, the Karlheinz Company, and John Elmsly. It initiates many performances and plays an integral part in the city's musical life.

Heath Lees.

Christchurch

Music at Canterbury University College (founded 1873) began modestly when in 1891, G. F. Tendall, organist of the Anglican cathedral, was appointed a part-time lecturer. After a successful year's teaching his position was made permanent. Christchurch initially had more success than Auckland in producing music graduates. In 1901 it was proposed that a Conservatorium of Music be established in what was considered New Zealand's most musical city. Dr J. C. Bradshaw, cathedral organist and choirmaster, who had been appointed lecturer in music in 1902, vigorously supported the campaign, but after the drafting of a detailed scheme in 1910, appeals to the Canterbury public and to the Government proved fruitless. During his long reign, which lasted until 1941, the Canterbury College Music Department produced a number of excellent musicians and an outstanding composer in Douglas Lilburn. Bradshaw's rigorously academic teaching methods resembled those of Thomas in Auckland. Lilburn noted ruefully that 'because the Doctor was a formidable teacher, any composing you happened to do was done in the vacations and usually not mentioned'.[49]

In 1942 Thomas Vernon Griffiths (1894-1985) became Professor, having already

Professors of music in flight—the four musical heavyweights (left to right) Drs Edgar Ford and Victor (Henry?) Lyon (visting examiners), Professors Victor Galway and Vernon Griffiths. Date unknown. *David Sell, School of Music, University of Canterbury*

David F. Sell, Chairman of the School of Music, University of Canterbury

made his mark in schools and educational music.[50] He brought the Department closer to the city by organizing regular concerts and encouraging communal activities. His espousal of English music and conservative tastes imparted a particular flavour, yet his dedication to the musical life of his adopted country showed itself in his editing of *Music in New Zealand* and his 1936 declaration in *Tomorrow*, that 'Our children have as much potential ability for wonderful musicianship as the children of any other nation.'[51] In 1962 John A. Ritchie (b. 1921), a New Zealander, whose musical abilities had been encouraged while a pupil of Griffiths in Dunedin, succeeded him. Ritchie had wide interests as a composer and conductor, and founded a String Orchestra under his own name. During his regime, the permanent staff grew from four to eleven, and the Department pioneered the appointment of resident chamber ensembles—the University of Canterbury Trio, the Alard Quartet, the Prague, the Alberni, and the Czech. In 1974 the School moved into the first building specially designed for university music at the new Ilam campus, and afterwards set up a separate electro-acoustic studio under John Cousins. Since Ritchie's resignation as Head of Department in 1981 (and from the University in 1985), the School of Music has operated on the system of an elected Head, at present (1988) David Sell. B. Mus. courses now allow for specialization in composition, music education, musicology, or performance, all of which may be continued to Honours or Masters level. Consistent with the historical emphasis stemming from Vernon Griffiths, Canterbury set up the first degree course in music education in 1965, and now offers a full range of qualifications in this subject from B. Mus.(Hons) to Ph.D.

Dunedin

In 1925 English-born Dr V. E. Galway, with a doctorate from the University of Melbourne, was appointed to a lectureship in music at the University of Otago, under a benefaction in the will of John Blair. Galway had come from Brisbane in 1919 to be organist of First Church. He directed performances of many major works by Bach, Handel, Haydn, Mendelssohn, Stanford, Parry, Elgar, and others. Charles Brasch described him as 'a rotund bald bouncing genial Englishman . . . sanguine, high-spirited and good company'.[52] In 1926 music was offered as part of the B.A. degree. In 1928 a B. Mus. course was initiated, and in 1939 Galway was appointed Blair Professor of Music. City organist from 1930, he gave regular recitals which attracted large audiences. He also gave lectures on music appreciation for Adult Education.

Dr Galway was a highly trained and extremely accomplished musician, whose naturally conservative tastes brought him into conflict at times with contemporary styles, as in the famed marking controversy of 1948, when he disagreed violently with the standards acceptable at Victoria University College. Of one candidate, now a leading composer and university professor himself, he wrote:

> I insist on my students modelling themselves on the classics. What they do thereafter is a matter for themselves, but at the University they must write according to the universally accepted canons of taste. But we are moving towards autonomy. If you [Professor Page] and Lilburn accept and teach this style of writing it is not for me to say you nay. The exercise shows plenty of ability and if you wish to pass it I will agree. But I can assure you it would not be accepted in Otago or Canterbury.[53]

John Drummond, Professor of Music, University of Otago, Dunedin

The candidate was David Farquhar.

A similar experience befell the young composer Edwin Carr: 'I think it was at an end of the year tea party that he played a gramophone record of one of the vocal fugues from the B minor Mass. I had just bought the Stravinsky Symphony of Psalms conducted by the composer, and he very reluctantly played it at my request. He was in agony throughout.'

In 1957 Peter Platt (b. 1924), an Oxford graduate, accepted the Chair, and during the next seventeen years built up an influential department, musicologically distinguished under John Steele, which identified itself strongly with regional and national musical needs.[54] The establishment of the Mozart Fellowship in 1969 was the first such recognition for New Zealand composers. An executant performing course was set up in 1971. John Drummond, from the University of Birmingham, became Professor in 1976. He developed operatic activities, and built up an archive of music in Otago. He has also composed an opera himself, *Plague upon Eyam*, with lecturer Patrick Little as librettist.

Wellington

Professor Frederick Page, Professor of Music, Victoria University of Wellington, 1967-71. *Tom Shenahan*

When Sir Thomas Hunter, Principal of Victoria University College, summoned Frederick Page from Christchurch in 1946 to start a Music Department, the latter became the first New Zealander to hold such a position.[55] Page rapidly made it a centre for contemporary music and for New Zealand composers. Douglas Lilburn joined him in 1947, to be followed by David Farquhar, Jenny McLeod, Ross Harris, and Jack Body.[56] Although initially regarded as wayward by the English-orientated departments elsewhere, the fruits of its work began to tell and the Department's influence grew beyond all expectations. It attracted many students from other parts of New Zealand, including some who were to become leading composers in their own right, such as Gillian Whitehead, Denis Smalley, and Ross Harris. Lilburn established the first electro-acoustic (electronic) music studio in Australia or New Zealand in 1966 and directed it until 1979. An executants' course was established in 1965: 'Our ideal is to produce highly-skilled performers whose talent is supported by a thorough education in music', commented Dr Peter Walls.[57] Its performance course makes good use of the resources of the city: most of the executant teachers are principals in the New Zealand Symphony Orchestra. The School supports a choir, a chamber choir, and a chamber orchestra, and almost every year mounts an opera production. From time to time the University Orchestra combines with the Schola Musica and the Wellington Polytechnic Orchestra. Its composers have developed the tradition established by Lilburn and Farquhar, its musicologists have been deeply involved in performance, and importance has been given to Asian music, under Alan Thomas, exemplified in the increasing expertise of its gamelan orchestra, unique in New Zealand. The newly formed New Zealand String Quartet (1988) are in residence, and give classes in chamber music. Walls defines the role of the School as one of 'cooperation between performers, composers and musicologists'. It moved from the old Hunter building into an impressively designed new School in 1989.

At present, the balance between British and New Zealand-born professors and staff within the university music system is about equal. After many trials and not a few errors, the teaching is a combination of English, European, and American approaches and influences, with an infusion of New Zealand and the Pacific. The rise of a school of New Zealand composition, with leading composers on the staff or in residence, as with the Mozart Fellowship in Dunedin, has meant that a more indigenous approach has evolved. The university music department is still a principal workplace for composers. Its present executive training courses have established themselves: 'Historically, university music

Peter Walls rehearsing the Victoria University of Wellington's School of Music orchestra in the Adam Room, June 1989. *John Casey*

departments accepted a responsibility for advanced performance training because there were no other institutions in New Zealand who could do the job', commented Dr Peter Walls. On his 1987 visit to New Zealand, Basil Tchaikov, Director of the National Centre for Orchestral Studies in the United Kingdom, gave strong support to the existing system, with its advantages of a more broadly-based education than a conservatorium could provide.[58] Each New Zealand university music department now has its own character and specialities, its own opportunities for growth.

The Nelson School of Music

The traditions initiated by Michael Balling continued after his departure even if on a less intense level. The preference for German-born principals was maintained and the School saw its principal function as assuming a leading role in the musical life of the community. In 1898 the School affiliated itself with the Associated Board whose examinations replaced the original certificates and diploma. An arrangement with the Girls' and Boys' College gave the School principal responsibility for the teaching of music. A fine organ was installed in 1913, funded by Thomas Cawthron, founder of the scientific Institute bearing his name. The School survived the loss of students during the war years and the vicious persecution of its then principal Herr Julius Lemmer (whose eldest son was killed at Gallipoli). It survived the depression and the strains of World War II. In 1944 Herr Lemmer resigned after forty-five devoted years to be succeeded by T. J. Kirk Burnnand.[59]

In 1952 the two colleges withdrew from their arrangement with the School and appointed their own teachers, a near-fatal blow which halved the student roll and brought about many difficult years. The appointment of Heaton Drake, an accountant of outstanding financial acumen and drive, as trustee and secretary from 1968-1975 turned its fortunes. The Drake Report of 1969 redefined the School's principal role as concentrating on group classes: henceforth individual tuition was to be on a private student/teacher relationship using the School's facilities. Closer links with national musical organizations were forged and a new role gradually emerged, strengthened during the regime of Dr Raymond White (1970-1978), especially by his abilities in choral music.

In 1981 the School was recognized by the Ministry of Education as an organization of continuing education and since then it has acquired a high reputation for its seminars and composers' courses and residencies. Donald Maurice, the eighth principal (1980-1983), stimulated orchestral and chamber music activities as Dr Raymond White had done with choral. Mary Grodd, an accomplished German-born flautist succeeded him (1983-1986), with her husband Uwe, experienced on the same instrument and as a teacher. Unique amongst the musical organizations within New Zealand, the Nelson School of Music has amazingly survived in an environment in which the ideal of a conservatorium has never taken root. Balling would surely feel vindicated.

Notes

[1]   Martin, M. 'Music, the worst taught subject'. *MNZ*, 10 March 1937, 9-10
[2]   Page, 29-31
[3]   Clark, M. (ed.), 117
[4]   These comprised Canterbury (1897), Auckland (1902), Otago, Timaru, Oamaru, and Southland (*c.* 1906), and Wellington (1907)
[5]   Initiated by Mr E. C. Cachemaille, New Zealand Resident Secretary of the Associated Board of the Royal Schools of Music, London
[6]   Robert Parker became president and Cachemaille secretary
[7]   See Jennings, *The Music Teaching Profession in New Zealand*, for a full account of the history of the Bill and related matters
[8]   He died three weeks later
[9]   See, however, 'Forward from the famous five', Proceedings of the 6th National Conference, Australian Society for Music Education (1986) 89. See also 'Five Englishmen', *Studies in Music Education*, vol. 1 no. 1, 1986, 15, where Sell examines the effectiveness of the English influence
[10] This section is based on notes prepared by the late Marion Rayward, a highly valued colleague, lecturer in music at Wellington Training College, who drew on an M.A. thesis by G. E. Jansen
[11] Jansen thesis, 2
[12] Ibid., 4
[13] See also Chapter XXIV
[14] Harry Wells, the first to be appointed, was succeeded by G. F. Tendall, J. C. Bradshaw, and C. Foster Browne
[15] Appendices to the Journals of the House of Representatives, 1885-1962, quoted in Rayward

[16] Jansen thesis, 10

[17] Quoted in Jansen thesis, 18, from unpublished article (1974), expanded in Sell, 'Five Englishmen', *Studies in Music Education*, vol. 1 no. 1, 1986, 3-18

[18] Tayler, 12

[19] Sell attributes this partly to Tayler's idealistic approach, often couched in flowery language pitched too high to make effective contact with actual school conditions. He considered subsequent journal articles to be too highly technical

[20] Jansen thesis, 16. Tayler's 'resignation' put forward in personal communication from Jansen to author, 30 April 1988. Tayler died in California in 1932. See also Vernon Griffiths' tribute 'Leading New Zealand musicians', *MNZ*, 1 August 1931, 89-91

[21] Sell points out their lack of contemporary works in 'Forward from the famous five', 90

[22] See Jansen thesis for excellent summary of Tayler's influence

[23] 'Forward from the famous five', 90

[24] Communication to author, 1 May 1988; see also *Third Stream*, March 1968, 10

[25] Renwick, W. L. 'Music Education: a time for stocktaking', Proceedings of the National Music Education Conference, Wellington, 26 August 1983, 2-3

[26] See his *An Experiment in School Music-making*

[27] Griffiths' scrapbooks, etc., are in the University of Canterbury Library. Frank Callaway, who succeeded Griffiths, later became Professor of Music at the University of Western Australia, Perth. Afterwards he became President and Treasurer of the International Society of Music Education, President of the IMC, and received a knighthood

[28] See Elizabeth Wemyss' 'The Changing Pattern'

[29] Jennings, *Let the Children Play*

[30] 'Walden-Mills was quite the right person for the job', said W. L. Renwick in 'Music Education' (1983) 5, which assesses the influence of Walden-Mills. Many teachers felt otherwise

[31] The Arts Council did not support publication. The survey was strongly criticized for a variety of reasons, including its use of current educational technological jargon

[32] See especially *Canzona*, vol. 7 no. 20, 1985, 17-24 for critical appraisal by Elizabeth Kerr; also various individual evaluations by composers

[33] Steve Rosenberg's recorder books, for example, proved extremely popular. Since 1975 Ian Dando and David Sell have written *Listening Guides* associated with set works at 5th, 6th, and 7th Form levels

[34] See 'Finding the key' in Thomson, *Into a New Key*, 127ff.

[35] Communication to author, 1 May 1988

[36] See Beeby, C. E. 'The influence of the Carnegie Corporation' in McKinnon (ed.) *The American Connection*, 48

[37] See Hall, D. *New Zealand Adult Education*, 62ff. and elsewhere; also Beeby, 'The influence of the Carnegie Corporation', 38-51

[38] Hall, J. H., 118-19

[39] Ibid., 127-33

[40] He had emigrated in the 1860s to Auckland, where he conducted the Choral Society and founded a Young Ladies' Orchestra

[41] Brochure from the Centennial Music Festival, Auckland (1940) 38; also Nalden, '1888-1899 — A Troubled Decade' in *History*

[42] Quoted in Nalden, 36, from General Correspondence 1900, No. 182

[43] Nalden, 37

[44] Ibid., 38

[45] Ibid., 41

[46] *A Century of Music, the story of the first 100 years of the Auckland Choral Society.* Auckland (1955) 9

[47] R. B. Hollinrake to author, 21 June 1982

[48] Nalden, 83

[49] Lilburn, *A Search for Tradition*, 17. See also chapter VIII, 1

[50] See above, 'The Griffiths-Jenner era'

[51] *Tomorrow*, 15 January 1936, 7-9

[52] Brasch, *Indirections*, 184

[53] Letter to Frederick Page in the author's possession

[54] See his stimulating inaugural lecture, 'Music history as a living study'

[55] The appointment was at the instigation of Sir James Hight, Rector of Canterbury University College (communication from Frederick Page)

[56] See Page, chapter 5, 'Wellington'

[57] Communication to author, 1988

[58] Communication to author, 1988

[59] The present author, pupil of Miss Carty of the Nelson School of Music during much of his time at Nelson College, recalls vividly the personalities of these devoted teachers, including also Miss Jarmy and Herr Lemmer himself.

Appendix 2: Instrument making in New Zealand

Research concerning the part played in the history of music in New Zealand by western musical instruments and instrument makers is meagre. Recent work[1] to identify makers who have worked in this country has identified about 150 between around 1860 and the present time, but few surveys have been made concerning the instruments themselves and how they arrived here. From our knowledge of musical activities and from known surviving instruments of the early colonial period, some conclusions can be drawn, but they do not present a comprehensive picture.

Before the arrival of the first colonists (1840), European whalers, sealers and missionaries had visited this country. The development by the Māori, probably in the first half of the 19th century, of their pōrutu and rehu (end-blown and side-blown flutes), showed a clear European influence in their length and shape, although the three fingerholes of their traditional flutes (kōauau and nguru) were retained. One mechanical organ, now in Wanganui Museum, is known to have been brought by missionaries in 1829.

When Bishop Selwyn arrived here with his wife in 1842, they brought with them not only religious music, but also much popular and keyboard music of the 18th century, including harpsichord lessons, both volumes of which show evidence of much use. This collection is held in St. John's College in Auckland. We do not know whether they brought a harpsichord, but they did bring a square piano by the English maker, Broadwood. From specimens in museums and in private hands, we know that square pianos made as early as the 1820s still exist here.

Easily transported instruments such as violins and flutes would have arrived in New Zealand with their owners from an early stage. Some evidence in respect of woodwind instruments exists in the early flutes and other woodwind instruments assembled by one collector entirely in New Zealand. These include a number of woodwinds dating from the late eighteenth and very early nineteenth centuries.

The internationally known Zillah and Ronald Castle collection of musical instruments in Wellington—more than 500 instruments—contains a large number connected with New Zealand's pioneers, many of which have been generously donated by descendants. These include a rare seventeenth century tenor recorder by Thomas Stanesby (sen.) which was brought to this country in an old Scotch chest, and presented by descendants of the original owner who was a minister of the church. Another rare instrument, found in the attic of an old house in Petone, is a philomela (technically, a bowed zither).

James Hewitt (1867-1936), violin maker of 18 Swanson Street, Auckland, in his workshop. *David McClury Young. Auckland Institute and Museum*

The earliest date in the Index of instrument makers is 1861, when Charles Begg arrived in Dunedin. In 1865 he exhibited a piano he had made in the Dunedin Exhibition.[2] Although he complained of difficulties in obtaining suitable and adequately seasoned woods, his firm evidently persevered as they are recorded as having turned out their 1000th piano in 1927. Begg also became a major importer of pianos and other musical instruments. Nine other piano makers from the colonial period have been identified, mostly in Auckland and Dunedin. Several of them took part in the great exhibtions of the late nineteenth century in New Zealand, Australia, and London.[3] Nevertheless, pianos do not appear to have been made in significant numbers until the establishment of Bishop & Co in Auckland in 1913. Linked with the music firm of Lewis Eady & Co. Ltd., they made several thousand upright pianos, a number of which are still in use. Economic conditions forced the closure of this firm in the early 1930s.

Within two decades of the founding of Beggs in the early 1860s, sixteen music shops had been opened, nine in the main centres, and seven in five provincial towns. By 1909, the four main centres shared no fewer than fifty-one music dealers, while another fifty-five had been established in thirty provincial centres. Of these, eleven included the word 'Piano' in their names, suggesting the popularity of this instrument. Hire purchase was well established with the Dresden Piano Company advertising in 1898 pianos at 20 shillings, and organs at 10 shillings a month. In 1909, upright pianos were advertised from £42.10s to £80. At this time, Beggs advertised Starck flutes from 1s.9d to 12s.6d, Starck concert flutes from 33s.6d to 87s.6d., and Strad. model Dolling violins, 'with case, bow, resin and spare set of strings' for 50 shillings.

The Webster organ. *Auckland Institute and Museum*

An important area of musical activity was the church. Although early activity was largely choral and instruments scarce, emphasis always lay on the acquisition of an organ or a harmonium, rather than the more readily available square piano. Organ builders were well spread throughout the country by the 1870s, eleven of whom have been identified, mainly from advertisements in contemporary newspapers and journals. While many of the organs they installed were imported, they all seem to have built a number of important early pipe organs for both church and civic use. Unfortunately, many of the early organs have been repaired and modified extensively, perhaps beyond restoration to their original form. Smaller centres would have tended to acquire harmoniums, the European manufacture of which had expanded rapidly from about 1840. Again, the number of such organs in museum collections and private hands supports this.

One of the more important early pipe organs built in New Zealand was that of James Webster. Arriving in Wellington in 1840, accompanied by sawmilling equipment, he established himself in the Hokianga. He began building a small organ in 1845 as a wedding present for his daughter. It was completed in 1850, and today is in the Auckland Museum, where it is played regularly. It has a mechanical tracker action, four stops and three ½ octaves. Webster used mainly local woods, and did the metal work in his own forge; the white keys are of whale tooth ivory obtained by trading in the Bay of Islands.

New Zealand developed an early interest in both pipe and brass bands. A high level of interest was to persist for almost a century. By the 1930s it was a small community indeed which did not have a brass or a pipe band, or even both. There is still much interest in both brass and pipe bands, with competitions taking place regularly. However, many of the bands in smaller centres have now disappeared. While most of the necessary instruments—thousands of them—must have been imported, there is a record of a pipe maker, William

Simpson, in Invercargill who exhibited Highland pipes in four international exhibitions in Melbourne, London and Dunedin between 1880 and 1890.[3] Bagpipe makers continue to this day to be represented among known instrument makers, but, as far as can be established, brass instruments have never been made in New Zealand, and very few brass repairers are recorded.

Music played a substantial part in life on the goldfields of Otago and the West Coast, as well as on the gumfields in North Auckland. Several overseas museums have ample evidence of the ingenuity of musicians in such situations where clearly the lack of instruments led to improvisation such as the use of kerosene tins, the musicality of which must remain open to doubt. It seems that violins were a favoured instrument for the amateur to try his hand on. Some were copied from pictures, but equally some were made from memory, and while few could have been the equal of professionally made instruments, they filled the gap and provided music of a sort. While local examples have not emerged, it seems highly likely that the diggers of gold and gum would have been among New Zealand's earliest instrument makers.

Mechanical instruments were known from the earliest colonial days. These fell into several groups, mechanical pipe organs, familiar from the eighteenth century, musical boxes with mechanically turned cylinders fitted with pins which plucked tuned teeth of steel combs, and, by the middle of the 1800s, mechanical pneumatic reed organs. The limitation with all these instruments was the need to change the pinned cylinders which dictated the tunes, often an awkward procedure which could easily damage the pinning on which the usefulness of the cylinders depended. For the organs, both pipe and reed, the invention in the 1850s of a perforated card system was a major advance, but the musical box had to wait until the 1890s before a simple interchangeable disc was developed in Germany to replace the cylinders. This provided for an almost unlimited repertoire and rapidly displaced the cylindrical type of musical box, only to be displaced in its turn by the early gramophone within a decade or so. Examples of all these instruments are fairly widespread in museum collections, as well as still being found in private hands. A mechanical organ brought to New Zealand in 1829 is today in the Wanganui Museum. Although not in perfect order, it can still play. Player pianos began to emerge in Europe in the 1890s. The early ones consisted of a rather cumbersome cabinet which was put in place in front of an ordinary piano. It had a row of felt-covered wooden 'fingers' projecting over the keyboard, and was actuated by a music roll or note sheet passing over a tracker box with slots for each note. When a perforation uncovered a slot in the tracker box, suction generated by pedals drew air through the slot and actuated a valve and lever, forcing the 'finger' down onto the piano key. By the turn of the century, this mechanism was built into the piano itself, and it was gradually improved to the point where it could reproduce the performance nuances of concert pianists. This type of instrument reached its heyday in the 1920s, gradually decreasing in popularity with the increased use of the gramophone and radio. Nevertheless, the advertising columns of the daily newspapers show that considerable numbers of player pianos are still being bought and sold.

The Index of Musical Instrument Makers now includes some 150 names. Of these, about fifty relate to the first hundred years after colonization, while the remaining two thirds have been active since 1940. It is surprising to find that so far, only two are women. This record is incomplete and it is unlikely that it can ever be regarded as definitive. Contemporary publications, even specialist journals relating to music, tended to concentrate on performers and performances, and scant regard was paid to those whose activities made performances possible. At the same time, it must be said that the contribution made by local makers is miniscule in relation to the numbers of instruments brought into the country by settlers and imported by music firms.

Nevertheless, of the 150 makers so far identified, seventy-one have been violin makers. Predominantly amateurs, often self-taught from books and from experience, quite a number have been eminently successful, attracting support not only from local players, but in some cases selling their instruments to overseas professionals. An early English-trained maker, C. J. Bowman, worked in Dunedin and Christchurch for a number of years. He interested, encouraged and trained James Hewitt, widely regarded as perhaps New Zealand's first professional violin maker. Hewitt who was born in Otago in 1867, first set up in business as a maker in Dunedin in 1913. He later moved his business to Auckland where after many years of making and repairing, he trained Norman Smith whose instruments also carried a good reputation. This business eventually became the Stringed Instrument Company, which still serves the musical community.

One Auckland amateur, Ron Beatson, who, incidentally, experimented widely with local woods and innovative designs, sold one of his conventional violins to Alan Loveday who used the instrument in a Royal Command performance in the Festival Hall in London in 1953. A Wellington professional trained in Cremona, Nigel Harris, was sufficiently successful internationally to lead him to set up as a luthier in Europe. A Hamilton maker, Ian Sweetman, who began as an amateur, has now been making for more than forty years. In the 1960s he received an Arts Council grant which enabled him to study overseas. His instruments, violins and violas, are not only widely sought-after throughout New Zealand, but can be found in Europe, Australia and the United States, mostly in the hands of professional orchestral players. Many others have produced quite large numbers of instruments — surely a reasonable proof of acceptable quality. Among earlier makers of good repute, can be listed Robert Thain, William Zettwitz, who exhibited in the Auckland Exhibition in 1913/14,[4] H. T. Kidson, Charles Johnson, Eric Meier, and James Williamson. Modern makers working professionally include Noel Sweetman (Waikato), Malcolm Collins (Wellington), and, probably the most highly trained and experienced

Kim Webby, Whangarei harp maker. *Northern Advocate*

maker and restorer, Adrian Studer of Nelson. Neville Whitehead of North Auckland, worked in London for ten years with the famed double bass maker, Gimple Solomon, and is now established as a specialist double bass maker, much of whose work goes overseas. The earliest recorded violin maker dates from the 1870s in Canterbury, and the remainder are well spread through the country and fairly evenly divided over the intervening years, with some fifteen known to be making currently.

Rising interest since the 1950s in the early music movement has led to a number of makers becoming involved in the making of modern reproductions of historic instruments. One such, Alec Loretto, who spent several years assembling early keyboards, harpsichords, virginals, clavichords, etc., later turned to renaissance and baroque recorders and has gained an international reputation both as a maker and as a teacher. Another current recorder maker in Auckland, David Coomber, has a secure and widespread international market for his instruments.

Several makers specialize in assembling historic keyboards. One however, Paul Downie, builds his harpsichords from the raw material stage, using professional drawings of actual historic instruments. He is gaining an international reputation as a maker of fine instruments and may well be the only restorer of historic keyboards with appropriate overseas training and experience in this field. There are also several makers of viols, both renaissance and baroque.

A young harp maker, Kim Webby of Whangarei, whose sister wanted to learn the instrument, made one for her in 1980. He has now completed more than sixty harps of varying designs and sizes, including a double action pedal harp designed by himself. He, too, is rapidly gaining an international reputation, having recently (1990) exhibited a full size double action concert harp of his own design in Paris.

Other early musical instruments made locally range from three-hole pipes and tabors, dulcimers, both plucked and hammered, hurdy gurdies, lutes, mandolins and zithers. There are a number of guitar makers, many of whom concentrate on the folk and pop music scene. Several, however, such as Peter Madill of Auckland, and Raymond Mercer of Wellington, have been sufficiently successful to have guitars bearing their names sell overseas.

A characteristic of many of these makers is experimentation, often successful, with indigenous woods, which has prevailed from the earliest times. In the early stages, importation of traditional instrument-making woods must have required great patience and involved delays of more than a year between order and receipt. Even today, importing quality tone woods can be difficult.

Some of the local woods found suitable for the backs and ribs of bowed stringed instruments, both tonally and in their decorative appearance, include curly Southland beech (*Nothofagus menziesii*), mangeao (or tangeao) (*Litsea calicaris*), and pigeon-wood (*Hedycarya arborea*). No local wood has been found satisfactory for bellies, although some early makers used New Zealand cedar (*Libocedrus doniana*) and kauri (*Agathis australis*) with moderate success. Woodwind makers have found a greater variety of acceptable, and even desirable woods. Among those used successfully are rata (*Metrosideros robusta*), tawa (*Beilschmiedia tawa*), puriri (*Vitex lucens*), black maire (*Olea cunninghamii*) and kauri (*Agathis australis*). One maker, Paul Whinray of Auckland, has had considerable success with manuka (*Leptospermum scoparia*), a notoriously difficult wood owing to the frequency with which it splits during seasoning.

In a community in which music has played such a prominent part during the last 150 years, the growth of interest in making a wide range of instruments is not surprising. Few makers trained overseas are known to have established themselves here, and few intending makers are able to take advantage of the established European instrument-making schools. Despite this, many have reached high standards, and almost without exception, are eager and willing to pass on their knowledge and skills to others. In a country in which surveys suggest that one person in every six is involved with some form of craft work, it seems certain that musical instrument making will continue to make a valuable contribution to music in New Zealand.

JUSTINE OLSEN
LEN STANNERS

JUSTINE OLSEN, BA, has been Curator of Applied Arts in the Auckland Institute and Museum since 1988.

L. S. STANNERS, CBE, has worked with musical instruments at the Museum since 1985, and has been the Honorary Curator of Musical Instruments for the last three years.

Notes

1 *Index of Craftspeople, Designers & Manufacturers*, Auckland Institute & Museum
2 *Catalogue of New Zealand Exhibition*, Dunedin, 1865
3 Exhibition Catalogues, Melbourne International Exhibition, 1880/81; Centennial International Exhibition, Melbourne, 1888; Colonial and Indian Exhibition, London, 1886; South Seas Exhibition, Dunedin, 1889/90.
4 Auckland Exhibition Catalogue 1913/14 — Zettwitz exhibited a violin, viola and a cello

Bibliography

Anon. *Introduction to New Zealand*. Wellington 1945.

———. *Letters from Settlers and Labouring Emigrants in the New Zealand Company's Settlements of Wellington, Nelson and New Plymouth, 1842-1843*. London 1843.

———. *The New Zealand Goldfields, 1861*. Victorian New Zealand: a reprint series, no. 1. Dunedin 1976.

———. *The Maori Population*. Victorian New Zealand: a reprint series, no. 3. Dunedin 1977.

———. *The Pakeha and the Treaty: Signposts*. Church and Social Community of the National Council of Churches in New Zealand. Christchurch 1986.

Adams, Peter. *Fatal Necessity: British Intervention in New Zealand, 1830-47*. Auckland 1977.

Airey, Elisabeth. *Renwick: The Story of a Pioneer Family*. Wellington 1979.

Alda, Frances. *Men, Women and Tenors*. Boston 1937.

Alington, Margaret. *Frederick Thatcher and St Paul's: An Ecclesiological Study*. Wellington 1965.

Allan, Ruth M. *Nelson: A History of Early Settlement*. Wellington 1965.

Alpers, Antony. *The Life of Katherine Mansfield*. New York 1980.

Andersen, Johannes C. *Maori Music*. New Plymouth 1934.

Anderson, Bruce. *The Story of the New Zealand Record Industry*. Wellington 1984.

Anderson, Grahame. *Fresh about Cook Strait*. Auckland 1984.

Anderson, Hugh. *The Colonial Minstrel*. Melbourne 1960.

Arnold, Rollo. *The Farthest Promised Land*. Wellington 1981.

Ashton-Warner, Sylvia. *I Passed This Way*. Wellington 1979.

Awatere, Donna. *Maori Sovereignty*. Wellington 1984.

Bailey, Rona, and Herbert Roth (eds.) *Shanties by the Way*. Christchurch 1967.

Baillie, Isobel. *Never Sing Louder than Lovely*. London 1982.

Barker, Lady. *Station Life in New Zealand*. London 1871.

———. *Station Amusements in New Zealand*. Leipzig 1874.

Barrow, Terence. *Traditional and Modern Music of the Maori*. Wellington 1965.

Bathgate, Alexander. *Colonial Experiences*. Glasgow 1874.

Baxter, Archibald. *We Will Not Cease*. Whatamongo Bay (Cape Catley) 1983.

Beaglehole, Ann. *A Small Price to Pay*. Wellington 1988.

Beaglehole, J. C. *New Zealand: A Short History*. London 1936.

———. *The Discovery of New Zealand*. Wellington 1939.

———. (ed.). *New Zealand and the Statute of Westminster*. Wellington 1944.

———. *The Life of Captain James Cook*. London 1974.

Belich, James. *The New Zealand Wars and the Victorian Interpretation of Racial Conflict*. Auckland 1986.

Bell, Leonard. *The Maori in European Art*. Wellington 1980.

Bertram, James. *Charles Brasch*. Wellington 1976.

Best, Elsdon. *Games and Pastimes of the Maori*. Wellington 1976.

Best, Ensign A. D. W. *Journal, 1837-1843* (ed. Taylor, Nancy M.). Wellington 1966.

Binney, Judith. *A Legacy of Guilt: The Life of Thomas Kendall*. Auckland 1968.

————, Gillian Chaplin. *Nga Morehu: The Survivors*. Auckland 1986.

Bird, John. *Percy Grainger*. London 1976.

Bodell, James. *Reminiscences* (ed. Sinclair, Keith). London 1982.

Boorstin, Daniel J. *The Americans 1: The Colonial Experience*. London 1965.

Boston, Canon Noel, Lindsay G. Langwill. *Church and Chamber Barrel Organs*. Edinburgh 1967.

Boyd, M. B. *City of the Plains: A History of Hastings*. Wellington 1984.

Brake, Brian, James McNeish, David Simmons. *Art of the Pacific*. London 1979.

Brasch, Charles. *Present Company: Reflections on the Arts*. Auckland 1966.

————. *Indirections: A Memoir, 1909-47*. Wellington 1980.

————. *The Universal Dance*. A selection from the critical prose writings of Charles Brasch (ed. Watson, J.C.). Dunedin 1981.

Barrington, A. C. *The Predestined Choice: Samuel Butler in Canterbury*. Christchurch 1972.

Brewer, N. H. *A Century of Style: Great Ships of the Union Line, 1875-1976*. Wellington 1982.

Brown, Gordon H. *Colin McCahon, Artist*. Wellington 1984.

Brusey, Phyllis. *Ring Down the Curtain*. Wellington 1973.

Buck, Peter. *Vikings of the Sunrise*. Philadelphia 1938.

Bunbury, Major Thomas. *Reminiscences of a Veteran* (3 vols.). London 1861.

Burdon, R. M. *The New Dominion. A Social and Political History of New Zealand between the Wars*. Wellington 1965.

Burney, James. *With Captain James Cook in the Antarctic and Pacific, 1772-3* (ed. Hooper, Beverley). Canberra 1975.

Busch, Glenn. *Working Men*. Wellington 1984.

Butler, Samuel. *A First Year in Canterbury Settlement*. London 1923.

Butterworth, Graham. *Sir Apirana Ngata. New Zealand profiles*. Wellington 1968.

Callaway, Frank, David Tunley. *Australian Composition in the Twentieth Century*. Melbourne 1978.

Campbell, A. E. *Educating New Zealand*. Wellington 1941.

Campbell, John Logan. *Poenamu*. Auckland 1881, 1973.

Campbell, Margaret. *Music in Dunedin*. Dunedin 1945.

Cape, Peter. *New Zealand Painting since 1960: A Study in Themes and Developments*. Auckland 1978.

Carman, A. H. *Birth of a City, Wellington 1840-43*. Wellington 1970.

Carner, Mosco. *The Waltz*. London 1948.

Carrington, C. E. *John Robert Godley of Canterbury*. Christchurch 1950.

Carroll, Brian. *Australian Stage Album*. Melbourne 1976.

Cattell, John (compiler). *Historic Buildings of Wellington*. New Zealand Historic Places Trust. Wellington 1986.

Challingsworth, Nell. *Dancing Down the Years: The Romantic Century in Australia*. Melbourne 1978.

Chapple, L. J. B., H. C. Veitch. *Wanganui*. Hawera 1939.

Chew, V. K. *Talking Machines*. London 1981.

Clark, Margaret (ed.). *Beyond Expectations: Fourteen New Zealand Women Write about their Lives*. Wellington 1986.

Clark, Paul. *'Hauhau': The Pai Marire Search for Maori Identity*. Auckland 1975.

Cleveland, Les. *The Songs we Sang: A Collection of New Zealand Army and Service Ballads*. Wellington 1959.

Cole, Hugo. *The Changing Face of Music*. London 1978.

Colles, H. C., John Cruft. *The Royal College of Music: A Centenary Record 1883-1983*. London 1982.

Collins, Ken G. *Broadcasting Grave and Gay*. Christchurch 1967.

Colquhoun, Neil (ed.). *New Zealand Folksongs: Songs of a Young Country*. Folkestone 1973.

Condliffe, J. B. *A Short History of New Zealand*. Christchurch 1927.

———. *Te Rani Hiroa: The Life of Sir Peter Buck*. Christchurch 1971.

Courage, Sarah Amelia. *Lights and Shadows of a Colonial Life*. Christchurch/Wellington 1896.

Covell, Roger. *Australian Music: Themes of a New Society*. Melbourne 1967.

Cowan, James. *The New Zealand Wars* (vol. 1: 1845-64; vol. 2: 1864-72). Wellington 1983.

Coward, Sir Henry. *Round the World on Wings of Song. An Account of the Tour of the Sheffield Music Union Through the British Dominions, March-September 1911*. Sheffield 1933.

Crosby, Alfred W. *Ecological Imperialism: The Biological Expansion of Europe 900-1900*. Cambridge 1986.

Curteiss, G. H. *Bishop Selwyn*. London 1889.

Dalton, B. J. *War and Politics in New Zealand, 1855-1870*. Sydney 1967.

Dalziel, R. M. *The Origins of New Zealand Diplomacy*. Wellington 1975.

Dando, Ian, David Sell. *Listening Guide 1979-81*. Wellington 1979.

Davidson, Janet. *The Prehistory of New Zealand*. Auckland 1987.

Dennan, Rangitiaria, Ross Annabell. *Guide Rangi of Rotorua*. Christchurch 1968.

Dennis, Jonathan (ed.). *'The Tin Shed': Origins of the National Film Unit*. New Zealand Film Archive, no. 1. Wellington 1981.

Disher, Maurice Willson. *Victorian Song: From Diva to Drawing Room*. London 1955.

Docking, Gil. *Two Hundred Years of New Zealand Painting*. Wellington 1975.

Domett, Alfred. *Diary 1872-1885* (ed. Horsmann, E. A.). Oxford 1953.

Downes, Peter. *Shadows on the Stage: Theatre in New Zealand, the First Years.* Dunedin 1975.

———. *Top of the Bill: Entertainers Through the Years.* Wellington 1979.

———, Peter Harcourt. *Voices in the Air: Radio Broadcasting in New Zealand: A Documentary.* Wellington 1976.

Drogheda, Lord, Ken Davison, Andrew Wheatcroft. *The Covent Garden Album: 200 Years of Theatre, Opera and Ballet.* London 1981.

Duff, Oliver. *New Zealand Now.* Hamilton 1956.

Duff, Roger. *The Moa-hunter Period of Maori Culture.* Wellington 1977.

Dumont d'Urville, Jules Sebastian César. *New Zealand 1826-1827.* (tr. Wright, Olive). Wellington 1950.

Dunn, Michael. *John Kinder: Paintings and Photographs.* Auckland 1985.

Duperrey, Louis Isidor. *Visit to New Zealand in 1824* (ed. Sharp, Andrew). Wellington 1971.

Ebbet, Eve. *In True Colonial Fashion: A Lively Look at what New Zealanders Wore.* Wellington 1977.

Eccles, Alfred. *The First New Zealand Exhibition of Dunedin in 1865.* Dunedin 1925.

Elder, J. R. *The History of the Presbyterian Church of New Zealand 1840-1940.* Christchurch 1940.

Eldred-Grigg, Stevan. *A Southern Gentry.* Wellington 1980.

———. *Canterbury: A New History.* Dunedin 1982.

Entwistle, Peter. *Hodgkins, William Mathew and his circle.* Dunedin 1984.

Evans, J. H. *Churchman Militant: George Augustus Selwyn, Bishop of New Zealand and Lichfield.* London 1964.

Fairburn, A. R. D. *Letters* (ed. Edmond, Lauris). Auckland 1981.

Fairburn, Miles. *The Ideal Society and its Enemies.* Auckland 1989.

Fanning, C. S. *Pictorial History of New Zealand and South Seas Exhibition, Dunedin 1925-6.* Dunedin [1926].

Fell, Alfred. *A Colonist's Voyage to New Zealand.* London 1926, Christchurch 1973.

Fingleton, David. *Kiri.* London 1983.

Fitton, E. B. *New Zealand: Its Present Condition, Prospects and Resources. . . .* London 1856.

Fitzroy, Robert. *Remarks on New Zealand.* London 1846, Dunedin 1969.

Foster, Roland. *Come Listen to my Song.* London 1949.

Freedman, Sam (arr.). *Maori Songs of New Zealand* (text by James Siers and W. T. Ngata). Wellington 1974.

Fresne, Yvonne du. *'Farvel' and other stories.* Wellington 1980.

Froude, J. A. *Oceana.* London 1886.

Fry, Christopher (introd.). *Charlie Hammond's Sketch-book.* Oxford 1980.

Fulton, R. V. *Medical Practice in Otago and Southland in the Early Days.* Dunedin, 1922.

Gardner, W. J. (ed.). *A History of Canterbury* (2 vols.). Christchurch 1971.

Gardner, W. J., E. T. Beardsley, T. E. Carter. *History of the University of Canterbury 1873-1973*. Christchurch 1973.

Gardyne, Stuart. 'The transition in architectural style from Beaux-Arts to Bauhaus, Wellington between the wars 1918-39. BArch Thesis, Victoria University of Wellington, 1981.

Garrett, Jane. *An Artist's Daughter: With Christopher Perkins in New Zealand, 1929-34*. Auckland 1986.

Gibbons, P. J. *Johannes C. Andersen and Catherine Andersen*. Hamilton 1985.

Godley, Charlotte. *Letters from Early New Zealand 1850-1853* (ed. Godley, John R.). Christhcurch 1951.

Gordon, John. *All the World's a Stage*. Wellington 1981.

Grey, Sir George. *Polynesian Mythology and Ancient Traditional History of the New Zealanders*. London 1922.

Griffiths, Vernon. *An Experiment in School Music-making*. Christchurch 1942.

Hadden, J. Cuthbert. *Modern Musicians*. London 1913.

Hall, David. *Portrait of New Zealand*. Wellington 1955.

————. *New Zealand Adult Education*. London 1970.

————. *The Golden Echo: Some Aspects of New Zealand Social History*. Auckland 1971.

Hall, J. H. *The History of Broadcasting in New Zealand 1920-1954*. Wellington 1984.

Harcourt, Peter. *A Dramatic Appearance: New Zealand Theatre 1920-1970*. Wellington 1978.

Harris, Valerie, Philip Norman (eds). *Douglas Lilburn: A Festschrift for Douglas Lilburn on his Retirement from the Victoria University of Wellington, 31 January 1980*. 2nd ed. Wellington 1980.

Harrop, A. J. *England and New Zealand: From Tasman to the Taranaki War*. London 1926.

Harvey, D. R. (compiler). *A Bibliography of Writings About New Zealand Music, Published to the End of 1983*. Wellington 1985.

Hayward, Bruce W., P. Selwyn. *Cinemas of Auckland 1896-1979*. Auckland 1979.

Hayward, H. J. *Here's to Life! The Impressions, Confessions and Garnered Thoughts of a Free-minded Showman*. Auckland 1944.

Heaphy, Charles. *Narrative of a Residence in Various Parts of New Zealand*. London 1942, Christchurch 1972.

Heenan, Ashley. *NZBC Schola Musicum*. Wellington 1974.

Hewlett, Awdrey, *Cause to Rejoice: The Life of John Bishop*. Adelaide 1983.

Hillary, J. H. *Westland Journal of John Hillary, 1879*. Sculthorpe 1979.

Hitchcock, H. Wiley. *Music in the United States: A Historical Introduction*. New Jersey 1974.

Hocken, Thomas Morland. *Contributions to the Early History of New Zealand*. London 1898.

Holt, Elizabeth. *Popular Entertainment*. Hove 1975.

Hoskins, Robert. *Goldfield Balladeer: The Life and Times of the Celebrated Charles R. Thatcher*. Auckland 1977.

———. *An Annotated Bibliography of Nineteenth-century New Zealand Songbooks*. Christchurch 1988.

Howe, Clement (compiler). *Schola Cantorum, Wellington, New Zealand, 1936-1950*. Wellington 1951.

Howell, Arthur R. *Frances Hodgkins: Four Vital Years*. London 1951.

Hurst, Maurice. *Music and the Stage in New Zealand, 1840-1943*. Auckland/Wellington 1944.

Hursthouse, Charles F. *The New Zealand Emigrants' 'Bradshaw'*. London 1861.

Hutchens, Frank. *See* Jobson, Sandra (ed.).

Ihimaera, Witi. *Pounamu, Pounamu*. Wellington 1972.

Innes, C. C. *Canterbury Sketches*. Christchurch 1879.

Irvine, R. F., O. T. J. Alpers. *The Progress of New Zealand in the Century*. London 1902.

Jennings, John M. *The Music Teaching Profession in New Zealand: A Jubilee History of the Music Teachers' Registration Board of New Zealand*. Wellington 1978.

———. *Let the Children Play: The First Twenty-Five Years of The Christchurch School of Instrumental Music 1955-1980*. Christchurch 1988.

———. *Song of the Music Makers: An Account of the first Fifty Years of Primary School Music Festivals in Christchurch*. Christchurch 1989.

Jensen, Owen. *NZBC Symphony Orchestra*. Wellington 1966.

Jillett, David. *Farrell: A Biography*. Auckland 1985.

Jobson, Sandra (ed.). *Frank Hutchens*. Sydney 1971.

Johnson, David. *Music and Society in Lowland Scotland in the Eighteenth Century*. London 1972.

Julius, Harry. *Theatrical Caricatures: Marginal Anecdotes by Claude McKay*. Sydney 1912.

Keith, Hamish. *New Zealand Art: Painting 1827-1890*. Wellington 1968.

Kennedy, David. *Kennedy's Colonial Travel*. Edinburgh 1876.

Kenyon, Nicholas. *The BBC Symphony Orchestra 1930-1980*. London 1981.

King, Michael. *Te Puea: A Biography*. Auckland 1977.

———. *The Collector: A Biography of Andreas Reischek*. Auckland 1981.

Knight, C. R. *The Selwyn Churches of Auckland*. Wellington 1972.

Knight, Hardwicke. *Photography in New Zealand: A Social and Technical History*. Dunedin 1971.

———. *Dunedin Then*. Dunedin 1974.

Lee, Edward. *Folksong and Music Hall*. London 1982.

Lee, John A. *Early Days in New Zealand*. Martinborough 1977.

Lilburn, Douglas. *A Search for Tradition*. A talk given at the first Cambridge Summer School of Music, January 1946. Wellington 1984.

————. *A Search for a Language*. University of Otago open lecture, 12 March 1969. Wellington 1985.

Limbrick, Warren E. (ed.). *Bishop Selwyn in New Zealand, 1841-68*. Palmerston North 1983.

Lindauer, Gottfried. *Maori Paintings: Pictures for the Partridge Collection of Paintings* (ed. Graham, J. C.). Wellington 1963.

Love, Harold. *The Golden Age of Australian Opera: W. S. Lyster and his Companies, 1861-80*. Sydney 1981.

Low, David. *Low's Autobiography*. London 1956.

Luscombe, H. C. *Plain Words on Music*. Auckland *c*. 1945.

Macandrew, Jennie. *Memories: Musical and Otherwise*. Auckland 1941

Maconie, Robin. *Stockhausen*. London 1976.

McCormick, E. H. *The Expatriate: A Study of Frances Hodgkins*. Wellington 1954.

————. *New Zealand Literature: A Survey*. London 1959.

————. *Omai: Pacific Envoy*. Auckland 1977.

————. *The Inland Eye: A Sketch in Visual Autobiography*. Auckland 1979.

————. *Portrait of Frances Hodgkins*. Auckland 1981.

McEldowney, Dennis. *Frank Sargeson in his Time*. Dunedin 1976.

McGill, David. *Pioneers of Port Nicholson*. Wellington 1984.

McIntosh, A. D. (ed.). *Marlborough: A Provincial History*. Blenheim 1940.

McIntyre, David, Michael Field, Christine Quinn. *Cook's Wild Strait*. Wellington 1983.

McKay, F. M. *Eileen Duggan*. Wellington 1977.

McKay, Ian K. *Broadcasting in New Zealand*. Wellington 1953.

MacKenzie, Barbara and Findlay. *Singers of Australia from Melba to Sutherland*. Melbourne 1967.

McKinlay, Ernest. *Ways and By-ways of a Singing Kiwi*. Dunedin 1939.

McLean, Mervyn. *Maori Music*. Wellington 1971.

————, Margaret Orbell. *Traditional Songs of the Maori*. Wellington 1975.

McNeish, James. *Tavern in the Town*. Wellington 1984.

Main, William. *Bragge's Wellington and the Wairarapa*. Wellington 1974.

————. *Maori in Focus: A Selection of Photographs of the Maori from 1850-1914*. Wellington 1976.

————. *Auckland Through a Victorian Lens*. Wellington 1977.

————. *Wellington Through a Victorian Lens*. Wellington 1980.

Makereti (Guide Maggie Papakura). *The Old-time Maori*. Auckland 1986.

Maling, Peter Bromley. *Samuel Butler at Mesopotamia*. Wellington 1960.

Mann, Shonadh. *F. G. Gibbs: His Influence on the Social History of Nelson, 1890-1950*. Nelson 1977.

Mansfield, Katherine. *Collected Stories*. London 1945.

————. *Journal*. (ed. Murry J. Middleton.). Albatross Library. Rome 1950.

————. *Letters and Journals: A Selection*. (ed. Stead, C. K.). London 1977.

————. *Collected Letters* (ed. O'Sullivan and Scott). Vol. 1, 1903-17. Oxford, 1984.

Martin, Lady. *Our Maoris*. London 1884.

May, Philip Ross. *Hokitika: Goldfields Capital*. Christchurch 1964.

Meredith, John, Hugh Anderson. *Folk Songs of Australia and the Men and Women who Sang them*. Sydney 1985.

Miller, John. *Early Victorian New Zealand: A Study of Racial Tension and Social Attitudes, 1839-52*. Wellington 1974.

Mitcalfe, Barry. *Maori Poetry: The Singing Word*. Wellington 1974.

Moncrieff, Gladys. *My Life of Song*. Adelaide 1974.

Moorehead, Alan. *The Fatal Impact*. London 1968.

Morrell, W. P., D. O. W. Hall. *A History of New Zealand Life*. Christchurch 1957.

————. *The Provincial System in New Zealand 1852-76*. Christchurch 1964.

————. *The Anglican Church in New Zealand: A History*. Dunedin 1973.

Morton, Harry. *The Whale's Wake*. Dunedin 1982.

Mulgan, Alan. *City of the Strait*. Wellington 1939.

————. *Literature and Authorship in New Zealand*. London 1943.

————. *Great Days in New Zealand Writing*. Wellington 1962.

Mulgan, John. *Man Alone*. Hamilton 1960.

Munz, Peter (ed.). *The Feel of Truth: Essays in New Zealand and Pacific History*. Wellington 1969.

Nalden, Charles. *A History of the Conservatorium of Music, University of Auckland, 1888-1981*. Auckland 1981.

Nash, Walter. *New Zealand: A Working Democracy*. London 1944.

Neel, Boyd. *The Story of an Orchestra*. London 1950.

Newcomb, S. P. *Music of the People: The Story of the Band Movement in New Zealand*. Christchurch 1963.

————. *Challenging Brass. 100 Years of Brass Band Contests in New Zealand, 1880-1980*. Takapuna 1980.

Nicholas, J. L. *Narrative of Voyage to New Zealand, 1814, 1815* (2 vols.). London 1817.

Norman, Philip. *Bibliography of New Zealand Compositions: Vol. One*. 2nd ed. Christchurch 1982.

Oliver, W. H. *The Story of New Zealand*. London 1960.

————. *Towards a New History?*. Hocken Lecture 1969. Dunedin 1971.

————, B. R. Williams. *The Oxford History of New Zealand*. Wellington 1981.

Olssen, Erik. *A History of Otago*. Dunedin 1984.

Orange, Claudia. *The Treaty of Waitangi*. Wellington 1987.

Orchard, Arundel. *A Distant View*. Sydney 1943.

Orbell, Margaret. *Maori Poetry*. Auckland 1978.

Ord-Hume, Arthur W. J. G. *Clockwork Music*. London 1973.

O'Sullivan, Vincent. *James K. Baxter*. Wellington 1976.

Owens, J. M. R. *Prophets in the Wilderness: The Wesleyan Mission to New Zealand, 1819-27*. Auckland 1974.

Paderewski, Ignace Jan, Mary Lowton. *The Paderewski Memoirs*. London 1939.

Page, Frederick. *A Musician's Journal* (ed. Thomson, J. M., Janet Paul). Dunedin 1986.

Palethorpe, N. B. *Official History of the New Zealand Centennial Exhibition, Wellington, 1939-40*. Wellington 1940.

Papakura, Guide Maggie. *See* Makereti.

Parkyn, G. W. *Sight of that Immortal Sea*. Combs-Lopdell Memorial Address, 1964. Wellington 1964.

Paul, Janet, Neil Roberts. *Evelyn Page: Seven Decades*. Christchurch/Wellington 1986.

Pearsall, Ronald. *Victorian Popular Music*. Newton Abbott 1973.

———. *Edwardian Popular Music*. New Jersey 1975.

Peaks, R. E. *Music-making in the School and Home*. Wellington 1965.

Peters, Marie. *Christchurch—Saint Michael's: A Study in Anglicanism in New Zealand*. Christchurch 1986.

Phillips, A. A. *The Australian Tradition: Studies in a Colonial Culture*. Melbourne 1958.

Phillips, Jock (ed.). *Biography in New Zealand*. Wellington 1985.

———. *A Man's Country?* Auckland 1987.

———. (ed.). *Te Whenua, te Iwi/The Land and the People*. Wellington 1987.

Pirani, M. R. *A Short History of the Cathedral of Saint Paul the Apostle*. Wellington 1958.

Platt, Peter. *Music History as a Living Study*. Dunedin 1959.

Platts, Una. *The Lively Capital: Auckland, 1840-65*. Christchurch 1971.

Pleasants, Henry. *The Great Singers*. London 1981.

Plischke, Ernst. *Design and Living*. Wellington 1947.

Plowman, Peter. *Passenger Ships of Australia and New Zealand: Vol. 1, 1876-1912; Vol. 2, 1913-1980*. Auckland 1980.

Pocock, J. G. A. (ed.). *The Maori and New Zealand Politics*. Auckland 1965.

Ponder, Winifred. *Clara Butt: Her Life Story*. London 1928.

Porter, Frances (ed.). *Historic Buildings of New Zealand: North Island*. Auckland 1979.

——— (ed.). *Historic Buildings of New Zealand: South Island*. Auckland 1983.

———. *Born to New Zealand: a biography of Jane Maria Atkinson*. Wellington 1989.

Porter, Hal. *Stars of Australian Stage and Screen*. Adelaide 1965.

Pound, Frances. *Frames on the Land*. Auckland 1983.

Pritchard, Brian W. *Words and Music: A Jubilee History of the Christchurch Harmonic Society*. Christchurch 1977.

———. *Selected Source Readings on Musical Activity in the Canterbury Settlement,*

1850-80. Canterbury series of bibliographies, catalogues and source readings in music. Christchurch 1984.

Radic, Thérèse. *G. W. L. Marshall-Hall: Portrait of a Lost Crusader*. Perth 1982.

Ramsden, Eric. *Sir Apirana Ngata and Maori Culture*. Wellington 1948.

Rees, C. B. *One Hundred Years of the Hallé*. London 1957.

Reeves, W. Pember (ed.). *Canterbury Rhymes*. Christchurch 1883.

————. *The Long White Cloud*. London 1898.

Reid, Charles. *Malcolm Sargent*. London 1968.

Reid, J. C. 'The Contribution of the Arts'. *Auckland Yesterday and Tomorrow* (ed. Simpson, Frank). Auckland 1971.

Reischek, Andreas. *Yesterdays in Maoriland* (tr. Priday H. E. L.). London 1930.

Reith, J. C. W. *Into the Wind*. London 1949.

Ricketts, Harry. *Twelve New Zealand Poets in Conversation*. Wellington 1986.

Roddick, Alan. *Allen Curnow*. Wellington 1980.

Rolleston, Rosamond. *William and Mary Rolleston: An Informal Biography*. Wellington 1971.

Ross, R. M. *New Zealand's First Capital*. Wellington 1946.

————. *A Guide to Pompalier House*. Wellington 1979.

————. *Melanesians at Mission Bay*. Wellington 1983.

Russell, Thomas. *Philharmonic Decade*. London 1944.

Rutherford, James, W. H. Skinner (eds). *The Establishment of the New Plymouth Settlement in New Zealand, 1841-3*. New Plymouth 1940.

Sablosky, Irving C. *American Music*. Chicago 1969.

Scholefield, G. H. *Notable New Zealand Statesmen: Twelve Prime Ministers*. Christchurch 1946.

———— (ed.). *The Richmond-Atkinson Papers* (2 vols.). Wellington 1960.

Scholes, Percy A. *The Mirror of Music, 1844-1944* (2 vols.). London 1947.

Seeley, J. R. *The Expansion of England*. Chicago/London 1971.

Selwyn, Sarah Harriet. *Reminiscences* (ed. Evans, Enid A.). Auckland 1961.

Servant, Father C. *Customs and Habits of the New Zealanders, 1838-42* (tr. Glasgow, J., ed. Simmons, D. R.). Wellington 1973.

Sewell, Henry. *Journal 1853-71* (2 vols.) (ed. McIntyre, W. David). Christchurch 1980.

Sharp, Andrew. *Crisis at Kerikeri*. Wellington 1958.

————. *Voyages of Tasman*. Oxford 1968.

———— (ed.). *Duperrey's Visit to New Zealand in 1824*. Welllington 1971.

Shaw, Bernard. *Shaw's Music* (3 vols.). London 1981.

Shennan, Jennifer. *The Maori Action Song*. Wellington 1984.

Shirley, Henry. *Just a Bloody Piano Player*. Auckland 1971.

Siegfried, André. *Democracy in New Zealand* (tr. Burns, E.V.). Wellington 1982.

Simpson, F. C. *A Survey of the Arts in New Zealand*. Wellington 1961.

Simpson, Adrienne (ed). *Opera in New Zealand: Aspects of History and Performance*. Wellington 1990.

Sinclair, Keith. *A History of New Zealand*. Wellington 1959.

——— (ed.). *Distance Looks our Way*. Hamilton 1961.

———. *Reeves, William Pember, New Zealand Fabian*. Oxford 1965.

———. *Walter Nash*. Auckland 1976.

———, Wendy Harrex. *Looking Back*. Wellington 1978.

———. *A History of the University of Auckland, 1883-1983*. Auckland 1983.

Smith, Bernard. *European Vision and the South Pacific, 1768-1850*. London 1960.

Sowry, Clive. *Film-making in New Zealand: A Brief Historical Survey*. New Zealand Film Archive. Wellington 1984.

Spellman, Doreen and Sidney. *Victorian Music Covers*. London 1969.

Stackpoole, John. *William Mason, The First New Zealand Architect*. Auckland 1971.

———. *Colonial Architecture in New Zealand*. Wellington 1976.

Standish, M. W. *The Waimate Mission Station*. Wellington 1962.

Stewart, Adela. *My Simple Life in New Zealand*. London 1908.

Stewart, Douglas. *Springtime in Taranaki: An Autobiography of Youth*. Auckland 1983.

Stewart, Nellie. *My Life's Story*. Sydney 1923.

Stravinksy, Igor. *Poetics of Music, in the Form of Six Lessons*. Cambridge (Mass.) 1970.

Stuart, Peter. *Edmund Gibbon Wakefield in New Zealand*. Wellington 1971.

Surville, J. F. M. de. *Extracts from the Journals Relating to the Visit to New Zealand of the French Ship* St Jean Baptiste *in December 1769 Under the Command of J. F. M. de Surville* (tr. Ollivier, Isabel, Cheryl Hingley). Wellington 1982.

Sutch, W. B. *The Quest for Security in New Zealand, 1840-1966*. Wellington 1966.

Swainson, William. *Auckland, the Capital of New Zealand*. London 1853.

Tait, Viola. *A Family of Brothers*. Melbourne 1971.

Tayler, Douglas E. *A Complete Scheme of School Music Related to Human Life*. Wellington 1927.

Taylor, Arthur R. *Brass Bands*. London 1979.

Taylor, David M. *The Oldest Manuscripts in New Zealand*. Wellington 1955.

Taylor, Nancy M. (ed.). *Early Travellers in New Zealand*. Oxford 1959.

——— (ed.). *Journal of Ensign Best*. Wellington 1946.

———. *The Home Front: The New Zealand People at War; New Zealand in the Second World War, 1939-45* (2 vols.). Wellington 1986.

Temperley, Nicholas. *The Music of the English Parish Church* (2 vols.). Cambridge 1979.

———. *The Romantic Age, 1800-1914: The Athlone History of Music in Britain*. London 1981.

Temple, Philip. *Wellington Yesterday*. Wellington 1980.

Thomas, Allan, Ross Clark (eds). *Asia Pacific Voices*, special issue of *Canzona*, Vol. 7, No. 24. Wellington 1986.

Tocqueville, Alexis de. *Journey to America* (tr. Lawrence, George). London 1959.

Tombs, H. H. (ed.). *A Century of Art in Otago*. Wellington 1978.

Thompson, G. E. *Official Record of the New Zealand and South Seas International Exhibition, Dunedin 1925-26*. Dunedin 1926.

Thompson, Paul. *The Voice of the Past: Oral History*. London 1978.

Thomson, Arthur S. M. D. *The Story of New Zealand, Past and Present — Savage and Civilized* (2 vols.). London 1859.

Thomson, J. E. P. *Denis Glover*. Wellington 1977.

———. *New Zealand Drama, 1930-80: An Illustrated History*. Auckland 1984.

Thomson, John Mansfield. *A Distant Music: The Life and Times of Alfred Hill 1870-1960*. Auckland 1980.

———. *Into a New Key: The Origins and History of the Music Federation of New Zealand, 1950-1982*. Wellington 1985.

———, Janet Paul (eds). *Frederick Page: A Musician's Journal, 1905-1983*. Dunedin 1986.

——— (ed.). *The Attentive Ear: A Work-book on Music Criticism*. Wellington 1987.

———. *Biographical Dictionary of New Zealand Composers*. Wellington 1990.

———. *Musical Images: A New Zealand Historical Journey 1840-1990*. Wellington 1990.

Tonks, Joy. *The New Zealand Symphony Orchestra: The First Forty Years*. Auckland 1986.

Tomory, P. A. *New Zealand Art: Painting, 1890-1950*. Wellington 1968.

Torlesse, Charles Obius. *The Torlesse Papers: The Journals and Letters of Charles Obius Torlesse, 1848-51* (ed. Maling, P. B.). Christchurch 1958.

Trevelyan, Charles Philips. *Letters from North America and the Pacific, 1898*. London 1969.

Trevelyan, G. M. *History and the Reader*. London 1945.

Tripp, Ellen Shephard. *My Early Days*. Christchurch 1916.

Trollope, Anthony. *Australia and New Zealand* (2 vols.). London 1873.

Tucker, F. K. *J. C. Bradshaw: A Memoir*. Christchurch 1956.

Tullett, J. S. *The Industrious Heart: A History of New Plymouth*. New Plymouth 1981.

Turnbull, Michael. *The Changing Land: A Short History of New Zealand*. 2nd ed. Auckland 1975.

———. *The Land of New Zealand*. London 1964.

Urville, Dumont d'. *See* Wright, Olive.

Wakefield, E. J. *Adventure in New Zealand* (2 vols.). London 1845

———. *Hand-Book for New Zealand [A Late Magistrate of the Colony]*. London 1848.

———. *Adventure in New Zealand*. Abridged edn, (ed. Stevens, Joan). Wellington 1955.

———. *The London Journal, 1845-46* (ed. Stevens, Joan). Wellington 1972.

Wall, Arnold (compiler). *The First Ninety Years of the Nelson School of Music*. Nelson 1984.

Ward, Alan. *A Show of Justice: Racial Amalgamation in Nineteenth Century New Zealand*. Auckland 1974.

Ward, Edward. *Journal of 1850-51*. Christchurch 1951.

Ward, L. E. *Early Wellington*. Wellington 1929.

Wards, Ian. *The Shadow of the Land*. Wellington 1968.

Warner, Marina. *Queen Victoria's Sketchbook*. London 1979.

Webb, Beatrice, Sydney Webb. *The Webbs in New Zealand 1898* (ed. Hamer, D. A.). Wellington 1974.

Wedde, Ian, Harvey McQueen (eds). *The Penguin Book of New Zealand Verse*. Auckland 1985.

Weir, J. E. *R. A. K. Mason*. Wellington 1977.

Westra, Ans. *Notes on the Country I Live in*. Wellington 1972.

Wheeler, Mr. *The New Zealand Goldfields 1861*. Victorian New Zealand: A Reprint Series, No. 1. Dunedin 1976.

White, John. *Ancient History of the Maori*. Wellington 1887.

Wiata, Beryl Te. *Inia Te Wiata: Most Happy Fella*. Auckland 1982.

Wicksteed, M. R. *The New Zealand Army: A History From the 1840s to the 1980s*. Wellington 1982.

Williams, Barry M. *Structures and Attitudes in New Zealand Education, 1945-75*. Wellington 1978.

Willox, J. *Willox's New Zealand Handbook*. Liverpool 1859.

Willson, M. Disher. *Victorian Song*. London 1955.

Wilson, Helen. *My First Eighty Years*. Hamilton 1959.

Wilson, Ormond. *From Hongi Hika to Hone Heke*. Dunedin 1983.

————. *An Outsider Looks Back*. Wellington 1982.

Wilson, Phillip. *The Maorilanders: A Study of William Satchell*. Christchurch 1961.

Wood, F. C. W. *New Zealand in the World*. Wellington 1940.

————. *This New Zealand*. Hamilton 1946.

Wood, June A. *Victorian New Zealanders*. Wellington 1974.

Woollaston, M. Toss. *The Far-away Hills: A Meditation on the New Zealand Landscape*. Auckland 1962.

————. *Sage Tea*. Auckland 1980.

Wright, Olive (tr.). *New Zealand 1826-1827*, an English translation of the voyage of the *Astrolabe*, from the French of Dumont d'Urville. Wellington 1950.

Yate, Rev. William. *An Account of New Zealand*. London 1835.

Private Papers

1.   Alexander Turnbull Library, Wellington
Anderson, Bruce. ATL MSS, 82-11, folders 1-9.
Anson, H. V. MS Papers 327.
Bradshaw, Dr J. C. Scrapbook. ACC 81-119.

Donne, T. E. Scrapbook and MS Papers, 1387.

Elliot, Archibald, J. Papers, 1937-1974. MS Papers 1573.

Gladstone-Hill, H. Autobiography. ACC 76-251.

Lilburn, D. G. MS Papers 2843.

Page, Frederick and Evelyn. MS Papers 3903: 1/1/8.

Prouse, Oliver Richard. Papers [*c*. 1940]. MS Papers 463.

Woods, John Joseph. Papers on musical composition *God Defend New Zealand*, 1877-78, 1897, 1932. MS Papers 355.

2. Auckland Public Library

Bennett, John F., musician. Memoirs, 1867-1930, by one of his pupils, Ivy F. Smytheman. 70-13979. 780.92 R.

Williams, H. Williams Papers 1822-64.

3. Hocken Library, Dunedin

Sinton, Walter. Programme Scrapbook 1879-96. 4 vols., MS 1226 A-1, 8-2.

Squarise, Raphael. Scrapbooks. VVw55.

Articles, pamphlets and bibliographies

Abraham, Gerald. 'Creating a musical tradition'. *Journal of the Royal Society for the encouragement of Arts, Manufactures and Commerce*, London, May 1967, 417-29.

Annabell, A. 'New Zealand folksong research'. *Continuo*, June 1975.

Beattie, David. *A Calendar of References to Music in Christchurch Newspapers, 1851-1860*. The Canterbury series of bibliographies, catalogues and source documents in music, No. 2. Christchurch 1986.

Butler, Samuel. 'Samuel Butler Number'. *Life and Letters*, London, Vol. 7, No. 41, 1931.

Heenan, Ashley. 'A way of life'. *Challenge in Music Education*. ISME Conference Papers, Perth 1974, 249-254.

McCredie, Andrew D. 'Alfred Hill (1870-1960): Some backgrounds and perspectives for an historical edition'. *Miscellanea Musicologica*, Adelaide Studies on Musicology, Vol. 3, 1968.

————. 'Alfred Hill' in *Australian Composition in the Twentieth Century* (eds Callaway, Frank, David Tunley). Melbourne 1978.

McLean, Mervyn. 'An analysis of 651 Maori scales'. Yearbook of the International Folk Music Council, 1969, 1123-64.

————. An Annotated Bibliography of Oceanic Music and Dance. Wellington 1977; supplement, Auckland 1981.

————. 'Future directions in the study of the arts of Oceania'. Papers of 1979 symposium. *JPS*, Vol. 90, No. 2, June 1981.

————. 'Preservation of the indigenous music heritage of New Zealand'. *Continuo*, Vol. 10, Nos 2 and 3, 1981, 21-30.

————. 'Towards a typology of musical change: missionaries and adjustive response in Oceania'. *World of Music*, Berlin, Vol. 28, No. 1, 1986, 29-43.

Moore, Dallas. *Old St Paul's: The First Hundred Years*. Wellington 1970.

Orbell, Margaret. 'Songs of the first Maori Christians'. *Landfall*, March 1984, 70-9.

————. 'Aotearoa's written history'. *NZL*, 23 February 1985.

Petre, Robert. Bibliography of printed music published before 1801, held in the Rare Book Room and Bishop's House Collection in the Auckland Public Library. Unpublished paper, Auckland Public Library, 1977.

Prestcott, Elizabeth. 'Places where music was made in Christchurch'. *Historic Places in New Zealand*, December 1987, 16-17.

Reid, J. C. 'The Contribution of the Arts'. *Auckland Yesterday and Tomorrow*, City of Auckland Centennial Lecture Series, 1971, Auckland 1971, 8-20.

Sargison, Patricia A. *Victoria's Furthest Daughters: A Bibliography of Published Sources for the Study of Women in New Zealand, 1830-1914*. Wellington 1984.

Seaman, G. 'Early music periodicals in New Zealand'. *Continuo*, Vol. 6, 1976.

Simpson, Adrienne. 'This country may well be proud of her': Frances Alda's 1927 tour of New Zealand: *MNZ*, Spring 1989, 36-41.

————. 'Boyd Neel and after: a tale of two orchestras', *MNZ*, Autumn 1990, 36ff.

————. 'The Simonsen Opera Company's 1876 tour of New Zealand', *TLR*, October 1990.

Standish, M. W. 'The Waimate Mission Station' in *Bishop Selwyn at Waimate*. Wellington 1962, 28-33.

Taylor, Hilda. 'English folk-dancing in New Zealand'. *Art New Zealand*, June 1940, 209.

Thomson, John Mansfield. 'A question of authenticity: Alfred Hill, The Chevalier de Kontski, Ovide Musin and the Wellington Orchestral Society 1892-6'. *TLR*, Wellington, October 1980.

————. 'From Bayreuth to the Urewera: Michael Balling and the viola-alta'. *TLR*, October 1990.

Towards Maturity, Turnbull Winter Lectures. R. Quentin-Baxter, Bert Roth, Sydney Moko Mead, James Bertram. Wellington 1982.

Trave, J. E. *New Zealand Studies: A Guide to Bibliographical Resources*. Wellington 1985.

Wentzel, Anne. 'Early composers in Australia'. *Quadrant*, Vol. 6, No. 2, 1926, 29-36.

Williamson, Malcolm. 'How Australian can Australian music become?' *Journal of the Royal Society for the encouragement of Arts, Manufactures and Commerce*, London, June 1970.

Concert programmes and brochures

A Century of Music, the story of the first 100 years of the Auckland Choral Society. Auckland 1955.

McLeod, Jenny. *Under the Sun*. Palmerston North 1971.

NZBC Symphony Orchestra. Australian tour, October 1974. Wellington 1974.

NZSO. *Concord of Sweet Sounds: The NZSO at 30* (ed. Hambleton, Keith). Wellington 1977.

Sonic Circus. Wellington 1987.

Art and exhibition catalogues

Angus, Rita. National Art Gallery, December 1982-March 1983.

The British Sailor. An exhibition of rare and current books, manuscripts, and prints. National Book League, London, October-December 1959.

Collier, Edith, in Retrospect. Biographical essay by Janet Paul. Sargeant Gallery, Wanganui 1980.

Cook: A Hundred Years After (Foreword by J. C. Beaglehole). New Zealand House, London, June 1956.

Hodgkins, Frances: Exhibition of Paintings in the Centennial Year of her Birth. Hocken Library, University of Otago 1969.

Hoyte, J. C. Auckland City Art Gallery, June-July 1957.

McCahon, Colin: A Survey Exhibition. Auckland City Art Gallery, March-April 1972.

———. *Religious Works, 1946-52*. Manawatu Art Gallery 1975.

———. *McCahon's 'Necessary Protection'*. Govett-Brewster Art Gallery, New Plymouth 1977.

McIntyre, Raymond: A New Zealand Painter. Auckland City Art Gallery 1984.

New Zealand Art: A National Centennial Exhibition. Wellington 1940.

Omai, The Two Worlds of. Auckland City Art Gallery 1977.

Tempsky, Gustavus Ferdinand von: The Man and the Artist. Waikato Art Museum, May-June 1978.

Unpublished theses, etc.

Annabel, Angela. 'Music in Auckland 1840-55. M.A., University of Auckland.

———. 'New Zealand's Cultural and Economic Development Reflected in Song', Ph.D., University of Auckland, 1975.

Baughen, G. A. K. 'C. N. Baeyertz and the *Triad*'. B.A.(Hons.) in History, University of Otago, 1980.

Bornet, C. P. 'Anglican Church Music in Canterbury, 1850-1900'. M.A., University of Canterbury, 1973.

Burt, Gordon. 'Talks on New Zealand Composers'. Concert Programme, Radio New Zealand, Alexander Turnbull Library.

Elphick, Judith. 'Auckland 1870-74: A Social Portrait'. M.A., University of Auckland, 1974.

Harkness, Susan A. 'History in Song: The Nature and Historical Development of New Zealand Folk Music'. B.A.(Hons.), University of Otago, 1980.

Jansen, G. E. 'The History of School Music in New Zealand'. M.A., Victoria University of Wellington, 1966.

Mitchell, C. H., 'The Arts in Wellington, 1890-1912'. M.A., Victoria University of Wellington, 1959.

Moriarty, J. M. 'Wellington Music in the First Half-century of Settlement'. M.A., Victoria University of Wellington, 1967.

Murray, Susan M. 'A Survey of Music and Drama on Stage in Auckland, 1900-14'. M.A. research essay, University of Auckland, 1983.

Norman, Philip. 'The Beginning and Development of a New Zealand Music: The Life and Work (1940-1965) of Douglas Lilburn'. Ph.D., University of Canterbury, 1983.

Pearson, Ethel (Margaret Campbell). 'A History of Music in Dunedin to 1925'. M.A.(Hons.), University of Otago.

Phillips, J. R. 'A Social History of Auckland 1840-53'. M.A., University of Auckland, 1966.

Pritchard, B. W. 'Societies in Society: A Case Study in the Historical Sociology of Music'. M.A.(Hons.), University of Canterbury, 1965.

Walsh, B. 'A Survey of Orchestral Activity in New Zealand'. M.A., Victoria University of Wellington, 1967.

Watson, Helen. 'Music in Christchurch'. M.A., University of New Zealand (Canterbury), 1948.

Wentzel, Ann (Ann Carr-Boyd). 'Music in Australia, 1788-1888'. University of Sydney, 1966.

Index

The index is of persons active in New Zealand's musical life as composers, conductors, critics, educators, ethnologists, impresarios, instrument-makers, music-lovers, musicologists, patrons, performers, or publishers, and it is necessarily somewhat selective. In particular, the names of some members of opera companies (e.g. the Pollard company), and of some other musicians mentioned briefly in passing, are excluded. The abbreviations 'ill.' or 'with ill.' refer to an illustration or illustrations.